A History of Migration from Germany to Canada, 1850-1939

Jonathan Wagner

A History of Migration from Germany to Canada, 1850-1939

UBCPress · Vancouver · Toronto

15 14 13 12 11 10 09 08 07 06   5 4 3 2 1

This book is printed on ancient-forest-free (100% post-consumer recycled) paper
that is processed chlorine- and acid-free, with vegetable based inks.

Library and Archives Canada Cataloguing in Publication

Wagner, Jonathan F. (Jonathan Frederick), 1940-
    A history of migration from Germany to Canada, 1850-1939 / Jonathan Wagner.

Includes bibliographical references and index.

ISBN-13: 978-0-7748-1215-3
ISBN-10: 0-7748-1215-X

    1. Germany – Emigration and immigration – History. 2. Canada – Emigration
and immigration – History. I. Title.

IFC106.G3W25 2005   325'.243'0971   C2005-905690-8

Canadä

UBC Press gratefully acknowledges the financial support for our publishing
program of the Government of Canada through the Book Publishing Industry
Development Program (BPIDP), and of the Canada Council for the Arts, and
the British Columbia Arts Council.

UBC Press would also like to acknowledge the financial contribution of the
International Council for Canadian Studies through its Publishing Fund. The Press
also acknowledges the assistance of the Minot State University Development Fund.

Printed and bound in Canada by Friesens
Set in Stone by Artegraphica Design Co. Ltd.
Copy editor: Sarah Wight
Proofreader and indexer: Deborah Kerr

UBC Press
The University of British Columbia
2029 West Mall
Vancouver, BC V6T 1Z2
604-822-5959 / Fax: 604-822-6083
www.ubcpress.ca

To my bookend sons,
Nathaniel and Robert, lights of my life.

Contents

Acknowledgments

In this book's preparation and production, I owe a debt of gratitude to many people in many archives and libraries in Germany, Canada, and the United States. I regret not being able to acknowledge all the small and great favours that so many accorded me. Several persons, however, must receive their due. Special thanks go to Dr. Peter Gabrielson of the Staatsarchiv Hamburg and to Herr Paasch of the Archiv des Kirchenkreis Alt-Hamburg in der Nordelbischen Evangelisch-lutherischen Kirche, also in Hamburg. These gentlemen were most responsible for making my research trip to Hamburg so rewarding. In Ottawa Mr. Ghislain Malette of the Library and Archives Canada staff accommodated me most graciously during my visit to Canada's capital city. In Minot, North Dakota, I wish to note my gratitude to the Olson Library staff and Jane LaPlante in particular for all the extra time and effort she expended securing not only numerous books but also documents and microfilm from other libraries and archives in Canada and the United States. Likewise, I want to thank Minot State University's administration and especially Dr. Nancy Hall for supporting my work with both funding and encouragement.

Finally, I must thank the editors and staff at UBC Press for their efficient handling of my work from first submission of the manuscript, through the reviewing and editorial process, to publication of the book. My chief editor, Emily Andrew, who directed these efforts throughout, was a joy to work with. Without her wise advice, intelligent criticism, and steady encouragement, I would not have finished as I did. My gratitude extends as well to production manager Camilla Blakeley for her patience and efficiency in handling many details in preparation for publication of this book. To copy editor Sarah Wight goes my sincere thanks for her painstakingly thorough reading of the entire manuscript and her many helpful suggestions for its improvement.

Any errors of omission and commission are my responsibility entirely. Where German sources have been used, the translations are my own.

A History of Migration from Germany to Canada, 1850-1939

Introduction

> The journey to Montreal [after disembarking at St. John, New
> Brunswick] was magnificent. Large lakes, fantastic rock formations,
> open areas alternating with conifer groves mixed with alders and
> birches. The landscape resembled something right out of Cooper's
> Leatherstocking tales ... On the trip west to Winnipeg [after the
> stopover] I saw nickel mines and other mining operations that
> promised untold riches. The scene was again characterized by
> frequent lakes, swamps, wild rock formations ... huge conifers,
> birches, and alders. The strange spectacle made me think that I
> was traveling through an antediluvian land.[1]

So wrote the young immigrant Manfred von Bresler to his parents in Germany in September 1927. Manfred's awestruck response typified the reaction of many German immigrants upon first encountering North America's largest country. Many experienced the same romantic ecstasy, appearing overwhelmed by all-encompassing, primitive nature. Just as fundamentally, Manfred's response exhibited awareness of Canada's difference from his own native land. To those experiencing Manfred's shock, Canada appeared to be arrested at some unrecognizable stage of the past. On its frontier, which appeared so ubiquitous and proximate, Canada often seemed not even vaguely contemporary. Canada's undeveloped state compared to Germany ultimately played a crucial role in the history of German-Canadian migration, influencing not only how Germans responded to Canada but also how Canadians conceived of themselves and of the immigrants they favoured recruiting.

As Dirk Hoerder and other contemporary migration scholars have often pointed out, movement involving change of residence, or migration, has been a prominent theme in human existence for hundreds of years.[2] Over the centuries, these globally dispersed migrations have been made over short or long distances; they have been carried out within state boundaries, across them, and even when no boundaries existed. Migrations have been temporary and permanent; they have been circular, linear, and seasonal; they have been undertaken by people individually and in groups. Some have been coerced; others have resulted from freer choice. They have occurred in virtually all the inhabited areas of our world, for many different causes. In "this bewilderingly complex pattern of tidal currents,"[3] to quote Frank Thistlethwaite, the movement of Germans to Canada occupies only a small part. Within the global context, German migration to Canada formed part of a regional mass movement occurring between 1800 and 1939 that involved millions of Europeans leaving their historic homes in the old country to take up permanent or temporary residence, or to secure seasonal work in the Atlantic economies.[4] In that Atlantic mass odyssey, Germany represented only one of the European donors, while Canada was a single receiving state among several, including the United States, Australia, Argentina, and Brazil.[5] Connecting Canada's German movement to these more general patterns provides context, perspective, and the basis for comparisons and insights into the migration's larger significance and meaning. Nevertheless, as Moch and Jackson have emphasized, we must not "allow our concern for understanding migration as a core historical phenomenon to blind us to its link with distinct regional and national histories."[6] Like all human experiences, Canada's German migrations remain special and unique. In this book I have tried to describe this uniqueness while at the same time expanding the picture of human world migration.

Tracing the course of German-Canadian migration from 1850 to the outbreak of war in 1939, I describe how that migration reflected the modernization processes then at work in the sending land, Germany, and in the receiving country, Canada. In other words, as the social orders, political systems, economic arrangements, and ideological assumptions and commitments in the two countries altered, the migration, a fundamental part of the social history of both countries, closely mirrored these alterations. The 1850-1939 migrations are distinguished from earlier movements by the new features and forces characterizing and determining them. In short, a portion of the new world emerged as a result of the Industrial Revolution. The different processes and paces of the changes wrought by the Industrial Revolution's spread in the two countries determined the nature and extent of the migration to Canada. Because Canada's economy industrialized later and less completely than Germany's over the period 1850-1939, Canada's recruiting of immigrants to provide for its own perceived needs could not win converts in the more industrialized Germany.

I use the terms "modern" and "modernization" differently from the way in which sociologists, economists, or political scientists normally employ them.[7] By referring to modernization, I am not attempting to fit Canadian and German events into some kind of predictable model that applies generally to societies experiencing modern economic innovation. Rather, I am employing a synonym for change related to industrial transformation. Similarly, when I refer to "traditional" I do not intend to convey a condition of frozen status, rigid form, or inflexible mindset but customary and usual practices. Anyone familiar with the evolution of Anglo-American common law (that is, law based on custom rather than legislative statute), for example, knows that change has always been inherent in the common law. Likewise, traditional or preindustrial European society never remained totally static; it always exhibited movement or migration. But generally accepted customs and long-hallowed traditions, whatever the opponents of modernization theory may claim, normally changed more slowly before the great watershed of industrialization than after it: industrialization introduced a speeding-up uncommon to earlier times. Hence, I use "traditional" and "modern" only as general adjectives to describe customary (time-tested) and more innovative (post-Industrial Revolution) conditions. Between 1850 and 1939, in both Canada and Germany the customary ways of doing many things changed, and new procedures were introduced in politics, economics, social conventions, and patterns of thinking. All of these areas, as I shall show, affected German migration to Canada, and all mirrored the effects of contemporaneous industrial revolutionary changes.

Before 1850, the stages of economic, social, and political development in both countries showed greater parity than at any other time until after the Second World War. Germany and British North America both had overwhelmingly rural, agriculture-based social and economic systems. Smallholding farmers, artisans, and modest merchants composed the majority of each society.[8] The two lands nevertheless evolved differently because of the varying pace of economic development. Advancing more rapidly and completely into the industrial age, by 1900 Germany had become a world industrial powerhouse, while Canada continued to rely more heavily on the products of its fields, mines, and forests than on the fruits of its modest industry.[9]

Just how much the two societies shared before 1850 becomes apparent by considering briefly their economic structures. In the first half of the nineteenth century, British North America's economy depended almost entirely on the bounty nature provided. Agricultural products and the traditional primary sector staples of fur, fish, and timber constituted the economy's base. A more specific sectoral breakdown for 1851 shows the following distribution: farming employed 32 percent of the labour force, and forestry, fishing, trapping, and mining another 14.8 percent. The total for the primary sector (46.8 percent) thus dwarfed both manufacturing and the tertiary sector, each with 18.9 percent. Export-import statistics underline the importance of renewable resources to this pre-Confederation economy: in

1851 agricultural produce, animal products (e.g., fur and hides), wood, and wood derivatives including paper constituted over 88 percent of British North America's exported goods; finished iron products and textiles made up 40 percent of imports. Finally, labour categories tell the same story. Data available for 1851 show 75 percent of the Canadian labouring population engaged as farmers, lumbermen, miners, fishermen, or trappers. Most obviously absent here are the first practitioners of modern industry. Commenting on this facet of British North America's pre-1850 economy, Marr and Paterson write, "While non-primary occupations grew and expanded from 1763 to 1851 – foundries, boot and shoe factories, brickyards, tobacco factories, banks, furniture plants, and shipyards to name a few – the working population was concentrated in the primary occupations during the first half of the nineteenth century, and the proportion in these occupations may have increased from, say, the 1790s."[10]

The general features of Germany's economy at midcentury appeared quite similar to those of England's North American colony. As in Canada, an estimated three-quarters of Germany's population inhabited small rural villages and derived their livelihoods from agriculture or related activities. Indeed, the German peasantry was not far removed from the traditional feudal past, for in some German states peasant emancipation had not been completed as late as the 1840s. Although railroads had already made their appearance in Germany by 1850, the modern factory system and accompanying proletariat remained inchoate. Despite the existence of some proto-industry in Germany, artisans produced what industrial goods there were. David Blackbourn sums up the German scene cogently: "The number of weavers grew from 315,000 to 570,000 between 1800 and 1850 but over 90 percent of looms were hand-operated. Within the overall economy, industry proper continued to be eclipsed by outworking and handicraft production, and even more by agriculture."[11]

The earliest German settlements in what would eventually become the Dominion of Canada had been established in the eighteenth century. The colony's oldest German settlements were located in the Maritimes; small but thriving permanent centres of German population were formed in Halifax and Lunenburg shortly after 1750. Assigned land upon which to settle by the British government, the original settlers were farmers. Over the years, however, they and their progeny turned from the land to the sea to make their livelihoods. As a result, the Germans in Nova Scotia gradually became subsumed into the majority English community, though still as primary producers.

The American Revolution prompted additional Germans to move to Canada during the late eighteenth century. Among these immigrants, there were three main groups. First, 2,400 German mercenaries employed by King George III elected to move into Canada rather than return to Germany.

Known in the revolution as Hessians, but originally from several petty German principalities also including Brunswick, Anhalt-Zerbst, Waldeck, and Ansbach-Bayreuth, 1,400 of them settled in Quebec. The remaining 1,000 chose Ontario, New Brunswick, or Nova Scotia, where they took up farming, like their compatriots elsewhere in Canada. Another group of Germans came north with those who had remained true to the king during the American rebellion. Known as the United Empire Loyalists, this mostly English group nevertheless included some Germans among its ranks, most of whom settled on the land in Upper Canada. Pennsylvania's Mennonite settlements provided the last and most numerous group of German migrants from the south. Several thousand of these pacifist people abandoned the American colonies during or after the Revolutionary War because of sympathy with the British cause or dissatisfaction with the course of the new republic.[12]

Augmented by natural growth plus the influx of American Mennonites, Ontario's Mennonite communities grew steadily in the early years of the nineteenth century. As Gerhard Bassler points out, "From 1805 until the War of 1812 and throughout the 1820s an uninterrupted stream of Mennonites on foot, on horseback, and in Conestoga wagons drawn by four- and six-horse teams moved along a 400 mile trail from different parts of Pennsylvania to the secured German Company Tract on the Grand River." Like the earlier migrations, this later Mennonite immigration concentrated in Waterloo County and adjacent areas of southwestern Ontario. Thus, by 1840 Upper Canada possessed 5,400 Mennonite settlers.[13] Their success in establishing their farms and villages prompted other Germans to follow. In the 1830s Lutherans and Catholics began to arrive from Germany. This trend continued until nearly midcentury. According to K.M. McLaughlin, "One result of this development was that by 1833 the area surrounding the original German Company Tract was cleared and settled, a German newspaper had been initiated and a variety of German religious congregations formed. In the midst of this activity the central village in the original Mennonite settlement was re-named Berlin to commemorate the presence of so many newcomers from Germany."[14]

Thus, in 1850 most of British North America's German community resided in two general areas, Nova Scotia (15 percent) and Waterloo County in Upper Canada (60 percent). The remaining 25 percent were scattered about Quebec, the Ottawa Valley, and Montreal and Toronto. A community profile at midcentury shows them to have been in large measure faithful to the traditions of their past. A substantial majority of Canada's Germans lived either on their own farms or in small settlements, where they raised their families and worked the land upon which they or their forebears had settled. Those who had moved off the land lived in villages where they plied traditional handicrafts, trades, or small businesses. By modern standards these villages appear quite small. Berlin, the focal point of Waterloo

County's German population in 1850, numbered only about 1,000 souls. Of these Berlin residents, Udo Sauttner claimed that more than 100 artisans worked at various trades.[15]

Although eastern Canada did receive additional immigrants from Germany in the 1830s and 1840s, they were too few to alter the general shape of Canada's German community. Canada's German centres remained modest in number, composed mostly of Germans who had lived in North America for some time. The majority exhibited distant rather than immediate connections to Germany proper. This distant connection and small size limited their ability to act as centres for later chain migration from Germany.[16] Moreover, virtually all the German residents of British North America in 1850 had migrated prior to or in the earliest stages of industrialization in Germany and the United States. Because industrialization proceeded rapidly in Germany after the middle of the nineteenth century, subsequent German-Canadian migration was affected by the forces associated with the new industrial technology and the resultant economic, social, and political change. Because the Reich German migrants considered in this study belonged to the post-1850s migrations, they are fundamentally distinguishable from their predecessors.

In distinguishing the post-1850 immigrants, I analyze them and the migration phenomenon from several vantage points. First, the push-pull metaphor describes the larger immigration scene in both the "community of origin" (Germany) and the "community of destination" (Canada). This includes not only broad economic trends (recession or expansion) but demographics and particular political structures as well. As shall be shown, official immigration policy in both Germany and Canada nearly always reflected such broad themes. Some forces, for example, were pushing the would-be emigrant out of Germany, while concurrent influences at home were pulling in the opposite direction to keep the migrant from leaving.[17] Besides taking into consideration push-pull factors, I have adopted from Marcus Hansen four additional categories to account for emigration: 1) the legal freedom to migrate outside the country, 2) the means to do this, 3) the desire to move, and 4) the existence of an acceptable receiving land.[18]

In German-Canadian migration these four factors played significant roles. To start with, the laws facilitating or prohibiting migrant ingress and egress changed significantly over the period 1850-1939. The means to migrate include such matters as transportation opportunities, publicity or propaganda to induce movement, agents soliciting Germans for Canada, and facilitation agencies assisting emigrants to leave. Motivation to leave, the third category, relates to available opportunities to depart as well as awareness of the advantages of departing. Most often, the desire to abandon the old land stemmed not only from unhappiness or frustration at home but also from the belief in existing opportunities abroad. That is, how the would-be migrant perceived the receiving land is crucial. This perception, in turn, relates to the important role played by image in Canada's migration drama. Consequently, the following chapters contain considerable discussion of the various images that supporters and detractors ascribed to Canada, and their effects. The actual status of Canada as a viable receiving land for Reich Germans is also discussed, along with how the image of Canada as a home for immigrants evolved in relation to other receiving lands and particularly the United States.

Finally, a major portion of the discussion is allotted to analyzing the nature of German migration to Canada and the ideologies employed to support or oppose it. By nature I mean not only vital statistics categories such as sex, age, vocation, residence in Germany, and marital status but also how the immigration occurred. Did it involve basically family units – married parents with children – or did single individuals make the move to North America independently? Did German migration to Canada exhibit the chain characteristics so often true of German movement to the United States? Ideological considerations are discussed as reasons for supporting or opposing, for justifying or rationalizing migrations in and out. As shall be shown, these arguments included everything from nationalist expansionism through liberal idealism to racist obstructionism.

In treating the period 1850-1939, I divide the German-Canadian migration story into four major chronological segments: the twenty years following 1850, the two decades from 1870 to 1890, the watershed years from 1890 to the Great War, and the interwar period from 1919 to 1939. Although admittedly arbitrary, this division seemed not only convenient but justifiable for several reasons. To begin with, it corresponds to four readily recognizable stages in the political development of both countries. To discuss migration through a structuring political context makes sense because in both countries migration influenced and also was influenced by political posturing and policy making. These four political periods also exhibit economic and social features distinctive enough to merit separation and individual scrutiny. Certainly, social and economic developments related closely to political developments, functioning often as both cause and effect. The labour migration historian Carl Strickwerda encapsulates the intimacy between politics and economics: "International migration is thus always an economic and political phenomenon. The major determinants of international migration have been the economy and the state. The economic forces impinging on migration are demography, technology, the level of wages, and access – geographical proximity, transportation, and communications. The state is the confluence of social and political forces within countries which define, encourage or curtail, and regulate movement across borders. The interaction between these two factors creates the complexities of international migration."[19]

The first of the four periods, 1850-70, was a time of unification in both Canada and Germany. At the end of these two decades, in Canada in 1867 and then in Germany in 1870, a tenuous but clear politically unified nation-state was successfully established. Besides the creation of new political forms, political unification made a national system of economics feasible. Such a system ultimately included not only a national market but new commercial codes, tariff policies, transportation systems, and common weights and measures. In Germany more than in Canada these developments facilitated rapid economic advances in new industry and commerce. Even agriculture was affected. Consequently, German labourers and labouring were transformed as new social classes were created and old ones made redundant. After midcentury, the Industrial Revolution spread in Canada, albeit more slowly than in Germany. Throughout the 1860s and 1870s, Canada's economy remained agrarian and natural-resource based. Not so in Germany, where the rapid and profound changes in politics and economics influenced nearly all facets of people's lives. The social upheaval associated with developing industrialization and rapid demographic growth increased the number of Germany's potential emigrants. At the same time in traditional Canada, the developing national movement became increasingly aware of its need for more citizens. Hence, in the period 1850-70 in both Germany and Canada the potential for major changes in migration policies, procedures, and makeup developed naturally, and the groundwork for the evolution of truly national migration programs was laid. Chapter 1 describes how these several issues affected German-Canadian migration.

Corresponding to the era of two dominant political figures, Otto von Bismarck in Germany and Sir John A. Macdonald in Canada, Chapter 2 covers the two decades from 1870 to 1890. During this period, two apparently unrelated developments occurred that affected the possible movement of Germans to Canada. The first, a serious economic slowdown in the German Empire, saw the end of the rapid growth and expansion of the previous years as well as the emergence of serious social problems in conjunction with the economic downturn. Massive social and economic dislocation created enough difficulties to greatly expand Germany's potential emigrant pool. The second development was Ottawa's acquisition of the extensive Hudson's Bay lands lying between Ontario's Lake of the Woods and British Columbia. Overseen and inspired by Macdonald, this addition completed the physical development of the dominion by adding the North-West Territories. Besides binding west to east, this expansion also presented the dominion with new challenges, not the least of which was how to people the new lands with adequate numbers loyal to Ottawa. From this time, Canada was faced with a much more extensive immigration problem than in any previous age.

Between 1890 and the outbreak of war in August 1914, Canada received more immigrants than in either of the two periods just discussed. The people most responsible for this impressive turnaround were the Liberal prime minister Sir Wilfrid Laurier and his minister in charge of immigration, Clifford Sifton. Recognizing, as Macdonald had, that the West could not survive as a vital part of Canada unless it were populated, Laurier and Sifton deviated sharply from Macdonald's traditional emphasis upon seeking new immigrants among the English-speaking population of the British Isles and the United States. The Liberal government committed substantial resources and effort to soliciting settlers for the North West among non-English peoples, particularly those residing in central and eastern Europe. As a direct result of their liberalizing efforts, large numbers of Slavs and Germans from Russia and the Hapsburg lands made their way to Canada's newest frontier. Although the new Laurier-Sifton policy applied to Reich Germans as well, it enjoyed very limited success there. Chapter 3 treats the migration events and developments occurring during the two and a half decades before 1914.

Although the Great War halted German migration to Canada, it resumed not long after the conflict ended. Chapter 4 covers this period, ending with the second absolute cessation of that movement in 1939 at the outbreak of the Second World War. Although from 1919 to 1939 significant numbers of Reich Germans were admitted to Canada, most migrated there between 1923 and 1929. In those seven years, young Germans particularly flocked to Canada and other receiving lands because postwar conditions in the Weimar Republic were so politically unstable, socially chaotic, and economically uncertain. When the worldwide Depression commenced, out-migration ceased to exist as an option for the down and out. This was due less to the failing will of Germany's intended migrants than to the changing conditions in the receiving lands. Themselves suffering from the Depression, Canada, the United States, and the other traditional receiving lands effectively closed their doors to immigration. Germany's solution to both the Depression and the desire of its people to emigrate came in the form of Hitler's public works and rearmament program. As a result, the often expressed need for a way to relieve social pressure caused by a faltering economy, which emigration had previously fulfilled, disappeared as well.

This study was never meant to be a complete account of German migration to Canada or a history of Germans in Canada. I have deliberately not gone into detail on how German immigrants were received by the non-German Canadian community, nor attempted to describe how they were assimilated or integrated into Canadian society. Their role in Canadian life and their contribution to Canada represents an entirely different subject. Furthermore, I do not deal with all the different groups of German speakers who immigrated to Canada between 1850 and 1939. Although on occasion

I have discussed the so-called *Volksdeutsche,* those German speakers who before their migration to Canada resided outside of Germany proper, such as in Austro-Hungary, Russia, or the United States, I have concentrated on Germans hailing from "traditional" Germany, that is, from the Holy Roman Empire, the German Confederation, Bismarck's and then Wilhelm II's Second Empire, the Weimar Republic, and to a very limited extent Hitler's Germany. Because I am concerned equally here with events in Germany and in Canada, the work is intended to be a contribution to migration studies in general.

Moreover, I have not attempted to treat remigration, or *Rückwanderung;* that is, the returning of immigrants from Canada to Germany. Certainly, remigration represents an important element in the general migration story. The volume of recent literature devoted to it attests to this.[20] Just as clearly, a number of Canada's German immigrants did migrate back to Germany during the period 1850-1930. Indeed, some Canadian "immigrant trunks" also returned home to the old country as "a piece of that dream which once drew an emigrant across the sea."[21] In several places, I note examples of such remigration during the interwar period.

Nevertheless, I have dealt with Canada's returning Germans peripherally for two basic reasons. First, the subject remains particularly elusive because the available relevant statistics are notoriously unreliable and incomplete for both Germany and Canada. Confronted with the same statistical quandary for computing America's German remigration for the period up to 1890, Walter Nugent could only surmise that America's German migrants, who were in the majority farmers, probably showed low levels of return migration. In this regard, they appeared to resemble their fellow Irish and Scandinavian immigrants and to differ from America's British and Italian non-farmer, labour-seeking immigrants, who exhibited much higher levels of return migration.[22] Since the majority of Germans who came to Canada between 1850 and 1914 were, as we shall see, by official definition land seekers, what Nugent deduced about Germans in the United States very likely paralleled what happened in Canada.

Second, the subject's scope and scale exceeds the limits of this work. To treat Canada's German *Rückwanderung* appropriately would have required a much more extensive investigation into the circumstances surrounding the immigrants in Canada: the host society's responses to them, their assimilation or adjustment as immigrants, in short, their fate while living amid Canadian society. Since my effort has been directed at disclosing the causes and forces that prompted and facilitated the original move to Canada, a discussion of remigration appeared inessential to my main object, namely explaining why and how German migration to Canada occurred as it did.

Finally, the book makes no pretence to provide an in-depth history of either Canadian or German migration policy. Nevertheless, in each section

I have tried to include information about basic migration policies in the two lands to provide a workable theoretical framework for understanding how migration was viewed and why it was pursued or opposed by the governors in both countries.

This book is about Germans from Germany migrating to Canada between 1850 and 1939. More to the point, it deals with the reasons why Germans from Germany selected Canada as their receiving land, how the Canadian government both perceived and dealt with them as immigrants, why they left Germany, who assisted them in leaving and, finally, how they made the trip across the ocean to Canada. As such, it concerns itself with what happened in Germany as much as with events in Canada. From its inception then, the work was intended to be a contribution to migration studies more than to the literature of Germans in Canada.

1
Migration in the 1850s and 1860s

In the two decades after 1850, the movement of Germans to Canada became increasingly distinguishable from earlier migrations. The explanation for this is straightforward: in both British North America and the German Confederation the first modernizing effects of the Industrial Revolution were being felt. Although more apparent in Germany than Canada at this time, the Industrial Revolution nevertheless affected economic growth, technological advances, social restructuring, and political evolution either directly or indirectly in both lands. In so doing, it necessarily influenced migrant makeup, motivations, and opportunities. Because for generations governments had considered the movement of their subjects important and consequently had sought to control such movement, it seems appropriate to begin by considering the political context for the movement of peoples from the German states to British North America at the midpoint of the nineteenth century.

The Political Background
In the generation after midcentury, Canadian and German politics reveal some interesting and suggestive parallels. Both states had experienced political upheavals in the second quarter of the nineteenth century, Canada in 1837 and Germany in 1830 and 1848. Both countries were politically disunited in 1850 and tugged at by opposing political forces: Austria and Prussia for the multiple German states, and England and the United States for the several parts of British North America. After 1850 both countries, although divided by regional and religious differences, nevertheless experienced the rapid growth of modern national consciousness in the two decades; in both countries the threat of war pushed the unity movement forward; and finally, by 1870 both Germany and Canada had forged the first stages of successful political unification. All these political developments helped shape the traditional push-pull forces influencing German-Canadian migration.

Despite the political reaction that dominated Germany in the 1850s, the defeat of the 1848 liberal nationalists had not quashed the ideal of German unification.[1] The unity movement re-emerged with new vigour after 1860. Indeed, the period from 1860 to the proclamation of the German Empire at Versailles in January 1871 witnessed a dramatic reduction of traditional German particularism. The old, loose German Confederation was replaced first by the North German Confederation and then by the Empire of Bismarck and Wilhelm I.[2] By the time Wilhelm I acceded to the imperial office in 1871, the German states had suffered through two decades of revolution, reaction, war, and precipitous unification. Now the daunting task of forging administrative and political unity remained. Although the country's political state following the Franco-Prussian War may have satisfied nationalists, Prussians, or converted liberals, other significant groups including socialists, Catholics, doctrinaire liberals, and South Germans viewed the future with less equanimity.[3] Unsurprisingly, the years between 1850 and 1870, with their early stifling political oppression, followed by the uncertainty of multiple wars and major political reshuffling, and finally the abrupt imposition of new political institutions, saw the continuation of mass migration out of the German homeland to new political environs in the United States, Australia, and Canada.[4]

At the same time that Bismarck was crafting the new Germany, British North America was experiencing political transformation. The historic conflict between English Upper Canada and French Lower Canada, the independent attitudes of the Maritime provinces of New Brunswick, Nova Scotia, and Prince Edward Island, as well as Newfoundland, and the sheer distance of British Columbia from the east continued to frustrate national unity. In Canada, the most populous province, the sectional and religious split between the two founding national groups, institutionalized in the province's system of political dualism, had all but paralyzed politics at midcentury. This paralysis in Upper and Lower Canada in some ways paralleled the German North-South, Prussian-Austrian stand-off taking place at roughly the same time. Despite these political problems, fundamental forces for changing the political order in British North America were at work, just as they were in the former Holy Roman Empire.[5]

Moreover, in British North America as in Germany, an external state unduly influenced political developments. In British North America, the United States exerted the pressure for change. Caught up in its own sectionalisms, which inspired an aggressive expansionism not only into the Mexican-controlled southwest but also to the north and west, the United States in the 1840s and 1850s assumed an ever more menacing posture to many British North Americans. Manifested earlier in the Oregon and Maine boundary disputes, the American threat now appeared in an aggressive expansion onto the northern plains adjacent to the unsettled British-controlled lands stretching from Lake of the Woods to the Crown colony in British Columbia. The American Civil War intensified the apparent threat to the point where the several parts of British America felt endangered enough to draw together.[6]

Although fear of war with the United States did much to bind British Americans together emotionally and to stimulate a nascent nationalism, by itself hostility toward the United States was insufficient to effect political unity. Other, less emotional factors contributed to the development of a viable Canadian unification movement at the beginning of the 1860s. British willingness to support self-determination in British North America was one. The repeal of the Corn Laws in 1846, the grant of responsible government in 1848, and the removal of the Navigation Acts in 1849 all provided evidence of such willingness. Furthermore, the reciprocity treaty that Canada negotiated with the United States in 1854 indicated an expanding British North American desire for increased self-determination. Of even greater importance to the feasibility of British North American unity, however, was the appearance of new technology, in the form of the steamboat and what J.B. Brebner labels that "great, impersonal, international engine of earth conquest, the railway itself."[7] Appearing initially in British North America in the 1840s, the railroad expanded significantly in the next decade. By 1856 the plans for the Grand Trunk Railway, a rail link from Lake Huron to the Atlantic Ocean, had been laid out and the central section from Toronto to Montreal was already completed. The physical barrier of distance that had separated the region since its settlement had thus begun to come down, making the vision of a united British America seem plausible for the first time. Finally, the social context seemed favourable; as David Gagen argues, a social crisis in Canada West involving inadequate land for new settlers plus declining opportunities for those already settled had generated "popular interest in confederation and its territorial objectives."[8]

With the stars thus in conjunction, efforts to realize this vision began in the early 1860s. Several dramatic events facilitated the union movement. A new coalition government in Canada led by John A. Macdonald of Upper Canada and George-Étienne Cartier of Lower Canada, the publication by this government of a proposal for a general British American federation, and the surprising willingness of the Maritime provinces (Nova Scotia and New Brunswick in particular) to allow representatives from Canada to attend their constitutional conference in Charlottetown in September 1864 constituted "the greatest breakthrough in British American political history."[9] The Charlottetown meetings were followed over the next several years by additional conferences in North America and in London, culminating in July 1867 with the establishment of the Dominion of Canada. The dominion originally comprised three provinces: Canada, New Brunswick, and Nova Scotia.[10] With a Canadian federal framework in place, Macdonald, the first prime minister of the new dominion, lost no time in developing not only the ideal but the reality of the Canadian nation-state.[11] Under his leadership, the province of Manitoba and the North-West Territories were added to the dominion in 1870, British Columbia in 1871, and Prince Edward Island in 1873. All these lands, but particularly the newest areas of Canadian settlement in the west, needed economic development and people to make them viable political entities.

Confederation supporters understood the importance of immigration. Initially the British North America Act placed immigration and agriculture under the concurrent jurisdictions of the federal and provincial governments. This linking of agriculture and immigration followed logically from the assumption that the vast majority of those ultimately settling the West would be farmers. It did not take long to recognize that the federal government should be granted more extensive powers in controlling and directing immigration, and the first federal Immigration Act, passed in 1869, placed regulating immigration squarely in the hands of the federal government. Ottawa could now regulate conditions on board ships landing immigrants in Canada, as well as restrict undesirables such as paupers, criminals, or the disabled from entering the country. In addition, the Dominion Lands Act of 1872 placed control of the western lands exclusively with the federal government. Thus, a system to receive immigrants and to provide for them was in place when the Macdonald government unveiled its National Policy in the next decade.[12]

The Economic Context
Whether enough people could be induced to migrate to Canada and settle the West depended on a variety of factors. For German migrants, two of the most significant were the material promises of Canada and the concurrent economic conditions in Germany. Like the political order, the German economy experienced great changes in the period 1850-70. Although its widely hailed industrialization process had begun well before, the real industrial take-off period in Germany did not begin until the 1850s.[13] Equally fundamental alterations in agricultural procedures and output paralleled the far-reaching changes happening in industrial organization and production. The two spheres of agriculture and industry had reciprocal influences on each other and both were in turn profoundly affected by a Europe-wide demographic revolution that increased Germany's population by nearly 60 percent between 1816 and 1865.

A dynamic and complex affair, German industrialization produced in the first two decades after midcentury a market economy growing at a rate of over 2.5 percent a year. A significant heavy industrial sector of iron, steel, and coal developed. Closely associated with these burgeoning industries, as both cause and effect, was the huge expansion of Germany's railways.[14] With the spectacular growth of the rail system came, in turn, expansion in subsidiary industries such as engineering, metallurgy, and building construction. Consumer goods production took off as well; textiles, leather goods, glassware, and ceramics all experienced rapid expansion, as did the food and drink processing industries. Investment capital from a newly developing banking system financed both industrial and consumer goods production. And to accommodate the economy's increased scale and complexity, new and more sophisticated business forms emerged, such as joint stock companies and interlocking directorates.[15]

As new factories and businesses appeared in record numbers, the demand for labour grew proportionately. While creating some job opportunities, these new factories rendered obsolescent much traditional industrial work. For example, proto-industries such as linen cloth manufacturing were ruined, causing deindustrialization in rural areas of Germany heavily dependent on such cottage work.[16] Labour became more fluid as record numbers of workers moved into newly developing occupations. This changed Germany's traditional residential patterns, as Germans seeking industrial opportunities migrated from rural settings into towns or from towns into larger cities. This rural to urban migration signalled an equally profound transformation in German agriculture.[17]

Recent studies have emphasized the fundamental, concurrent, and even parallel changes in agriculture that both stimulated Germany's industrial transformation and developed as a response to it. In effect a kind of agricultural revolution occurred at the same time industrialization took off. The basis of this agricultural revolution lay in the widespread introduction of root-crop cultivation. J.A. Perkins succinctly insists that "the really outstanding feature of German agriculture from the 1850s was the considerable expansion of the acres devoted to root-crops and in particular to potatoes and sugar beets."[18] The widespread introduction of root crops greatly speeded up the transition from traditional open field cultivation to enclosed holdings, which tended to be more extensive. The movement toward increased scale or size occurred not only in the east but in central and western Germany as well. With the switch to root crops came changes in procedures for working the land, and reliance on fertilizers, especially potash, spread. Expanding root-crop cultivation also meant new sources for livestock fodder, which in turn expanded animal husbandry. Finally, these changes, like the concurrent innovations in industry, created new demands for capital to finance the transformation. As a result of this rush to root-crop cultivation, Germany's agriculture became "permeated with capitalist attitudes and practices."[19]

As landholding practices altered, crop rotations became obsolete, and production costs increased, agricultural labour changed also. Large-scale grain growing in the east and the spread of root-crop cultivation elsewhere affected labour practices and labourers in two fundamental ways. First, where large-scale capitalist-inspired cultivation existed, the traditional peasant ways of farming tended to disappear. With the abolition of serfdom, completed by 1850, Germany's former serfs had been set free not only from obligations to their lords but from certain rights to the land. Without the customary security of place, the newly emancipated peasant was forced to fend for himself, and peasants were gradually replaced by wage labourers. Second, because the old ties had been severed at the same time that new agricultural processes appeared, Germany's farmers were able to move on to new work. Although migration of agricultural workers had occurred for centuries in Germany, the scale of the movement now surpassed earlier levels, as migratory, often seasonal, agricultural labour became typical. The mass movement of displaced agricultural workers also expressed itself in new migratory patterns, especially in movement from east to west. Displaced or redundant, they abandoned their ancestral homes to seek work in other agricultural districts or in the new urban industries. Many of those hired for farm work as wage labourers thus became rural replicas of those who toiled for wages in the new factories. Unfortunately, the employment opportunities in the new industrial and revamped agricultural sectors were inadequate to absorb the surplus labour force created by the demographic upswing and the recent developments in agriculture and industry that had displaced so many artisans and agricultural workers.[20]

During the two decades after 1850, Canada's economic development appeared neither as dramatic nor as innovative as Germany's.[21] Canada's slower growth had much to do with the strength of the traditional conservative myth that envisioned Canada as primarily "a pastoral society composed of sturdy yeoman farmers surrounded by comfortable houses and a real sense of community."[22] In fact, at Confederation 80 percent of Canadians laboured in the primary spheres of fishing, farming, and lumbering. Canada did develop some new industry in this period: in Lower Canada paper products, leather goods, glassware, and steam engines were being produced. Elsewhere in British North America, however, proto-industries appeared far more common than modern enterprises. As late as the 1860s "grist mills and sawmills, which were linked so closely to the old staple trades, still accounted for forty percent of British American manufacturing."[23]

Although Canada's industrial development appeared modest compared to Germany's, the country showed, as noted above, an impressive advance in transportation technology and infrastructure. Although limited resources had hampered railroad construction before 1850, the subsequent period witnessed a veritable railroad boom.[24] The expansion of the rail system, in turn, stimulated growth not only in related industries but also in agriculture. By tying the distant parts of the Canadian farm economy to the country's growing population centres, rail lines greatly advanced marketing possibilities for formerly isolated frontier producers. The use of steamships also grew proportionately, further facilitating the flow of goods and services to the west along the St. Lawrence River and on the Great Lakes. New roads hacked into the country's undeveloped areas opened up additional opportunities for developing farms, mines, and timber operations. And as these changes occurred, the population of British North America increased by 50 percent, rising from 2.4 million to 3.6 million between 1850 and 1870. This growth decreed that if the economic advances of the previous decades were to continue, Canada would need to locate new lands to settle and additional people to settle them.[25]

Canadian Immigration Policy

Although crucial to Canada's existence, Canadian immigration policy was plagued from the beginning by what Reg Whitaker describes as a "persistent lack of clarity on the one hand" and "a diffusion and fragmentation of responsibility for formulating, executing and enforcing immigration policy between the public and private sectors and between the federal and provincial levels of government" on the other.[26]

Such an absence of clarity and apparent fragmentation certainly existed in the period 1850-70, as evidenced by the public pronouncements of Canada's politicians. For example, when the subject of immigration was broached in the debates of the Legislative Council of the United Province of Canada in the early 1860s, the commentators indicated either concern over the absence of a forthright government policy or limited expectations from any program that might or should exist. To those who complained that not enough was being done to solicit immigrants or to provide opportunities for them once in Canada, immigration opponents responded that the role of government included neither sponsoring nor chaperoning such people. They argued that the country did not need to recruit new settlers nor, once the newcomers had arrived, "to provide them with the means of subsistence, to watch over them, and to see that they did not suffer by their want of success in clearing their farms." In brief, "all that could be expected from the Government was that they [the government] should open up roads into the unsettled lands of the Crown and to offer these lands at a reasonable price." While some urged sending agents to Europe to solicit, skeptics wrote the idea off as foolishly counterproductive: "To send agents to the old country to lecture to the people, and tell them that the Government was ready and anxious to give them large tracts of good land, if they would but spend their little all in reaching these shores, and to have large numbers of people act upon this information, only to be disappointed and disgusted and perhaps, to starve to death, was the very best way possible to check immigration." To be successful, the critics argued, immigration must be induced by private sources, not government officials: "The best immigration agents were those who immigrated to the Province many years ago, and who, in writing home letters to their friends, were in a position to tell them of the advantages the country possessed in the way of bettering the condition of those who might come here."[27]

With Confederation, the immigration debate intensified. As the pressure mounted for Canadian expansion westward, advocates began calling for a more aggressive immigration policy. Senators voiced concerns that local governments could not provide the cheap lands required to convince immigrants to settle in the dominion, and demanded that Ottawa intervene actively with both a new federal lands policy promising such cheap land and a new approach to immigrant solicitation in Europe. The parliamentary debates for May 1868, for example, reported that while visiting Europe Senator Macpherson had noted how

> emigration was conducted there [by the Americans]. He found at all the leading ports both consuls and shipping agents very busy in inducing men to emigrate to the United States. Numerous placards were posted up, offering free lands in the most attractive part of the United States to those who would emigrate and the consuls were acting as emigration agents as all should do. It was a great mistake made by this country in not having qualified emigration agents in Europe; if we had sent such agents there as were sent by the United States, the Minister of Immigration would not have had to make the mortifying statement which he had had to make today, [namely, that] the tide of immigration is now setting strongly towards the Western States and it would be very difficult to change it.[28]

Unfortunately for Macpherson and those who shared his views, the unclear or nonexistent Canadian immigration policy in Germany and Europe continued for several more years.

The lack of a German recruitment policy in Canada prompted private Germans to volunteer their immigrant-proselytizing services to Ottawa. Some of the proposals included explicit policy guidelines. For example, in the fall of 1868, Dr. Becker, a former British army surgeon and veteran of the Crimean War living in Colchester, England, wrote to Governor General Viscount Monck to suggest that "if Ottawa would only offer 100 acres of land to every head of a family and to every male child by 18 years old," this would "induce thousands of people, instead of going to the United States to settle in British territory." The surgeon continued, "It would without a shadow of a doubt revolutionize the present immigration," causing "thousands to ascend the St. Lawrence and Ottawa Rivers and settle, wherever the Colonial Government should see fit." The people Becker had in mind were his own Germans: "It is particularly the German population which I intend to choose Canada as their future home. They are small people, of small means, but still industrious and honest, not likely to shirk back from the first year's hardships." He concluded by offering his own professional services: "The scheme would work well under an appointed general Agent who by his personal knowledge of the different localities in Germany and their people, would be able to demonstrate to them the advantages of a colony under British rule, rather than under a Republican government. All this I would do with pleasure and come with them if the Government would allow a free passage for me and my family."[29]

Another epistle from March 1869 to the minister of agriculture from William Raich, editor and publisher of the *German Canadian* in Waterloo, Ontario, echoed Dr. Becker's sentiments. Raich urged Minister Jean-Charles Chapais that "if Your Honor has not agreed upon any certain plan [for soliciting German immigrants in Germany] I would offer my services to you and encourage my countrymen in Germany to come to Canada." Claiming to have been in Germany in 1867 delivering public lectures on behalf of several western US states, Raich assured the minister that he was not only thoroughly informed on matters in Germany but on Canada as well. "I am most sure," he insisted, "that this [a public lecture] is the best way of routing information to the Germans and they are a pretty good class of settlers, which we want in Canada." And the cost of his services would be most reasonable: "The Salary, Traveling Expense, Printing ... would amount to about $7.00 per day or $2500 per year for which I could deliver about 200 lectures in the different cities of North, Middle and South Germany and give all information required by those who want to come to Canada."[30] Letters like these did not cease until a more clearly enunciated immigration program took shape.

Migration Morphology: Nature and Causes

Unlike Canada, Germany suffered no dearth of people in 1850. As noted, the German states had been experiencing the larger European demographic revolution for nearly a century. Although many causes have been suggested to explain this population increase, a declining mortality rate seems to have been the most significant factor for Germany, as elsewhere. In any case, between 1816 and 1865 the population of the German states (Prussia plus the Confederation) grew from about thirty-two million to fifty-two million, an increase of over 60 percent. Population density in the individual states expanded accordingly, although considerable variety existed in growth rates from state to state. As the century progressed, a pattern describing this population explosion appeared in the form of regional shifts. In the two decades after 1850, the movement shifted away from the northwest, south, and southwest toward the Rhineland and the northeast.

As with the general population expansion, the suggested causes for the regional variations have been several. Although increasing fertility rates or sympathetic public policy may have contributed to the faster growth of some regions, local and internal conditions were not the only determinants. External factors such as migration often played equally significant roles. Indeed, the movement of people across the landscape, whether as external emigration or as internal movement from one part of Germany to another, particularly distinguished the second half of the nineteenth century. Migration within Germany could be traditional, as when agricultural workers travelled from one rural setting to another to find work, or it could be into the cities or towns offering new employment opportunities. Involving more effort and greater distances, emigration represented an even more dramatic change of circumstances. Although overseas emigration had occurred at earlier times, the new feature in the mid-nineteenth century was the volume of those moving out of Germany entirely. The first great surge of emigration began in 1845 and continued into the mid-1850s. In 1854 alone over a quarter of a million departed. Over a million people left Germany between 1845 and 1858. Then numbers declined until 1864, when a second major movement began. Continuing until the economic crisis of 1873, this renewed exodus saw another million leave.

The abolition of traditional strictures designed to prevent emigration proved to be crucial to this enhanced movement. Customarily, Europe's mercantilists had equated the state's well-being (its wealth and power) with healthy population numbers. Mercantilist theory therefore justified any state act that would guarantee such numbers, including limiting the movement of individual subjects. The legacy of eighteenth-century liberal political as well as economic and social theory clearly undermined the mercantilist belief in the state's power to manipulate population to the state's benefit. Although the post-Napoleonic period witnessed an effort to restore the *ancien régime*, with its hierarchical social order and controlled economy, the liberal concept of free movement advanced nevertheless. This liberal advance also occurred in the newly created German Confederation.

There, the decline of the state's documentary control over individual movement, which extended back to the fifteenth century, moved forward step by step as the nineteenth century itself advanced. Although the several German states were quite reluctant to abandon police surveillance, visas, passports, and residency requirements, the labour needs of the emerging capitalist economy necessitated a relaxation of such controls. Deregulation progressed from a modest loosening of the process by which passports were acquired, to agreements among several states authorizing limited movement (e.g., the Pass Card Treaty of 1850) to outright abolition of passports by several states including Saxony, Bavaria, and Württemberg in 1865. This progressive relaxation climaxed with the decriminalization of movement in the Passport Law passed by the North German Confederation in 1867. The German elimination or reduction of passport restrictions was duplicated elsewhere in Europe. This widespread opening-up contributed directly

to the great Atlantic migration that reached its crescendo in the two generations preceding the Great War.[31]

Emigrants' reasons for leaving Germany varied. The usual explanations
included seeking political asylum, religious freedom, opportunities for adventure, social security, or economic opportunity. All emigrants, however,
had to make the wrenching decision to sever ties with their native land. As
Peter Marschalck describes the process, "Whatever the motives – as various
as they were – they could only lead to emigration if the would-be emigrant
had resolved to cut himself loose from the homeland and if a land existed
elsewhere that offered him the same employment opportunities in agriculture or handicrafts that had existed previously in the old country."[32] The
specific motives prompting Germans to leave in the period 1850-70 were
generally not religious, political, or adventuresome, but basically social and
economic. The rapid population growth, plus the changes in landholding
practices and the decline of the artisan trades described above, all exerted
pressure on the traditional social and economic systems. Germany's rural,
small-village population, and most notably small landholders and landless
agricultural workers, together with marginalized artisans and redundant
proto-industrial workers, experienced the most intense economic pressure
to emigrate.[33] Klaus Bade sums up the situation thus: "The immigrant ships
were filled with those social groups caught up in the maelstrom of social
and economic change who tried to escape the misery which characterized
the reserve army of the hopelessly unemployed."[34] Because the recently begun industrialization had not advanced far enough to absorb these declassed
groups, they had few options other than leaving.

These emigrants were mostly family units. In general, families migrated
after having been pushed out of their native land more than because they
were pulled to the new homeland. Overwhelmingly, the first wave of Germans leaving in the early 1850s was composed of small peasants and artisans fleeing the economic distress that burdened the overpopulated rural
southwestern states of Baden, Württemberg, and the Palatinate. The second emigrant wave, beginning in the 1860s, again included significant
numbers from agricultural areas in the west, but increasingly former peasants from the east and northeast appeared among those leaving. By the
end of the 1860s, for example, Mecklenburg, the eastern provinces of Prussia, and Saxony had all lost nearly a third of their agricultural workers to
migration.

As the geographic origin of the emigrants shifted to the north and east,
typical immigrant family and marital status changed also. Although statistics from the period 1850-70 are more incomplete than those of later times,
enough partial data exist to allow a measure of sex and age determination.
The available data indicate that persons under the age of ten made up about
20 percent of the emigrant population between 1850 and 1870. The impli-

cations of this are clear: families, rather than individuals travelling alone, composed the majority of German emigrants in the first several decades after 1850. The prevalence of children further confirms the picture of small freeholding families leaving Germany because "they could not, despite the existence of cottage industry, earn enough to survive."[35] This preindustrial emigration declined only toward the end of the 1860s, when the number of independent small farmers and artisan families among the departing started to drop off. Meanwhile, as Germany's industrialization progressed, the proportion of unmarried, landless agricultural workers and factory labourers in the emigrant population expanded.

The overwhelming majority, nearly 85 percent, of Germans emigrating in the decades 1850-70 headed for the United States, where they believed the best opportunities in agriculture or the traditional handicrafts lay. But a significant proportion of the remaining 15 percent selected the British provinces as their North American destination. Marschalck estimates that between 1851 and 1870 some 1,749,200 Germans immigrated to the United States while Canada received 52,400 new Germans.[36] And Canada, as noted, needed people. In 1850 British North America, which in size exceeded the whole of western Europe, possessed a population of less than two and a half million. Despite steady immigration from Europe, which between 1850 and 1870 totalled just under half a million souls, the population of Canada grew relatively slowly after 1850. The large numbers of Canadians migrating to the United States during this period offset the immigrants entering the dominion.[37]

Migrants and Images

Although the vast majority of the half-million immigrants entering Canada at this time hailed from the British Isles, a small percentage emigrated from Germany. A precise calculation of Germans who settled permanently in British North America is difficult to make. Many ship ledgers recording immigrants coming to Canada did not describe their German passengers as Germans.[38] On British ships there were only four nationality categories: English, Scottish, Irish, and Foreigner. Moreover, many of the "foreigner" Germans who landed in New Brunswick or Quebec headed straight for the United States, using Canada only as a transit zone. Nevertheless, some of the arrivals remained in Canada. The best estimates suggest that about a third of those immigrants who either landed in Canada directly from Europe or entered from the United States settled in British North America. This low German retention rate nevertheless greatly exceeded that for the Norwegian migrants who entered Quebec as part of the contemporaneous Norwegian-Canadian timber exchange. Almost all of the nearly 100,000 Norwegian immigrants who landed at Quebec between 1850 and 1874 moved on to homesteads in Wisconsin and Iowa.[39]

For the Germans, a report covering the years 1846 to 1861 described 50,644 Germans disembarking at Quebec. Of these, 16,370 stayed on in Canada. The vast majority of newly arrived Germans who did put down roots between 1850 and 1870 ended up in Upper Canada, where they joined the majority English-speaking element residing along the shores of the St. Lawrence River and the Great Lakes to the west. In his report for 1863 the Prussian consul in Quebec, Gustav Beling, listed only 672 of 23,578 German-born residents in Canada as living in French-speaking Lower Canada.[40] Most who migrated to Canada in this period came as immigrant families rather than as individuals. For example, of the passengers delivered to Quebec in 1868 from Bremen, 39 percent were under ten years old; from Hamburg in the same year the figure reached almost 49 percent; while in 1869 children under ten constituted just over 18 percent of passengers from Bremen.[41]

Why Germans chose British North America in general and specifically Upper Canada depended on several factors, including chance. As with nearly all transoceanic migrations, the decision was influenced by the general economic conditions in the sending and receiving lands and the political climate affecting whether they would be able to leave the old world and enter the new. Free Canadian land available for any intended settler certainly acted as a powerful inducement, but the reasons many emigrants ended up in Canada can only be described as fortuitous. Those, for example, who intended to settle in the United States but landed in Quebec rather than New York and then decided after disembarking, for whatever reason, to remain in Canada would qualify as fortuitous emigrants. Evidence indicates significant numbers of these. Reasons for remaining in Canada ranged from insufficient funds to finish the original journey, to fatigue or sickness caused by the voyage from Germany that prevented further travel, to approval of the country and people encountered in Canada that induced them to stay on.

Besides the absence of a clear Canadian immigration policy, three main reasons explain why so few German emigrants heading for North America chose Canada for settlement: the nearly irresistible lure of the American republic for many Germans, the deep-seated ignorance of Canada and things Canadian in Germany, and the negative image of Canada held throughout much of Germany during the first half of the nineteenth century. The powerful, indeed magnetic, draw of "America," which could be traced back several generations, provided the basis for the successful recruitment of German emigrants by the several US states. Compared to Canada, Michigan, Wisconsin, and Missouri had developed by midcentury much more comprehensive and sophisticated recruitment practices. Canada could simply not compete on the same level. The ignorance of Canada and the negative image problem in Europe and Germany were interrelated, and both had existed for some time. Fundamental to this negative image was climate, which, as Mabel Timlin puts it, "for many years had been an enemy to Canadian immigration."[42] In England, Kipling's vision of Canada as "Our Lady of the Snows" held sway long before he published his poem. In France, Voltaire's popularization of Canada as a frozen land inhabited by savages endured. In nineteenth-century Germany, the popular view considered Canada merely "a land of snow and ice with bears, wolves, and reindeer," a frozen, wild, primitive place "unsuitable for European settlement or culture."[43] An article in Rudolstadt's *Allgemeine Auswanderungszeitung* (General Emigration Newspaper) in August 1865 complained how difficult it was to counter the popular prejudice in Germany that in Canada "it is so cold the blood stops circulating and even the mercury [in the thermometers] freezes."[44]

When one ponders the real motivations behind the emigration at midcentury, Canada's negative image in Germany assumes even greater importance. Most historians who have considered this emigration agree that fundamental social and economic forces in Germany drove the outmigration: the threat of pauperization and precipitous social decline pushed these emigrants out of Europe. They migrated to America, as Rheinhard Doerries puts it, not because they were pulled there by outstanding opportunities but because they were literally driven out of their native land. In America at midcentury economic and social conditions were not appreciably better than they had been before 1850. If the American pull were, as Doerries contends, not determinative, why then did so many Germans head for the United States and ignore settlement opportunities in Canada? All things being equal on the pull side of the equation, it would seem that more Germans should have been ready to try Canada as their new homeland. That they did not can be explained not only by the absence of a clear German immigration policy in Ottawa but also by the widespread ignorance of Canada in Germany and by the negative associations that British North America conjured up in the minds of many Germans.[45]

Before Canada could improve its drawing power, it had to be able to compete with the United States. From the beginning, this posed a serious, if not insurmountable, obstacle because the American apologists had been aggressively promoting the United States in Germany for more than a generation before Canada's officials decided to commence soliciting emigrants there. The version of America then circulating in Germany was both older and based upon more varied sources, which complicated the Canadian task of creating an image as attractive as the American one. The fascinating, and for some compellingly attractive, picture of America circulating in Germany in 1850 owed its existence not only to official American accounts but also to the efforts of Germany's own literary figures.

The majority of official American accounts designed to lure German settlers were produced not by the federal government but by individual states seeking to fill their undeveloped lands. State officers believed, as Philip Taylor writes, that the state's "growth and prosperity depended largely upon the contribution immigrants could make in settling its land and building up its industry."[46] Michigan and Wisconsin set the pace, but many other states, including Minnesota, Iowa, Missouri, Texas, Ohio, West Virginia, Oregon, Nebraska, Louisiana, and Tennessee, joined in the promotion effort, and competition among them could be intense.[47] In the period 1850-70, the several states advertised most often for agricultural immigrants, although after the Civil War industrial workers were increasingly sought by some. Not until the closing of the American frontier in 1890 did solicitation begin to switch over from agricultural to large-scale industrial immigration. After 1850 the railroads and steamship lines joined the states in the solicitation effort. Often the states and the transportation companies published their own brochures and advertised in German newspapers. The American image was also conveyed throughout the eighteenth and nineteenth centuries by letters from immigrants living in the United States to friends and relatives back home.[48]

Most often, propaganda emphasized the high standard of living enjoyed by Americans, and specifically the economic advantages of migrating to the United States. In its publications, for example, Wisconsin described the state's natural resources, population, vocational opportunities, and land policies rather than political institutions or educational traditions.[49] American prosperity, these sources emphasized, derived in large measure from the land's natural wealth. The country had extensive mineral deposits, valuable timber reserves, and superior soil for growing everything from wheat to apples. In the United States, land was available to the would-be settler either free of charge or for a nominal sum. Any immigrant, regardless of personal wealth, could realize material well-being in this "land of unlimited opportunities"; the only requirement for success was determination and hard work. And once ensconced in America, the new citizen would enjoy a social equality and mobility unlike anything available in Europe. As one immigrant wrote home, in America "no one takes off his hat to another as you do in Germany."[50]

Nearly equal in importance to the propaganda produced by the states and transportation firms for shaping German opinion was the romanticized frontier literary tradition exported to Germany from America. Although not the first to write about the US frontier, James Fenimore Cooper was nevertheless "the first to seize upon and exploit this immeasurable wealth of literary material."[51] Cooper's works, which described noble Native Americans and rough, natural frontier people, gave Europeans a supposedly in-depth look at frontier life in the new republic across the sea. Such novels as *The Pioneers* (1823), *The Prairie* (1827), and *The Last of the Mohicans* (1826) spread Cooper's fame throughout Europe, and a kind of Cooper mania swept

Germany in the second quarter of the nineteenth century.[52] Cooper's German readers included not simply the educated middle class but large numbers of society's literate lower orders as well.

Cooper's popularity in Germany may be attributable to several causes. One factor was the contemporary German political context, for the years between 1815 and 1848 were characterized by repression and reaction. The chaos of early industrialization and economic change no doubt also played a role. To youthful spirits suffering in Germany's stifling climate, the primeval forests of Cooper's novels appeared as a fresh, invigorating, free place for vicarious escape. This period also witnessed the flowering of Germany's own romantic literary movement. In such an environment, the image of Cooper's American Indian, presumably a more realistic version of Rousseau's noble savage, fit in nicely. Cooper's picture of the wild, untrammelled American frontier, and its strong, energetic, natural, and free inhabitants, appealed to Germans who had become disenchanted with their own land; it appealed to what has been labelled the *Europamüdigkeit* (Europe fatigue) of those weary of Germany's allegedly effete civilization.[53] Julian Schmidt, a literary historian writing at midcentury, explained the German fascination for Cooper and other depicters of the American wilderness: "From the misery of our own circumstances arises the yearning for primeval forests, Indians, and other products of nature."[54]

The American frontier literary tradition that Cooper introduced to Germany inspired a number of native authors to follow his example, creating a German school of American frontier novelists and travel writers. The five most prominent authors to elaborate on what Cooper had begun were Charles Sealsfield, Otto Ruppius, Friedrich Gerstäcker, Friedrich Armand Strubberg, and Balduin Mollhausen. All these authors had lived in America and experienced the frontier personally before writing about it. Charles Sealsfield (1793-1864), the first German author to write an Indian novel, created in *Der Legitime und der Indianer* (The Lawful and the Indian, 1833), for example, his own version of Cooper's heroes Hawkeye and Chingachgook.[55] Otto Ruppius (1819-64), who lived on the US frontier for a dozen years, returned to Germany in 1861. In the three years before he died, he produced eight novels celebrating German immigrants on the American frontier. A contemporary of Ruppius, Friedrich Gerstäcker (1816-72), was even more productive, turning out nearly 150 volumes of travelogues and novels dealing with the new world. His most famous work, *Nach Amerika! Ein Volksbuch* (To America! A People's Book) described real-life German immigrants in America. But he also wrote about Indians, frontiersmen, and America's natural landscape. Indeed, A.J. Prahl claims, "Nature and freedom are the two key words which again and again appear in Gerstäcker's writings which deal with the people of the Middle West." Gerstäcker glorified the primitive life led by the westerners in contrast to the unnatural life of city dwellers and people in Europe, particularly in Germany. Nature and freedom produce in the backwoodsmen and farmers the qualities Gerstäcker admires: "They are affable and courteous, hospitable and subtle, brave and frank, free of earthly anxiety."[56]

Friedrich Armand Strubberg (1806-89) lived a number of years in Texas before starting his literary career in 1858. His first work, *Amerikanische Jagd und Reisenabenteuer aus meinem Leben in den Westlichen Indianergebieten* (American Hunting and Travel Adventures in the Western Indian Territories) described what the title promised – Indians and the frontier. In the twenty years thereafter Strubberg published more than fifty novels dealing with the moving American frontier. Finally, Balduin Mollhausen (1825-1905) also authored over 150 volumes of travel books and novels describing America and concentrated on the frontier. Having lived with Native people and worked for the government as an explorer in the wilderness, Mollhausen came closest to imitating Cooper. *Der Halbindianer und der Majordomo* (The Half-Indian and the Major-domo), for example, contains a version of Cooper's Natty Bumpo.[57]

The great productivity of the Cooper imitators and the widespread enthusiasm for the works of Cooper himself testify to the popularity of the American frontier in mid-nineteenth-century Germany. To the romantic appeal of youth, nature, and adventure that this literature provided for those who felt stifled or weary of their own German context must be added the blood connection. Preston Barba sums up this nexus well: "The demand for such literature is easily explained when we remember that there was hardly a family, even in the remoter villages of Germany, which did not have a member, friend, or relative seeking his fortune in America."[58] This onslaught of frontier literature supplemented the propaganda materials disseminated by state governments and transportation companies, and personal letters from emigrants, which begins to explain how knowledge of America became so widespread in Germany. This dissemination created not only interest in the United States but also an image of America that combined the promise of wealth and abundance with the titillating challenge of frontier adventure and violence; elements of danger, excitement, and novelty merged with concrete material awards. In short, from the works of the immigration publicists and Cooper-inspired novelists, America emerged, in Ray Billington's words, as a "Land of Savagery, Land of Promise."[59] This negative/positive image dichotomy was the challenge Canadian apologists confronted.

To contest the American success at winning German emigrants two preconditions had to be fulfilled. First, a real desire to recruit Germans as Canadian settlers was needed; Canadian recruiters had to extend their recruitment vision beyond the British Isles. Second, and less difficult, was the creation of a new image for Canada. Such an image had already begun to emerge in the decades after 1850, and it appeared in Germany almost from its inception. Because Canada lacked the advantages of a Cooper-style literary celebration, printed sources disseminating the new image consisted almost exclusively of newspaper accounts and brochures published by agents of Canada to promote emigration. The majority of these reports trumpeted the virtues of Canada. What these virtues were and how they were presented to German audiences remained, as shall be shown, largely consistent throughout the period described in this book.

In general, the new vision of Canada was based on two often contradictory sets of assumptions. On the one hand, apologists repeatedly presented Canada in romantic fashion as a uniquely unspoiled and natural land, wild and beautiful, mysterious and spiritual; on the other, it was described as a progressive, dynamic, and, most of all, civilized society. This dual presentation accorded with the ambivalence regarding tradition and change so apparent in the mid-nineteenth-century Western world, including Germany. The romantic and wild version of Canada thus could appeal to the allegedly spiritual and nonmaterialistic German who rejected the crassness and shallowness of the modern age in favour of the unspoiled and natural, while the dynamic, civilized rendition supposedly attracted Germans who embraced the progress and material advances associated with modernization. For the Faust types who were torn between the spiritual and material, Canada could be doubly fascinating.

In nearly every romantic description of Canada that appeared in Germany from the period before the Hudson's Bay lands were added to the dominion, the country appeared as a huge, sparsely settled land dominated by primeval forests *(Urwald)*. Europeans were present, but their settlements had barely scratched the surface of the vast uncharted land. At this time, the broader concept of Canada included not only Upper and Lower Canada (later Ontario and Quebec) but also the eastern provinces New Brunswick, Nova Scotia, Newfoundland, and Prince Edward Island. The great North West, stretching from Ontario to the colony of British Columbia, was only beginning to be treated as part of the Canadian whole. The allusions to Canada appearing in mid-nineteenth-century Germany referred primarily to Lower and Upper Canada, which still possessed extensive tracts of virgin lands. These undeveloped areas, and especially the wild, unsettled areas of Ontario, appealed strongly to the German romantic's fascination with pure nature, and their descriptions in the German press afford the most common and complete presentations of the Canadian romantic ideal.

In their undisturbed and natural state, the virgin tracts of northern and western Ontario, it was claimed, contained an overabundance of natural resources. For example, in 1852 the *Deutsche Auswanderer-Zeitung* (German Emigrants Newspaper), which appeared in Bremen, touted the province's mineral wealth as including lead, iron, silver, gold, tin, and copper "in huge quantities."[60] The same article reported that in similar fashion the seemingly endless forests of oak, maple, birch, elm, ash, hickory, butternut, cherry, poplar, cypress, hazelnut, sycamore, white pine, spruce, chestnut, and black walnut trees formed storehouses of valuable timber. Furthermore, these woods teemed with an extensive list of wild animals, some suitable for food, others valuable for their fur. Besides the edible deer, moose, and rabbits, there were innumerable ducks and geese for table fare. The passenger pigeons were so abundant that when migrating south in the fall they "filled the sky like clouds." The forests also contained such exotic furbearers as wolverines, foxes, martens, minks, weasels, beavers, and muskrats. Wolves and bears were also present, but "not to be feared" because they kept to themselves in the undeveloped areas of the country. In addition, Ontario's untracked north and west possessed extensive rivers and countless lakes filled with prize trout, pike, bass, and salmon.

Distinct from European custom, this abundant wild game was not the preserve of a special, privileged class. Accounts of life in the Canadian wilds nearly always pointed out the spectacular hunting and fishing opportunities available to all Canadian residents. For example, a letter from a German settler in northern Ontario that appeared in May 1871 in the *Allgemeine Auswanderungszeitung* contained the following report: "If he is fond of hunting, the landowner in his free time can stock in a good supply of meat for the winter. The woods are full of deer and smaller game which in some cases have valuable pelts. Feathered game, such as spruce grouse, are present in some areas in unbelievable numbers."[61] Thus, for the immigrant in Canada, hunting and fishing were both a right and a privilege, bringing the resident of Canada's wilds into direct and intimate contact with elemental nature. To succeed at living off the land by hunting or fishing, one had not only to live in the midst of the animals being pursued; one had also to know their secrets in the same way the Native Americans did. Hunting in Canada might turn one into another Natty Bumpo, Cooper's natural man in tune with the primeval forest and its creatures. In so promising, Canada offered the romantic imagination an experience every bit as alluring as the American one.

While the popular press and recruitment brochures depicted nature in Canada as untamed and uncharted, another more benign version also appeared. In the benign account, Canada's climate was neither as harsh nor as forbidding as so often claimed. Canada's apologists repeatedly insisted that the country's climate and particularly its winters were not unbearably cold. Both Upper and Lower Canada were often described as having milder winter months than many of the bordering American states. An article appearing in December 1854 in the *Deutsche Auswanderer-Zeitung* asserted, "The climate in Canada is milder than that of New York, Illinois, Ohio and Wisconsin."[62] Admittedly the Canadian winters brought ice and snow, but these represented blessings, not burdens. Canadians used the snow to their advantage, for "snow accompanied by hard frost turns the country's roads into the most beautiful thoroughfares" and upon these enchanting streets horse-drawn sleighs travel with ease. Even when some concessions were made to the serious cold of Canada's winters, its negative effects were de-emphasized. A pamphlet from 1858 designed to inform potential immigrants about Canada admitted that "the north wind is the coldest wind of winter" but insisted that this wind was "not rough but gentle."[63] Even when the winters appeared in print accurately as both long and bitterly cold, they were still defended as more beneficent than those of either America or Europe. "The [Canadian] winter" the *Allgemeine Auswanderungszeitung* reported in 1865, "may be harsh and severe, but it offers its special advantages such as the absence of fog and dampness which in milder climates are detrimental to health."[64]

The supposed advantages of Canada's unspoiled natural environment and salubrious climate were continually emphasized. The bracing Canadian weather, apologists argued, contributed to the absence of disease, making Canada a healthier place than either the United States or Europe. Another 1858 pamphlet designed to lure Germans into emigrating summed up the Canadian advantage as follows: "On the whole, Canada's climate is very beneficial to both humans and plants. As a result, those living in Canada have a thoroughly healthy appearance. Sicknesses common in other countries are absent in Canada. Malaria, for example, so common in the United States is seldom found in Canada. Therefore, the mortality rate in Canada is lower than in any other country."[65] During a period when many Europeans suffered not only from malnutrition but also from a multitude of maladies including cholera, typhus, and tuberculosis, the emphasis on Canada's favourable mortality rate in immigration recruitment literature made sense. An article in the *Allgemeine Auswanderungszeitung* in January 1862 purported to show just how superior the Canadian environment really was with a list of the mortality rates for ten European countries and Canada. Russia, with 1 in every 26 persons dying per year, appeared at the top of the list; at the very bottom came Canada, with a mortality rate of 1 for every 102 persons. Incidentally, Prussia and Austria were next in line after Russia, with rates of 1 per 30 and 35, respectively.[66] Lower mortality rates meant that people were living longer, and, according to the *Deutsche Auswanderer-Zeitung,* Canada proved the point. Drawing its figures from the 1851 Canadian census, the paper added up the number of people then living in Canada older than 80 years. The results tabulated as follows: 73 Canadians were 100 or more years old, 208 had lived between 90 and 100 years, and 2,664 fell into the 80-to-90-year-old group. "No country on earth with a population of only 2 million," the article concluded, "can boast a similar number of persons so old. A land in which so many reach such an age must have a climate highly conducive to good health. Whoever wants to live a long time should emigrate to Canada."[67]

Not surprisingly, a climate fostering longevity would also create favourable conditions for successful agriculture. Most brochures and articles that sought to win converts for Canada depicted the country as essentially pastoral. "Agriculture in Canada," a Canadian apologist wrote in the *Allgemeine Auswanderungszeitung*, "is far more a livelihood issue than in the United States. Since we possess neither extensive nor large-scale industry ... our independence from foreign control, the increase in our general well-being, and the existence of our commerce depends essentially on the development and products of our land."[68] Between 1850 and 1870, Canadian agriculture produced grains, meat and dairy products, fruits, and vegetables. Virtually every report sent back to Germany by consuls or other observers described the Canadian agricultural scene as flourishing. These reports showed steady increases in the amount of land under cultivation and the volume of agricultural products produced. Importantly, farmers working their own land produced the agricultural products so necessary for the country's existence. The romantic ideal of the simple, self-reliant, self-respecting peasant landowner was thus being widely realized in Canada.

Moreover, these independent Canadian farmers wrested more than a meagre living from the soil. Toiling happily on their own land, they turned the wilderness into enchanting little Arcadias. An 1865 report in the *Allgemeine Auswanderungszeitung* nicely described what happened after a settler had taken possession of the land: "In the course of a few years an unbelievable transformation takes place. The previous wilderness is transformed into fertile fields. One after another, the tree stumps are uprooted and removed and the plow given free reign. The [primitive] blockhouse is replaced by a more elegant one of stone or wood. A garden is put in which provides vegetables for the family table. An orchard is planted: apples, pears, plums, cherries, and in some areas, splendid peaches are grown. Nowhere in the world do apples reach such impressive size, such beautiful coloration, such wonderful taste as in Canada."[69] The humble Canadian farm held out the promise of paradise; under the right management it could become a veritable Garden of Eden in the North American wilderness.

This flattering transformation incorporates the before and after theme used extensively by American propagandists. A Wisconsin solicitation brochure from 1881 provides an example of this technique. In it, two houses are depicted on one page. The "old farmhouse" is a simple log cabin in the forest with the family members busy at humble tasks: the father chops down a tree, while the mother stands over a cooking fire in the clearing before the house. The page's lower portion presents the "new farmhouse," an elaborate two-storey home with a second-floor balcony, arched windows and doors in both levels, a pillared porch extending off the building's right side, and appropriately elaborate outbuildings behind the main house. No one is working about the house. Rather, a carriage with a driver is drawn up before the front door as if waiting for the master's appearance.[70] The lesson here is not subtle: If you migrate to Wisconsin, you can expect to progress from crude to finished, to rise from bare sufficiency to real wealth and comfort.

The Garden of Eden in Canada was not realized without significant homesteader effort, however. Accounts describing the process of creating a farm, particularly house building and clearing the land, appeared frequently in the popular press. Clearing the land, the most difficult single task confronting the immigrant-farmer, was often depicted in detail. Interested readers and would-be immigrants learned not only about felling trees (dangerous and difficult work) but also about how to remove the logs and stumps, how to stack the felled trees and brush in long rows, and then how to burn this mass of discarded wood. Finally, the reader received instruction on the retrieval of potash from the bonfire's remains.[71]

The portrayals of land clearing showcase a different version of nature from the benevolent, romantic picture described above. In this interpretation, as in the distant Germanic past, a hostile, even threatening, nature confronts humanity. To survive, settlers must strive against nature and force it to do their bidding. The struggle could become heroic. "To be sure," editorialized the *Allgemeine Auswanderungszeitung* in August 1865, "cutting down the forest and clearing the land is hard and often very frustrating work. Nevertheless, because the [settler's] stake in the cutting and clearing is so substantial and the satisfaction derived from it so great, the work unavoidably becomes a kind of labour of love. In a sense then, the axe is swung like a conquering sword. For the settler, mastering the forest is like vanquishing an enemy upon whose defeat the settler's future livelihood and well-being depends."[72] In the aftermath of this battle between settler and primeval forest, civilization could and did enter the picture. Indeed, by 1850, apologists for Canada increasingly emphasized the progress Canada had made in advancing this civilizing process. Thus, the second facet of Canada's image, the civilized one, made its appearance in Germany.

In the period 1850-70 Canada was advertised as a civilized land in a variety of ways. To begin with, it appeared as a progressive country with a huge, almost limitless potential for economic development. To foster the development of both the country and its citizens, Canada fortunately possessed a responsible, responsive, and above all free political system. Although excluding women, this government closely protected the rights of its free males, making citizenship available to any honest man. Good citizenship, it was assumed, followed from informed citizens, so Canada also boasted a comprehensive and enlightened educational system. Thus, at midcentury Canada enjoyed a free, peaceful, and orderly existence in comparison with the United States. Although the United States also offered free land and political participation, these did not come without risks. Aggressive, expansionist America, with its tradition of war (the 1840s had seen the war against Mexico and continued expropriation of Native lands) and its burden of Southern slavery, contrasted sharply with Canada's less belligerent, less frenetic ways. Canada apologists never tired of pointing this out to their German audience.

Although promotional literature usually described Canada as a tradition-bound agrarian paradise, other accounts available in Germany showed its economic system as forward moving. If the country did not equal Great Britain, the United States, or even Germany in industrial activity, it never appeared economically comatose. The introduction of the railroad showed life; so did the frantic building of roads into the bush and the new patent activity apparent in midcentury Canada. This latter development disproved the "hewer of wood and drawer of water" Canadian stereotype by showing, as one enthusiast put it, that "a remarkably acute sense for mechanical matters and a profound understanding of related sciences" existed in Canada.[73] The future development of Canada's economy therefore seemed promising. Among other things, the abundance of fast-running rivers assured an available power source for the country's coming factories.[74] By midcentury, Canadian time had developed that new speeded-up dimension so often associated with modern economic life. "As recently as 14 years ago," an observer noted in 1867, "it took the mail service 10½ days to carry a letter from Quebec to Detroit. Now it can be done in 30 hours."[75]

Nevertheless, apologists not only admitted outright that Canada's industry was more traditional than modern, they even celebrated this traditionalism. Pre-Confederation lists of employment opportunities for Germans in Canada nearly always included positions available in the artisan trades. An 1861 brochure from a Canadian agent in Berlin listed some 15,000 job openings in Upper Canada. Although about three-quarters of these solicited either farmers or domestic servants, some 1,500 alleged openings called for skilled craftsmen such as carpenters, masons, tailors, goldsmiths, and shoemakers.[76] In the same vein, another agent reporting from Quebec in 1867 insisted that "those who enjoy the best chances for employment in Canada are farmers, blacksmiths, masons, locksmiths, tailors, day labourers and housemaids."[77] There were also opportunities in proto-industries such as linen production. Advancements in Canadian flax growing and the linen cloth industry were frequently pointed out and exaggerated claims were not uncommon. An anonymous correspondent to the *Deutsche Auswanderer-Zeitung* in 1853, for example, claimed linen manufacturing had advanced so far in Canada that "flax taken green from the field in the morning could be turned into sturdy cloth by evening of the same day."[78]

This progressively conservative and civilized Canadian economy could only have developed, so propagandists argued, in a supportive political environment. Both small independent farmers and artisans fit easily into Canada's political order, which not only protected individual rights but also relied on citizen participation to make the system function. Thus, the promotional commentaries on Canada's government appearing in Germany during the period 1850-70 emphasized two major points. First, individual Canadians enjoyed extensive personal freedom. They lived, as one commentator put it, "free as a fish in water."[79] Although Canada in 1850 remained tethered to England's monarchy, Canadians enjoyed the same rights and privileges as free Englishmen: "Despite the fact that Canada is a royal province," a German immigrant wrote home in 1853, "it nevertheless enjoys a freedom and independence that does not exist in continental Europe. As England, the mother country of this colony, possesses the freest institutions in Europe, so Canada enjoys the same rights and freedoms. Furthermore, between the independence of the United States and Canada there is no essential difference. For we [Canadians] have the same personal freedom, the same independent law making power, the same protections afforded by the law, and the same free press."[80]

Second, the political system that provided such personal freedom represented its citizens in model fashion. The explanation for this was simple: Canadians enjoyed self-government because they could vote. An 1860 brochure broadcasting Canada's merits explained its broad suffrage: "The right to vote is nearly general. Every man who pays 30 dollars property tax in the cities or who pays 20 dollars tax in the country is permitted to vote." In addition, the pamphlet continued, "All public offices and seats in the legislature are open to any candidate who has the trust of his fellow citizens, owns property, and is a British subject."[81] Immigrants acquired citizenship with all its privileges through naturalization, available to them after a three-year waiting period. Impressive examples of self-government existed throughout the Canadian political system. At the highest level, citizens elected representatives to a legislative council and house of assembly, both modelled on the British parliamentary division between House of Commons and House of Lords. For the average farmer or immigrant, even more obvious expressions of Canada's celebrated self-government appeared at the county and municipal levels, in the citizen's control of taxes. "The municipal taxes," the *Allgemeine Auswanderungszeitung* proclaimed in June 1857, "are raised from a tax on all [real] property in the township or county" and "must be expended for the general welfare." Furthermore, "no special tax could be levied without the prior approval of the municipality's residents."[82]

The very substantial public monies devoted to schools proved convincingly that Canadians supported their revenue-raising system.

Virtually all accounts arguing the advantages of Germans immigrating to Canada focused attention on its impressive system of public education. Supported, as seen, by public monies, this system included grammar schools in each township and county high schools. As settled areas expanded, so did the school system. Between 1842 and 1855, the German press reported, the number of grammar schools in Upper Canada increased from 1,721 to 3,325.[83] To provide instructors for these schools, the provincial government created a normal school, "a highly effective and necessary institute for educating teachers which graduates each year 100 to 150 young men and women who are systematically trained ... so that in Upper Canada a grammar school system has been established that promises great things."[84] To accommodate teachers and students, significant tracts of land were set aside in the townships for schools. The *Deutsche Auswanderer-Zeitung* reported in 1853 that the provincial and local governments in Upper Canada "have made extraordinary outlays for the support of education ... Nearly 500,000 acres have been reserved for educational institutions."[85]

Finally, to emphasize Canada's civilized condition, apologists used the United States as a foil, particularly in the 1860s when civil war and chaos reigned there. The theme of slavery repeatedly appeared in these moral comparisons. Even before the outbreak of the War between the States, the existence of slavery in America was condemned as hypocritically inconsistent with American claims of being a free society. In contrast, Canada not only had no legalized slavery but thousands of escaped slaves living there as free Canadian citizens. "Coloured people," the *Deutsche Auswanderer-Zeitung* pointed out in 1853, "in the British-American provinces enjoy the same rights as whites, and not merely on paper but in fact. For example, one can see mulattoes and Negroes sitting next to their fellow white citizens on juries rendering judgment on whites. A citizen of the United States would find such a proceeding tainted. He would consider a trial in which whites were judged by Negroes or descendants of Negroes not only unusual but hateful."[86]

Canadian recruiters and agents saw the American Civil War as a splendid opportunity to promote Canadian immigration at the expense of the United States. To Germans who themselves had experienced war and revolution, Canadian apologists now offered a peaceful alternative: "During this time of civil war in America, Canada offers the immigrant a homeland where he will enjoy full freedom to move about and to pursue his livelihood undisturbed."[87] Free expression also existed in Canada to a greater degree than in war-torn America. "The violent passions sweeping both the southern and northern United States and the summary proceedings through which opinions are controlled," the *Allgemeine Auswanderungszeitung* editorialized in May 1861, "stand in dramatic contrast to the freedom of discussion to which the immigrant is accustomed in Canada. Indeed, there are numerous examples of men who, harbouring the wrong ideas, have settled in the United States and been either lynched or subjected to other abuses because they dared to exercise a right guaranteed in Canada, namely the right to free speech." The article pointed out that the violent limitations on free speech extended to the press as well: "In both the North and South the mob has established itself as censor"; the oppression "is no worse in New Orleans than in New York, in Baltimore than in Buffalo."[88]

In Canada the violence of intolerant opinion, the terrorist acts of brutal men, and the tyranny of a government that taxed for war and drafted young innocents for battle were mercifully absent. Because civilized Canada exhibited peace, not war, freedom, not slavery, her "social relations, morals, and customs offered more to the European immigrant than did the Yankees." And because the Civil War's moral corruption was likely to continue even after the guns fell silent and the physical destruction stopped, Canada's advantage over the United States as a place for immigrants would remain into the future. In July 1862, the *Allgemeine Auswanderungszeitung* described the American fall from grace that could only advantage the British portion of North America: "Even if this unholy war ends, its effects will not. The magical spell which once surrounded the world-renowned Union has forever been broken." Canada's superiority, the paper claimed, was so "obvious no elaboration is necessary."[89] Despite the truth in much of this, the number of emigrants heading for Canada during the Civil War did not increase dramatically. Although immigration to the United States fell off, Canada's attracting power had not increased enough to exploit the American decline.[90]

In sum, the image created for Canada in the period 1850-70, although modelled in many ways on that of the United States, remained distinct. Despite the fact that both countries touted their free, productive land and their civilized institutions and customs, major differences existed. To the hope for greater wealth and personal freedom, to the promise of low taxes and free public education, the American image added an element absent in the Canadian version, namely, that of adventure or even danger. The America of frontier rough-and-tumble, duels over honour, Indian wars, and mining town prostitutes allegedly did not exist in Britain's North American colony. On the contrary, Canada's promotional materials, composed almost entirely by paid emigration propagandists, were meant to appeal to peaceful, hard-working, sober, responsible types only. The savage land, "Wild West" image bandied about by American apologists and German fiction writers never materialized for Canada. Presumably such a violent, disordered model would not have properly reflected British institutions, customs, or law.

Although printed promotional materials described Canada as a superior choice for would-be immigrants, just how much the propaganda influenced migration remains difficult to measure. The image just described mirrored the ideals of the sturdy, respectable bourgeoisie, reflecting middle-class values prevalent at midcentury in England, Canada, and Germany. Most German emigrants to Canada in the period 1850-70 did not belong to Germany's *Bildungsburgertum*, that is, the wealthy, educated upper middle class, but rather were part of the lower middle class or petty bourgeoisie, being former landowning peasants, agricultural labourers, small craftsmen, and the like. Yet many of these people shared the middle-class values being promoted in the Canada image. Presumably the promise of free land would have influenced them, as Monckmeier recognized: "The most powerful attraction in the new world is the surplus of land which offers the possibility of easy acquisition of one's own place ... The wish to possess one's own land has been the goal of Germany's petty bourgeoisie, skilled craftsmen, and farmers who make up the majority of those who emigrate."[91] How much these same groups were moved by free political institutions, comprehensive education, or social tranquility is more difficult to know. Finally, the romantic image of untamed, wild, spiritual Canadian nature may have appealed to a member of the *Bildungsburgertum* who read Novalis or Goethe on nature, or perhaps James Fenimore Cooper on North America, but most likely not to a ruined freeholding peasant or marginal artisan. The issue of promotional effectiveness is tied not only to socioeconomic class preferences and cultural proclivities but also to image dissemination. This in turn relates directly to the role played by agents and agencies in facilitating immigration.

Agents and Agencies to Assist Migration

For migration historians, who have long recognized the push-pull factors affecting movement, the role played by immigration agents and agencies as a possible third force between the push-pull forces remains problematic. Although sources for accurate assessment of agent work are rare, a good deal is known about what nineteenth-century agents and agencies did to foster immigration. Before 1850, immigrant recruitment had normally been unsystematic, often haphazard. Burgeoning immigrant numbers and the increasingly apparent profits to be made by those in German lands and ports facilitating emigration changed this. The rapid expansion and development of official agencies, agents, and sales staffs promoting migration occurred in conjunction with the changeover from sailing ships to steam power. In the words of the Danish migration historian Kristian Hvidt, "The introduction of regular traffic routes between Europe and the United States and the consolidation of Atlantic shipping in large, well-financed steamship companies in England and Germany necessitated a thoroughly organized, permanent sales organization."[92] In North America the new sales organizations and their agents appeared first in the United States; Canada experienced the change more slowly and tentatively.

During the 1850s the use of government agents to promote German immigration to Canada was strictly limited. Several factors accounted for this. The absence of a coherent, general migration policy for the provinces of British North America contributed. In Britain the prevailing liberal ideology decreed that no explicit governmental involvement in designing or implementing an active migration policy for British North America would be forthcoming. Further, the political uncertainty in Upper and Lower Canada, which made immigration a potentially divisive issue, did not favour active governmental promotion. The economic downturn in the middle of the decade also played a role by reducing the numbers of migrants coming to Canada and thus the need for government personnel to serve them. Despite these unfavourable factors, a small number of German immigrants continued to seek asylum in Canada. To assist these newcomers, some service-rendering agents had to exist, as limited as their numbers might be. In general, agents employed by the Canadian government could be divided into two main groups: domestic and foreign. The former were basically appointees stationed in Canada to assist immigrants who had just arrived; the representatives positioned outside Canada in the British Isles or continental Europe were charged with both recruiting and then assisting their charges in the migration process. Despite the paucity of foreign agents, enough of their domestic counterparts were in place in British North America at mid-century to provide German immigrants with settlement assistance.

Stationed at different locations in Canada, domestic agents provided a large variety of services. Agents at the disembarkation ports informed the new arrivals on such matters as train schedules and ticket prices, temporary housing, short-term employment, and even exchange rates for currency brought from Germany. In addition, most areas being opened up for settlement had domestic agents assigned to assist immigrants in locating and beginning a homestead.[93] Ontario agents were listed by name for those areas offering free land. For example, the German emigrant press announced in July 1856 that "the provincial government has recently opened up three main roads ... and has surveyed the land through which these roads traverse or which lies near them and marked off lots for settlement. Furthermore, it has published information on the roads in the several regions and the agents the government has appointed to administer them for settlement. The roads are known as the Ottawa and Opeongo Road, the Addington Road, and the Hastings Road." For the Ottawa Road the agent "who transfers land is Mr. T.P. French, who lives in Mount St. Patrick." The agent for the Addington Road was a "Mr. C. Perry, who lives in the village of Flints Mills." For the Hastings Road, settlers were to contact "Mr. M.P. Hayes, residing in Hastings Village about 28 miles north of the town of Belleville." These agents, the article concluded, would be able "to provide whomsoever wants to settle all the information necessary" to secure a free homestead.[94] In short, Canada's domestic agents were expected to look after the newcomers upon their arrival in Canada, to ensure safe travel to their intended place of settlement, and to provide the new immigrants with advice and assistance in establishing their homesteads.

In the 1850s William Sinn was Canada's most prominent domestic agent serving German immigrants and the one best known in Germany. A native Prussian, Sinn received an appointment in 1853 as agent in Quebec to assist A.C. Buchanan, long-time head of the Royal Emigration Department's branch there. Located on Quebec's Gibb's Wharf, Sinn's office invited new arrivals to stop in. As described in an 1853 flyer circulated in Germany, agent Sinn was "to dedicate his entire activity to the well-being of his fellow landspeople [Germans] and to provide them with all necessary information on the cheapest and best opportunities for travel inland, real estate availability, and the prospects for securing such property." In cases of complaints about abuse of immigrants during the passage over, he was "to see that steps be taken to guarantee that those guilty of such abuses be held responsible."[95] An announcement that appeared in the German migration press in August 1853 also emphasized Sinn's caretaker, watchdog role. Buchanan, the *Deutsche Auswanderer-Zeitung* announced, had appointed the German-speaking Sinn to thwart con artists and so-called runners who over the past few years "had swindled many German families out of their hard-earned money."[96] Sinn, an 1860 brochure assured intended Canadian immigrants, would be easily recognizable because "he had only one eye."[97]

Correspondence Sinn maintained with the Württemberg Ministry of the Interior in the mid-1850s reveals his actual activities in serving German immigrants. On occasion he cashed the money drafts which the emigrants brought with them from Württemberg. He also made special efforts to assist immigrants in reaching their intended places of settlement as expeditiously as possible. His letters to the Württemberg ministry describe how he successfully secured reduced fares or free train tickets for some. Indeed, Sinn's close relationship with the Grand Trunk Railway contributed to the belief in Quebec that he served as an agent for the railroad as well as the emigration department. In addition, Sinn assisted many newcomers to find jobs on farms or as servants. "To avoid the ordeals of Liverpool," Gerhard Bassler writes, "Sinn recommended use of the equally cheap Hamburg shipping line Knorr & Holtermann about whose past six years of direct services to Quebec not a single complaint had been registered." Sinn's close working relationship with the Württemberg government "led to his being considered for the position of that state's consul in Canada."[98] A. Schumacher, the German consul in Baltimore, who visited Quebec while on vacation in the fall of 1854, also attested to the effectiveness of Sinn's activities. From his interview with Sinn, Schumacher concluded that the Canadian authorities did more to assist German immigrants than their counterparts in the United States.[99]

Nevertheless, in this period immigrant agents often received little respect from the public. For example, Norman Macdonald found hostile sentiment in Great Britain, where Canadian immigrant agents were commonly thought of as "noisy, boasting, bragging, blustering ... story tellers" who lied about Canada "beautifully and plausibly."[100] Similarly, the *Allgemeine Auswanderungszeitung* in Rudolstadt published a series of reports listing immigrant dissatisfactions with Sinn's work. These included accusations of selling railway tickets at inflated prices and using his job as Buchanan's assistant to advance his career.[101]

In the end, the accusations against Sinn were refuted in an article in the *Deutsche Auswanderer-Zeitung*. Buchanan, the respected head of the immigration office in Quebec, vouched for Sinn, insisting that he was neither a "phoney nor hypocrite" guilty of exploiting immigrants. Furthermore, the *Deutsche Auswanderer-Zeitung* reported that Sinn had also received written approval "complete with official seals from the consuls for the Hansa cities, Belgium, and Prussia."[102] This appeared to be sufficient proof of his respectability. The Bremen paper's conclusion seems borne out by the fact that Sinn remained in office. Five years later in a promotional pamphlet, Buchanan included testimonials from Prussian immigrants extolling Sinn's contribution to their successful settlement in Upper Canada.[103] In 1868, the year of Buchanan's death, William Sinn remained the interpreter and record keeper for German immigrants arriving in Quebec.[104] The controversies that characterized Sinn's term in office reflected not only his personal credibility problems but the uncertain and undefined state of Canadian immigration policy and practice. The shifting parameters of Sinn's job frequently created conflicts of interest as he sought to fulfill roles as both private businessman and paid civil servant.

Gradually, in the late 1850s modest support developed for the belief that the recruitment of immigrants in Europe needed a fresh approach. The previous system of sending private persons as temporary missionaries to win converts for Canada or of relying on ship captains or shipping firms in Germany or England to solicit emigrants on an ad hoc basis seemed inadequate. Immigration had become pressing because increasing numbers of Canadians, both English and French speakers, had moved south to the United States. Responding to this hemorrhaging population, the legislative assembly of the Province of Canada in 1857 appointed a series of committees to investigate and find a solution to the population drain. According to Paul Gates, "The first important step in what was to develop into a great campaign to secure immigrants for Canada was taken in the latter part of 1859 when A.B. Hawke ... was sent to England to begin work there." He was specifically charged "to open an office at Liverpool where persons planning to emigrate might obtain information and ... to advertise in such papers as *The Times, The Liverpool Times, Bell's Weekly Messenger*, and *The*

Field, calling attention to his office and the information and literature available there ... and to circularize the rural papers by sending them copies of the pamphlets and other advertising literature with which he was provided."[105] Thus, the Canadian government began sending permanent agents to Europe to establish offices for recruiting future settlers and assisting them in their journeys to Canada. Overwhelmingly, the government based its agents in the United Kingdom: at the beginning of the 1860s Reverend Henry Hope was sent to London, John A. Donaldson to Londonderry, and Alexander McLachlan to Scotland. A.C. Buchanan was transferred in 1861 from Quebec to take over Hawke's work in Liverpool.[106] At the same time, in a significant departure from its earlier practices, the Canadian government appointed a German-speaking agent to reside in Germany, where he could personally direct would-be immigrants to Canada.

The first representative of this policy, the Prussian native and naturalized Canadian William Wagner, received his appointment to head a newly established bureau in Berlin on 30 January 1860. Born in 1820 in Grabow (Posen), Wagner had studied geography and surveying in Breslau, Posen, and Berlin before emigrating to Canada in 1850. A government land surveyor in Upper Canada, he had also gained some experience as an independent agent. For example, in June 1859 he "visited Prussia and North Germany to recruit immigrants for settlement in Canada." On that tour, he provided information about Canada on land acquisition, climate, and the legal system. Thus his background and experience seemed especially appropriate for this German appointment. As an emigrant himself, he knew from personal experience the complexities and difficulties in both leaving Germany and shipping to Canada. Having resided in Canada for nine years before accepting the Berlin post, he was a credible authority for those interested in moving to Canada. Finally, he possessed useful journalistic skills, knowing how to write persuasively in the German language. Examples of his journalism appeared at the outset of his Berlin appointment: in 1860 he published the pamphlets *Über die unentgeldliche Hergabe von Land in Canada* (On the Acquisition of Free Land in Canada) and *Über den Verkauf von Regierungs-Landereien in Canada* (On the Purchasing of Government Lands in Canada), and in 1861, *Anleitung für Diejenigen welche sich am Ottawa Flusse Niederlassen Wollen* (Guide for Those Seeking to Settle on the Ottawa River).[107] At the time of his Berlin appointment, Wagner was instructed by Ottawa "to encourage small farmers and agricultural laborers, but not mechanics, to migrate to Canada."[108]

As publicist, salesperson, and recruiter, Wagner travelled throughout Prussia and northern Germany. In February 1861 he reported home that he had secured permission from the commissioners of the Berlin-Hamburg Railway "to display a map of Canada at stations along the line." In 1862 Wagner claimed that he had "advertised in papers with a joint circulation of 400,000 copies, distributed 3,500 pamphlets, displayed 222 maps of Canada in railway stations, pubs, etc." As well, he lectured in Frankfurt am Main, Berlin, Breslau, Hirschberg (Silesia), and Erfurt. Between January and March of 1862, he informed his superiors that he had "answered 178 letters of inquiry from prospective emigrants."[109] How successful his activity was in garnering actual immigrants for Canada cannot be known, but it was insufficient for the legislative committee that investigated his work in 1862 and found the returns for the $6,000 invested in his efforts unsatisfactory.[110] Although in 1866 the Montreal German Society pushed Wagner's candidacy for the recently vacated immigration agent position in Quebec, by then his star had set.[111]

Although Wagner represented the new salaried governmental functionary charged with recruiting and looking after immigrants, the old private practitioners still dominated the field. Private transportation firms continued their efforts to solicit paying customers. For example, the Allan Shipping Line stationed a permanent man in Liverpool who advertised his services for would-be German emigrants in the *Allgemeine Auswanderungszeitung*.[112] Canada's Grand Trunk Railway also had representatives in Liverpool selling tickets that would carry immigrants from Liverpool to Quebec and beyond to the places of intended settlement. In 1869 the railway sent agents to Hamburg to sell such tickets there. (The Hamburg city government refused the request to allow these sales, claiming the impossibility of guaranteeing the validity of such tickets once the immigrant reached Canada.)[113] Advertising land in eastern Ontario for fifty cents an acre in the German press, the Canadian Land and Emigration Company in 1866 dispatched its agent Mr. Bechel to Germany to travel through Hanover, Hesse-Kassel, Brunswick, and part of Prussia soliciting emigrant purchasers.[114] This unsystematic and often chaotic mixture of private persons and public officials competing with one another in selling tickets, soliciting emigrants, and providing information on how to emigrate persisted throughout the decade. Although the several types of agents frequently worked at cross purposes, they generally used the same sales techniques.

To complement the work of the emigration agents but also to protect against unscrupulous agents, agencies designed to facilitate and to reduce the hazards of immigration multiplied in Europe as the emigration movement mushroomed. Secular and religious emigration assistance organizations appeared in Germany, the United Kingdom, and Scandinavia. For example, in England during the last half of the nineteenth century over sixty such agencies worked to promote and justify emigration to Britain's numerous colonies.[115] The National Emigration Aid Society, formed in 1867, which provided information covering the whole process of migration from departure to settlement, was representative. In Germany, the first such agency, the Giessener Auswanderungsgesellschaft (Giessen Emigration Society), had been founded in 1833.[116] Those that followed, both public and private, varied considerably, with some functioning for profit, some for altruistic or nationalist motives. During the 1840s in particular their numbers increased dramatically. Peter Marschalck lists twenty-seven German immigration agencies active in the period 1833-50, of which twenty were established in the 1840s.[117]

The most important of these was the National Verein für Deutsche Auswanderung und Ansiedlung (National Society for German Emigration and Settlement). The program of the National Verein appeared first in the weekly publication *Der Deutsche Auswanderer* (The German Emigrant) in December 1847. This impressively detailed document articulated many of the themes and goals characterizing emigration assistance agencies throughout the period 1850-1939. For example, the society's program considered poverty and the role of the poor in emigration; it discussed the importance of German ports and shipping companies transporting emigrants; it analyzed emigrant categories, from the wealthy seeking new business opportunities to the paupers desiring only to exchange their hopeless condition in Germany for a new chance abroad; it reflected on the possibility and desirability of establishing closed colonies of Germans overseas; it listed the kinds of printed materials, such as itineraries, maps, and money exchange rate tables, emigrants should be provided with before departing from Germany; it described what earlier German immigrants already established in the United States could do to assist newly arriving countrymen; it made suggestions for monitoring conditions aboard emigrant ships in German ports; and it proposed the establishment of a dozen branch offices of the National Verein throughout Germany.

Several such branch offices did materialize, in Hesse, Württemberg, Baden, Kurhesse, and Nassau. The National Verein branch office in Baden was representative. Founded in 1849, this agency was empowered by statute with several tasks: to establish a central office in Karlsruhe to oversee and coordinate emigration matters, to provide information for emigrants on travelling out of Germany and settlement overseas, to appoint agents at various locations along the routes used by emigrants, to monitor travel contracts, and to support emigrants without means by raising money to pay for their exodus from Germany. Closely allied with Baden's government (eight of the nine-member executive committee directing the agency were civil servants), the agency supported the policy of reducing the numbers of the duchy's paupers by using public monies to pay for their emigration. The agency's activities increased as the tide of immigration swelled to a peak in 1854. After that, its effectiveness decreased dramatically.[118]

During the same period a number of similar societies not closely affiliated with the National Verein appeared in Saxony, Silesia, Berlin, Hamburg, Bremen, and Frankfurt, such as Der Frankfurter Verein zum Schutze der Auswanderung (The Frankfurt Society for the Protection of Emigration), formed in 1850. With a membership fluctuating between 200 and 300 throughout the 1850s and 1860s, the association exhibited both material and philanthropic motives. The society's members, for the most part important political and economic figures in the city, wished to protect emigrants passing through Frankfurt from swindlers and others intent upon exploiting them. The city fathers strongly believed that if the emigrants fared well in Frankfurt, not only would the reputation of the city be upheld but the business community would also benefit. To this end, the city government passed protective regulations. Agents and others engaged in serving emigrants received close and ongoing police scrutiny. Moreover, solicitation of emigrants was prohibited on the Main River docks, in train stations, and even in public houses. Beyond ensuring a safe environment, the society saw its mission as providing information and advice. According to Hartmut Bickelmann, "The office [of the society] dispensed both written and verbal information on all questions pertaining to emigration, on the suitability of some lands for immigration, on the types of transportation available, and on travel and settlement conditions overseas. They often worked closely with the assistance bureaus in Bremen and Hamburg as well as with the German societies in the United States."[119] The society's yearly reports indicate that in the early 1850s, its busiest period, the society advised over 2,000 emigrants a year.

Berlin, Germany's largest city in 1850, had its own emigration agency, Der Berliner Verein zu Centralisation deutscher Auswanderung und Colonisation (The Berlin Society for the Centralization of German Emigration and Colonization). Founded in 1849, this private association differed from most other emigration aid organizations and the National Verein. From its inception, the society's directors had close connections to Prussia's conservative elements. These wealthy merchants, bankers, high-up bureaucrats, and particularly large landowners were all strongly opposed to German labour and wealth leaving the country. Viewing German emigration critically, the Berliner Verein considered a major part of its mission to be dissuading would-be emigrants from leaving. If emigrants could not be convinced to stay home, then the society tried to steer them to a closed German colony that would maintain close economic and political ties to the fatherland. Specifically, it promoted settlement areas and colonies in Central and South America, such as Nicaragua's Mosquito Coast. The Berliner Verein disapproved of settlement in North America and especially the United States, because Germans who had emigrated there became too assimilated and thus lost to the fatherland. To convince future emigrants to avoid the United States, it circulated disparaging reports about American settlement opportunities; its publications frequently detailed how often disillusioned German immigrants had failed in their efforts to settle there. The Berliner Verein also assumed the traditional role of defending emigrants from unscrupulous agents and swindlers by providing practical advice and assistance. During its five-year existence, the society allegedly advised over 15,000 souls. Although this service could be considered successful, the society's other objectives of dampening emigration desires and promoting German colonies remained unfulfilled.[120]

In Canada, a network of immigrant assistance agencies developed only slowly. Founded in 1835, the Deutsche Gesellschaft Montreal (German Society of Montreal) was the earliest and most prominent of such organizations. Originally a social club, the society became involved with Canada's German immigrants in the late 1840s when their numbers increased so dramatically. These augmented numbers reflected not only the economic and social crises of those years but also the opening in 1847 of a direct route for sailing ships between Bremen and Quebec. With more and more German immigrants in the city, the society began to serve the neediest. For example, it gave indigents funds for further travel, covered medical bills, and provided educational support. In 1852 the society effectively petitioned the Canadian government to appoint Adolphus Schmidt, one of its members, "to serve under Buchanan as the first German subagent and interpreter for German immigrants in the port of Montreal."[121] In the period 1850-70, the society increasingly assumed the task of representing and defending the interests of fellow Germans.

Propaganda to Induce Migration

Of the printed materials used to sell Canada in Germany, the two most common were articles in German newspapers and German-language information brochures. What appeared in the newspapers repeated what the brochures described, only in more detail. The first Canadian promotional brochures appeared in the mid-1850s. In 1854 William Hutton, secretary of the Bureau of Agriculture, produced a pamphlet entitled *Canada: Its Present Conditions, Prospects, and Resources, Fully Described for the Information of Intending Emigrants,* which circulated not only in England but also in translation in the German states.[122] The Canadian brochures circulating in Germany during the period 1850-70 were typical of the genre for North America generally, providing similar information about the how, where, and when of migration and developing common themes dealing with present and future immigrant prospects. Whether created by the government or private firms, Canadian brochures imitated US efforts, for the Americans had developed the promotional pamphlet to a high degree. The following content analysis of representative brochures promoting Upper and Lower Canada includes references to brochures and pamphlets produced between 1853 and 1862.

From their title pages, most of the brochures left little doubt that they conveyed facts on Canada for immigrants. The brochures' authors always insisted that the information provided constituted neither an apologia for Canada nor an attack on Germany. Rather, their object was simply to inform those who had already decided to leave. Beginning with the "hardest facts," the brochures usually started with a description of Canada's size. In 1850, for example, Upper and Lower Canada, together totalled "350,000 square miles ... more than a third greater than France and three times the size of Prussia." Within this huge land mass one found a varied and fascinating topography – vast forests, abundant rivers and lakes, and even mountains. The brochures nearly always described the climate as temperate, the population of several million as tiny compared to Europe's, the beauty of the landscape as astonishing, and the plants and animals as valuable and multifarious. The country's history was among these hard facts.[123] Founded by French explorers in the sixteenth century, it was first settled by their transplanted countrymen, and then by the English. The conflict between the French and English reached a resolution in 1761 with the English finally defeating the French. From then on, Upper and Lower Canada, which were united politically in 1840, had remained tied to Great Britain. Undeterred by revolution and sometimes invasion from the south, Canada had stubbornly retained its independence from the United States up to the present.

Besides giving such general information, the brochures usually described Canada's political and economic systems. The resulting picture of Canada's politics conformed closely to the promotional image described above: that is, Canada's free political system and generous citizenship provisions guaranteed broad individual participation in and close identification with the system. From such identification and participation followed its low taxes, religious tolerance, impressive educational program, and individual economic opportunity. This last feature became a constant theme in Canadian brochure literature. Like most American promotional brochures from the same period, the pamphlets pointedly described opportunities in Canada exceeding those available in Germany.[124] This emphasis testified to the recognition among brochure producers that the economic motive appealed most powerfully to would-be immigrants.

The brochure portrait of Canada's economy normally included natural resources, commerce, industry, transportation, and agriculture, and the last two logically received the most attention. Developments in the period 1850-70 in Canada's transportation system included extending the system of roads, building canals, expanding steamboat travel on the St. Lawrence and the Great Lakes, and introducing the railroad. Canadian promotional pamphlets frequently cited canals as artful engineering feats linking Canada's wonderful system of lakes and rivers. Announcements of new roads to open up undeveloped areas of the country for settlement also appeared in virtually all Canadian brochures. As well as showing growth and expansion of the settled portion of the country, these announcements broadcast the location of new lands available for homesteading. For example, William Wagner's 1860 pamphlet listed, besides the Ottawa-Opeongo, Addington, and Hastings Roads, eight additional highways in Upper Canada being extended at that time.[125] To reach the newly created roads with speed and a minimum of discomfort, the brochures proudly pointed out, Canada's rapidly developing steamship and railway system lay at the immigrants' disposal.

In the extensive promotional literature produced by the several American states competing for German immigrants at this time, the railroads were also elaborately described and celebrated. As Ingrid Schöberl has pointed out, in US immigration propaganda the railroad was intended to represent "a measuring rod of civilization." Furthermore, the American state railroads "in their connections to other interstate lines and in their plans for expansion proved that the state was not cut off from the outside world."[126] Similarly, nearly all the brochures produced to solicit immigrants for British North America emphasized the significance of the railroad for Canada's present and future. William Wagner boasted to his German readers that Canada already possessed 1,876 miles of track, and thus "exceeded the mileage in Ireland or Scotland" and was "more than that in the three states New Jersey, Delaware, and Maryland or in the two states North and South Carolina."[127] In 1853 Buchanan produced a three-page flyer that included tables for some three dozen railroad routes connecting centres in Upper and Lower Canada. These tables listed for each route the number of miles of completed track, the mileage under construction, and the distances approved for construction. He even put an asterisk before those routes "which either ran through or passed close to German settlements."[128]

Canada's transportation infrastructure developed so rapidly after mid-century to facilitate the growth of the Canadian economy. As already noted, in the period 1850-70 agriculture and agricultural products constituted the most important part of that economy. The promotional brochures puffing Canada for potential German immigrants reflected this fact by devoting significant space to information about agriculture and the opportunities it afforded new settlers. Although Canadian agriculture in the two decades after 1850 included dairy farming and truck gardening, most Canadian farmers concentrated on growing wheat. "The chief product of agriculture," an anonymous pamphlet reported in 1858, "is wheat, and the enormous quantity of this valuable commodity exported as grain and flour proves how extensively it is cultivated."[129] In Wagner's brochure Canada's wheat received an even more enthusiastic review: "One should not forget that Canadian wheat grown near Toronto won first prize at the Paris exhibition." He further asserted that "the quality of Canadian wheat is so excellent that American millers buy it to mix with American wheat to improve the quality of their export flour."[130]

In addition to providing such positive descriptions of Canada's farmland, the brochures indicated how and where an immigrant could secure free, readily available acreage for growing such superior crops. For example, a pamphlet entitled *Canada 1862: Zur Nachricht für Einwanderer* (Canada 1862: Information for Immigrants) described free land grants of up to 100 acres in Upper Canada along seven specific roads including the Addington, Ottawa and Opeongo, and Hastings Roads. As well as providing the names and addresses of the agents for those roads, it indicated what means of transportation to use to reach the free land. In addition, the brochure included individual, informative reports from the land agents providing details on local conditions and developments. For the Addington Road, the agent Ebenezer Perry of Tamworth described available free Crown land and partially cleared land for seventy cents an acre. He mentioned the rich sandy loam of the area and the many kinds of trees that grew locally, and he reported on the ethnic makeup of the immigrant population and how well they got along.[131]

Some pamphlets offered more information for homesteaders than just land prices and locations. The more comprehensive brochures sometimes described what expenses the settler would incur after he had taken up possession of his free farmstead. William Wagner's brochure, for example, projected the food needs for a family in Canada during the first year of homesteading, including eight barrels of flour, eighty bushels of potatoes, and thirty pounds of tea. Widening his scope, Wagner calculated other living expenses, such as seed amounts and costs for planting potatoes, wheat, and oats. Wagner also estimated necessary personal, household, and work articles, such as dishes, pots, and pans, clothes for the family, and farming tools. After all his listing and figuring, Wagner concluded that immigrants to Canada should bring at least 300 Prussian thalers. With any less cash, Wagner warned, they "would be unable to establish a viable home in Canada."[132]

Although the average brochure may not have dispensed advice to the extent Wagner did, most pamphlets nevertheless provided suggestions on what to do after arrival in Canada. This included more than simply providing boat and train schedules and ticket prices. Brochure authors knew the vulnerability of naive immigrants upon their arrival in North America. As a result, the pamphlets offered solicitous advice on everything from what clothes to pack, what amount of cash to take for the trip to Canada, where to exchange German currency in Canada (and what amount to expect in return), where to go in Quebec to find reliable help or guidance for the continuation of the journey, and what kinds of people to avoid to keep from being defrauded or swindled. On this latter subject, Canada pamphlets frequently emphasized how much less of a problem swindlers posed in Canada than in the United States.[133]

To lessen immigrant fears about how they would fare once settled in Canada, the brochures offered two general assurances. First, they predicted the Canadian reception awaiting the newcomers would be friendly, encouraging, and helpful. A Canadian pamphlet from 1862 asserted in its opening lines that the German immigrant was especially valued: "Canada is almost the only land where the German immigrant is treated both before the law and in practical matters just the same as any native-born Canadian."[134] Second, the brochures described success as highly probable for the would-be German settler. In Canada the social gradations and inequalities of privilege and status that prevailed in Europe simply did not exist, and the only qualities a settler needed were industry, diligence, and skill. In short, merit prevailed. "There were," Wagner wrote, "no monopolies, no exclusive privileges, no great unbridgeable divisions between social classes to prevent or delay the advancement of an honourable and hard-working man ... In truth, Canada is a land of hope that disillusions no man."[135]

To validate such claims, the brochures included testimonials from immigrants ensconced in Canada. For example, in 1862 the agent William Sinn reported in a promotional brochure the fates of ninety-five German families he had helped settle in County Renfrew, Upper Canada. According to him, forty had made great progress with their farmsteads within eighteen months of landing in Canada. After adding up the cost of the groups' farms and their farming expenses from the time they took up residence, Sinn calculated that each family had made a $220 profit. The agent followed this analysis with a statement by his charges: "We all are satisfied with the government land we purchased. It has yielded bumper crops. If in the beginning we had little means, we easily found paid employment on the surrounding farms. Thus we were able to secure what was necessary until our own farms provided for us." Appended to this statement appeared the names of the forty German farmers who had, in their own words, "signed and given [the testimonial] in our homes in the townships of Alice and Wilberforce in the month of October, 1860."[136]

Besides employing brochures, German agents promoting emigration to Canada used the immigration press. In the period 1846-75 eight different newspapers devoted to emigration appeared in Germany, the two most significant being the *Allgemeine Auswanderungszeitung* and the *Deutsche Auswanderer-Zeitung*. Published in Rudolstadt with a circulation estimated at between 500 and 1,000 copies, the *Allgemeine Auswanderungszeitung* appeared three times a week from 1846 to 1871. The Bremen-based *Deutsche Auswanderer-Zeitung* appeared each Monday from 1852 to 1875, and its circulation approximated that of its Rudolstadt competitor.[137] Both papers published long, informative articles describing Canada's institutions, traditions, and natural conditions. Canada's agents not only had their views printed in these newspapers but on occasion even had their services delineated. These apologists regularly submitted letters allegedly written by their clients in Canada to relatives or friends in Germany. Generally, such letters painted rosy pictures of prosperity and contentment in the wilds of British North America.

The following examples from the *Deutsche Auswanderer-Zeitung* are illustrative. Beginning in December 1852 and continuing into the next summer, the Bremen weekly ran a series of fifteen letters from "C.B." Written by one whose language betrayed a sophistication beyond that of the usual farmer or artisan correspondent, these letters describe nearly everything a typical brochure did, but with markedly more enthusiasm.[138] Apparently no pretext existed for the paper to restrain the author's hyperbole, because C.B. professed to report as a Canadian citizen writing the truth about Canada to a personal friend in Germany. And the truth was mighty indeed. The letters described a beautiful land richly endowed with renewable resources, blessed with a dynamic and civil population, and governed under a sympathetic and responsible political system. Individuals enjoyed personal freedom, low taxes, excellent schools, and helpful and friendly neighbours. In short, the epistles painted a blissful picture. For any immigrant who truly tried to make a go of it, failure was virtually impossible. "Only those farmers," C.B. wrote in the letter of 11 January 1853, "will fail who believe they can live a life of luxury on the income of a small holding ... On the other hand, those who understand work and attempt to create viable farms with their own resources rather than with someone else's money will make a successful go of it."[139]

Although the immigrant press reproduced some actual correspondence from Canada, most letters home to Germany usually circulated in their original form among relatives, friends, and hometown folk. The exact volume of such letters remains unknown, but copious correspondence was produced by nineteenth-century German immigrants in the United States.[140] Because the German-Canadian community in this period was much smaller and generally of less recent origin than America's Germans, the volume of letters sent home from Canada would have been much smaller. Reduced volume probably translated into less influence, but how much less influence in stimulating or inducing others to leave for Canada is impossible to know. Whether desire to leave was produced by family members beckoning to be joined in North America, agent agitation, newspaper editorials, or persuasive brochures, migration to Canada in the middle of the nineteenth century still represented a costly and uncertain undertaking.

Emigration and Immigration: The Role of Governments

Regardless of the source of the desire to leave or of the role played by agencies in assisting departure, the emigrant had to be legally free to depart before actual movement out of Europe could occur. Essentially, the freedom to leave was a political issue involving the position of the individual

German state governments on emigration. During the nineteenth century the emigration policies of the several governments passed through various phases reflecting support, hostility, and indifference. In the first phase, from the eighteenth century into the early years of the nineteenth century, emigration was viewed in purely mercantilist terms: it represented a threat to the state's military and economic potential and was therefore opposed. Evaluating the history of Germany's emigration in the early nineteenth century, the scholar Eugen von Philippovich wrote in 1886 that German states that allowed their subjects to emigrate were always "pressured by the spectre of economic and military disadvantages associated with emigration." In this nightmarish vision, "the 100,000 emigrants that Germany each year sends abroad form a splendidly equipped army that leaves the country and then disappears without a trace."[141] Reflecting this fear of losing wealth and potential, many state governments tried to prevent their subjects from leaving through licensing, passports, departure taxes, and bureaucratic dissuasion. In the southwest, where the hemorrhaging was most intense, even more extreme measures were applied. For example, in 1817 Baden's government expressly prohibited its subjects from emigrating between the months of May and November.[142]

The second phase of emigration politics commenced in the middle of the 1830s in response to a dramatic increase in emigration, particularly to North America. Lack of either an adequate emigration policy or appropriate official regulations in the several German states led to many abuses that in turn caused much suffering among the departing. Eventually public disapproval forced the abandonment of official efforts to prevent emigration and the adoption instead of regulations assisting emigrants in leaving. The Hansa embarkation centres Bremen and Hamburg led in establishing regulations to protect emigrants from exploitation and to facilitate their exodus. The impact of the new acceptance and assistance policy remained modest, however, as most state governments, if no longer hostile, tended to be passive observers. But any vigorous state intervention in emigration required that the earlier mercantilist hostility be abandoned, which occurred only gradually after 1830. Thus, official state involvement remained for the most part restricted to monitoring agent activity or warning off would-be emigrants from leaving Germany.[143]

Not until the hungry forties were these lingering interferences replaced by much greater governmental acceptance along with expanded assistance for those departing, marking the third phase of German emigration politics. Because the economic crisis and resultant social upheaval of the 1840s stimulated out-migration, public awareness and discussion of the "emigration problem" increased accordingly. According to Klaus Bade, three schools of thought about emigration emerged. First, there was what he labelled a "romantic-volkish" one which lamented out-migration as a loss of national potential. For this group, emigration constituted a kind of bloodletting with serious consequences for the nation's future. A second group viewed emigration as an important tool for coping with the social and economic exigencies caused by Germany's recent population explosion. For them, emigration constituted a safety valve that could relieve the pressures threatening social stability and property. A third faction argued for aggressive state regulation of emigration through appropriate laws, and the encouragement of private associations to organize and direct the flow of those leaving to Germany's advantage. Specifically, this group favoured the creation of closed German settlements in the emigrant receiving lands or the establishment of outright German colonies overseas. Such settlements would benefit the fatherland just as British or French overseas possessions advantaged those nations.[144]

From such debate, emigration emerged in the late 1840s as an important political issue. Thus, in the 1848 revolution, the Frankfurt National Assembly decreed that the freedom to emigrate constituted a fundamental right for all Germans. Although the National Assembly's constitution was never promulgated, numerous German states later recognized this right and incorporated it into their laws. Even conservative Prussia included a provision in its constitution of 1850 that "the freedom to emigrate can only be limited by military obligations. Departure taxes may not be charged."[145] Thus after the 1840s no German government supported prohibiting emigration outright. Indeed, the opposite became the rule, particularly among local and regional public functionaries who increasingly espoused the "safety valve" policy. These officials viewed the rising number of indigent and unemployed as potential social problems endangering both the region's peace and the local government's solvency. As a result, programs providing public funds to pay for the emigration of paupers and petty criminals expanded. Paid emigration proponents claimed that funding out-migration cost far less than maintaining such misfits on the public welfare rolls.[146] Few provisions, if any, were made for those dumped abroad. The small cash payments emigrants received from their German sponsors on landing in Canada, for example, usually turned out to be inadequate. In effect, they left as paupers and arrived in their new homelands in the same condition.[147]

Paid emigration programs appeared in the states of Baden, Württemberg, and Hesse. Of these, the Grand Duchy of Baden developed the most complete system for paying emigrants to leave, a direct result of the disastrous economic conditions plaguing the duchy after 1845. Through financial support of emigration, the government hoped to reduce the skyrocketing costs of supporting its growing number of indigents. Although often badly organized and administered, this state-supported emigration helped reduce the duchy's overall population by over 3 percent between 1852 and 1855. Paid emigration supporters claimed that reduction of the pauper and

petty-criminal class through emigration led to a substantial decline in serious crimes, a drastic reduction in the number of beggars, and an increase in
work opportunities and wages for labourers at home. To the extent that this
was true, "Baden's emigration politics," Christine Hansen concludes, "were
very successful."[148]

In Württemberg and Hesse, funding for paid emigration fell largely to
local parishes and communities, although Württemberg backed private agencies and local officials with state funds as well as encouragement. The Hessian government in Darmstadt did not go as far in providing monetary
assistance, but local communities seeking to export their poor had
Darmstadt's blessing. Successful local initiatives in sponsoring emigration
were common. For example, in Württemberg in 1852 the authorities in
Gotzingen financed thirty-two paupers to Peru. From the early 1840s in
Hesse, local parishes actively raised money to sponsor emigration. Occasionally, such sponsorship included the out-migration of whole villages.
The Grosszimmern Affair of 1846 is illustrative. From Grosszimmern, a small
town east of Darmstadt, 600 to 700 paupers and petty criminals were exported en masse to New York, the total cost being only 50,000 gulden.[149]
Hesse's efforts at eliminating its poor normally included payment only for
transportation out of Germany, stranding immigrants in their new homeland without enough funds to avoid the local poorhouse. The failure to
provide for their charges' welfare after leaving Germany revealed that the
"parishes were intent above all on freeing themselves of their 'troublemak-
ers' as quickly as possible and what happened to them after departure was
of no interest. Any responsibility for the emigrants had been rejected."[150]

In Prussia would-be emigrants, whether petty criminals or paupers, received no official state aid to leave. Despite considerable emigration from
its western lands in the 1840s, Prussia's rulers never developed a clear emigration policy. Conservative circles may have discussed, for example, German colonies backed by Prussia, but officially Berlin expressed a healthy
skepticism, if not overt hostility, toward any kind of emigration throughout the period 1850-70. The official disapproval notwithstanding, local Prussian communities, especially in the economically hard-hit Rhineland, did
occasionally support exporting their poor. Conversely, in extreme cases
Prussia's central government intervened to prevent emigration. As a response
to the abuses of the Brazilian plantation system, Prussia in 1859 prohibited
its subjects from migrating to that country.[151] With the decline of emigrant
numbers in the late 1850s, the emigration problem ceased to be a major
concern in Prussia. In 1860 William Wagner reported from Berlin to his
overseers in Canada that he had met with the Prussian minister of trade
and a senior Berlin police official and that they had agreed to allow him to
carry on his recruitment work unimpeded.[152] Apparently Canada was per-

ceived as neither a bad place to live nor a land where large numbers of Prussians would head. Later in the 1860s the crisis in Prussian domestic politics and then the wars of Bismarck overshadowed all else, and the emigration issue became nearly moot, as elsewhere in Germany. As Mack Walker puts it, "Germans did not do much analyzing or theorizing about the *Auswanderung* between 1855 and the unification."[153]

While the migration policies in the German states in the two decades after 1850 shifted from hostility to acceptance to indifference, Canadian governmental policy reflected no such wild swings but rather a lack of direction and uncertainty about how to respond to or indeed create immigration. As noted above, much of this uncertainty related to the general political and economic situation in British North America. Economic weakness, political stalemate, and the failure of the laissez faire British government to provide leadership decreed that forceful and innovative immigration policies would not materialize. Regulations for British subjects migrating to Canada remained virtually nonexistent. Even in the terrible midcentury famine years, when thousands of destitute Irish and Highland Scots sought refuge in Canada, the British and Canadian governments did nothing to regulate the flood of indigents pouring into the country. Canada also received some German immigrants with insufficient funds to support themselves.

The emigration from Baden and Württemberg to Canada in the early 1850s affords a good example of the confluence of German and Canadian emigration policies at this time. As noted, in the late 1840s and early 1850s southwest Germany suffered grievously from economic collapse and social turmoil. Both Baden and Württemberg dumped some of their poor in Canada. Compared to the United States, where several thousand paupers were delivered in the period, Canada received modest numbers. The immigration agent in Quebec recorded thirty paupers from Baden landing in 1853 and 422 in 1854. William Sinn noted that of the 11,012 persons who had landed in Quebec in 1854 "473 of them were so far as I could make out proletarians or beggars, whose emigration costs had been paid by their local communities. Moreover, 425 [of the 473] were from the Grand Duchy of Baden. As support money, they received from their home towns on arrival in Canada ten gulden or about four dollars."[154]

The landing of such indigents did not go unnoticed. The British government protested in February 1855 to the Presidium of the Diet of the German Confederation that during 1854 Baden had sent 422 paupers to Quebec. These persons, the testy British note pointed out, "presented an appearance of such squalor and destitution, scantily clothed, ignorant of our language, without any particular destination in view and possessed of but a small sum, paid to each on landing here, which at most would be barely sufficient for a week's support." The note condemned the audacity of "a foreign state to relieve itself of paupers already physically ill adapted to labour and thrown on a country requiring the aid of a robust and energetic emigration."[155] In December 1855 the British minister Alexander Malet sent a similar protest to the authorities in Bremen, Frankfurt, and Württemberg decrying the recent landing of indigent emigrants from Württemberg in Saint John, New Brunswick. The note informed the German authorities that ninety poverty-stricken immigrants had been sent at the public expense to Canada via Rotterdam and Liverpool. Fifty-seven of them had been so indigent that they had to be sent to the poorhouse, where they became public charges.[156] This aggrieved British response rings not altogether convincing, since the British themselves had been dumping paupers, orphans, and other undesirables in Canada on a regular basis from the time of the social upheavals associated with the post-Napoleonic years right through the Irish potato famine crisis.[157]

In his study of assisted emigration from Württemberg to North America, Gerhard Bassler notes that among the paupers dumped in Canada in the mid-1850s were "beggars, former convicts, unmarried women with children, all kinds of trouble makers and wards of the community but also large numbers of individuals and families who had been prosperous until ... reduced to utter poverty by forces beyond their control." Bassler's examples include a forty-three-year-old former owner of a turner's shop and a fifty-nine-year-old blacksmith who had formerly owned a forty-acre estate. Both men had lost all their real property and personal wealth; both had families (the smith had nine children and a wife) for whom they could no longer provide; both had been reduced to utter despair by their abject conditions. Distraught in the extreme, both men saw no other alternative than emigration, and petitioned their community for assistance to leave the district of Weinsberg. The local officials granted their requests and sponsored their journey to Saint John, New Brunswick, where they were promptly placed in the poorhouse.[158]

Canada could not prevent such dumping until its immigration policies had been more clearly defined, and that had to wait until Confederation. In 1868 Ottawa acted. Using public health and the prevention of disease as justifications, Parliament passed an act regulating immigrants landing at the port of Quebec. The act provided that any vessel arriving in Quebec would be immediately inspected by a government-appointed physician who would examine not only the health of immigrants but also their material assets in order to determine whether they could pay their own way to their final destination. If the doctor determined that an immigrant had sufficient assets, he would grant a permit to land in Canada. If an immigrant were deemed to be without the necessary funds, the landing permit would be withheld. Any ship's officer who allowed the landing of persons without the necessary permit would be subject to a heavy fine.

The Mechanics of Migration: Travel from Germany to Canada

Emigrating from Germany to Canada involved three stages: departure from Germany, the sea voyage to North America, and the journey in Canada to the place of settlement. Each stage of an emigrant's odyssey was unique, fraught with problems, difficulties, and dangers. Throughout, the migrant had to adjust to frequently frustrating procedures and new, often hostile surroundings. The process lost some of its worst nightmare-like qualities after 1850, with the introduction of new transportation technology and the development of more sympathetic attitudes in government and society toward migrants in both the sending and receiving lands. Nevertheless, into the twentieth century emigration remained a taxing ordeal for those brave or desperate enough to undertake it.

In emigration's first stage, the migrant had to find transportation to the coast. In the early nineteenth century, migrants journeyed by foot, horse-drawn wagon, and river barge for several weeks to reach the ports of embarkation. Frequently their seaward travel was interrupted by long waits for proper transport, and once on the Rhine the numerous toll stations along the river prolonged their trip even more. After 1840 the railroad and river steamboats greatly speeded up the process. As the volume of migrant traffic increased from the 1840s, it concentrated in centres such as Mannheim, Frankfurt am Main, Cologne, Leipzig, and Berlin. These centres, where emigrants transferred between modes of transportation, posed their own dangers. Bickelmann describes the hazards: "Businessmen who made a living from emigration found here a rich field for activity. Emigrants were surrounded by agents, representatives of the shipping and railway companies, porters, moneychangers and hawkers of all kinds, who attempted to beguile them into purchases or services of every possible kind. Trickery by hotelkeepers and transport firms, which the emigrants had always had to reckon with, were a part of daily life in such places, as a result of the sheer volume of emigrant traffic."[159]

Although in the first decades of the nineteenth century, Antwerp, Le Havre, and Rotterdam functioned as the main places of embarkation, Bremen emerged in the 1830s as an important port for Germans travelling to North America. Bremen's original advantage derived from its 1832 requirement that ship owners provide food for the emigrants during the voyage. In 1851 Bremen also established an information bureau for emigrants (Nachweisungsbureau für Auswanderer). This office provided information on such matters as lodging, food, and other travel-related expenses while also protecting the emigrants from being swindled. Hamburg, which had originally viewed poor emigrants as potential social problems and consequently restricted their entry into the city, soon recognized the profitability of the emigrant trade. After rescinding its discriminatory law in 1837, Hamburg quickly developed into a significant rival for Bremen, even setting up its own emigrant assistance office in 1851. To this was added the Hamburg Deputation, a commission for dispute resolution charged with seeing that contracts were upheld and that emigrants received legal protection.[160]

From these beginnings, both Hamburg and Bremen gradually established more comprehensive laws to protect emigrants in their cities. The Hamburg authorities established a branch office of the information bureau in the main train station to advise emigrants as they arrived. Travellers needed such assistance because they were usually met as they departed their trains by local hotelkeepers or their agents competing, sometimes in fraudulent fashion, for business. To counter this, the information bureau officials passed out leaflets and put up posters instructing emigrants to come directly to their station office for assistance. Eventually hotel personnel were banned from the railroad station altogether, leaving the information office staff and the police as the only reception committee. In 1868 Hamburg increased its protective measures by licensing hotelkeepers dealing with emigrants and requiring minimum sanitary conditions for housing and feeding emigrants in the city's hotels. In 1870 Hamburg's hotel owners were required to post price lists for room and board and for any tickets, utensils, or other supplies offered for sale to emigrants.[161]

Measures to protect the emigrants developed differently in Bremen. Compared to Hamburg, Bremen suffered from an obvious disadvantage in attracting emigrants: the port of Bremerhaven was at least a day's journey down the Weser River until 1862. To make the Bremer/Bremerhaven option more attractive, a building specifically designed to house waiting emigrants was constructed in Bremerhaven in 1850. This did much to solve the problem of delays in shipping out due to inadequate winds. The introduction of steamships to ply the Weser in the late 1850s, and even more important the opening of a railroad line from Bremen to the coast in 1862, greatly facilitated the journey to Bremerhaven. This allowed emigrants to remain in Bremen until the day their ships departed for the new world. Like their Hamburg counterparts, the Bremen city authorities sought to ensure the well-being and fair treatment of travellers during their sojourns in the city. The room and board arrangements in Bremen, however, were controlled by contract between the information bureau and the various hotelkeepers. Bremen's hotel owners contracted for the right to house and feed the emigrants. In exchange, they agreed to allow the bureau to set standards for housing and general hygiene. Together the hotel owners and bureau personnel agreed upon prices to be charged for rooms, food, and other services.[162]

In 1850 sailing ships still carried most emigrants to North America, although ships driven by steam power existed. The new technology gradually won out in the next two decades. In his account of nineteenth-century emigration from Great Britain to Canada, Edwin Guillet claims, "Sailing-vessels predominated until the end of the 1863 season, during which 55 percent patronized them; but in subsequent years the steamship quickly assumed the lead, and by 1870 the number of sailing-ship passengers was negligible."[163] For the port of New York the shift to steam was equally dramatic. "In 1856," Birgit Gelberg writes, "only 5 percent of those who landed in New York came by steamship; in 1870 that number had increased to 88 percent."[164] The Hamburg-American Line (HAPAG) started a steamship route to New York in 1856, and Bremen's North German Lloyd did the same a year later.[165] Günter Moltmann reports that the last sailing ship to ferry emigrants from Hamburg to North America completed its voyage in 1873.[166]

The transition to steamships in the German carrying trade to Canada occurred more slowly. In fact, it appears that throughout the period 1850-70, if Germans travelled to Canada on steamships, they were non-German ships. For example, in the four years from 1858 to 1861 Hamburg sent twenty ships to Quebec, all of them under sail.[167] Consul Gustav Beling's report for 1863 listed a total of 148 ships bringing emigrants from Great Britain and Germany to Canada in that year, 77 powered by steam and 71 by sail. The twelve of these ships from Germany were all sailing vessels.[168] Data from Bremen from the late 1860s illustrate just how completely the sailing vessel still reigned. In 1867 eight ships, all of them sailing vessels, made the voyage from Bremen to Quebec. In 1868, thirteen Bremen ships made the same crossing, and in 1869 Bremen sent only two vessels to Quebec, all powered by sail.[169] Over the years 1861 to 1867 a total of 5,231 passengers travelled to Quebec from Bremen on twenty ships. The number of passengers per ship averaged just over 260. During the same seven-year period, New York received 212,191 passengers on 653 Bremen ships with an average passenger load of 325.[170] In this much more extensive and lucrative New York business the steamship played the leading role. The small passenger volume to Quebec, plus the more limited opportunities for return carriage, determined the use of sailing vessels, for wind-driven craft cost considerably less than steamships to run.

The major disadvantage of sailing vessels lay in the greater length of the voyage by sail. The journey from Bremen or Hamburg to Quebec, New York, or Baltimore by sailing ship typically lasted six to eight weeks. Of the eight ships that sailed to Canada from Bremen in 1867, the fastest made Quebec in thirty-three days, the slowest in fifty-five. Most of the other ships required between forty-five and fifty days to complete the crossing. Fluctuations in the weather caused the varying length of sailing voyages, because ships were always at the mercy of the wind. Often sailing vessels could not leave on their scheduled departure date because there was no wind or, worse, an ill wind. Steamships, even the early ones, reduced the average duration of the Atlantic crossing by two-thirds. In 1867 steamers crossed from Bremen to New York in fourteen days on average. Steamships that left from Liverpool managed the crossing in even less time.[171]

Compared to steamships, the disadvantages of sailing ships were apparent in nearly all aspects of the voyage. The duration of the voyage by sail exacerbated the problems caused by inadequate sanitation facilities. As a consequence, cholera, typhus, and other serious illnesses occurred substantially more often on sailing ships. Mortality rates among immigrants making the Atlantic crossing declined dramatically after the adoption of the steamship. Providing food for the passengers on sailing vessels posed greater problems than on steamships. The radically shortened trip by steamer allowed passengers access to greater amounts of fresher, more nutritious food. The rations of hard bread and salted meat characteristic of the age of sail ceased to be regular fare.[172]

Regulations protecting emigrants in port developed before adequate measures were adopted for the ships themselves. Since the migrant trade had been largely incidental in the early nineteenth century, with passengers travelling individually or in small numbers on freight vessels, protective regulations had not seemed necessary. The upsurge in emigrant numbers after 1830, and particularly during the 1840s, led to ships devoted mostly to passenger transport. In the period 1850-70, most emigrants heading to North America travelled as steerage passengers, the steerage area being located directly below the main deck and extending for most of the ship's length. To maximize profits, shipping concerns attempted to convey as many passengers as possible on each ship, so the ship's steerage was characteristically overcrowded.

Primitive accommodations, little ventilation, and almost no illumination complicated the problem of overcrowding. The water furnished to passengers was frequently contaminated. "Water," the migration historian Marcus Hansen reports, "was stored in old sugar hogsheads, in oil casks which had never been cleaned, in vinegar, molasses and turpentine barrels ... Even under the most favorable conditions, the contents were almost undrinkable before the end of the journey. On some vessels gunpowder was sprinkled in the barrels as a preservative. This gave the water a blackish appearance and a repulsive taste which increased with time."[173] Most sailing ships (and many steamers), moreover, lacked any arrangements to provide food. Steerage passengers had to prepare their own meals with food brought on board with them. Again to quote Hansen: "No matter how dull life might be elsewhere on board, there was always fighting around the stove, and philosophically minded Germans quietly waiting their turn compared the government to the anarchy of the medieval empire when '*Faust Recht*' alone prevailed. Under such conditions breakfast was not ready until noon and dinner until night; and before the end of the journey both breakfast and dinner might be several days late."[174]

Summing up the problems in 1866, the *Allgemeine Auswanderungszeitung* called for governments to establish and enforce definite regulations to curb abuses of passengers. There must be, the paper insisted, "strict separation of male and female passengers, regular cleaning of the sleeping quarters, adequate provisioning of the ships with food of good quality and sufficient quantity, and appropriate measures to provide medical care for the sick."[175] Although many abuses continued unabated, some efforts were made to alleviate them.

In regulations to improve food on board, Bremen and Hamburg led the way. As early as 1832 both cities required that their ships provide prepared food for their passengers. (This regulation was not adopted elsewhere until much later.) The first attempts to solve the oppressive overcrowding came in 1850, when Hamburg passed a law requiring that the height of the ceiling in steerage be at least five and a half feet. To this was added a regulation allotting to each passenger twelve square feet (3.67 square metres) as individual space. Regulations mandating bed size followed. The lack of fresh air in steerage led to a requirement in 1868 that ventilators be installed to provide adequate air circulation. To reduce sexual abuse and the accusations of rampant immorality prompted by the mixing of the sexes in steerage, the Hamburg Senate enacted a regulation in 1868 dividing the ship's steerage into three parts. Single men were placed in the forward portion, families allotted the middle section, and single women assigned to the stern. On the basis of Hamburg's success, Bremen adopted the same regulation in 1870. These rather timid moves did alleviate the more obvious abuses but they did not reduce the dangers passengers encountered from improper sanitation. Lavatory facilities remained totally inadequate, with as many as fifty persons typically assigned to one toilet. Arrangements for bathing and washing clothes, or even eating utensils, did not exist.[176]

Given inadequate food and water, overcrowding, and the altogether primitive sanitary arrangements in steerage, conditions on most, if not all, immigrant vessels during the two decades after 1850 were horrendous. Nearly a hundred years before, Gottlieb Mittelberger, a German travelling to Pennsylvania, had described his steerage crossing:

> Howbeit, during the passage there doth arise in the vessels an awful misery, stink, smoke, horror, vomiting, sea-sickness of all kinds, fever, purgings, headaches, sweats, constipations of the bowels, sores, scurvy, cancers, thrush and the like, which do wholly arise from the stale and strongly salted food and meat, and from the exceeding badness and nastiness of the water, from which many do wretchedly decline and perish. Thereto come also the dearth of provision, hunger, thirst, cold, heat, damp, fear, want, janglings and lamentings, with other hardships, inasmuch as lice do often breed and proliferate, most of all upon the sick, so that a man may brush them off his body.[177]

Accounts describing the filth, the smells, the sickness, and the sufferings of steerage passage in the mid-nineteenth century had hardly changed from Mittelberger's time. In 1847, for example, Stephen E. DeVere, an Irish land-owner who travelled to Canada as a steerage passenger in a sailing ship ferrying Irish immigrants, described conditions in the following terms:

> Before the emigrant has been a week at sea he is an altered man ... Hundreds of poor people, men, women, and children of all ages are ... huddled together without light, air, wallowing in filth and breathing a fetid atmosphere, sick in body, dispirited in heart, the fever patients lying between the sound ... The food is generally ill-selected and seldom sufficiently cooked, in consequence of the insufficiency of the cooking places. The supply of water, hardly enough for cooking and drinking, does not allow washing. In many ships the filthy beds, teeming with all abominations, are never required to be brought on deck and aired.[178]

The most infamous German sailing vessel of the period, the *Leipzig* out of Hamburg, earned the title "ship of death" when it arrived in New York in January 1868 with nearly a fifth of its passengers dead from cholera contracted during the voyage. The *Leipzig*'s negative reputation caused "such anger and commotion among the public that the Hamburg owner changed the ship's name to *Liebig*."[179] The *Leipzig* case may have been worse than most, but death from malnutrition and especially contagious diseases such as cholera, typhus, and even smallpox occurred all too often on the immigrant ships of this period.

Although few, the voyages to Canada offered the same problems as other passages to the new world in the period 1850-70. A report on immigration to Canada for 1854, for example, listed 11,012 immigrants taking passage to Quebec that year. Of that number, 226 had died at sea; of these 192 were children under fourteen years of age. An additional 17 immigrants died in the quarantine station at Grosse Isle. Most of the victims died from cholera.[180] Twelve years later in 1866, the quarantine station at Grosse Isle reported similar news. Between April and October 1866, ten ships from Hamburg and Bremen transported 2,897 emigrants to be processed at Grosse Isle, all but 9 of whom travelled in steerage. Of the total, 71 perished at sea; another 81 arrived in Canada "sick." The vast majority of the deaths occurred during three voyages: on the *Pallas* 55 (11.2 percent) of the 491 passengers died, on the *Main* 12 (3 percent) of the 381 steerage travellers succumbed, and on the *Neckar* 22 (4 percent) of the 522 passengers were lost. The Grosse Isle inspectors attributed the deaths on the *Pallas* to measles – all the victims were children – on the *Main* to "cold and debility," and on the *Neckar* again to measles.[181]

The absence of adequate governmental supervision, particularly in the German lands and ports from which the emigrants set out, explains why such conditions persisted into the 1860s. Since most German states at this time, with the obvious exceptions of Hamburg and Bremen, still held ambivalent views on emigration, positive emigration policies had not been widely adopted in Germany. Without state protection, Germany's migrants to Canada and elsewhere were exposed on their journeys to a variety of abuses. Writing at the end of the nineteenth century, a melodramatic German patriot condemned the disastrous failure of Germany's governments to look after its departing sons and daughters: "The history of the care accorded to Germany's emigrants is a story of suffering, it is to a great extent a true martyr's history. This story dramatically illustrates the tragedy of our earlier political weakness and division. Ship fever decimated the emigrants until the 1860s. The journey to New York was a trip through the hell of immorality, misery, and lamentation." This description of the New York crossings apparently applied as well to some of the journeys ending in Montreal or Halifax.[182]

One obvious problem involved securing timely legal recourse for abuses suffered at sea. For example, the *Gellert* left Hamburg on 18 April 1860, scheduled to sail directly to Quebec. On the way, the ship made an unplanned seventeen-day stopover in St. John's, Newfoundland, causing much inconvenience and expense to its passengers. When the ship finally landed in Quebec on 2 July, the passengers, including some Prussians en route to Wisconsin, sought to recover the extra expenses caused by the layover. In their petition to the Prussian consul at Quebec, eleven of the disgruntled emigrants claimed that the unscheduled delay had caused them "to lose the opportunity to plant potatoes and other vegetables this summer due to the loss of so many working days."[183] Although their cause of action was sound, they received no compensation for their losses. The Prussian consul in Quebec, George Pemberton, reported in August that the passengers had not pursued damages because "the necessity of keeping the passengers here [in Quebec] to give evidence would have put them to so much inconvenience and expense that it was better to abandon the claim altogether."[184]

The case of the *Emil* involved more serious matters. The *Emil*, outfitted in Bremen but sailing under the flag of the North German Confederation, left Geestemunde on 3 April 1869 with 320 steerage passengers bound for Quebec. For this voyage it carried enough provisions for eighty days at sea. The passengers had been examined by a physician on the day of departure and all been found to be free of disease. Seven weeks later the ship arrived at Grosse Isle: several passengers had died; some had become sick enough to be hospitalized at Grosse Isle; and many were so weakened that further travel was impossible. After twelve of *Emil*'s passengers appealed for help, the Deutsche Gesellschaft in Montreal set up a committee to look into the matter and uncovered serious abuses. To begin with, the passengers, who had originally intended to emigrate to New York, found that when they arrived at the place of embarkation the ship they were to have travelled on was booked up. Agents at Geestemunde convinced them to take the waiting ship *Emil* to Quebec because Quebec "was very close to New York." Once on board, they discovered worse accommodations than anticipated. One passenger told the committee that "the food was of such limited amount and such poor quality and fresh water so sparse that two male passengers died because of it."[185] Indeed, the deliberate withholding of food became the most serious problem faced by the travellers, who believed malnutrition contributed directly to the sickness which began to plague large numbers in the third week of the voyage. The committee also heard bitter complaints about abuses received from the crew. For example, one immigrant told of how after arriving in Quebec's harbour, they "had to wait on board for hours before receiving permission to disembark. During all this time, they received no food. Then just as they were leaving, the ship's cook in a mocking gesture blew the whistle announcing meal time."[186]

Montreal's Deutsche Gesellschaft also provided assistance for indigent *Emil* passengers stranded in Montreal. Soliciting help from other people and organizations in the city, the society made arrangements to cover the medical and other maintenance costs for those who were too sick or weak to continue their journeys. When the dust had settled, the society protested publicly in the *Montreal Gazette*:

> These immigrants were landed at Quebec in direct violation of the law forbidding the landing of paupers; the Society has therefore brought these facts under the notice of the authorities at Quebec, so the law in question may be properly enforced. The experience of last summer ought to have sufficed to prompt the government to rigidly prohibit the landing of all immigrants unable to pay their passage inland ... Steps are also taken by the Society to urge the government of the North German Confederation through its consulate here of the imperative necessity to pass strict regulations for the carrying of immigrant passengers. The alleged inhuman treatment of the passengers on board the above named vessel will also be strictly inquired into.[187]

Although both the Canadian and German authorities received news of these abuses, nothing was done either to indemnify the victims or to punish the culprits.

After a long, uncomfortable, and often dangerous voyage, the first view of North America, normally the coast of Newfoundland, appeared as a welcome sight indeed. Reaching Newfoundland's shores, however, did not signal the trip's end, for several hundred hazardous miles, or a week or two of sailing, remained before docking in Quebec. Once out of the treacherous coastal waters off Newfoundland and into the Gulf of St. Lawrence, the emigrant ship had to negotiate such rocky hazards as St. Paul's Isle and Anticosti Island. Thirty-three miles below Quebec City, the ship passed through the quarantine inspection at Grosse Isle. Established in 1831, Grosse Isle had quickly earned an unsavoury reputation for its inadequate facilities to care for the sick and debilitated. By 1850 housing and medical arrangements had been markedly improved, and many of the abuses that had contributed to its earlier label as the "isle of death" abolished.[188]

Because of continuing abuses and safety hazards throughout the period 1850-70, Ottawa finally acted to ensure the safety of passengers coming to Canada and to prevent the spread of disease once the immigrants landed. The Immigration Act of 1869 sought to protect immigrants in two ways. First, the statute was intended to guard travellers from health risks encountered during the voyage from Europe. To this end, for example, the statute imposed limits on the number of passengers a ship could carry. Second, in the spirit of the reforms instituted by Bremen and Hamburg a generation before, Canada's Immigration Act of 1869 addressed exploitation by unscrupulous innkeepers and merchants, who traditionally offered their services to the newly arrived. Those soliciting immigrant business had to be licensed, and hotel and boarding-house owners were required to post their price lists prominently. To fend off probable trouble, the act also prohibited the landing of indigents and imposed penalties on the ship captains who did so. Finally, Ottawa tried to make the immigrants' reception in Canada less bewildering by appointing government agents to meet the immigrant ships as they arrived and to assist newcomers in arranging temporary housing and travel on the next leg of their Canadian odyssey.[189]

During the period 1850-70, the travel arrangements within British North America advanced considerably over earlier times. Steamboats replaced sailing ships and bateaux on lakes and rivers; the St. Lawrence canal system had been completed in the 1840s; railroad construction had made great strides; and passable, well-maintained roads into the interior expanded stagecoach travel. In 1851 James B. Brown, the author of a popular guidebook, wrote that "on arriving at Quebec emigrants may go direct from the ship's side on board of commodious steam vessels, without its being necessary for them to go on shore or to spend a shilling for transporting their luggage, or for any other purpose: and in those steam vessels they can be conveyed to their destination, to any of the main ports on the St. Lawrence or the Great Lakes without trans-shipment, and with great rapidity."[190] In 1854 A.C. Buchanan, who was first appointed resident superintendent and government agent for immigrants in Quebec in 1828, advertised combined train and steamboat fares that would take the newly arrived immigrant from

Quebec to Hamilton and on to Detroit or Chicago in only five days.[191] Despite these undeniable advances, problems persisted. As late as 1867, the Deutsche Gesellschaft zu Montreal complained to Ottawa that the Grand Trunk Railway had recently transported a group of German immigrants from Port Levi west in boxcars with no ventilation, inadequate drinking water, and no water closets. Buchanan wrote the railway authorities denouncing the abuse and demanding an appropriate remedy. The railway promptly issued a circular requiring all agents and conductors "to do all they can for the comfort of the emigrants in route ... with particular attention ... to the comfort of emigrants obliged to travel in ordinary box cars."[192]

Conclusion

In the two decades 1850-70 German emigration to British North America, which had expanded significantly in the desperate 1840s, continued but at a much less impressive pace. This slowdown reflected the larger economic, political, and social trends apparent in both Germany and Canada. In Germany the economy, plagued by crises in the late 1840s, improved after 1850 as the new industrial processes associated with the Industrial Revolution took off. At the same time rapid demographic growth continued. An expanding population coupled with fundamental economic change that made some occupations redundant and completely abolished others prompted large numbers of Germans to think of leaving home. New technology in the form of railroads and more efficient passenger ships (both sail and steam-powered vessels) made travel out of Europe and within Canada faster and far less difficult as well. New, more sophisticated advertising and solicitation techniques by those promoting emigration to Canada brought the country to the attention of increasing numbers of Germans. Finally, the laws affecting migration had caught up to its social and economic realities. In the German states, freedom of movement became a legal right as the last vestiges of earlier restrictions on individual movement disappeared. The German lands therefore offered excellent recruiting grounds for possible migrants to Canada.

Despite all these apparent advantages, Canada failed to lure significant numbers of new immigrants from the German states. In Canada the political system had been altered fundamentally during this period, but the country's economy and society had not. Traditional habits prevailed in immigration. Canada's governments continued to prefer British immigrants over "foreigners" and devoted most of their funds and efforts to winning converts in the United Kingdom. Nevertheless, in the decade of Confederation, Canada's leaders gradually concluded that if the country were to survive the threat of annexation by the United States and populate the newly acquired western lands it had to assume a more active role in promoting immigration beyond the mother country. As a result, the timid beginnings of a policy supporting more non-British immigrants were seen, including the first modest efforts to solicit emigrants in Germany and elsewhere on the Continent. The recognition that non-British immigrants were required for Canada's future also strengthened the belief in the need for a new, more alluring Canadian image to replace earlier negative stereotypes.

In these various ways, the period 1850-70 adumbrated what would develop in the ensuing two decades: earlier trends were consolidated and developed and new approaches tried as pull and push forces continued to be exerted from Canada and Germany. Although a clear, forceful policy in favour of either British or Continental immigration had not emerged by 1870, migration from Germany to Canada continued apace because governmental policy became somewhat more supportive and less prohibitive. In addition, solicitation techniques developed, technology improved, and facilitation networks became more sophisticated. Because of its inchoate immigration policy, Canada could not immediately compete with the United States, which had a huge lead in solicitation experience, resources, and success. Canada did, however, begin to emerge from the unknown and assert its claim as a home for Germany's emigrants. Although Canadian success in Germany remained modest, the romantic wilderness touted for its untapped natural wealth and its superior human institutions finally began to attract some attention.

2
Migration in the Age of Bismarck and Macdonald, 1870-90

Movement from Germany to Canada during the twenty years after 1870 evolved in accordance with social, economic, and political developments in the sending and receiving lands. The patterns of movement, migrant profiles, technological changes in transportation and communication, and the new advertising campaign to induce emigration all progressed apace. Cultural preferences and assumptions influenced both efforts to sell Canada and the effectiveness of the campaign in Germany. The expanded image of Canada that had emerged in the 1850s and '60s was honed and more widely promoted after 1870. The migration policies of Canada's and Germany's governments assumed more importance as migration became increasingly associated with and affected by the modernization processes occurring in both countries. Political developments in both countries formed the context for these changes.

The Political Background

The period from 1870 to 1890, like the preceding decades, revealed parallels in Canadian and German politics. The political scene in both countries was dominated by strong-willed conservatives: Sir John A. Macdonald and Otto von Bismarck. Both countries, so recently united, strove to define themselves as national entities and to establish their roles in the international order. Both faced disapproving neighbours. For Germany, France represented the envious threat; for Canada, it was the overconfident United States. Domestically, both countries struggled with similar problems as well. Most obviously both had to deal with sectional discontent with the newly established federal order. In Canada forces in both east and west resisted Ottawa's and Ontario's domination; in Germany the south and west chafed under the rule of Bismarck and Prussia. Furthermore, in both countries religious differences assumed major proportions: Quebec and ultramontanism roused heated opposition in the predominantly Protestant provinces and especially in Ontario, while Protestant Prussia led the resistance to the Catholic south and the ultramontane opponents of Prussianization. Despite these broad similarities, opposing positions on migration emerged in Germany and Canada. In Germany, support appeared to be growing for restricting emigration to prevent a weakening of the state in the face of the French threat. Meanwhile, in Canada potential immigrant settlers for Canada's west came to be viewed as increasingly crucial to the new dominion's effort to prevent US expansion across the forty-ninth parallel.

In Bismarck's Germany, the dominant political climate combined the conservative with the innovative. From the onset of the empire in 1871, Bismarck faced the formidable task of replacing former loyalties with new ones. The unification proclamation constituted less an established fact than a potential. To begin with, the new German state was not unitary, but a federal system with the Prussian king as emperor. Although Prussia dominated the system, the new Germany resembled the former federal order because the several German states that had united under Prussian leadership retained much of their previous independence, including their own representative institutions and the power to levy their own taxes. The largest states even exchanged ambassadors and determined their own emigration policies. Consequently, many Germans considered unification incomplete and found themselves suffering what Gordon Craig calls "an identity crisis." To effect a credible unity, Bismarck had to make the parts transcend their past sectional differences and accept the new Prussian-dominated system.[1]

To rally support for the Prusso-German constitution with its three anomalous features of absolute monarchy, representative parliament, and democratic plebiscite, Bismarck manipulated the system to Prussia's advantage. On the one hand, he courted those he thought would support the system; on the other, he persecuted alleged subversives and enemies of it. For example, to win favour with the liberals, he campaigned against Germany's Roman Catholics.[2] When Bismarck no longer needed liberal support, he curried favour with the Reich's conservative and agrarian elements by outlawing Germany's socialist movement. To placate the empire's working class, which had become increasingly identified with that socialist movement, Bismarck then introduced the world's first set of social insurance laws.[3] Although the campaigns against the Catholics and socialists alienated many from the empire, Bismarck's repressions did not weaken the new order as much as might have been expected. By the 1880s the new system had developed enough popular support, or acquiescence, to move forward.

Indeed, institutional consolidation progressed almost inexorably. A loyal civil service was in place; a national German army, albeit Prussian-dominated, had been created; common weights and measures had been established; an integrated railway system had appeared; and a unitary German postal system had replaced the various earlier systems. The new Reichstag had become a central organ of the German state if only by virtue of the sheer volume of its legislation. Under Bismarck, liberals, socialists, and other outspoken advocates of greater democracy remained frustrated, but nationalists and imperialists fared better. By the time of his removal in 1890, the idea of a powerful German national state had become fact. German colonies in Africa and the Pacific, Germany's presence as a player in the contest for China, and Bismarck's dominant role in the Berlin Conference of 1885 all lent credence to this fact. Thus, by 1890 the emigration of Germans appeared increasingly inappropriate for a German Empire with worldwide political aspirations.[4]

Similar problems of making the new unity work and creating a nation-state out of the abstract dominion concept dominated the Canadian political scene. In 1870 the overwhelmingly rural and conservative British North American population, which numbered over 3.6 million, was hardly united. The pivotal political figure in transforming the country's sectionalism into a greater Canadian national identity was John A. Macdonald, who, but for five years in the mid-1870s, remained prime minister until his death in 1891.[5] Faced with a continued annexationist threat from the south, Macdonald moved to frustrate the Americans.[6] To begin with, he expanded the original dominion membership to include the new provinces of Nova Scotia and Manitoba plus the extensive lands formerly controlled by the Hudson's Bay Company. Realizing, as the Argentine political thinker Juan Bautista Alberdi put it, that "to govern is to populate,"[7] Macdonald set about filling the newly acquired western lands with loyal Canadians. Extending federal control over these lands, Macdonald's government at the same time introduced an enlightened land tenure program. Taking his cue from the US Homestead Act of 1862, he led the passage of the Dominion Lands Act in 1872.[8] This crucial piece of governmental activism granted free homesteads to those families who pledged to settle on the land and improve it for three years. Although Canada's act did not trump that of the United States, it seemed especially generous when compared to the policies of the other major Western Hemisphere receiver states, Argentina and Brazil, which sought not freeholders to populate their open spaces but renters (sharecroppers) and day labourers.[9] With the Dominion Lands Act passed, Macdonald then campaigned for a transcontinental railway to tie the newly acquired lands and their homesteaders to the Canadian nation. Finally, as appropriate for an emerging state with imperial designs, Macdonald's government abrogated the reciprocity treaty with the United States, leaving the new dominion free to create a national economy. The protective tariffs introduced in 1879 to shelter fledgling Canadian industries and to stimulate agriculture represented a major step in this direction.[10]

Known as the National Policy after 1878, Macdonald's program bore fruit in the following decade.[11] The national railroad was realized in 1886 when the Canadian Pacific Railway completed its line over the mountains to connect Ontario with British Columbia.[12] With Canada linked from sea to sea, settlers began moving onto the newly available western lands. Initially most homesteaders were British and sought to create Ontario-style agricultural settlements.[13] They were soon followed by a trickle of non-British immigrants, including some Germans, who came to establish homes in the newest part of Canada. Louis Riel's aborted and anticlimactic North-West Rebellion of 1885 bore witness to the success of Macdonald's western policies.[14] Although sectionalisms persisted in other areas of the country after Riel's protest,[15] by the end of Macdonald's time in office the Canadian national ideal appeared more plausible than ever before. Still, continued political success depended on holding the country together. To do this, the dominion needed more citizens for its greatly expanded territories. This meant increasing immigration to Canada.

The Economic Background

As we have seen, the German economy that emerged in the last quarter of the nineteenth century to rival the British one had grown spectacularly during the two decades after 1850.[16] Although expansion continued in the first years of the new Reich, by 1873 it had been replaced by a major economic downturn. Known as the "Great Depression," this deflationary period lasted into the mid-1890s.[17] During this time, industrial recession and reduced agricultural prices coincided with a steadily increasing population that grew from 43 million in 1870 to 48 million in 1890. Economic change and growth in Germany had not ceased altogether; rather it had slowed to what Volker Berghahn labels a kind of "retarded growth."[18] The social effects of this "retardation," however, were significant. The economically advantaged and powerful – cartel members, large landholding aristocrats, and even wealthy peasants – may have experienced little adversity during the recessionary decades 1875-95 but many smaller people suffered. For example, in Prussia's east the plight of the agricultural worker deteriorated measurably. Declining wages, decreasing numbers, and increasingly harsh working conditions caused many to emigrate or to abandon the land for the country's rapidly growing cities. Likewise, many smaller businesses, both industrial and commercial, failed during these economically troubled years. The period of recession in the 1870s and 1880s thus saw both significant innovations and adaptations in many areas of the economy and considerable social exploitation and suffering.[19] The disparity between rapid population growth and the slower pace of industrial change decreed that not enough work opportunities were created to satisfy the work needs of the people. Unemployment, displacement, and frustration resulted.

An article in the 24 June 1872 issue of the *Deutsche Auswanderer-Zeitung* (German Emigrants Newspaper) captured the sense of frustration felt by the

"little people." According to the anonymous author, Germany's modernizing economy adversely affected not only small independent peasants and
dependent agricultural workers but also traditional craftsmen: "The industrial development of our age has ruined the traditional trades in the towns
and destroyed the small industrial cottage industries." The cost of agricultural production had increased dramatically while prices for the goods produced had not. Thus, smallholders as well as the landless had lost out, and
the traditional bonds linking employer and employee had been destroyed.
For example, the critic noted, the work day had been abnormally length-
ened, worsening the plight of the agricultural labourer. Any liberality a land-
owner might show his workers was now considered "uneconomic charity."
Thus, the article continued, the native village had lost its charm and fortune; life had become more and more difficult as earnings became increasingly meagre. The probable fate of their children led peasants and artisans
to an inevitable conclusion: "either move to the city to seek factory work
where wages were better or emigrate to the new world." The disillusioned
author concluded his diatribe bitterly: "Toward the machine-like modern
state with its bourgeois ideology and catchwords, its feckless legislation, its
colossal bureaucracy, the little man feels nothing but indifference and alienation ... the national enthusiasm for Kaiser and Empire and for heroic military deeds which may appear splendid and comforting to the rich and
educated, [the little man] does not understand in the least."[20] Although
hyperbole clearly marks this passage, the author correctly identified how
difficult and painful was the demise of the former agrarian and artisanal
world and how much the birth of a new industrial order disturbed German
economic and social life.

As it had Germany, the economic downturn of the 1870s and 1880s also
affected Canada. Although recent Canadian scholarship has suggested that
the period may not have been as bleak as earlier thought, Canada's economy
nevertheless fared considerably better both before 1873 and after 1896.[21]
Between those years, industrialization continued but at a slower pace. Business failures and unemployment appeared in various locations, and the
number of Canadians moving to the United States reached unprecedented
levels.[22] In agriculture, the dramatic advances anticipated for the Canadian
prairies had not materialized; agriculture's position in the country's economy
appeared to be declining after 1870.[23] Nevertheless, in spite of the slowdown in industry, the losses to emigration, and the delayed opening of the
West, significant numbers of industries not only survived the downturn but
even managed to expand. The secondary industries of lumber processing,
cheese making, meat packing, and flour milling grew. So too did some heavier
industries turning out the likes of iron castings and agricultural machinery.
The adoption of the protective tariff in 1879 stimulated some older industries
while opening up opportunities for new ones.[24] These industrial advances

and structural changes notwithstanding, the Canadian economy remained at the end of the 1880s dominated by its traditional staple products: lumber, agricultural products, fish, and minerals.

The opening up of the West promised further expansion in these areas. The neomercantilist policies of the Macdonald government, which sought to protect domestic industry from foreign competition, also aimed at exploiting the West's great agricultural and natural resource potential. The extent of the federal government's commitment to western development can be seen in the special status and privileges bestowed upon the Canadian Pacific Railway, charged with the building of the transcontinental railroad.[25] These included tax breaks, land grants, and monopoly rights. Such generous concessions provided not only the profit incentive but also encouragement for "the CPR to attract immigrants to the west and thus increase the value of their unsold lands as well as produce traffic for the road and markets for central Canadian businessmen."[26]

According to Warwick Armstrong, Macdonald's choice to develop the West's resources and particularly its wheat economy meant that Canada embarked on an economic program clearly distinguishable from that of either Great Britain or the United States. Labelling this program "Dominion capitalism," Armstrong saw it as leading to a kind of partial industrial development. Within the international economy, Canada became an "efficient and capital intensive specialist producer of raw materials and foodstuff exports." Macdonald's protective tariffs, Armstrong concluded, were designed "less to promote an indigenous class of Canadian manufacturers than to encourage industries on Canadian soil." Such industries could be and in some instances did become branch plants for expansive foreign-based industry. Under this program, Canadian industry expanded most often as "small-scale, manufacturing activities associated with agricultural production." The Eastern bankers and commercial interests supporting Macdonald's program were not interested in developing a strong national manufacturing class but rather in advancing an indigenous Canadian industry to serve the country's staple export economy. In short, Canadian industry was tailored to fit the needs of "medium scale farmers with middle means less in need of imported capital or luxury goods." Canada's farmers would turn to "local manufacturers for their fertilizers, fencing wire, and agricultural machinery."[27] As shall be shown, this partial industrial strategy influenced immigration policy decisions well beyond Macdonald's day, and Canada continued to seek agricultural rather than industrial immigrants right up to 1930.

Canada's Immigration Policy
Between 1870 and 1890, Canada's immigration policies manifested more structure and certainty than in the preceding period. The escalating national

ambitions and anxieties endemic to the new dominion explain why Canada's politicians began to allot more energy and resources to immigration. Western settlement, which Macdonald and his supporters viewed as vital to the nation's development, became a crucial element in federal immigration policy.[28] Settling the West meant bringing in farmers to till the virgin soil. The 1877 report of the Parliamentary Committee on Immigration and Colonization stated the government's position clearly: "The class of immigrants required by Canada, at the present time, is confined to those who are able and willing to work, principally on land, or those who have means. The class of professional men, or of men only fitted for special pursuits, should not be advised to come to Canada to seek employment, as they would probably meet with bitter disappointment."[29] In keeping with the country's British traditions, the same report indicated that the government intended to recruit the vast majority of the necessary farmer-immigrants in the British Isles. Consequently, ten of the fifteen immigration agents on Canada's European staff were based in the United Kingdom, and recruitment funds were apportioned overwhelmingly to agents in England, Scotland, and Ireland.[30]

The government's rationale for weighting its program so heavily toward Britain extended beyond the usual cultural and political arguments offered in favour of British subjects as most appropriate for Canada's society and traditions. The belief that sufficient agriculturalists could be recruited in the United Kingdom rested on the expectation that long-term economic trends in the British Isles would produce a pool of available and willing migrants for Canada. John Lowe, secretary in the dominion's Department of Agriculture, explained, "Reports lead us to believe there is a tendency in the United Kingdom to an enlargement of farms, which throws many small farmers out of their holdings. It is found that altered circumstances in agricultural practices require the investment of much more capital per acre. The farmers are, therefore, to a great extent in a transition state." Quoting an English authority, Lowe predicted "that farming capital, by the substitution of steam for horse power in agriculture, as it has been in manufactures, locomotion and navigation, must be very greatly increased. Tenant-farmers thus thrown out of their holdings, and also by the operation of converting farms into parks, will be likely to emigrate if they see they can do better."[31]

Despite such strong pro-British feeling, many Canadian government personnel considered the "industrious" Germans an attractive and plausible alternative if British immigrants were unavailable. Lowe's view, expressed in 1879, that "German immigrants have been found to be specially adapted for settlement on the Prairies of the North West of the Dominion" appears quite representative.[32] So long as they were not indigent, Germans were welcomed as immigrants into Canada during the period 1870-90. Indeed, Macdonald himself reflected the growing support in the dominion for Germany's people becoming Canadians. His favourable response to the

Deutsche Gesellschaft zu Montreal's memo to the secretary of agriculture in 1872 discussing the issue of German immigration illustrates the prime minister's early sympathy for the German cause.

The German Society suggested a number of avenues Canada could pursue to secure more German immigrants. To begin with, the society proposed to expand the knowledge of Canada and its advantages "by circulating [in Germany] supplements to newspapers and other pamphlets containing such information." Second, it suggested Ottawa pay its agents in Germany "as a remuneration for distributing information respecting the Dominion" a bonus of "$2 per capita per adult immigrant to Canada." Third, the society recommended that the Canadian government set aside a township in Manitoba for a German settlement. If Ottawa were to do this, the Montreal society pledged to use its contacts in North Germany "to bring out annually a certain number of families possessed of some means and settle them in that township." Finally, the society urged that a "conductor speaking the German language" should be established in Winnipeg to provide for the immigrants upon their arrival in the North West.[33]

By the end of Macdonald's tenure as Canada's leader, most of these suggestions had been incorporated into Canada's German immigration policy, at least experimentally. Canadian agents were sent to Germany, and German agents hired there, to solicit agriculturalists for the dominion. The agents employed, as instructed, various forms of propaganda including advertising in newspapers and publishing German-language pamphlets. As well as receiving salaries and expense accounts, Canada's agents were rewarded with bonuses for successful recruitment. And separate areas were even set aside in Manitoba for German-speaking settlers. Despite these positive steps, the new policy, as shall be shown, did not enjoy much success in Bismarck's Germany. The mixing of private and government personnel, indicative of the federal government's reluctance to assume a dominant role in immigration, represented part of the problem. The good intentions of the policy makers were not enough to offset a lack of imagination and will. The trials and tribulations of Elise de Koerber illustrate this.

In September 1875, de Koerber, a German native, was appointed to act as "agent of the Department of Agriculture to Germany and Switzerland to facilitate female emigration to Canada."[34] Prior to this she had resided in Canada as the wife of a former Austrian army officer who had himself spent twenty years working for the Canadian government in the Crown Lands Department. An energetic, determined, exceedingly forceful personality, de Koerber committed herself religiously to winning converts for Canada. Establishing a base in Berne shortly after receiving her commission, she devoted her initial energies to soliciting Swiss emigrants but soon extended her efforts into Germany. Supremely self-assured and organized, she moved boldly into realms where angels might have feared to tread. In early 1877 in

Baden, a German state close to Switzerland, she encountered her first serious difficulties.

De Koerber's problems in the Grand Duchy of Baden centred on the Karlsruhe government's refusal to receive her mission. She tried three times to secure an audience with the duchy's minister of the interior, only to be rebuffed each time. Exactly why she was refused is not entirely clear but one may speculate: aside from her aggressive style, her views on migration were considerably more advanced and enlightened than usual. In brief, she believed that both the Canadian and German governments should be willing and active partners in supporting emigration not only for humanitarian reasons but also as "a rational means of remedying many of the social evils in Europe."[35] Hence, she advocated a "protected" migration, one that required more governmental commitment and support than most European and Atlantic states were willing to provide at that time. Despite the "rude and overbearing" behaviour of Baden's minister, the determined de Koerber appealed to the English ambassador in Berlin, Lord Odo Russell, for help in forcing her recognition in Karlsruhe.[36] He refused, claiming "he did not feel at liberty to intercede in her behalf with the German government without special instructions" from London.[37]

Frustrated by the lack of support in Europe, de Koerber returned to Ottawa and in early 1879 launched an effort to rally support at home that would enable her to conduct her immigration mission properly. First she appealed to the Canadian government to adopt her immigration program. In a series of letters addressed to the governor general, de Koerber pleaded for a more comprehensive and vigorous policy for soliciting immigrants in Germany. Each of her epistles emphasized the shortcomings of the dominion approach to immigration. Although she admitted that Ottawa had done some positive things, such as assisting "the agents of the Allan and Dominion Lines residing in Hamburg and Bremen ... and [giving] them the assistance of a resident government agent," this was clearly insufficient. "It is utterly impossible," she wrote, "to make German emigration to Canada a success under the existing circumstances." Unless the Canadian government intervened more explicitly in Berlin, "all the goodwill of the German Government towards Canada will be of no avail." She considered it highly "impolitic if the Canadian government does not do all in its power to meet it [the German government] halfway."[38] Since "an emigration [out of the Reich] already exists," all Ottawa had to do was intercede diplomatically to prevail upon the German government to promote that "emigration to Canada instead of going elsewhere." She remained convinced "that if politely asked by the Canadian government, it [Berlin] would give a polite reply."[39]

To convince Ottawa to allocate the necessary resources and make the requisite moves in Berlin, de Koerber described the attractive pool of available

German emigrants. For example, she reported that she had been approached on more than one occasion by the mothers of young officers "who were obliged to leave the army." Through no fault of their own but rather because of failing family fortunes, their futures had been jeopardized. These young worthies, she insisted, would make good farmers for Canada's North West, and only their lack of farming expertise prevented them from coming to Canada. To remedy this, Madame de Koerber suggested the following:

> Let a committee of [Canadian] gentlemen take this matter into consideration; they will then select good land in Canada for the establishment of a kind of agricultural school; they will get the means of putting up the necessary buildings and sending out a thoroughly trustworthy director, who will not only direct the work but will also exercise a good moral influence on the young men. When such sad cases occur as those mentioned, the committee sends them to that school where they will undergo a training of 1 to 2 years and with the assistance and advice of the director they will ultimately establish themselves on their own land.[40]

Not to neglect her own special sphere of interest, namely Germany's young women, de Koerber went on to point out the advantages Canada would receive from Germany's surplus females. "Honest working women," she preached, "would not only be a boon to [Canada's] households but the industrious and thrifty German women should also make capital wives for the settlers already in this country or coming to it."

In addition, the indefatigable de Koerber began to organize a grassroots movement among her fellow Canadians for support of her proposed immigration changes. Emphasizing her original role as solicitor of female immigrants, in April 1879 de Koerber set about establishing a central committee of respectable and influential citizens in Ottawa, the Committee for the Control and Protection of Female Immigration, to organize the migration of European women to Canada. Once established, the Ottawa organization set up branch committees in Halifax, St. John, Montreal, Toronto, and Winnipeg. These organizations were charged with "finding out in Canada by communication with the various parts of the country what may be from time to time the special wants of special localities in the way of governesses, nurses, skilled or ordinary servants and to take the necessary steps to supply such special wants and not to countenance ... further indiscriminate female immigration."[41] With its structure in place, de Koerber's committee proceeded to make even more specific proposals to Ottawa: that a permanent $5 bonus system for female immigrants be established, that bonus vouchers be placed in the hands of the central committee's European representatives for dispersal, that Ottawa provide free passage through the country to whomever the various committees might recommend as appropriate immigrants, that for the protection and well-being of young women immigrants the dominion government establish a halfway house in Ottawa for the newly arrived, and that this house be staffed with teachers to provide instruction in homemaking skills.

Unfortunately, de Koerber's efforts at organizing a more rational and humane immigration failed in Canada as they had in Europe. All her elaborate planning, petitioning, and pleading with government officials for federal support ultimately met with polite skepticism and inaction. For example, her proposal for an agricultural school to train young German officers in farming techniques was considered too much of a major "undertaking" for the dominion government to be realistic. By May 1879 she recognized that her efforts were "embarrassing" I.H. Pope, the secretary of agriculture. "Politics," she sadly admitted, "had become too much of a barrier."[42] Her assessment was accurate. Even in 1890, Canada's immigration policy had not yet developed to the stage where the kind of systematic, rational approach she promoted appeared either appropriate or acceptable. Ottawa was unprepared and unwilling to support the extensive federal role, with its necessarily augmented funding and staffing, that the precocious German woman demanded.

The Migrants

During the Macdonald era, with its tentative and often timid immigration policies, the pool of German emigrants potentially available to Canada increased by about a third over the earlier two decades. Between 1870 and 1890 nearly two million emigrants left Bismarck's Reich, an increase of nearly half a million over the period 1850-70, as insufficient labour opportunities drove people out of the country. The flow of emigrants out of Germany fluctuated, with the periods of most intense emigration being the first half of the 1870s and the 1880s. The years from 1885 to 1890 saw a tapering-off of movement, but nearly half a million more Germans nevertheless emigrated in this period as well. As earlier, the overwhelming majority leaving the Reich between 1870 and 1890 headed for the United States. Of the two million or so who left Germany, Canada received only about 20,000, or approximately 1 percent. In fact, German emigration to destinations other than the United States was likewise modest. Brazil, the second-most popular destination, welcomed only 50,000 new German immigrants, while Argentina received 10,000.[43] During this twenty-year period, Canada admitted just under 1.5 million immigrants of all nationalities and ethnic backgrounds. In this total, the component from Imperial Germany again represented a small minority of slightly more than 3 percent.

Contemporary witnesses noted how slight the trickle to Canada had become. For example, the *Deutsche Auswanderer-Zeitung* reported that between 1871 and 1873 Bremen sent to Quebec a total of four ships with only 1,001 passengers.⁴⁴ In 1885 the diplomat Carl Peterson informed Berlin that the numbers of Germans going to Canada were "not meaningful." He estimated that between 1871 and 1884 only 9,754 Germans migrated to Canada.⁴⁵ Finally, the German historian Monckmeier, writing in 1912, claimed that between 1871 and 1890 only 5,175 emigrants departed Bremerhaven and Hamburg for Canada. He asserted that in the heavy emigration years of the 1880s North Germany's ports sent a total of 3,874 German immigrants to Canada, compared with over 1.2 million to the United States.⁴⁶

Although the accuracy of the Canadian government's estimates on the numbers of Germans arriving via the St. Lawrence River and the numbers recorded by the German authorities of those bound for Canada are both suspect, they do concur that the totals were small. Duncan McDougall's more systematic and probably more accurate analysis also projects modest numbers: he estimates that between 1871 and 1890 only 10,000 emigrants from Germany and Poland arrived in Canada.⁴⁷ Furthermore, those who stayed on after landing in Canada represented a small minority of the immigrant total, because in the 1870s and 1880s most Germans disembarking in Canada travelled on to the United States. For example, in his year-end report for 1881, the Reich's consul in Montreal, Wilhelm C. Munderlow, claimed that of the 30,238 immigrants that year entering Canada via the St. Lawrence River only 530 were Reich Germans. His report included a summary of an article from the *Montreal Gazette* bemoaning the fact that according to Canadian census figures, between 1871 and 1881 the total of German residents in Canada who had been born in Germany "increased by a mere 588 souls." This small figure contrasted dramatically with the huge number of Germans immigrating during this decade to the United States. And what was worse, the article claimed, the number of Germans coming to Canada had recently decreased.⁴⁸

Most Germans emigrating between 1870 and 1890 reflected earlier patterns in terms of place of origin, occupation, age, and family status. Of those departing Germany, 60 to 65 percent hailed from northeast Germany and Prussia or from the southwestern states of Baden and Württemberg.⁴⁹ Likewise the occupational background of Germany's emigrants remained relatively constant for nearly three-quarters of the two decades considered here, with farmers, agricultural workers, and artisans making up between one-half and two-fifths of the total sample. After 1885, artisans and farmers among the emigrants declined to 30 percent, while industrial workers and those with no particular skills or training increased proportionately. By 1890 they represented 60 percent of the total leaving Germany. According to Marschalck, adverse social and economic conditions in the country's cities inspired increasing numbers of labourers to abandon Germany's industrial centres for new opportunities and a fresh start abroad.⁵⁰

The information available on sex, age, and marital or family status for the 1870-90 cohorts indicates migrants leaving not as individuals but as families. Males composed between 55 and 60 percent of the total, and so the number of females never dropped below 40 percent. High percentages of females among emigration samples normally equate with family migration. In terms of age, around 60 percent were between fifteen and forty years old, and children under the age of fifteen always made up about a quarter of those leaving. Like the number of women, such a high percentage of children indicates a majority of families in the emigrant group. The emigrant profile of families with children from the northeast or southwest who had previously been engaged in agriculture or skilled handicrafts remained typical until the end of the 1880s. Then the numbers of single males with industrial work backgrounds or no vocational skills increased dramatically and altered the emigrant patterns that had held true since the 1860s.[51]

In the period 1870-90 Germans from the Reich were not the only German speakers seeking admission as settlers into Canada. A significant number of ethnic Germans migrated to British North America from lands in Europe well beyond the borders of Imperial Germany, such as the Hapsburg Empire, Romania, and Russia. For example, in the mid-1870s about 7,000 German-speaking Mennonites made the journey from southeastern Russia to take up farming in Manitoba, setting a precedent later followed by thousands of eastern European Germans. A decade after the first Mennonites arrived, a group of German Catholics, also from the Black Sea in south Russia, settled in Saskatchewan. Three years later the first group of German Lutherans from Russia followed the Catholic example and settled in Saskatchewan as well. From Galicia in the Hapsburg Empire another group of German Lutherans migrated to Saskatchewan in 1889, and in 1890 German Baptists from the Romanian Dobruja followed.[52] The precise volume of this eastern European German migration into western Canada is impossible to know for certain, because German, Canadian, and American statistics all offer different figures. According to Heinz Lehmann, who researched this topic most thoroughly, about 4,000 non-Mennonite, eastern European Germans came to Canada's newly opened West between 1880 and 1889. During the six years 1884-90 in Saskatchewan alone, they established settlements in Strasbourg, Edenwold, Langenburg, Josephtal, Ebenezer, Landshut, and South Qu'Appelle.[53]

For the most part, these eastern European Germans came from farmer or peasant backgrounds; that is, they had either owned or aspired to farms in Europe before they emigrated. Therefore, the majority migrated to Canada intending to farm. The Mennonites represented this agrarian commitment, as did the other Germans who settled the towns in Saskatchewan described above. In this regard, they contrasted with the emigrants from the Reich, whose occupational profile included, besides farmers and agricultural workers, those from the skilled handicraft trades and even some industrial workers. The gender, age, and family profile of the eastern Germans followed closely that of the Germans from the Reich, for these ethnic Germans also migrated as families rather than single persons. In their ranks, females were only slightly outnumbered by males, the percentage of children was high, and the majority tended to be relatively young, that is, under forty-five.[54]

Although the eastern Germans resembled the emigrants from the Reich demographically, their motives for leaving differed. Social and economic influences were present, but many emigrants had strong religious and political reasons to abandon their homes in Russia or the Hapsburg Empire. The German-speaking Mennonites who left Russia for Canada in the mid-1870s illustrate how Russification policies induced out-migration. Their ancestors had left West Prussia at the end of the eighteenth century to settle in the newly conquered Crimea, at the behest of Tsarina Catherine II, and been followed by more Mennonites in the first quarter of the nineteenth century. To persuade these successful farmers to leave Germany and settle on the Russian frontier, Russian governments beginning with Catherine's offered several inducements besides cheap land: the Mennonites received guarantees that they would be able to administer their own affairs, practise their religion freely, and be excused from any military service. Because the group had been from its inception in the sixteenth century dedicated pacifists, the Mennonites considered this last privilege essential. Thus, the abrogation in 1871 of their historical right not to serve in the military and the imposition of mandatory military service in 1874 prompted 20,000 Mennonites to leave successful farms and homes in south Russia. The 7,000 immigrants who settled in southern Manitoba beginning in 1874 constituted part of this emigration. A few years later, more Mennonites as well as some Lutheran and Catholic Germans also abandoned Russia for western Canada in response to the Russian government's restrictions on landownership, German-language schools, and local political rights.[55]

According to Lehmann, the newly opened Canadian west attracted far fewer Germans from the Reich than from eastern Europe. He estimates that between 1875 and 1914 two-thirds of the Germans settling in western Canada had emigrated either from Russia or the Austro-Hungarian Empire, and only 12 percent from the Reich. Lehmann attributes the failure of the Canadian west to attract Germans from Germany proper to the nature of the western landscape and its undeveloped state: "The Canadian prairies appealed to Russian Germans who had become accustomed to the steppes, but not to Germans from the Reich. The latter preferred to settle in the forested American Middle West with its plentiful water because this was more like their homeland. They deliberately shied away from the treeless prairies." Lehmann also cites the harsh climate, the economic insecurity, and the cultural backwardness of the western frontier as additional reasons Reich Germans lacked enthusiasm for Canada's newest area of settlement.[56] He might have added that the push factors affecting the eastern European Germans differed substantially from those in the Reich. Neither the strong nationalist nor the religious pressures inducing emigration out of Russia and the Hapsburg Empire were apparent in Bismarck's Germany. Nevertheless, the majority of Reich Germans heading for the United States during Macdonald's era were also farmers who could have fit into the Canadian scheme of things. Those migrating clearly lacked the desire to emigrate to the dominion, and this related, as Lehmann recognizes, to Canada's image problems.

Remaking Canada's Image

Contemporaries such as Otto Hahn attributed German lack of interest in Canada less to aversion than to ignorance. According to him, Germans in the 1870s and '80s were largely unfamiliar with Canada, and particularly the recently opened West. Ignorance of the West was, he argued, in large measure due to the policies of the Hudson's Bay Company, which had controlled so much of the region before 1870. During its period of sovereignty, the Hudson's Bay Company had deliberately discouraged settlement because it would have interfered with business. In Hahn's words, the fur-trading company's directors believed that "the animals fled before the settler's axe and his dogs." This disturbance directly interfered with the hunting or trapping of furbearers and thus adversely affected the company's profits.[57] Hahn's analysis appears to have been largely accurate, for as Doug Owram has shown, the prevailing pre-Confederation image of the Hudson's Bay territories had not been positive for settlement. Rather, British North Americans for decades had perceived the North West as a distant, wild, inhospitable subarctic land in which only trappers, Native people, and the animals they hunted or trapped were at home.[58]

By the time of Confederation, the region's negative image had been altered by the scientific expeditions dispatched to the North West during 1857 and 1858. The first, under Henry Hind and sponsored by the Canadian government, and the second, led by John Palliser and commissioned by London, both returned with favourable reports, especially for those supporting Canada's annexation of these seemingly limitless western lands. The two explorations showed that the North-West Territories were much more than a barren, ice-locked wasteland. Concentrating their efforts on the southern portion of the Hudson's Bay lands, the explorers found a fertile belt that stretched from Lake of the Woods to the Rocky Mountains. Passing north of the Great American desert, these prairies possessed not only excellent soil but enough water to support large-scale agriculture. The Hind and Palliser reports also dispelled the traditional climatic prohibitions: the North West was temperate enough to support both agriculture and human settlement. As Owram puts it, "the image of the North West had changed from that of a howling wilderness to a fertile garden."[59] And it had become available for immediate colonization.

Once settlement appeared feasible, annexationists pushed hard for prompt incorporation of the Hudson's Bay holdings into Canada. By the late 1860s the West was being described as crucial for the country's future development, and expansionism had become inextricably intertwined with Canadian nationalism. The size and potential of this immense area fed the most exalted dreams of empire. The West, as Owram writes, "was no longer seen through the eyes of the fur trader or the missionary but through those of the potential farmer. The possibility of agriculture was not only no longer ignored as it had been in the past, but became the first priority to those who would make observations on the west."[60] Since successful agriculture needed farmers, immigration emerged almost immediately as the key to western development. Thus, the promotion of immigration became a central theme for annexationists on the eve of Confederation and remained so for their imperialist progeny long after the dominion had become a reality.

The image of Canada accompanying the propaganda employed in the 1870s and '80s in Germany to induce migration to Manitoba, Saskatchewan, or the North West again emphasized both the romantic and civilized images of Canada described in Chapter 1. Of the two versions, however, the romantic one appeared more prominently. Perhaps those who devised the propaganda believed that the romantic image of Canada would be more appropriate for German subjects. Also, in the Macdonald years the Canadian government directed its efforts at securing agricultural workers and peasants to settle and farm the virgin western prairie lands. Thus, the emphasis on the wild, unspoiled, free condition of Manitoba and the North-West Territories reflected real conditions: the physical accoutrements of civilization such as roads, schools, towns, or theatres were still undeveloped in the West. What there were of these, the railroad represented, and the railroad appeared in virtually every advertisement for Canada produced in this period. Nevertheless, just how heavily the official sources relied on the romantic image of Canada can be seen in the brochures that circulated in the German Empire in the age of Bismarck.

Like earlier romantic propaganda, the brochures of the period 1870-90 exaggerated the healthy climate and bracing weather, the unspoiled condition and natural richness of the countryside, and the personal freedom afforded by owning one's own land. A pamphlet from 1885 described the special benefits to be derived from Manitoba's climate: "For people who have weak lungs, there is no better climate than here. No one dies from respiratory diseases here. Whoever may have had lung problems before arriving is quickly cured. One often sees people who upon arrival look as if they were about to die yet only four weeks later appear as healthy as birds in the air!" Using the same freedom metaphor, the pamphlet went on to romanticize the Western farmer: "Who is the richest man on earth, not in Marks and Pfennigs but in all those things that make life pleasant?" The answer was the Manitoba farmer, for "he pays no rent; he knows no boss; he rises and retires when he alone chooses; he must watch no clock, nor heed any whistle. The best of everything is available to him: fresh vegetables, pure milk, rich cream, golden butter, freshly laid eggs, young chickens, fat geese, and well fed pigs. Moreover, his daily labour done near his home and in the fresh air renders his life exceedingly comfortable."[61]

In addition to dressing the old romantic images in new clothes – this time in terms of Manitoba and the West – the brochures of the 1880s also relied more heavily upon visual presentations. The cover page of a pamphlet from 1883, for example, contains six separate representations of Manitoba.[62] The top-left corner features a large, fat, satisfied-looking cow. Beneath this appear three smaller scenes depicting outdoor leisure activities: the first, entitled "Buffalo Hunting," shows a man on horseback firing a pistol into a herd of buffalo; the second, "Deer Shooting," portrays a man standing at the edge of a lake and shooting a rifle at a running deer; and the third, "Salmon Fishing," includes two men standing before their canoe, one holding a fishing rod, the other a gaff, and both displaying in their free hands two very large fish – presumably salmon. The cover's top-right corner pictures a farm scene including a sturdy two-storey wood frame house with a veranda, set in a neatly fenced-in yard. A recently harvested grain field complete with symmetrical rows of sheaves begins at the yard's edge and fills the scene's bottom half. Another field with carefully plowed furrows borders the grain field and extends into the picture's background, framed by a stretch of woods with a lake. On the cover page's bottom-left corner is a quarter-circle containing another water scene with flying ducks. On the shore in the foreground, standing amid tall grass, are stacked a rifle, a fishing rod, a canoe paddle, and a gaff's hook. The message conveyed by these images is unmistakable: come to Manitoba, where the farming is great and the fishing and hunting even better. Farmers in Manitoba could count on the land rewarding their labours handsomely. Wealth enough to ensure well-being and respectability would follow naturally from diligence and effort. Moreover, the wild rivers, forests, and plains afforded not only the chance to live in tune with nature but also the opportunity to enjoy its bountiful blessings. The successful farms in Manitoba would provide their owners with enough leisure time to hunt and fish.

In their proselytizing efforts, the agents in the service of Canada relied on such printed materials. Besides evoking the romantic image discussed above, the publications from the 1870-90 period also described specific material advantages to be gained by moving to Canada, many of which echoed earlier propaganda claims. The main emphasis continued to be on the free land or readily available farm property in Canada. The land offered to potential settlers was no longer in Waterloo County or the Ottawa Valley but in the new province of Manitoba and the prairie land to the west. The brochures employed superlatives to describe this prairie land, with its "deep black soil of unsurpassed richness."[63] Not surprisingly, such fertile land was claimed to produce the world's finest crops, and particularly the best wheat: "king wheat" reigned. The Canadian prairies west of Winnipeg, one pamphlet insisted, yielded "the highest average production of the American Continent and quite possibly of the entire world."[64] It was pointed out that Manitoba lay on the northernmost edge of the great North American wheat belt. Since in wheat growing, northern was better than southern, Manitoba wheat farmers were "in the position to bring the best quality number one hard wheat to market."[65]

According to Doug Owram, the enthusiasm for the North West that generated such hyperbole developed only after 1879, when a new interpretation of its agricultural potential surfaced. This was the result of renewed government surveys of the region conducted in the late 1870s, particularly the work and words of John Macoun. Macoun, a prominent eastern botanist, provided an updated and politically correct interpretation of the area of southwest Saskatchewan and eastern Alberta known as the Palliser Triangle. While the earlier accounts of Hind and Palliser had described this area as too arid to be of much value as agricultural land, Macoun and other revisionists argued the opposite in their reappraisals, claiming that even this portion of the North West offered great potential for successful farming. Supporters of western development immediately latched onto Macoun's analysis and incorporated it into immigration propaganda touting the North West as a settlement area. Hence, in Owram's words, "the final qualifications in the myth of the garden [were removed and] all restraints on the descriptions of the North West collapsed." Increasingly in the early 1880s writers began to view the region as something approximating a utopia. Like most utopias, the one imagined in the Canadian North West lacked certain elements of reality. The landscape became "the largest flower garden on the continent" and the climate so tame that it was "very much the same as it was in England 30 years ago."[66]

In addition to providing these wondrous agricultural opportunities, Canada's North West in 1880 also offered the same fringe benefits that had been attributed to British North America in the 1850s and 1860s, namely, low taxes, political freedom, and religious liberty. In response to the increasing xenophobia of Europe's national states on the one hand and the spread of American nationalism on the other, the brochures emphasized the cultural rights enjoyed by German settlers in Canada. The German Mennonites from Russia who had settled in Manitoba in the late 1870s allegedly afforded the best example, for they proved convincingly that Canada not only willingly received religious refugees but also welcomed those who desired to maintain their German ethnicity in Canada. Therefore the propaganda brochures argued that Germans coming to Canada might, if they so desired, remain German: "For the German, immigrant settlement in Manitoba has the great advantage that he enters as a German and can remain one without suffering the slightest diminution of his civil or political rights."[67] This beneficial condition contrasted with the plight of German immigrants in the United States: "If the German settler is annexed, classified, and incorporated body and soul into the United States, he must swear an oath to give up all his obligations to his fatherland. In Manitoba, on the contrary, he retains the unconditional freedom to enjoy all the advantages of a settler without having to deny his German origins, without having to alienate himself from the social as well as political traditions of his former homeland."[68]

The reference to English laws and government in Canadian immigration propaganda represents a muted expression of the traditional Canadian expansionist rhetoric that insisted the North West should remain British in institutions and culture. This assurance appeared in all of Canada's efforts to solicit immigrants from the British Isles. Expansionists and western annexationists had always been outspoken advocates of spreading British institutions and traditions into the North West. These new lands would receive British models for law, government, and social theory, so that Canada's west and the dominion itself would represent a valid extension of Britain. The British people (English, Scottish, and Irish), it was argued, were the most appropriate vehicles for advancing the desired British traditions into Canada's western empire. In a sense, they were not really immigrants at all but merely British subjects who had changed their residences within the empire. Obviously, to this way of thinking, German immigrants constituted a problem, since they could hardly function as ideal carriers of British traditions or culture. Nevertheless, they might be able to respect and indeed benefit from British institutions and the tradition of individual freedom. Canadian solicitation propaganda for Germans nearly always made this point.

As earlier Canadian immigrant recruitment propaganda had done, that of the Macdonald period emphasized the absence in Canada of disadvantageous conditions. Earlier publications had described Canada as a land without health problems, but later claims in this regard grew even more elaborate. Not only did Manitoba and the West have no problems with malaria and the other diseases that afflicted frontier America but the traditional causes or promoters of disease were absent as well. "In Europe," one brochure asserted, "the air oppresses the earth but here [in Manitoba] it sucks all the bad humours *(Dunste)* which men bring with them from other lands out of their bodies. Moreover, there are neither bogs nor swamps here, also no rats and fleas."[69] Nor did human misdeeds endanger the health and well-being of Canada's residents. As noted in Chapter 1, Canada's apologists during the 1860s had taken great pains to point out how life in Canada had not been poisoned by war, and how Canada had avoided the effects of the murderous US conflict between the North and the South. Now, the brochures emphasized how the peaceful Canadian frontier, free from Indian trouble, contrasted dramatically with the border wars being fought between the United States Army and the several Plains Indian tribes. Any effort to describe Riel's rebellion in Saskatchewan as comparable to America's upheavals, the apologists insisted, represented an egregious exaggeration and distortion of reality. Like the rest of the country, Canada's west remained secure and at peace under British law and good government.[70]

In the promotional pamphlets and brochures, testimonials frequently alleged German immigrant satisfaction with peaceful Canada, its land, its government, and its way of life. Although testimonials had been employed earlier, the period 1870-90 saw increased reliance on this propagandizing device. Logically enough, the recent Mennonite settlers were frequently called upon to bear witness to the blessings of life on Canada's western prairie. These sober, sincere, simple folk were believed to be especially credible. For example, a brochure from 1884 quoted several satisfied Manitoba Mennonite farmers. Kornelius Kornelson of Morris wrote, "I am a Mennonite from south Russia. In my opinion the healthy, hard-working, and thrifty person with God's help can make his future here." Cornelius Toews of Bergfeld asserted, "I consider this land very well suited for agriculture. Whoever wants to work will succeed here. But one must be hard-working." And Jacob Friesen from West Lyne testified that "taxes on land and property here are very low. There is no head tax. The schools are government supported. Agricultural tools and machines are available at reasonable prices. The hard-working farmer receives the most respect here."[71]

The picture presented in Canadian government-sponsored publications appeared in private German ones as well. For example, in 1887 Heinrich Lemcke, the editor and publisher of the *Deutsch-Amerikanische Correspondence* (German-American Correspondence) in New York, published in Leipzig a 200-page compendium on Canada and things Canadian entitled *Canada, das Land und seine Leute* (Canada, the Land and Its People). An experienced propagandist employed previously by the Department of Agriculture to write appropriate letters "in relation to Canada and particularly the North West" for publication in German-language newspapers, Lemcke intended his work to be definitive.[72] Thus, his narrative ranged over broad areas of Canadian life and the physical makeup of the country. Commencing with a historical sketch of Canada from its "discovery" by Europeans to the present, he moved on to portray Canada's climate, physical geography, institutions, and culture. The minutiae recounted are nearly overwhelming: the seven kinds of salmon in British Columbia, the German-language newspapers published in Canada, the fruits grown in Ontario, the country's weights and measures, the full names of all the government immigration officers and their postings. Lemcke described Canada's economy, including its industry, commerce, banking, and monetary system; he extolled the country's educational institutions and cultural activities; he noted Canada's German colonies and Native peoples; he enumerated the leading cities; he celebrated Montreal's Winter Festival. Canadian agriculture from animal husbandry to wheat growing to fruit cultivation was portrayed in lengthy, superlative passages. Fishing, hunting, trapping, mining, and lumbering received appropriate attention. At the end, Lemcke pointed out the areas of Canada still open for settlement, detailed the steps to be taken to secure free Canadian land, described how to leave Germany, painted a blissful picture of the voyage from Europe to North America, and instructed potential immigrants on what to do upon their arrival in Canada. He summed up his admonitions in what he called "The Golden Rules for Immigrants." These included such pithy advice as "Trust the word of no man," "Never buy land you have not seen in person," and "Never sign anything in a foreign language without consulting some reliable, knowledgeable person as to the exact contents of the document."[73]

In nearly all of this elaboration and detailing, Lemcke's encyclopedic account remains rather unremarkable. Puffing and boasting had become standard fare in such works, and his celebration of Canada and Canadians as being superior to the United States and Yankees was therefore not extraordinary. At times, Lemcke seemed to be carried away, as when describing the wonderful hunting opportunities in British Columbia: "Many Americans possess a special preference for killing and everything that crawls or flies they pitilessly shoot simply out of a sheer lust for blood *(Mordlust).*"[74] Nevertheless, Lemcke's imaginative efforts to silence the critics of Canada's climate set his work apart from most propaganda pieces.

In refuting the negative opinions about Canada's weather, *Canada, das Land und seine Leute* repeated earlier disclaimers about Canada's winters. For example, Lemcke asserted that Ontario had the same climate as New York, and that winters in Manitoba were no different from those in northeast Germany. But he went much further than these blandly false statements to describe how Canadians flourished amid their winters. He depicted, for instance, the life of a typical lumberjack, for "winter is the season for cutting wood." Ignoring the harsh realities of the lumber camp, the author painted a roseate picture of life in the Canadian north woods harvesting timber. It was "a beautiful sight," he informed his readers, to see a lumberjack at work: "With what ease the lumberjack swings the heavy axe over his head ... No blow falls in vain. At each blow the chips fly in all directions. Then the tree trembles, sways, and finally falls to earth with a mighty crash, which echoes through the primeval forest." Such work made lumberjacks supermen because "lumberjacking uses all the body's muscles" and as a consequence does "wonders for the health." Indeed, Lemcke pointed out that lumberjacks were distinguishable by "their healthy faces and Herculean bodies" upon which "there was not an ounce of fat, with every muscle being larger than normal size." Despite this imposing physique, the winter lumberjack possessed "a true, soft-hearted spirit." In romantic fashion, Lemcke insisted that this derived from the lumberjack's close contact with nature: "Nature is the guide for [the lumberjack's] life. It is the intermediary conveying to him awareness of a higher essence which in turn ennobles his spirit." These fortunate, happy, healthy men "led a merry and joyful life free from worries."[75] Real lumberjacks would not have recognized Lemcke's portrait of their backbreaking and extremely dangerous work in isolated lumber camps, with cramped living quarters and the most primitive sanitary conditions, sharing with their companions not only the fleas and lice but also the unforgettable smell of body odour, cigarette smoke, and bad camp food mixed together.

Lemcke's enthusiasm for his happy lumberjacks was bettered by his vision of Montreal in winter, detailed in a separate section of the work entitled "A Winter Visit in Canada." Lemcke began his encomium by describing his first impressions of Montreal after coming from New York. The latter, a dreary, dirty, and foggy city, could not possibly compare to Montreal, "a marzipan-like white city ... dressed in an ermine robe."[76] Canada's largest city was vibrating "with life and movement." Residents revelled in the snow blanketing the city, which in Lemcke's description assumed a unique, romantic guise: "If Canada is a land of wild animals ... so the people of Montreal in their furs look like animals ... One sees only bears, wolves, and seals moving about the city's streets. Everyone pulls his fur hat down as far as his eyebrows, turns up the collar of his fur coat to cover his ears or wraps a shawl about his face covering nose and mouth. Thus, what one normally sees are two eyes peering out." Exceptions to this rule did exist: for the benefit of each other, "coquettish girls and elegant men exposed their faces to the cold." From this practice, Lemcke argued, "Canadian ladies acquire their rosy cheeks, which make them readily distinguishable from their pale-faced American sisters."[77]

Canadians in general and Montrealers specifically turned the Canadian winter into a grand time of play. One became immediately aware of this in Montreal, Lemcke wrote, for despite the cold "splendid sleighs fly swiftly here and there about the city, their bells ringing continuously." Warmly dressed for the cold, Canadians found much pleasure, Lemcke observed, "in travelling through the snow ... The sleigh drivers are all dressed in furs ... their fur hats covering their ears, their hands buried in huge gloves, which could almost fit an elephant's foot." In Canada, sleigh rides could even be titillating for, as Lemcke pointed out, "many a young gallant when he takes his chosen young lady for a sleigh ride may invoke a long-standing sleigh tradition and kiss his girl at the ride's end."[78] Ice boating, tobogganing, and snowshoeing offered additional winter fun, but most of all, Canadians loved to skate: "Not only the men but also the women skate, and even small children have mastered the skating art ... One might even say that the entire Canadian people sail through life on ice skates."[79] Thus, the Canadian winters were not unbearably cold and boring, as so often alleged. Far from being a danger to health, Canada's cold winter was actually refreshing and stimulating, and made it possible for Canadians "to retain their youthful freshness right into old age." In brief, the Canadian loved the winter, which defined him. He considered the winter "the greatest of natural blessings"; to it he owed "the spiritual strength and creativity of his character."[80]

Besides the encyclopedic, semi-factual recapitulations in the style of Lemcke, other forms of pro-Canada materials written by Germans for Germans appeared in the period 1870-90. For example, *Canada: The Reports of Four German Delegates on Their Journey to Canada in the Fall of 1881,* edited by Dr. Otto Hahn of Reutlingen, appeared in that city in 1883. Like Lemcke, Hahn had served as an Agricultural Department agent for several years.[81] Thus, not surprisingly, the department paid for these reports, including the printing costs and the delegates' travel expenses.[82] Hahn's collection provided much the same kind of information as Lemcke's book, describing the land and its products, the Canadian people, including the country's German immigrants, prices and wages, the railroads and their future significance, the land still available for settlement, hunting and fishing opportunities, and the like. Again, Canada's climate was found to be milder than popularly believed, and again the United States fell far short of her northern neighbour – for example, Canada's women were better looking, her Indians more peaceful, her citizens more attached to the "good old morality."[83] But the four reports deviated from Lemcke's broader rendition by concentrating on Canada's west, and particularly Manitoba, which Hahn labelled "the farmer's El Dorado." Since Hahn had arranged the "experts" tour at the behest of the Canadian government to publicize settlement opportunities in Manitoba, this emphasis is understandable. More important, Hahn's collection included a discussion of the status of German agriculture and the contemporary German debate on emigration policy. Because, atypically, both discussions centred on Canada rather than the United States, Hahn's document is special.

Two of the four delegates, namely Hahn and Ludwig Glock, addressed German and Canadian agriculture and migrations in detail. Glock began his report by announcing, "In south Germany and also in a large part of the country's north, a reduction in the number of those engaged in agriculture is necessary in order for Germany to compete with North American agriculture." These labour surpluses created "excessively high labour costs" in relation to other lands.[84] Furthermore, the "inefficient and irrational" system of small holdings rendered the efforts of Germany's farmers unproductive and bound to fail: "No matter how hard he works, he [the German farmer] cannot stay afloat. The debts he contracts in bad times cannot be paid off even in the good years ... His fate is no longer in his own hands; the harvests of others in distant lands rather than his customers at home determine the price of his wheat." Because these ruined farmers would find no safety net in industry, which the author described as overburdened by overproduction, "they were destined to remain underemployed and in the end become a burden to the state."[85] According to Glock, the solution lay in finding new agricultural opportunities elsewhere, and only emigration could provide this. To try to prevent Germany's surplus agricultural population from leaving the country would be, in Glock's words, like "damming the Rhine." Or, using another popular metaphor, Glock insisted that preventing emigration would "create a volcano which would eventually erupt damaging all of society." Emigration would remove the unproductive forces from the German landscape, make German agriculture more competitive, and relieve social pressure.[86]

Glock answered the question of where to send Germany's superfluous agrarians unequivocally: they must go to Canada, where free government land was still available in both the east and west, especially in Manitoba. Glock's panegyric grew extreme: "Only Canada possessed in Ontario and the Northwest land enough to encompass half of Europe; only Canada permitted Germans to settle in closed colonies; only Canada has the same climate that Germans prefer; only Canada enjoys a system of morals and customs that correspond closely to those supported by respectable Germans." This final advantage was clearly absent in the United States where, Glock pointed out, "a mishmash of peoples has caused the loss of those [moral] sensitivities without which the German cannot live." Continuing this racial and cultural argument, Glock insisted that "no national group on earth stands so near to us as the English; none is more inclined to recognize [and value] the German essence; no national groups are so little separated from one another in morals and customs, in practical and religious attitudes than the English and the Germans."[87]

To these socioeconomic and cultural arguments, Glock added the German nationalist rationale. Since Germany lacked colonies, Canada offered the fatherland the opportunity to create proto-colonies in North America. Because Germans were permitted to settle in Canada in contiguous, homogeneous groups, emigrants would not be lost to the fatherland. In fact, "The new status of the German Reich will bind the Germans in Canada more closely than ever to the Fatherland." This binding would happen, however, only "if Germans were allowed to emigrate freely." Glock concluded his brief with this warning: "It is not the pressure to assimilate exerted on the German immigrant in his adopted foreign home that destroys the expatriate's attachment to his fatherland but much more the memory of a bad departure."[88] Although Glock used the same rationalizations as Friedrich Fabri and other pro-imperialists to justify emigration (i.e., relieving social tension while creating colonial possibilities abroad, as seen below), Glock's recognition of Canada as an appropriate place for Germans to settle differs from their anglophobic preference for South America.

Hahn's elaboration on the emigration theme appeared after Glock's report at the publication's end in a section labelled "the necessity for emigration." According to Hahn, emigration had become a burning issue in Germany. Everyone seemed to have a point of view and the opinions expressed ranged broadly. Some strongly advocated out-migration to avoid social chaos; others argued that German farming did not need to export its labour force but merely to change the crops being grown, that is, to switch from grain to other vegetables; still others sought to prohibit emigration entirely by using the police to prevent citizens from leaving. For Hahn, emigration appeared problematic because it involved two separate but interrelated difficulties: first, the problem of Germany's agriculture products being uncompetitive on the world market, and second, the social difficulties caused by surplus agricultural labour and low wages.

Hahn began discussing possible solutions to these dilemmas by insisting that Germany's agriculture could never be healthy until the labour supply and demand for it were roughly equal, for only then could a truly "free labour contract arise." If labour supply and demand coincided, then production costs would fall, ensuring adequate profits for landowners, and wages would rise, providing workers enough to live on properly. Hahn rejected as unrealistic other contemporary solutions to Germany's agricultural labour problems. He dismissed the traditional Christian argument that misery and the poor had always been and would always be present and thus Germany should accept poverty as part of God's plan. Likewise, he dismissed Germany's so-called cathedral socialists as misguided and too cautious to address the root causes of serious agrarian poverty. Hahn also scorned the classic liberal plans for self-help: "The poor possess the right [to act to improve themselves] but not the power [money or means to act] and thus this help is more a mockery of freedom than a real free choice." That the financial woes of German agriculture could be eliminated by following a "laissez-faire laissez-aller policy," he declared, "not even the stupidest politician believes any more." Finally, Hahn condemned the social democratic call for state intervention and property confiscation to alleviate the plight of Germany's agriculture workers.[89]

Hahn favoured some state intervention, but neither the massive private property reductions envisioned by the socialists nor the tinkering advocated by the cathedral socialists. Rather, he proposed modest state encouragement for emigration: "Emigration is necessary not only to increase the income generated by agriculture, to reduce the number of mouths to feed, and to raise production and rationalize the agricultural sector, but it is absolutely essential to reduce the number of agricultural workers and thus to bring down production costs and finally to lessen the number of those seeking to own and to live off the profits of agriculture."[90] Only by reducing the population through emigration, Hahn believed, could the natural laws governing the economy function properly again and equilibrium be restored. Germany, he repeatedly pointed out, had too great a population surplus in general and too many engaged in agriculture specifically. These surpluses, he argued, could not be absorbed by Germany's industrial sector because her industry had not advanced far enough for that to be possible.[91] Hence, the only viable alternative was increased emigration.

After concluding his justification for emigration, Hahn shifted his focus to consider the best land for Germans to seek out. Again Canada was ranked first. Emigrants, so crucial for Germany's future, Hahn emphasized, should avoid the United States. He essentially repeated most of the arguments employed by Glock: Canada had more abundant free land for settlers than did the United States; Canada's government was more sympathetic to Germans, allowing them to preserve their German customs and language; and Canadian morals and customs were more appropriate for Germans. Hahn even added a new twist to the hackneyed climate theme by claiming that the climate in much of the United States was too warm and thus unsuitable for Germans! Finally, Hahn repeated the racial claims that Canada offered more to German immigrants because in "the United States the mishmash of peoples there had accepted the customs of the Indians and Mormons, while in Canada these are completely separated from the rest of society."[92] Hahn failed to specify just exactly what Indian and Mormon customs the Americans had adopted.

These negative references to America's assimilating frontier customs are interesting. Both Hahn and Glock referred several times to Canada's frontier as peaceful and orderly, distinctly unlike its American counterpart. That this sober, orderly presentation was as attractive to Germans as its promoters believed remains doubtful. As noted in Chapter 1, Germans for several generations had been reading with relish about America's adventure-filled Wild West. Moreover, by the time Hahn published these reports, the most successful and famous of Germany's American frontier fiction authors had burst upon the scene. Born in Saxony in 1842, Karl May began his novel-writing career in 1875. Before he died in 1912, he produced some seventy books, forty of which dealt with America's Wild West. The millions of copies of his works circulating in Germany made him a household word well before the Great War. May's most famous and popular character, Old Shatterhand, the German equivalent of Cooper's Hawkeye, appeared at the very beginning of May's literary career. Tall, blond, muscular, catlike in his reflexes, common-sense smart, wise beyond his age, endowed with an acute moral sensitivity, this supposedly quintessential German was a marvel to all. Ernst Stadler describes May's hero as the paragon frontier man *(Westmann)*: "The greatest and best and bravest of all the white men is Old Shatterhand [who] runs like a storm, throws a tomahawk like the best of the Indians ... fights the grizzly bear with only a knife in his hand ... fires a second shot so quickly that it sounds like a single shot ... [yet] never strays from the paths of Christian charity."[93] In his seemingly endless battles with perverse Indians and bad white men, Old Shatterhand provided not only vicarious freedom, intense excitement, physical prowess, and cathartic violence but also an example of fantasized Germanic success in the Wild West. The apologists for sober, peaceful Canada faced a monumental task to substitute their own version of an ideal West for that of May and the other Cooper imitators so popular in Germany in the late nineteenth century.[94] That Hahn's version of Canada remained less than successful at winning converts for the dominion seems borne out by his ultimate fate: Secretary Lowe fired him in July 1888 because Hahn's agency "had failed in practical beneficial effect."[95]

Propaganda, Agents, and Agencies for Migration

The propaganda produced by German nationals like Hahn and Glock, as well as the Canadian government's own efforts, required distribution. The basic tool for this remained the individual agent. During the two decades after the Franco-Prussian War, the number of agents who distributed Canadian propaganda in Germany increased. The professionalization of agents, their closer ties with shipping firms, and the use of subagents to assist the agents in their work, all trends that had begun in the 1860s, expanded in the next two decades. Recruitment work for Canada in the Reich was carried on by agents working for the Canadian Pacific Railway and freelancing individuals, employees of other shipping firms, and agents working for the Canadian government. The CPR agents, however, were the best organized, best connected, and most pervasive Canadian promoters in Germany. They attempted to solicit their clients by direct contact in an extensive effort.

The work of the Dutchman R.R. Toe Laer, who ran the CPR's recruitment campaign from Amsterdam in the late 1880s, typifies its campaign to win immigrants for Canada. From his "tastefully decorated and comfortable office" in Amsterdam, which contained "representative products from Manitoba as well as its most recent newspapers," Toe Laer not only directed the flow of propaganda to Germany but also developed an elaborate network of agents and subagents to proselytize for Manitoba and Canada's west.[96] For example, in October 1887, Reichardt, the Reich's foreign minister, reported to Bismarck and Robert von Puttkamer, the minister of the interior, that the CPR had fifty-six agents at work in Germany. The list that Reichardt supplied, complete with names, addresses, and assigned areas for recruitment, reveals that the CPR had representatives in many German towns and cities, particularly in the north and east. Cities such as Hanover, Berlin, Frankfurt am Main and Frankfurt an der Oder, Düsseldorf, Breslau, Erfurt, Kiel, Cologne, and Königsberg were represented, as were many smaller centres.[97] The kinds of persons who functioned as agents, subagents, or unofficial distributors varied. Bismarck received information in July 1886, for example, that Toe Laer had been distributing propaganda on Manitoba and the Canadian west to innkeepers, agricultural society officers, master craftsmen, and threshing machine operators, in short, people who might know likely candidates for emigration among the working population.[98] These agents were not professionals engaged full-time in soliciting would-be emigrants, but recruited on the side. Toe Laer's subagents thus duplicated a pattern that Agnes Bretting and Hartmut Bickelmann found common among agents working in Germany, whether recruiting for the United States, Brazil, or elsewhere.[99]

The CPR provided its agents and spokesmen in Germany with pamphlets, folders, circulars, maps, and testimonials in German. According to the Reichardt document cited above, these agents normally had propaganda materials delivered to them in batches of several hundred copies. Typical examples include the CPR agent in Minden, Carl Heppe, who received in his 22 April 1887 delivery 600 pamphlets in German and another 600 folders; on 15 May 1887 Wilhelm Krausen in Düsseldorf obtained 850 German pamphlets, 100 maps, and 100 circulars; C.J. Bahr had delivered to him in the Heidenheim (Silesia) railway station 500 German pamphlets, 200 maps, and 200 testimonials. The agents were to distribute single copies to any individuals considering emigrating and to provide small numbers of copies, six or eight normally, to persons in positions likely to find other candidates. The *Gastwirt*, or innkeeper, was frequently called upon to fill this role.[100]

Although the CPR led Canadian railways in emigrant solicitation, others also actively recruited in Germany. The US railroads had developed effective recruitment tactics in Europe well before the Civil War and provided stiff competition for the CPR.[101] The Northern Pacific Railroad, which ran a line from Lake Superior to Puget Sound, was representative of these challengers. Like the CPR in western Canada, the Northern Pacific played a vital role in settling America's northern plains. By establishing towns and communities of small farmers along its line, it not only helped to make the land productive but also promoted its own carrying trade and real estate business. Working on its own and in conjunction with the northern plains states, Northern Pacific's recruitment in Europe and Germany included its own agents and pro-American propaganda every bit as extreme in its claims as the CPR's. One of its brochures claimed that "the only illness which even remotely touched the residents of Montana was the pangs of overeating, resulting from the excessive indulgence of the hearty appetite attendant upon the invigorating atmosphere."[102] The Northern Pacific supplied recruitment literature in large amounts to its European distributors. One historian claims that during 1882 in western Europe alone, 632,590 copies of Northern Pacific publications were distributed, including "pamphlets, circulars, folders, and letters ... printed in the principal Northern European languages."[103] To hand out these materials, in 1883 there were 124 Northern Pacific agents at work in western Europe and Germany. Furthermore, in 1884 the Northern Pacific advertised land and rail fares in sixty-eight German newspapers.

Although the Canadian Pacific enjoyed an immense advantage among Canadian recruiters from the scope of its operations and the support of the Canadian government, other transportation companies continued their efforts to recruit Germany's emigrants. Private, non-German steamship companies such as the Red Line and the Allan Line also solicited potential emigrants. The Allan Line's chief representative, Richard Berns, a former merchant from Linnich, embodied the promotional spirit favoured in the period of national expansion under Macdonald. In the early 1880s, he directed a stream of propaganda into Germany from his Antwerp office and ran subagents as well. Berns's inclination to proceed at his own pace regardless of precedent or official approval brought him into conflict with Richard Kind, the Reich's consul in Antwerp. As a result, Berns had his licence to solicit in Alsace-Lorraine, Germany's newest territorial addition, revoked in 1873.[104]

Although the Canadian government delegated a disproportionate amount of its immigration solicitation work to the CPR and other elements of the private sector throughout the Macdonald era, it did on occasion send its own representatives to Germany to act as recruiters. In 1872, for instance, Ottawa dispatched Wilhelm Hespeler from Waterloo, Ontario, to Berlin as its official agent. He was accompanied by Jacob Klatz, a native of Preston, Ontario, to work as his assistant and subagent out of their Berlin office.[105] Hespeler canvassed for immigrants not only in Germany but also in the Crimea and Bessarabia, where he played a major role in launching the emigration of the Mennonites who settled in Manitoba between 1874 and 1883.[106] After 1873, however, problems arose for Canada's resident agents. In February of that year John Dyke, a Canadian government agent stationed in Germany, was arrested and jailed for illegal solicitation.

John Dyke's story is a microcosm of the problems and inadequacies of Canada's German immigration policy in the early years of Confederation. Dyke, an energetic, sincere, and devoted servant of Canada, readily embraced his commission to recruit Germans for the province of Ontario when appointed to that task in December 1872. Stopping in London for instructions, the Ottawa native proceeded to Germany in late January 1873. After visiting Berlin, where he picked up a German assistant, Dyke moved out into the countryside to begin recruiting. Although his German assistant informed him that soliciting emigrants was illegal in Prussia, Dyke was assured that advertising in local newspapers as the US railroads had been doing was not forbidden. And so Dyke began contacting local newspapers to arrange for publishing propaganda on behalf of immigration to Canada. When his efforts became known to the authorities, he was summarily arrested on February 17 in the village of Stolp, in the Prussian province Posen. Hauled before the town's mayor, Dyke was first insulted. As he recounted later, the irate mayor called him a swindler *(Bauernanfänger)* and pig-dog *(Schweinhund)*. Then Stolp's Burgermeister charged him with having violated the state's antisolicitation law of 1853 and the statute against inducing emigration under false pretences. Thus indicted, Dyke was taken off to jail where, in his words, "as a common felon" he was "consigned to my cell 8 days, my bed being straw and a wooden pillow; my food ... being rye bread and water."[107] Vociferously asserting his innocence, Dyke immediately appealed for relief to Lord Russell, the British ambassador in Berlin. After several days, Dyke's 500 thaler bail was provided and the disgruntled young Canadian released on condition that he remain in Stolp until Prussia's Royal Court had heard and ruled on his case, which did not occur until June. Unable to prove Dyke's claims for Canada patently false, the Prussian court finally dismissed the charges, returned Dyke's bail money, and permitted him to leave Germany.[108]

Although sensational, Dyke's arrest and detention did not completely shut down Canadian efforts to solicit German immigrants. Ottawa shifted its recruiters working in Germany to residences beyond the Reich, normally in the United Kingdom and Belgium. Dyke was transferred to Liverpool, from where he continued recruiting in Germany. An October 1882 Agriculture Department memo to Dyke from John Lowe outlined the new, stricter procedures adopted by Canada's government for emigrant solicitation in Germany. To begin with, Lowe admonished Dyke to remain in close touch with the department's representative in London and to follow his instructions to the letter. At the same time, Dyke was urged to use his best judgment regarding immigration matters and "to make any suggestions which may occur to you and which may be suggested by your experiences in Europe." The note continued, "In order to take the most effective action ... to secure a German immigration to Manitoba or other parts of the North West during the approaching immigration season," Dyke should take all requisite steps to guarantee that "the necessary advertising [was] undertaken and expenses incurred for the circulation of publications, in such a way as is practicable or legal in Germany." Finally, Dyke was to pay special attention to uphold the arrangement that Ottawa had worked out with the Erie Railroad in New York for transporting German immigrants to Canada.[109]

This deal cogently illustrates the undeveloped and uncertain condition of Canada's German immigration policy during the Macdonald era. Its details are described in a letter Agriculture Secretary I.H. Pope sent to A.T. Galt, Canadian high commissioner in London, in March 1882. Because the Erie Railroad possessed well-developed contacts in the Reich, Pope believed it made more sense to have the Erie Railroad's general immigration agent in Europe "make the arrangements in detail with the Steamship agents in Germany" for securing the dominion's German immigrants. According to Pope, his department was obliged to turn to the US railroad for two reasons: first, "because of its very extensive connections and ramifications with Emigration Agencies in the German Empire," and second, because Canada had "no agency, nor was it possible for it to establish any, at least for the coming season [1882] in Germany." Ottawa agreed to pay the Erie Railroad a percentage of the immigrant's ticket price from Europe to Canada and to provide a five-dollar bonus to the railroad agents in Germany employed in soliciting successfully for Canada. A bonus had to be paid, Pope argued, because it was the best way to inspire appropriate agent effort on Canada's behalf.[110]

At the same time, in an effort to complement this indirect system, Ottawa continued to send ad hoc representatives to Germany on temporary immigrant solicitation tours. Thus, in March 1885 the Department of Agriculture dispatched Henry Eilber, an Ontario German, to act as agent "for diffusing information in Germany respecting the Dominion of Canada as a suitable field for German settlement." Employed for three months at a salary of $300, Eilber was specifically instructed to "offer a bonus of five dollars per adult ... to booking agents for all immigrants of suitable class from Germany upon their arrival in Manitoba."[111] A year later, the Canadian government sent two Winnipeg residents, D.W. Riedle and Adolf Christoph, to Germany on recruitment assignment. Naturalized Canadians, they were assigned to recruit in the areas of Germany where they had formerly resided. Riedle, a former resident of southwest Germany, was charged to work in "Alsace and the southern part of Baden," while Christoph, who had lived in Eschborn near Frankfurt, "was given as his field of activity the area around Frankfurt."[112] Copied from the practice of the American states, which had used it often and successfully, "the Yankee system" of sending German natives who had become naturalized Canadians on short-term recruiting trips became more common as the task of winning emigrants became more serious. Known as "return men," they were instructed to spread the good word about Canada among their former friends, relations, acquaintances, and village associates. As one historian put it, they were meant to function "as living promotional brochures."[113]

Besides such North American agents, various agencies existed within the German Empire to facilitate emigration. Both the Roman Catholic and

Lutheran Churches established a lasting commitment to helping Germany's emigrants. Inspired by Pastor Johann Heinrich Wichern, the Lutheran Church began ministering to emigrants in Hamburg in the early 1850s. From 1867 Hamburg's inner mission, established originally to assist paupers and other disadvantaged city residents, provided special religious services for departing emigrants. A year later Hamburg's Lutheran pastors started accompanying emigrants on their voyages out of Germany. In 1873 the church founded a special mission for ministering to emigrants, and because the mission's duties had grown so substantially, appointed a special emigration pastor to head this body. In the beginning, mission efforts were directed not only at rendering help in mundane matters such as ship's tickets or temporary housing but also at preventing emigrants from losing their religious commitment after settling in the new homeland. Thus, from its first years the Hamburg mission cultivated contacts abroad to whom it could send its charges.[114]

As in Hamburg, the Bremen Lutheran Church's involvement with emigrants evolved from its general effort to look after those displaced and pauperized by the new industrialization process. Although Bremen did not have factories producing proletarian poor as so many other German cities did at this time, by midcentury it did have enough poverty to merit the establishment of an inner-city mission to serve the city's disadvantaged. When the numbers of emigrants coming to Bremen to ship out exploded at the end of the 1870s, the Lutheran Church expanded the inner mission's charity work to include needy emigrants. This expansion seemed necessary because the number of emigrants cycling through the city rose from 9,300 in 1877 to 129,500 by 1881, and such high numbers continued for the rest of the 1880s.

The Lutheran inner mission in Bremen began modestly by providing religious tracts and sermons, but it quickly multiplied its services. Under the direction of Pastor Cuntz, a distinct emigrants' mission arose in 1881. A year later, Cuntz was joined in his work by Herman Krone. Carefully organized and administered, their emigrant assistance program flourished, becoming a model for other European assistance efforts. For emigrants already present in Bremen, Cuntz and Krone dispersed advice and information on emigration matters. They frequently secured tickets, arranged lodgings, and made ship's reservations for needy emigrants. They also distributed information publications and filled out documents for illiterate emigrants. They rendered assistance to the unsophisticated in need of protection from predatory agents and fraudulent tricksters. For the sick, for those separated from their families, and for countless other kinds of human needs they provided immediate help. Finally, for those who wanted to know, the Lutheran emigrants' mission provided information on where to locate the nearest Lutheran pastor in their new homeland. The confidence of emigrants in the mission was evidenced by the fact that increasing numbers entrusted their money to it either for safekeeping in Germany or for sending on to them after they had arrived in their new homeland. Indeed, in 1889 the mission reported that the money so entrusted to it had reached nearly a million marks.[115]

At approximately the same time that these Lutheran efforts commenced, Germany's Catholics also began to assist their fellows who had decided to leave for new homes abroad. The guiding spirit behind these efforts was the Limburg merchant Peter Paul Cahensly, who while working in Le Havre had become acutely aware of the misery and disappointment frequently experienced by emigrants. Presenting his plan before the general assembly of German Catholic organizations in Trier in 1865, Cahensly made three proposals. First, he called for the establishment in Hamburg, Bremen, Le Havre, and Antwerp of effective means to improve the conditions for emigrants at these embarkation points. Second, he proposed developing international cooperation for assisting migrants, specifically calling on Belgium's Catholics to participate. Third, Cahensly suggested that the Catholic diocese of New York make arrangements to look after Catholic immigrants landing there. These proposals received support not only from Germany's bishops but from the papacy as well. This led in 1868 to the formation of an ad hoc Committee for the Protection of Emigrants, which then established the St. Raphaels-Verein (St. Raphael Society) in 1871. The new society's lay directorate included the prominent aristocrat Count Furst zu Isenburg as president and Cahensly as general secretary.[116]

The "effective means" for assistance that Cahensly had called for in 1865 included not only advising emigrants on migration but also removing abuses and other potential and real problems affecting them both before and after their departure. Because, unlike its Lutheran counterparts, the St. Raphaels-Verein received no financial contributions from outside sources such as shipping firms and hotel owners but was wholly dependent upon membership contributions and support from the dioceses, its early efforts remained modest. Initially it lacked funds to staff its Hamburg and Bremen offices and had to rely on local priests and parish members to provide services to needy migrants. Nevertheless, as the society's success became apparent, its support increased. In 1872 in Hamburg and 1873 in Bremen, the society established resident officers to look after departing German Catholics. Besides offering advice, the society's agents campaigned tirelessly for regulations requiring hotels to charge reasonable rates and to provide clean rooms for their emigrant guests; they frequently boarded and inspected emigrant ships in Bremen and Hamburg to make sure of adequate provisions and accommodations. Their concerns extended to morality issues. The society fought successfully for the separation of the sexes in boarding houses and on emigrant ships. As Almut Mehner concludes, "The society's demands pertaining to how the emigrants were dealt with – separate sleeping quarters for the two sexes, no beds over one another, full and clear information on prices for room and board provided in several languages – were all incorporated into Hamburg's 1887 law and the regulations pertaining to emigrant accommodation."[117]

Cahensly's ambition to internationalize the St. Raphaels-Verein's efforts also enjoyed success, for by the end of the 1870s the society had put together a network of representatives beyond Germany. Agents were appointed in 1877 in Amsterdam, Antwerp, Rotterdam, Le Havre, Liverpool, and London. Shortly thereafter, the society established North American representatives in New York, Philadelphia, Baltimore, and Montreal.[118] These enabled the society not only to serve the needs of emigrants but also to keep its membership in Germany informed about conditions in the receiving lands. Beginning in 1886, the society published a newspaper, the *St. Raphaels-Blatt* (St. Raphael's Paper), which provided such information for the public.[119] In its first issue, the paper's mission statement reflected the society's international ambitions: "Through reliable coverage of the social and religious conditions in the various lands overseas, we intend to place our Catholic emigrants in a position from which they will be able to judge for themselves where the most satisfactory material and spiritual opportunities are, where they can find, besides suitable livelihoods, churches and schools."[120]

The Emigration Debate in Germany

The efforts of agencies like the St. Raphaels-Verein to facilitate emigration and protect emigrants did not go unnoticed by the German authorities. Indeed, in 1883 Prussia prohibited the society from advertising its services or publishing the addresses of its agents in either Catholic or non-Catholic papers.[121] Such a reaction illustrates the new significance emigration had assumed, which in turn had renewed debate on emigration's meaning and importance for the Reich. As noted, in the early 1880s Germany experienced both rapid population growth and massive emigration. Increasing numbers of Germans, both private citizens and public officials, came to view emigration with ambivalence. While the huge volume of emigrants appeared disastrous and incompatible with the nation's status as a world power, fear spread that Germany would be overwhelmed by paupers, revolutionary tinder that could ignite at any time. To avoid revolution, the country needed to export its superfluous masses; it needed the emigration safety valve. From these two apparently contradictory positions, a third developed. According to Klaus Bade, "The expanding population and emigration questions played a special role in the agitation for expansion and German colonial propaganda of the early 1880s."[122]

Friedrich Fabri, the so-called father of Germany's colonial movement, best represented this new position in the emigration debate. Fabri's support for emigration followed from his belief that Germany had too many people. To him, overpopulation threatened not only to explode in social upheaval but even more fundamentally to harm the material livelihoods of Germans in general. Fabri's solution to the population dilemma lay in exporting the country's excess to reside and work elsewhere. Because he was well aware that those departing represented valuable assets potentially lost to the nation for good, he supported turning the emigrants to Germany's advantage after their settlement abroad. Specifically, he proposed to control not only the process of out-migration but also to influence the settlers' affairs in their new residences abroad.

To effect this, Fabri advocated state-sponsored locations abroad where Reich Germans could settle together, ply their trades, and utilize their skills to establish profitable and rewarding economic lives, while remaining German in culture and national loyalty. Fabri envisioned two kinds of German colonies to accomplish these ends: agricultural settlements and commercial centres. For agricultural settlements, Fabri advocated sending Germany's emigrants to South America in general and to the ABC countries (Argentina, Brazil, and Chile) in particular. In these Latin American states, Fabri envisioned not only available and affordable land for Germany's emigrants but also a chance to control their own cultural and political affairs. In either the United States or Canada, he insisted, the German immigrant would be submerged in and assimilated by an unsympathetic cultural-political system that would destroy the immigrants' German qualities and loyalties as well as monopolize their economic contributions.

Fabri's second category of colonies, the mercantile ones, were not just vocationally different from the agricultural outposts. They were to be peopled by German emigrants from the Reich's middle and upper classes, who would pursue commercial and industrial livelihoods rather than of farming. Instead of homogeneous colonies of German farmers living together and working the land, the commercial colonies would be smaller in numbers and engage in more diverse activities. The commercial centres would also enjoy greater contact with local peoples, who could be exploited as labourers and as consumers of German manufactured goods. Thus, the mercantile colonies were to provide outlets for both Germany's surplus population and any overproduction in German industry. Because their business required more contact with non-Germans, Fabri saw his mercantile units as more dynamic than the agricultural colonies. Indeed, the mercantile colonies would be more mobile, with residents coming and going between the Reich and the foreign outposts; this traffic would have a liberating and uplifting influence on the fatherland. According to Fabri, non-agricultural settlement opportunities existed in such exotic places as Madagascar, the numerous islands of the South Pacific, and especially central Africa. Fabri fantasized a German colony similar to the Congo Free State so successfully and brutally being exploited by the Belgian king Leopold II.

While potential social unrest and overpopulation formed the material basis for his support of German imperialism, missionary zeal, social Darwinism, and German nationalism provided the ideological rationalizations. Throughout his writings and public addresses, Fabri described the German "right" to colonize as part of a larger European duty to civilize the uncivilized, a charge that came directly from God. His background in missionary work certainly contributed to this belief that colonization constituted God's work. He even interpreted the forced labour which colonized people had to endure as a civilizing influence: because it taught them the Christian virtue of hard work, it had to be divinely inspired. As a convinced social Darwinist, Fabri believed the laws of nature made the peoples of Africa, Asia, and South America inferior to Europeans. And as a German nationalist, he held that the recently united fatherland deserved colonies to accord with its new position as a world power.[123]

The emigration debate in which Fabri advanced these arguments inspired the establishment of a number of organizations in the early 1880s to promote the colonization cause. These included the Zentralverein für Handelsgeographie und zur Förderung deutscher Interessen im Ausland (Central Society for Commercial Geography and for the Advancement of German Interests Abroad), the Deutsche Colonialverein (German Colonial Society), the Westdeutsche Verein für Kolonization und Export (West German Society for Colonization and Export), the Verein für das Deutschtum im Ausland (Society for Germans Abroad), and the Alldeutsche Verband (Pan-German League). To restructure emigration to serve national ends, these societies launched major re-education campaigns. As the economist Karl Theodor Eheburg announced in 1884 before the assembled members of the Verein zum Schutze deutscher Interessen im Ausland (Society for the Protection of German Interests Abroad), positive changes in Germany's emigration could be accomplished only through dissemination of "objective and disinterested information." This would neutralize "the multifaceted damaging activity of the emigration agents" then soliciting in Germany. Such "objective and disinterested" advice, it was assumed, would have two effects: it would dissuade many from leaving Germany, and it would convince emigrants to avoid the United States and settle in German centres in South America. Only there, Eheburg concluded, could "the nationality and language of the immigrants be preserved."[124] To spread this kind of message, the several societies established information offices around the country. Despite such efforts, Germans who chose to emigrate still headed for the United States rather than Brazil or Argentina.

Although the pro-colonizing societies were less effective than their memberships had hoped, their activities and the public debates they inspired on colonies and emigration did affect emigration policy. To many concerned Germans, the policy of individual states setting their own standards on how much emigration to allow or on how to regulate out-migration began to appear dangerously obsolete. Belief grew that Germany needed a new national policy that would apply to all its parts.

Thus, early in 1878, Friedrich Kapp, a refugee from the 1848 revolution who had fled to the United States and then returned to Germany to become a Reichstag member, brought forward a plan to promote emigration abroad. Kapp's law proposed to set uniform bond rates for all Germany's agents and to require proof of German citizenship before issuing an agent's licence. But his legislation still allowed the individual states to determine the other rules and regulations pertaining to emigration. By requiring a measure of national uniformity while retaining some local independence, Kapp hoped to conform the emigration business and its applicable laws to the free market ideal. The outspoken liberal believed that healthy competition would ultimately reduce the numbers of inefficient and corrupt agents. Only in certain limited circumstances could licences be denied to aspiring agents, and only under set conditions could validly issued licences be revoked. Nevertheless, this mild proposal for some regulation from Berlin met with immediate opposition. To many, it seemed to infringe too far into the prerogatives of the individual states. Kapp's opponents argued that only if the individual state had complete control over the agents operating within its borders would it be able to prevent further mass migrations. On the basis of such opposition, Kapp's plan failed. Prussia's spokesmen, for example, declared it "absolutely unacceptable."[125]

The real issues blocking a uniform national emigration policy were economic. That is, different groups and different areas of the country viewed the entire emigration question from opposing vantage points. The conflict between the Hansa cities and Prussia best illustrates this. On the one hand, Hamburg and Bremen, which flourished from the trade in emigrants and from the unrestricted importation of cereals, supported liberal tariff and emigration policies for the country as a whole. Bismarck and his traditional landowning supporters in East Prussia, on the other hand, opposed the untaxed importation of foreign grain and a permissive policy toward those wanting to emigrate. For this group, the free importation of North American or Argentine grain threatened their profits, while increased numbers migrating out of the country and especially from the east threatened to exacerbate the shortage of agricultural workers already plaguing Germany's eastern provinces. As a result, Prussia's representatives and Bismarck balked at creating a uniform, more rational and liberal emigration law. They insisted on controlling their own emigration.[126]

German Efforts to Limit Out-Migration

Even though no national emigration law could be agreed upon, concerns about the effects of mass emigration continued. The agitations of persons like Fabri, the educational efforts of societies like the Deutsche Colonial-verein, and the debates in the Reichstag brought pressure to bear on the alleged main sources of the misinformation, namely, the emigration agents then at work in Germany. The specific activities of existing agents came under ever closer scrutiny, particularly in the 1880s. This scrutiny, in turn, meant that complaints about agent abuses began to receive more serious consideration. The response of the German authorities to a letter from the German Society of Montreal illustrates the new seriousness. Specifically, the July 1888 letter protested the "conscienceless agents" who had been recruiting indigent emigrants in Germany and then sending them on to Canada: "No week passes without people in the direst of conditions arriving here who then turn to the German Society for help." Most of these persons had come to Canada, the letter continued, having been assured by agents in Germany that once in North America they could easily move to the United States. After landing in Canada, they discovered they were hundreds of miles from their intended US destinations and that the United States had passed laws prohibiting indigents from entering the country. Thus, the indigents were stranded in Montreal with no means of support and no prospects except the poorhouse. The society's letter concluded with a demand that the guilty agents be stopped from recruiting.[127]

In response, the German emigration authorities sounded the alarm. In a letter dated 18 September, a foreign office official sent a note to Bismarck assuring the chancellor that not only had the foreign service been informed but also "the governments of Bavaria, Saxony, Württemberg, Baden, Hesse, Oldenburg, Mecklenburg-Schwerin, Mecklenburg-Strelitz and the senates of the Hansa Cities," and adding that the Montreal society's protest "had already been published in the press."[128] As a direct result of such complaints, the federal government and local authorities began to monitor more closely not only the emigrants but also those engaged in emigration facilitation. The stepped-up surveillance followed from the belief that before improper acts by agents, agencies, or emigrants could be thwarted, the authorities needed to know more about the entire process. This meant keeping track not only of agents and subagents but also of newspapers willing to print pro-emigration propaganda and of those agencies formed to assist would-be emigrants in leaving. The monitoring process thus grew in complexity and scale. By 1890 it included efforts by German consuls in Canada, governmental bureaucrats in Berlin, and local police magistrates in German towns and cities.

Monitoring usually involved observers working in tandem and keeping one another informed. Surveillance was carried out on groups of agents working for agencies and on individuals soliciting independently. An example of how the monitoring procedures were set up for the latter is illustrated by the case of a return agent from Winnipeg named Kirchheimer.

Monitoring began when R. Hoger, the German consul in Winnipeg, reported to Germany on 3 June 1887 that Kirchheimer, a native of Heilbronn with relatives in Baden, had recently left to sail from New York to Bremen with the intention of soliciting emigrants for western Canada. To prepare those in Germany who would have to keep track of Kirchheimer, the consul carefully described Kirchheimer's background and recent activities in North America. According to Hoger, who was personally acquainted with him, Kirchheimer had been living in Winnipeg for one year after spending nine years in the United States. Hoger claimed that Kirchheimer not only intended to solicit emigrants in Germany but that he knew solicitation to be prohibited in Prussia; Kirchheimer was bent on recruiting in the Thuringian towns of Abberode, Goslar, and Aschersleben. In addition, Hoger described Kirchheimer as having been "involved in a number of shady deals" which included "2-3 months in plying the prohibited liquor trade [he had been a bootlegger] in the far west, for which he had been punished by the law." To assist in surveillance, Hoger added a detailed physical description of Kirchheimer: he was thirty-two or thirty-three, of average height with broad shoulders and a squat build, and a full, oval face, dark brown eyes, blunt nose, wide mouth, full lips, all his teeth, and dark brown hair, as well as a full-bodied goatee.[129]

The warning about Kirchheimer that Hoger's June letter conveyed to the authorities in Glogau was in turn passed on to Puttkamer, the Reich interior minister in Berlin. Puttkamer then notified Bismarck as well as important governmental figures in Hanover and Mecklenburg. As a result, the local police were confidentially alerted about Kirchheimer, so that he would not suspect the police and state authorities of keeping tabs on him. Hoger's efforts to forewarn his associates in Germany were not unique. Indeed, the practice of German consuls in North America sending advance warnings about suspect agents travelling to Germany for emigrant recruitment became increasingly common in the last third of the nineteenth century, particularly after the several American states began to compete aggressively with one another in soliciting would-be immigrants.[130]

A January 1888 report from the internal security authorities in Düsseldorf affords another example of the monitoring process. Nine persons living in the area, suspected of illegally recruiting emigrants for Canada, were being carefully watched by the police for possible violations of the emigrant recruitment laws. Providing a list complete with names, addresses, and occupations, the report also included a brief summation of what the police investigators had been able to discover about the subjects' involvement in improper solicitation. For example, the first person named, Heinrich Andreas Jansen, was described as having assisted a young Hamburg man of military age to emigrate without having fulfilled his service obligation. Jansen also had been observed working for the Red Star Shipping Line recruiting emigrants in Düsseldorf and he was being investigated for his role in securing tickets for German emigrants leaving from Antwerp. The notes describing the other eight members of the group were more tentative, admitting that "up till now it has been impossible to convict them for such activities." In each instance the police were conducting "careful observation," assuming, as one of the reports put it, that the observed was living "a dark existence from which one could easily imagine that he was engaged in the facilitation of forbidden business."[131]

If efforts to catch the agent or subagent offenders with "the goods" presented problems, so also did prosecuting known violators. To begin with, the laws were not altogether clear on what constituted a violation. Moreover, the several German states applied the existing laws at their own discretion. These procedural difficulties were exacerbated by the problems of foreign citizenship or non-German residence. Return men practising "the Yankee system" were often in and out of the country before the authorities could act. Even with an arrest and conviction, collecting fines or enforcing jail sentences was often impossible. The Toe Laer case from the late 1880s illustrates just how difficult securing legal remedy against obvious offenders could become.

As noted above, Toe Laer, who both solicited himself and ran subagents, was the main Canadian Pacific agent working in Germany in the 1880s. The authorities in several German states had monitored his work closely, and some believed he had crossed the fine line that separated providing information from actual solicitation of emigrants. Calls arose in several places demanding action be taken against him for illegal advertising in Germany's newspapers and for distributing "direct or through subagents in various parts of the monarchy [Hanover] brochures and prospectuses" urging emigration to Canada.[132] Although Toe Laer violated both the licence requirement (he had none) and the antisolicitation laws, prosecuting him faced a serious problem, namely his Amsterdam residence. Legal opinions varied on whether to pursue him and how. Greifswald's city attorney argued against prosecution, claiming Toe Laer could not be held accountable to German law or court findings while residing in Amsterdam.[133] But such advice did not deter the state's attorney in Halle from pursuing Toe Laer until he secured a judgment in Halle for a small fine and a three-day jail sentence against the offending CPR agent. Halle's attorney knew full well, however, that the sentence could not be carried out with Toe Laer in Amsterdam.[134]

During this time, most of the German states engaging in clandestine surveillance or monitoring of emigration agents in the hopes of detecting criminal solicitation also scrutinized the propaganda materials that Canada circulated in Germany. The government watchdogs looked at brochures not only for illegal solicitation efforts but also for fraudulent claims. For example, in October 1884, the Interior Ministry in Prussia informed the Bavarian government that the brochure *Manitoba und der grosse Nordwesten Amerikas* (Manitoba and the Great Northwest of America) which had been circulating in Prussia, contained false information. Berlin reported that the brochure, which originated in Liverpool, included fraudulent letters from a Canadian immigrant to his parents in Germany. The forged letters purported to show that Julius Trapp, who had emigrated to Canada in 1879, not only owned his own farm there but also was making a grand success of it. According to Julius's father, his son lived not in "such splendid circumstances" but rather in entirely "miserable" *(kümmerlich)* ones. All Julius wanted, the father insisted, was to abandon his bad Canadian situation and return to Germany.[135]

As in their scrutiny of agent actions and brochure contents, the authorities especially sought evidence of actionable violations of the prohibitions against actively assisting in the recruiting process. Like censors in wartime, those who monitored the press looked for articles they believed were deliberately trying to win converts for emigration. When the authorities found something they considered actionable, they sometimes prosecuted. If the author of the suspect article could not be reached by the law, then the prosecutors frequently went after the paper's editor or publisher, sometimes both. Two cases from 1886 illustrate this particular tactic. Berlin's *Amerikanische Nachrichten* (American News) was prosecuted for violating the 1853 and 1871 laws against emigrant solicitation by publishing illegal articles advertising Manitoba in editions from June 1885 and January 1886. The *Amerikanische Nachrichten's* editor and publisher were hauled into court, tried, and found not guilty.[136] The same sort of charges and procedures were instituted against the editor and publisher of the *Schneidemühler Zeitung* (Schneidemühl Newspaper) also for publishing improper advertising about settlement opportunities in Manitoba. Since the allegedly illegal propaganda, which appeared in June and July 1886, originated with Toe Laer in Amsterdam, the prosecutors decided to go after "the responsible editor of the *Schneidemühler Zeitung* and the owner of the paper's press, the Schneidemühl native Gustav Eichstaedt." Like the *Amerikanische Nachrichten's* editor and publisher, Eichstaedt was found not guilty. The court decided that although "the advertisements may have contained an offer to dispense information on how to emigrate, this could not be determined for certain."[137]

Since securing a conviction was so difficult, skeptical prosecutors hesitated to press their cases. In another potential action against the *Neufelderslebener Wochenblatt* (Neufeldersleben Weekly), the Magdeburg state's attorney explained why he would seek redress from neither Toe Laer nor the editor of the paper. The advertising for Manitoba, he wrote, "did indeed contain an enticement to emigrate and it offered to provide further information about the acquisition of land in Canada; however, it did not offer emigration contracts, that is, contracts which aim to assist persons to go to foreign lands or to provide information on facilitating emigration. These are the only matters that are prosecutable under section 10 of the cited law [the law of 1853]."[138] Moreover, the effort might not have seemed worth much, since the numbers leaving Germany for Canada· were insignificant compared to the masses heading for America. As one monitor observed, Canada "appeared not as threatening as some other foreign lands."[139]

Unlike foreign solicitors, German agents operating in Germany could not avoid the courts, and had to observe the antisolicitation laws more carefully. In 1887, for example, the Hamburg-American Line (HAPAG) published a pamphlet of instructions for its agents in Germany. The brochure contained eighteen separate paragraphs that sought to inform HAPAG's representatives on the mechanics and the legal obligations involved in fulfilling the agent's role. Thus the list included both do's and don't's. The law strictly forbade trying to convince Germans to make the decision to leave Germany, and the HAPAG document instructed its agents explicitly to obey the law in its very first lines: "The first duty of every representative of the company is to follow the law strictly so that any conflicts with state officials or other interferences are avoided." Paragraph 3 addressed the most difficult problem for both agents and interpreters of the state's laws, namely, how to prevent the recruiting agent from "selling" his clients on the act of emigration and how to limit his role to providing information only: "It is not the task of the agents to encourage persons to emigrate. Agents are to limit their concerns only to such persons who have firmly decided to immigrate to America; they are to bring to the attention of those so resolved the advantages of our steamships and to recommend to them travel on those ships."[140]

Travel to Canada

Like the level of police and governmental scrutiny, the process of emigration had advanced considerably since 1870. With the ports of Bremen and Hamburg major centres for embarking emigrants, the emigration business assumed ever greater economic significance, and the arrangements for conducting it had become more sophisticated and organized. This held true also for the physical means of transporting emigrants out of Germany and across the seas. Since 1870, the German railway system had been extended further and travel made more convenient and easier to arrange. Likewise, in the two decades 1870-90, the transition was completed from sail to steam power for the transatlantic voyage. Although some ships continued to carry sails into the 1880s as insurance against mechanical breakdown, by 1890 sails had been dispensed with altogether. The development of the twin-screw ship in the 1880s obviated the insurance sails, and "sounded the death-knell of all the time-honored and romantic associations of the glistening sail and flowing sheet."[141] In addition, the introduction of the compound engine and improved condensers made for speedier and less expensive crossings after 1870. The use of superior and cheaper Bessemer steel replaced iron for ship construction, and ship length and tonnage increased significantly. Tonnage rose from 2,500 to range between 5,000 and 10,000, and length increased from 28-37 metres to 46 and above. Such augmented size and scale allowed ships to carry more cargo and passengers and to offer more than just first class and steerage accommodations.

As the steamship evolved, it became increasingly distinguishable from the sailing vessels of old. Superstructures topped with funnels replaced masts and sails; steel hulls succeeded wooden ones. With no masts and sails to make room for, the poop deck could be roofed over, allowing the possibility of building the ship up vertically. With steam power applied to steering, the wheelhouse could be moved forward so the helmsman could see to steer. These changes in design led to greater efficiency in performance, which in turn reduced costs. An observer writing in 1891 described how engineers had found ways to decrease coal consumption while at the same time increasing the steamer's power: "The old-fashioned paddle engine consumed 5 lbs of coal for each indicated horse power. The invention of the screw propeller reduced this to 3.28 lbs. The direct acting condensing engine reduced this again to 2.50 lbs; the compound engine brought the consumption down to 2 lbs; and the most recent form of triple engine using steam at 200 lbs. pressure only requires 1.25 to 1.82 lbs. of coal per indicated horse power, or to put it another way, the steamer of today can travel five times as far upon the same coal consumption as the steamer of 40 years ago."[142]

Most important, though, such efficiencies and innovations dramatically reduced the length of the voyage from Europe to North America, improving passenger comfort and safety. "In 1872," Günter Moltmann writes, "the average length of sailing voyages from Europe to New York was a little over 44 days; on steamers it was a little less than 14 days. The mortality rate on sailing vessels was one death to 184 passengers, on steamers one death to 2,195 passengers."[143] In effect, by reducing the length of the Atlantic's crossing to one-fifth of what it had been in sailing days, the steamship had rendered the voyage far less hazardous. In 1873 the US Marine Hospital Service's chief surgeon characterized the advantages of steam travel thus: "With the gradual supplanting of sailing vessels by steamers have come shorter voyages, increased space, improved accommodations, more light, better ventilation, more abundant supplies of more wholesome food and water, and a superior morale of officers and crews; though in this latter respect there is still much to be desired."[144] Despite continuing steerage abuses on some ships, the shorter time that passengers lived under adverse conditions significantly reduced the sickness and malnutrition characteristic of earlier periods. Discontent among German immigrants travelling to Canada had not disappeared entirely, as attested by a March 1882 letter to W. Wells, the government's immigration agent in Ottawa, complaining of German passenger baggage being roughly searched and damaged in Liverpool and Hull.[145] But the life-threatening dangers that had plagued travellers since the inception of transcontinental migration had ceased, to be replaced by minor inconveniences and particularly boredom.

Conclusion

The period from 1870 to 1890 witnessed the continuation of earlier economic and social trends in both Germany and Canada. In the old world, the traditional forms of agriculture and industry continued to be supplanted by more modern ones. The process, however, was complicated by a significant economic recession. Change and recession necessarily meant population movement and adjustment. To some Germans, the adjustment necessary to survive at home appeared neither possible nor desirable; a significant number of the disgruntled opted to emigrate. As they left, the debate on the meaning and significance of mass emigration again heated up. Many still harboured what had by now become a traditional view that emigration offered a convenient means for Germany to relieve itself of the social problems caused by the economic dislocations of the period. Increasing numbers of others, however, believed that emigration was more detrimental than had previously been thought, and that hemorrhaging emigration threatened Germany's national power and thus its political position in Europe and the world. As a result, the period 1870-90 saw the beginnings of much more serious efforts to monitor emigration and to levy some restrictions on those involved in assisting or promoting it. But despite the spreading concern over emigration, no consistent German national state policy emerged, and emigration remained a matter for the several German states and the local police. Such variation and indeed fecklessness among the Reich's local, state, and national authorities offered additional evidence of Germany's still-incomplete political unification.

The turmoil in Germany failed to bring a bumper crop of new immigrants to Canada. In fact, the overall volume of German immigrants arriving in Canada fell off during this period, despite the desperate need for new emigrants and the stepped-up efforts of the Canadian government and its agencies to lure new settlers to the North West. Certainly, the policy of free homestead land did not cause the failure. Compared to other Western Hemisphere rivals such as Brazil or Argentina, Canada's easy naturalization and land tenure programs seemed most attractive, closely resembling the hugely successful American policies. The reasons for the dominion's lack of success in attracting more German immigrants lay elsewhere. The prevailing economic climate in the 1870s and 1880s did not help, as the low price of wheat through most of this period provided no inducement to homestead farming. In addition, the Macdonald government's preference for British subjects as immigrants to the North West, to ensure that British institutions, culture, and traditions would prevail there, necessarily decreed that efforts to recruit German settlers would be both insufficient and inconsistent.

Another reason may have been detected by Lars Ljungmark in his study of Scandinavian migration to North America. In comparing American success at luring Scandinavians with Canada's failure to impress the same group, Ljungmark discovered that Canada's agents failed to convince Swedes to migrate to Canada because they had no evidence to draw upon of Swedes successfully residing in Canada. In other words, Swedish sources in Canada for developing a successful chain migration to Canada appeared to be lacking. Swedes, Ljungmark concluded, opted instead for the United States, because their countrymen and -women had already settled there and thus could provide future immigrants not only with evidence of successful settlement but also with assistance and guidance after the move.[146] This analysis more than likely applies to Reich Germans as well; that is, Canada's small and distant (i.e., far removed from Germany in time) German community may have had insufficient ties to inspire significant numbers to opt for Canada. The weak Canadian pull would have been particularly disadvantaged relative to the huge numbers of American Germans available at the same time for luring Germany's potential emigrants to the United States. Finally, throughout this period, Canada's German recruitment policies remained undefined and its propaganda exaggerated and unrealistic. The almost exclusive solicitation of would-be farmers clearly had limitations in an age of increasing industrialization. The depiction of Canada in romantic terms as a pristine, natural land waiting to be developed by agriculturalists failed to inspire the supposedly romantic Reich Germans to migrate to the dominion.

In short, although the numbers of emigrants leaving Germany increased during the period 1870-90, Canada continued to come in well behind the United States as the primary destination. What held true for Germany applied elsewhere as well. Indeed, the Macdonald immigration policy as a whole, that is, in the British Isles, the United States, and Europe, was unsuccessful, for throughout the period those emigrating from Canada exceeded the numbers immigrating into the dominion. A narrowly conceived and implemented immigration policy heavily favouring English-speaking farmers was an obvious failure. Although during the Macdonald era potential farmer-immigrants abounded in Europe, the most readily available ones were simply not solicited. For example, the thousands of Italian peasants displaced by the agricultural crisis that struck Italy from 1879 to 1883 emigrated to Brazil, Argentina, and the United States, not to Canada.[147] Furthermore, a Canadian immigration policy tailored to serve an economic program based on partial industrialization and staple exports could not offer enough inducement for those seeking other kinds of remunerative work. By 1890 it had become apparent that Canada needed to alter its immigration policy and expand its solicitation efforts even further – in Germany and elsewhere in non-British Europe – if the dominion were to receive what its proponents considered its rightful share of available immigrants. Canada needed to commit more resources and energy over a broader immigration field, and to make its immigration program more rational and structured. In short, it needed to do the kinds of things Elise de Koerber had advocated in the 1870s.

3
Migration in the Generation before the Great War, 1890-1914

Migration had taken on much of its modern shape by 1890, and in the two and a half decades before the Great War, its importance increased in both Germany and Canada. The solicitation of emigrants, the demographic and regional makeup and destination of migrants, the facilitation agencies in Germany, and the processes involved in leaving Europe and entering Canada were reconsidered carefully and debated publicly. In Germany much of this debate was influenced by the country's rapidly advancing industrialization and resultant modernization; emigration appeared increasingly linked to the country's burgeoning world power status. Although Canada's industrialization progressed more slowly than the Reich's, migration's apparent importance to the dominion also increased significantly in this period. And as in Germany, the perceived needs of the nation-state decreed this. Thus, in both countries political influences exerted greater pressure than previously on the policies dealing with the movement of people out of Germany and into Canada.

The Political and Economic Context
Although the period's politics displayed enough continuity with the past to be recognizable, important new themes and policies emerged in both lands. To begin with, the political leadership in Canada and Germany altered dramatically. The change in Germany from the Iron Chancellor to a series of lesser chancellors commencing in 1890 signalled a new age. Otto von Bismarck's successors not only lacked their predecessor's political skill, but they had to deal with an increasingly different political world. Most fundamentally, by 1900 the politicizing of Germany's masses had proceeded well beyond what Bismarck had known, and governing Germany had therefore become more complicated and more difficult.[1] Accompanying this expanding German political consciousness, the role of the imperial government also grew steadily. Expanding and increasingly interventionist, the governing process within Germany nevertheless often lacked coordination. Who

had the last word on many a political issue often remained a mystery.[2] At the same time, a new foreign policy emerged under Wilhelm II, as the Reich began to demand its "place in the sun." This meant a new *Weltpolitik;* that is, a concerted German effort to win recognition for the empire among the world's other leading powers.[3]

Although expansionist nationalism permeated politics, the new *Weltpolitik* was rooted in Germany's phenomenal economic growth. In the two decades before 1914 the German Empire matured as an industrial power. As one of the preconditions for this, Germany's population had grown dramatically. In 1890 there were 49 million Germans. By 1910 that number had expanded to 68 million, an increase of almost 40 percent. In 1880 German industry produced only half as much steel as Great Britain; thirty years later these roles were exactly reversed. Thus, in the course of a generation, "Germany passed from being Britain's favorite market to Britain's major industrial competitor."[4] On the eve of the Great War, the German Empire ranked as the world's second-most powerful industrial manufacturer, trailing only the United States. From such a position, Germany was poised to seek ever greater markets and economic influence.[5]

Industrialization transformed Germany from its formerly predominantly rural condition into a country where two-thirds of the population resided in cities. Migration to the urban centres was not only a response to the enhanced wages and improved material well-being promised by the new economy but also a flight from the land, which created a chronic farm worker shortage. As the traditional sources of agricultural labour dried up, arresting further flight from the land became a major concern for Germany's agriculturists.[6] Rapid economic changes and urbanization created or exacerbated social cleavages as well, intensifying social strife. To increasing numbers of the socially powerful, it appeared as if Germany needed an outlet for this growing social problem. *Weltpolitik* offered a chance to shift social concerns from the home front to the larger world stage. Like emigration at an earlier time, an aggressive foreign policy came to be viewed as a social safety valve.[7]

Bismarck's retirement also significantly affected migration policy. Throughout his tenure in office, Bismarck had disapproved of emigration and considered those who departed as forfeiting their rights to be considered Germans. "For me," he announced, "any German who casts off his fatherland like an old coat is no longer German and I cease to have any interest in him as a countryman."[8] Beginning with Georg Leo Count von Caprivi, Bismarck's successors abandoned this official attitude. Although Caprivi disapproved of emigration, he pragmatically recognized the inevitability of some out-migration. Hence, he supported Friedrich Fabri's idea of German commercial and agricultural colonies in South America as outlets for both surplus population and industrial products. Such colonies would provide, he and other policy makers believed, an answer to America's restrictive McKinley Tariffs, which were adversely affecting German industry. Neither Caprivi nor subsequent chancellors succeeded with these plans, largely because of inadequate support from other elements in the Reich's government.[9]

During this period, Canada's political scene changed almost as dramatically as Germany's. Although the Conservatives carried on as Canada's ruling party after Sir John A. Macdonald's death in 1891, they were replaced in 1896 by a Liberal government headed by Sir Wilfrid Laurier. Over the next fifteen years, Laurier fulfilled much of Macdonald's National Policy.[10] The single greatest political achievement of the Laurier years was the astonishingly successful settlement of Canada's west. From 1896 to 1914, 2.5 million immigrants entered Canada. The magnitude and significance of this influx can be seen in comparison with Canada's total population in the 1891 census, which numbered 4,833,239. Three decades later, that total had grown to 7,206,643, an increase of just under 50 percent. The 2.5 million immigrants made up most of the country's population increase, and 30 percent of these settled on Canada's western frontier. Another 20 percent, who chose not to homestead, found work in the West's expanding mines, mills, and railway construction.[11]

Several factors rendered the settlement of the West feasible at this time. First, European demand for Canadian agricultural products, especially wheat, made farming an attractive vocation for immigrants. The technical advances in shipping and the expansion of rail transport at the end of the nineteenth century drastically reduced the costs of moving grain to market and made Canadian products much more competitive. Second, the closing of the American frontier made Canada's free land more attractive. Third, continued pressure from the United States made western settlement a pressing issue for Canadian nationalists. Fourth, the cultivation of formerly marginal lands in significant portions of Saskatchewan and Alberta was made economically feasible by new "dry farming" techniques, which increased the yields from semi-arid lands, and by the development of new strains of wheat that matured quickly enough to be grown and harvested in short summers.[12] Finally, the West was ready for settlement. As H. Blair Neatby puts it, "The Indians had been located on reserves, the North West Mounted Police were enforcing the law, the Canadian Pacific Railway had been built, the land had been surveyed and municipal and territorial government had been established. Immigrants would not be coming to a turbulent and lawless frontier."[13]

Much of the success in western settlement could be attributed to Laurier's minister of the interior from 1896 to 1905, Clifford Sifton. Bringing great energy and commitment to the task of recruiting immigrants, Sifton, a westerner himself, seemingly stopped at nothing to carry out his charge.[14] He vigorously solicited settlers from such traditional recruitment areas as the United Kingdom and the United States but also looked beyond these English-speaking peoples. Aware of the special nature of the prairies, Sifton sought out potential farmer-settlers in the Hapsburg Empire and Russia, preferring Ukrainian, Polish, and Russian peasants, who he believed would be able to succeed on Canada's western plains better than most. Filling the allegedly empty prairies with essentially new ethnic groups from eastern Europe began a social transformation that within a short time significantly altered the makeup of Canada's population. Thus, on the eve of the Great War, Canada's society possessed a substantial element culturally and linguistically distinct from its two historical settling races, the French and English. The settlement of the former North-West Territories led to the creation in 1905 of the provinces Saskatchewan and Alberta. Together with Manitoba, the three Prairie provinces formed a new element in the Canadian political system.[15]

An expanding Canadian economy formed the backdrop for Laurier's political successes. Although regional growth rates varied, in general, the years from 1900 to 1914 represented one of the most dynamic periods of economic growth in the history of the dominion. In the east, manufacturing in both Ontario and Quebec grew steadily after 1895: the volume of manufactured goods more than doubled, while iron and steel production and the mining, lumber, and coal industries grew similarly. In the west, immigrants poured onto the prairies and the Macdonald-era expansionists' dream of a flourishing Canadian agriculture began to become reality. In its speed and scale, the settlement movement of the Laurier years dwarfed anything from the past. In 1871 fewer than 75,000 people lived on the prairies. Twenty years later there were 250,000, which by 1911 had quintupled to 1.3 million. From this population explosion followed the wheat boom of the prewar years, which Norrie and Owram labelled "perhaps the most dramatic ... of all the economic developments in Canada's first half-century."[16] As the virgin, fallow lands became expansive cultivated fields yielding bountiful grain crops, towns and cities sprang up on the once-lonely prairie. The development of the prairies had national implications: "Wheat," Norrie and Owram write, "was a national staple, and it transformed more than just the prairies and more than just the economy. Canadians far removed from the region earned their livelihood by preparing the region for settlement, supplying the equipment needed to produce the grain, transporting the grain to its markets, and providing for the needs of the farm families."[17]

Canada's Prewar Immigration Policy

By the end of the Laurier age in 1911, Canada's immigration policy had become more sympathetic, better funded and organized, and more inclusive than ever before, bringing to a climax many trends that had been evolving since Confederation. From the tentative policies developed in the

Macdonald era there emerged under Laurier a more forceful and ultimately more successful immigration program. Immigration had been the purview of the Department of Agriculture until 1891, when it was transferred to the Department of the Interior. Virtually no legal restrictions on immigration to Canada existed other than prohibitions against the diseased, criminal, and pauperized. The Alien Labour Act passed by Parliament in 1897 represented the lone exception here but it did not affect the agriculturists targeted by Sifton, and he thus did not have to alter the law to reach his ends. Instead, Laurier's first minister of the interior simply adjusted the government's administrative structure to make it more responsive and efficient in handling Canada's immigration. To streamline the immigration process and make it more productive, Sifton created within the Department of the Interior an independent Immigration Branch with its own director. To this office fell the task of "unifying all immigration activity under one administrative umbrella."[18] Sifton also simplified homestead acquisition and made the pre-emption of adjacent sections less expensive and less complicated.

Moving beyond these administrative changes, Sifton stepped up the promotional campaign to secure more immigrants. Most of Sifton's immigration program remained traditional; that is, he simply put more energy and resources into implementing policies popular in the past. Obvious continuities existed in the use of private and public appointees to conduct recruitment but also in three other areas: first, in soliciting for farmers almost exclusively; second, in devoting disproportionate amounts of activity and resources to securing immigrants in the British Isles; and third, in employing bonuses as an inducement in winning converts for Canada. To further his program, he increased the number of immigration agents from eleven in 1901 to nearly fifty in 1911. He also provided them with much more government-printed material touting Canada. Reflecting the growing sophistication and modernization of advertising techniques, Sifton's materials included market surveys, expanded brochures and pamphlets, maps, billboards, and conspicuous newspaper advertisements. Agents were encouraged to spread the good word about Canada through mailings, lectures, personal interviews, and newspaper advertisements, and to do what they could to assist their converts in finding homesteads, purchasing tickets, and moving to Canada. Sifton also offered steamship companies, railways, and colonization organizations bonuses for those they induced to migrate to Canada. Although most of these efforts were directed at populations in the United Kingdom and the United States, Sifton's campaign also included the Austrian, Russian, and German Empires. Since more restrictions existed on both recruiters and those being recruited on the Continent than in either Britain or the United States, Sifton pursued whatever avenues he could find to win agriculturalists for Canada.[19]

While Sifton preferred British immigrants, he realized early on that Canada would never recruit enough farmers in the United Kingdom to populate Canada's west. Hence, Sifton sought farmers elsewhere, even among the "less preferred" peoples of eastern and central Europe. The flood of non-British peoples created widespread anxiety among nativists who feared Canada's British character and institutions would be destroyed. (Generally, Canada's nativists adhered to the so-called Great Chain of Race theory, which ranked peoples on the basis of their closeness to the preferred British stock. At the top of this hierarchy were the Anglo-Celtic British peoples, the Irish, English, and Scots. After them came the Americans and then the Scandinavians. The Germans occupied the fourth-most desirable link in the chain, followed by the Slavs. Chinese, Africans, and American Native peoples were located at the very bottom.)[20] Sifton's successor from 1905 to 1911, Frank Oliver, also adhered to this social theory. While he shared Sifton's belief in the importance of immigration for Canada's future, Oliver did not share Sifton's fondness for eastern Europeans and particularly Slavs, insisting that "if in the future 'Sifton's pets' (i.e., the Slavs and other non-British peoples) wanted to migrate to Canada, they would have to do so on their own initiative."[21]

Oliver favoured making Canada's immigration laws more restrictive, and in both 1906 and 1910 laws were passed that greatly extended the powers of the Immigration Branch to reject immigrants. Under the new statutes, Canadian officials were able to exclude not only those traditionally rejected (the sick, criminal, and poor) but also other classes of people, on the basis of race and ethnocultural background. The undesirable race categories included Europe's Jews and Roma, African Americans, and "Orientals." This "lily white" Canadian policy was not unique among Britain's former colonies; the Australians had adopted the same racially restrictive immigration program even earlier and for the same reasons, namely to maintain the alleged "purity" of the British stock and the sanctity of its traditions.[22] To enforce the new restrictions, immigration officials could prohibit undesirables from disembarking on Canadian soil and require the shipping firm that brought them to pay for the unsuccessful immigrants' voyage back to their former homeland.[23]

Ottawa also gained new powers to deal with immigrants who had previously been admitted to Canada. The Immigration Acts of 1906 and 1910 augmented the federal government's powers to deport those considered undesirable. The government could deport landed immigrants who had been in the country more than a year. Although earlier deportations had been based chiefly on medical causes, the new laws applied to indigents, unemployed people who had become public charges, and convicted criminals. Actionable violations now included not only traditional criminal behaviour such as theft, robbery, or burglary but also vagrancy, picketing, being a nuisance, obstructing the police, and political subversion. With rigorous application of the new laws, deportation from Canada had evolved by 1914 from a makeshift, ad hoc process into a much more systematic and efficient political tool. Immigration officials had the discretion to judge when a violation had occurred and to deport summarily "those who did not meet the requirements of good citizenship within three years after arrival."[24]

At the same time, changes in Canada's naturalization process endowed Ottawa with new powers to act against alleged undesirables. For nearly fifty years after Confederation, naturalization requirements had remained relatively simple. The immigrant who had resided in Canada for three continuous years could apply for naturalization any time thereafter. The process involved appearing before a court official to swear an oath of allegiance, to prove the three years of residency, and to show "good character." In 1914 a new naturalization act expanded these conditions. The residency requirement was increased from three to five years, and the applicant had to prove not only good character but also sufficient knowledge of English or French. If satisfied at the hearing, the court referred the petition to the secretary of state for a decision, from which there was no appeal.[25]

The increasing restrictions on immigrants and immigration that Canada developed in Oliver's time were not unique to the dominion. Other receiving lands, including the United States and Australia, also exhibited strong nativist reactions to the global migrations characteristic of the age. In the United States, the same fear of being submerged by allegedly inferior non-Anglo-Saxon peoples had become widespread well before 1900. The Chinese Exclusion Act of 1882 was the first in a series of laws designed to halt the influx of foreigners deemed threatening to the US system. Similar attitudes prompted the Australian Immigration Restriction Act of 1901. Indeed, the Australian nativist response resembled Canada's reaction even more closely than did America's, as Freda Hawkins encapsulates: "The primary and identical motivation of Canadian and Australian politicians in trying to exclude first the Chinese, then other Asian migrants, and finally all potential non-white immigrants, was the desire to build and preserve societies and political systems in their hard-won, distant lands very like those of the United Kingdom ... The idea that other peoples, who had taken no part in the pioneering efforts, might simply arrive in large numbers to exploit important resources, or to take advantage of the earlier settlement efforts, was anathema."[26] Despite the more restrictive Canadian immigration policy and procedures under Oliver, however, the alterations and innovations of the Sifton years could not be entirely reversed.

The report of the Select Standing Committee on Agriculture and Colonization produced in late April 1908 illustrated both the new and older elements of Canada's immigration policy in the Laurier era. The report showed graphically how Canada's efforts at recruiting on the Continent had grown dramatically over the previous decade. For example, in 1897-8 expenditures for recruiting immigrants on the European continent totalled $31,000, and in 1904-5 that figure had increased by nearly 350 percent to $111,800. Likewise, the figures for homesteads entered into by new immigrants from the Continent had increased from 673 in 1897 to 7,260 for the fiscal year 1902-3, an increase of more than 1,000 percent. Although the annual homestead figures never reached this total again before the Great War, in the five years after 1902-3 they averaged above 4,500 per year.[27] These inflated homestead figures tell another tale beyond that of immigrants being solicited in new areas of Europe: despite Canada's significant industrial advances during this time, the preference in Ottawa for agrarians persisted.

Given this industrial growth, what drove the farmers-only policy, rather than one exhibiting more interest in industrial workers? Clearly, this agrarians-only policy harmonized with the priorities of partial industrialization to support a stable export economy discussed in Chapter 1. But publicly the federal government did not defend its strict agriculturalist policy and its refusal to sanction the admission of permanent industrial workers in these terms. Rather, it claimed that the majority of Canadians desired such a program. Sifton himself believed that immigrant mechanics and labourers posed a threat to Canada's stability. He did not wish to see, as Valerie Knowles puts it, "immigration swelling Canadian towns and cities for if this happened they would invariably develop many of the problems that he observed in their American counterparts."[28] But Donald Avery and others have suggested that the farmers-only policy had another, hidden agenda. According to Barbara Roberts, the reality of Canada's economic needs undermined the Sifton program from the outset. Often those who had been admitted as permanent agricultural settlers found themselves forced "into wage labor, either in the short term to accumulate the capital to start farming their own land or in the long term to supplant inadequate farm earnings."[29] Because immigrant farmers had to seek additional employment, Canada had in effect created a kind of temporary, fluctuating, migrant guest-worker system. Ottawa realized that these agricultural settlers fulfilled much of the country's mining, lumbering, and railway construction labour needs. Some former farmer-immigrants even ended up as members of Canada's permanent industrial proletariat. The advantages of such a guest-worker system for both employers and the state appeared obvious: the costs of maintaining, renewing, and supporting these migrant labourers were greatly reduced. Social service costs were virtually eliminated. Strictly speaking, the injured or incapacitated worker had no claim for support services because he was not a bona fide citizen. In short, Canada's farmers-only program also met the country's industrial labour needs and thus obviated the need for German industrial-worker immigrants. Hence, they were not solicited, and their indifference to or ignorance of Canadian employment possibilities apparently did not matter to Ottawa.

Another element of continuity in Canadian policy in the Laurier years was its British bias. As in the time of Macdonald, Canadian immigration policy continued to prefer Britishers and, after them, English-speaking Americans to occupy the developing West. The numbers of printed sheets advertising western homesteads revealed this preference: between 1901 and 1903, 15,000 were produced in Swedish, 10,000 in Danish, 5,000 in German, 2,000 in French, and 200,000 in English.[30] Data from the Immigration Report of 1908 likewise highlighted Ottawa's traditional priorities. The figures for the years 1897-1908 showed a huge disparity between amounts spent in England, Ireland, and Scotland and corresponding outlays on the Continent. In 1897 almost twice as much was spent in the British Isles ($61,000 versus $31,000); in 1907-8 the amount was four times as great ($174,000 versus $42,000). Even in 1904, when Canada spent over $100,000 on eastern and central European recruitment, the amounts expended in the British Isles still exceeded the outlay on the Continent by 40 percent.[31]

One innovation in Laurier's time was the more extensive use of recruitment bonuses. Although such bonuses had been in use in one form or another since 1882, they became a more firmly supported policy tool. Speaking for the government before the House of Commons Standing Committee in 1908, W.D. Scott articulated the new policy. Admitting that advertising in the press, distributing literature, and delivering lectures remained essential to Canada's recruitment efforts, he emphatically pointed out that "the payment of bonuses to steamship booking agents ... and to subagents in the United States, represents one of the principal methods adopted at the present time for bringing Canada's claims prominently before the emigrating population of suitable countries." The inconsistent and paltry bonuses of the past had been replaced by greater regularity and largesse in bonus granting. He proudly pointed out, for instance, that in 1908 the bonus paid on "continental immigrants had been increased from 10s. to £1 on adults and from 5s. to 10s. for children. Bonuses were even paid for domestic servants."[32]

Although Canada's recruitment remained directed at securing as many bodies as possible in the United Kingdom, Germans were nevertheless viewed consistently as valuable to Canada's overall immigration policy. Testimonials by immigration officials as to German worth were commonplace right up to the outbreak of war in 1914. John Lowe, secretary of agriculture, in 1891 eulogized the Germans as "the most desirable and on the whole the most successful immigrants to set foot on our soil."[33] Writing to Sir Charles Tupper, then minister of railways and canals in June 1893, the Immigration Branch's T. Mayne Daly echoed this opinion: "There is a large German population in Canada by far the most intelligent, prosperous and contented of the populations of foreign origin within the boundaries of the Dominion."[34] As a consequence, the bonus policy in effect in Britain was extended to include Germans as well. "We must stimulate the booking agents [in Germany] to work for Canada," Sir Charles wrote to Mayne Daly in 1895, "until we have a much larger nucleus of foreign settlements in Manitoba and the North West than we have now."[35]

No matter how highly Canada's policy makers may have valued the German element, recruitment in Germany aimed only at farmers, farm labourers, and domestic servants. The policy thus remained the traditional one designed to prolong Canada's Arcadian myth. In America, as Harold Troper has shown, Canada exclusively pursued "a narrow agriculturally based immigration policy," which between 1897 and 1912 induced over three-quarters of a million Americans to come to Canada to settle and farm. Troper concludes, "Of the Immigration Branch it is fair to concede that as an organization it achieved its goals. Immigration of farmers from the United States mushroomed, and settlement flowed and production boomed."[36] Canada duplicated in Germany the same advertising campaign that it had launched so successfully in the United States. Apparently, Sir Charles Tupper fully understood both the limitations of pursuing this successful American policy in Germany and the justifications for it. "In the United States," he instructed his associate Mayne Daly, "they have been able to absorb a comparatively large number of laborers speaking foreign languages ... In Canada, however, it has not been and is not easy to find employment for such people; the classes we have been trying to get are farmers with small capital but the bulk of the emigrants are naturally people who want to work for a living and to join their friends."[37] In the age of Laurier, this policy may have accorded with the emigration possibilities in the American states and the Romanov and Hapsburg Empires but it did not, as shall become clear, fit the prevailing German scene.

The Migrants

The new settlers Laurier and Sifton induced to emigrate to Canada differed from previous immigrant groups not only in ethnic makeup but in numbers. Besides those from the British Isles, the two other major groups were Americans and eastern Europeans. Of the approximately 2.5 million people who immigrated between 1896 and 1914, the British Isles yielded one million, the United States about three-quarters of a million, and eastern Europe just over half a million. In that half-million pool of eastern European immigrants, the ethnic German component was significant. According to Heinz Lehmann, about two-thirds of the entire German community in Canada's west in 1910 had come from the Austro-Hungarian Empire, Russia, or Romania. (The remaining third included Germans who had moved to Canada from the United States and those from Germany proper, at 18 percent and 12 percent, respectively.) More specifically, Lehmann calculates that between 1890 and 1914 nearly 50,000 Germans emigrated from various parts of Europe to western Canada, about 6,000 of them Reich Germans.[38] In 1905, Rudolf Franksen, the German consul in Montreal from 1905 to 1909, figured Reich Germans to be one-tenth of German immigrants.[39] Thus, Reich Germans who entered Canada in the Laurier years alongside the flood pouring in from the Austro-Hungarian and Russian Empires represented a relatively small part of the German total.

The eastern European German immigrants to Canada's west generally exhibited similar vocational, residential, and family traits. Before they departed, the vast majority had resided in small, ethnically homogenous German villages surrounded by a non-German majority, whether Slavic peoples, Hungarians, or Romanians. The Germans from the Russian Empire left areas around the Black Sea, the Russian-controlled portions of Poland, and the Volhynia. From the Hapsburg lands Germans migrated out of Galicia, Bukovina, and the Banat. Romania's Germans departed from the Dobruja. All of these regions were overwhelmingly agricultural. Thus, the eastern European German-speaking peoples who arrived in Canada at the end of the nineteenth and early twentieth centuries were basically peasants who had lived in villages close to the land they worked. These emigrants left their European homes as families, intending to acquire land in Canada and pick up where they had left off in Europe. Their reasons for leaving included a mixture of push and pull factors. Nearly all were lured by free or cheap farm land; the Mennonites from Russia left because their military exemption had been rescinded; those from the Banat departed because the new Magyarization program threatened their schools and potential property rights.[40]

While increasing numbers of Germans were leaving eastern Europe, the opposite trend developed in the Reich. In the period from 1895 to 1914 emigration from Germany dropped off dramatically. During the 1880s and in the first three years of the 1890s, nearly two million emigrants had gone forth from the Reich, in the third great wave of emigration Germany experienced in the nineteenth century. By contrast, the twenty years directly preceding the Great War saw only a quarter of that number depart. Between 1895 and 1914, emigration fell off to under 40,000 per year. Indeed, in 1914 the number departing had shrunk to about 12,000, just over 5 percent of the 220,000 who left in 1881. Emigration departure statistics from the Hansa cities Hamburg and Bremen, still the major German embarkation centres, reflect the dramatic decline of German overseas migration at the turn of the century. Between the peak emigration years 1880 and 1893, Germans composed 81 percent of all national or ethnic groups emigrating from the Hansa ports, but from 1894 to 1910 Germans were only 11 percent of the total.

One often-cited cause of the decline is the announced closing of the American frontier, which supposedly signified the end of free homestead land, since traditionally the United States had always received between 80 and 90 percent of the total German emigration. In reality, more fundamental forces were at work determining the flow of Germany's overseas migrants, the most significant being rapidly advancing industrialization. After 1895, German industrial growth had reached a stage where job opportunities in industry could finally keep pace with the nation's increasing population. Rising wages and improved material opportunities reduced the flow of out-migration to a trickle.

The Reich German emigrants between 1890 and 1914 differed substantially from their predecessors, who had tended to emigrate as families, as shown by roughly even gender ratios and the greater age range resulting from the numerous children among the families migrating. Although the percentage of families in the total had been declining ever since the shift in the sources of emigrants to the north and east in the 1870s and 1880s, not until 1890 did the percentage of single emigrants exceed the family totals. From 1891 to 1900 families made up 47.6 percent of emigrants from Germany; from 1901 to 1910 families dropped to 42.2 percent; and from 1911 to 1920 families declined again to 39.4 percent while single persons made up 60.6 percent of the total.[41] As the percentage of families fell, the proportion of men increased, while the reduction in the number of children increased the emigrants' average age.

The decline of family emigration signalled an alteration in the occupational profile as well. Traditionally, those families who migrated overseas from Germany's south and west had been independent small landholders (vintners, for example) or artisans. As the migration's focal point moved north and east, a substantial percentage of agriculturists remained among emigrants until the 1890s. These later emigrants from the agricultural sector, however, were overwhelmingly landless day labourers or cottagers, representing a kind of rural proletariat. The other large group of emigrants was categorized simply as workers, or those without a profession. These unskilled labourers performed a variety of jobs in traditional industry and in the new factories. At the end of the century and in the decade before the Great War, industrial workers began to appear more and more frequently among the emigrant pool. All of these new vocational types characteristically emigrated as single persons rather than as family members and, more often than not, they had goals distinct from those of their emigrant predecessors.[42] They sought remunerative, nonagricultural work which could be long term, short term, or seasonal. Furthermore, these young, single male or female migrants were inclined to migrate more than once: that is, they would travel overseas to work for a time and then return to their native land. This group, which

Frank Thistlethwaite labelled the "birds of passage," existed among Germany's migrants after 1890, but their actual numbers were quite low simply because the overall number of German emigrants had dropped off so precipitously.[43] Among migrating Poles, Hungarians, Italians, Greeks, and British, whose totals rose dramatically during the generation preceding the Great War, these "birds of passage" were common.[44]

In 1902 the director of the Hanseatic Colonial Society, Herr Sellin, described the new German emigrants:

> Earlier, it was basically would-be farmers who emigrated abroad in order to obtain their own farms, which Germany could not provide. Among the present group [of emigrants] those intending to become farmers are almost completely absent. Hailing most often from Germany's cities, they choose to leave the fatherland because of problems encountered in their urban employment. Many of these, originally agricultural workers, had previously migrated to the cities hoping to earn enough there to return to the land and secure small farms. But with most this desire has passed; they have lost interest in farming. Living in cities [in Germany] they have developed different lifestyles and needs. Frontier settlement [in North America], they have come to believe, could neither satisfy their needs nor make them happy. Thus those who emigrate do so either intending to return to Germany after living abroad for a while or to seek their livelihoods in the overseas cities.[45]

Another way to describe the alterations in Germany's emigration over the period 1865-1914 would be to employ the single versus chain migration typology. Generally, chain migration involved rural families leaving in times of heavy migration and possessing a relatively low level of wealth, education, or vocational training. They departed not by choice but were pushed out of their homeland by crushingly adverse circumstances. Individual emigration was engaged in by single persons, mostly young men, departing from the cities, leaving from areas or in periods of weak emigration, and possessing more wealth, education, and vocational training than those involved in chain migration. Individual emigrants, unlike chain emigrants, were not driven from Germany but rather chose freely to leave for a better job and life abroad.[46]

The decline in emigration of Reich Germans to Canada during the settlement of the Canadian west was part of a larger North American pattern. While total numbers were down, however, the proportions settling in the United States and Canada remained the same. Marschalck recorded that between 1890 and 1914 the United States received 87 percent of the total German overseas emigration. Working from the same set of figures, he estimated that Canada over the same period received only about 2 percent.[47] In actual number of persons, the German consul in Montreal reported that the number of Germans who had arrived in Canada and declared their intention to settle in the dominion totalled 563 in 1898 and 780 in the following year.[48] The United States received 25,000 to 30,000 Reich Germans yearly in the first decade of the new century. Meanwhile, in each year of that decade except 1906, which recorded 540, less than 500 German immigrants entered Canada. In 1901 only 11 people migrated from the Reich to the dominion.[49] It is noteworthy that the grandiose plans to create commercial and agricultural settlements in Brazil, which had greater support among Germany's officials than undirected emigration to Canada, likewise never materialized: from 1904 to 1914 Brazil never took in more than 400 German immigrants a year, or about 1 percent of the Reich's total emigration.[50] These low figures contrast sharply with the significant numbers of eastern European Germans arriving in Canada at the same time. Although, as noted, developments within the Reich accounted for the reduced flow of Germany's emigrants abroad during the two decades preceding the First World War, Canada's rather feckless solicitation efforts certainly did nothing to reverse this trend.

Canada's Efforts at Soliciting and Propagandizing

If circumstances in the Reich effectively reduced the pool of potential emigrants, Canada's immigration officials seemed to take little notice. The propaganda mills continued to turn out materials designed to convert Reich Germans into western Canadian farmers. Canadian propagandists still relied on traditional means and information to win converts. Basically they reproduced throughout the 1890s and the first decade of the new century the usual romantic/civilized image of Canada with some modern touches. Besides the abundant, rich, and, most important, free land, apologists continued to tout Canada's participatory political system, its free religious environment, superior schools, low taxes, and peaceful and orderly society tied together by a modern system of efficient transportation. A pamphlet from 1901 summed up the civilized advantages: "Canada is in the first instance a land for farmers and livestock growers. These will find there all that they need to pursue their livelihoods: the most fertile prairie land available in 160 acre grants to any 18-year-old, the healthiest climate in the world, excellent means of transportation on the country's lakes and streams with the steamboat and on land with the railroad, an ordered society with the lowest rate of robbery, murder, and theft anywhere, free schools for all children, and free churches with all denominations living together in peace."[51] Add to these advantages the social life described in a 1907 publication: "In the various private clubs in Canada there is always the opportunity for conversation with a good glass of beer."[52] The glorification of Canada's bountiful and unspoiled nature reproduced the traditional romantic picture: the mineral wealth, the vast forests, the beauty of the landscape, the sparkling lakes and rivers, the abundant animal life. A flyer from 1903 asserted on its first page that "hunting is completely free except for a few restrictions which apply only during closed seasons. Near settlements one finds deer, rabbits, doves, grouse, plovers, prairie chickens, geese, ducks and curlews. In the bush, further from the settled areas, there are bears, raccoons, minks, martens, otters, and sables."[53]

The modernized elements of Canada's propaganda that accompanied this traditional image mirrored changes that had occurred in both North America and Germany. Many of the brochures and flyers that circulated in Germany referred to an imagined "problem" of surplus population that had become a concern for many Germans, meaning the demographic revolution that by 1900 had so greatly altered the population of Europe in general and Germany specifically. To alarmists, social conservatives, imperialists, nationalists, and the like, overpopulation appeared to threaten both Germany's internal security and the country's place among the world's leading states. As a brochure from 1901 put it, only three means existed for resolving the dire threat to Germany posed by too many mouths to feed: Malthusian reduction through epidemic disease; the traditional depopulator, war; or emigration. No responsible or humane person, the pamphlet argued, would prefer the first two alternatives over the third: "Only through emigration can the surplus population be absorbed and the competition reduced to enable those who remain [in Germany] to feed themselves." Since emigration was necessary, only the question of where to send the threatening surplus remained.[54]

The obvious choice, Canadian propagandists insisted, was Canada. Although the United States traditionally had been the goal for the majority of Germany's overseas migrants, the brochures argued that by 1900 the American option was both unrealistic and problematic. To begin with, America itself suffered from overpopulation. The native population's natural increase plus the massive immigration of the past several generations had created in the United States an obvious overabundance of people. This in turn inevitably produced overproduction, unemployment, and the preconditions for continuing economic and social crisis. Canada's apologists argued that this explained the more restrictive immigration measures recently adopted by the United States. Like the American Civil War in the 1860s, America's alleged overpopulation in 1900 was hoped to deter those Germans who were considering migration to North America from settling in the United States. Canada, on the other hand, promised in 1900 what America had offered in 1800 – unlimited opportunities for all those with ambition and determination. More precisely, Canada, a land of 3.5 million square miles and a population of 5.5 million, still had, one brochure boasted, "room for over a million inhabitants."[55]

The closing of the American frontier in the 1890s had underlined the apparent US overpopulation. Canadian propaganda literature made a great deal of this, for it meant that the free land that had played such an instrumental role in populating America's west was no longer available. But the announcement of the frontier's closing also symbolized the end of the Old West, the subduing of that wild region with its warring Indians, brawling frontier towns, and lonely, peripatetic trapper-traders. That is, the romantic West that had fascinated Germans for so long, and which Karl May was still popularizing, had disappeared.[56] In Canada, on the other hand, the West was still just opening up. Abundant free land existed throughout the newly created western provinces and the virgin lands to their north. The traditional American agrarian myth of endless possibilities had been transferred to Canada, without the violence of the American frontier. With the North West Mounted Police keeping loose tabs on them, loner prospectors, trappers, and Native people still lived in and travelled peacefully about Canada's unsettled northern bush country. According to the author of a pamphlet entitled *Der deutsche Farmer in Kanada* (The German Farmer in Canada), the dominion had evolved into the "America of the present."[57]

In addition to Canada's less dense population and more abundant space, other "modern" reasons were proposed after 1900 to justify emigration to Canada. Europe's new imperialism had nearly completed its expansion at this time, and European colonies had been established in virtually all parts of Africa. In this free-for-all even the German Empire had managed to secure satellites in Togo, German East Africa, South-West Africa, and the Cameroon. Thus when the Canadian apologists tried to point out the advantages of North America, they described Canada as not only far less distant but also less dangerous than Germany's African colonies. In Canada, unlike "the tropical lands of South Africa and South America, there are fewer instances of tropical epidemic diseases ... which threaten to rob the hard-working man of the fruits of his labor."[58] Propagandists also played up the German settlements already established in Canada's west; new immigrants were not setting precedents but actually filling the empty spaces between like-minded German settlers. Again, these settlements proved that Canada allowed its German minority to continue to be Germans.

Almost as compelling as the push factor of overpopulation was the pull of economic advantage, and especially the wealth to be gained by growing wheat in Canada. As noted above, in the first decade of the twentieth century, Canada's western prairies were producing substantial amounts of wheat, for which ready markets had been secured. Reflecting this development, Canada's brochures trumpeted wheat as the new gold, more prevalent and easier to obtain than the metal gold then being sought in the Klondike. In 1903 the Canadian government produced a pamphlet entitled *Die Ernte in*

Canada (The Harvest in Canada), which opened with the claim that in 1902 Manitoba and the North-West Territories had produced 32 million tons of grain worth $55 million. Its second set of headlines proclaimed boldly that Canada offered "land, profitable employment, and a happy, carefree future for more than 100 million settlers."[59]

To verify its claims of immigrant success, the pamphlet included a list of twelve German farmers who had immigrated to Canada between 1880 and 1890, each a rags-to-riches story of the most dramatic type. For example, Steffen Christie began farming in Glenburn, Manitoba, in 1884 with three cows, two ponies, and no money. By 1902 he had accumulated forty head of cattle, 100 sheep, thirteen horses, fourteen pigs, 960 acres of land, a house, stalls, and machines worth $500. Even more impressive, however, was the story of Valentin Kauf, who started farming in Fort Qu'Appelle directly after his arrival in Canada in 1890 with absolutely nothing. In 1902 his possessions "included two and a half farms with 400 acres under cultivation, a house, garden, outbuildings, 3 wagons, 2 sleds, threshing, sowing and mowing machines, 2 plows, 3 harrows and many other machines, 6 horses, a great number of sheep, and poultry." Finally, the modest A. Klemke of Dominion City, Manitoba, started out in 1891 with exactly one dollar. His 1902 assets included "187 acres of land, property worth 2,500 dollars, and from the last harvest 2,600 bushels of grain." Following these astonishing accounts was a letter from a farmer who concluded his own success story and encomium of Manitoba by insisting that "if the people [in Europe] only knew how good the land is here, there would be no farmers in Europe. They would have to come here and make the wilderness tillable. The land here is so beautiful that all you need to do is plow and seed. Then everything is fine [*alles in Ordnung*]."[60]

Such Canadian brochure reporting was flawed not just because claims that "all you had to do was plow and seed" were obviously exaggerated. Even more important, the propaganda was directed at the wrong group of Germans. By the end of the nineteenth century most Germans lived in cities and worked at city jobs. If they or their forefathers had once been peasants, they were no more. The majority of those who had left their farms (*Bauernhof*) neither wanted nor were able to mend their broken ties to the land. Because the number of small peasants had shrunk so dramatically, Canada's efforts at finding agricultural immigrants in the Reich were bound to fail. Testimonials from eastern European German-speaking peasants exiled from the Hapsburg or Romanov Empires could not be expected to convert the man who worked in a factory, sang in a Social Democratic choir, and found himself at home in one of Germany's modern industrial cities.

Canada's Agents and Agencies at Work

As in the preceding periods, the brochure writers and newspaper propagandists were not the only ones touting Canada to would-be German emigrants. The generation prior to the Great War also witnessed continued emigration promotion by agents, although the process had become considerably more difficult: agent activities once permitted or ignored were now often prohibited. An official German report from 1900 pointed out that the "governments of Manitoba and the North-West Territories were vigorously pursuing emigrants in Great Britain, the United States, Belgium, France, Sweden and Austria by using both permanent and temporary agents and by circulating brochures." Germany had no such permanent Canadian solicitors because "the laws of Germany left little room for them to solicit." Possible legal retaliation, however, did not mean the end of Canadian recruitment efforts in the Reich but rather the implementation of new, less obtrusive selling techniques. Germany's officials were aware that Ottawa intended to continue recruitment. The 1900 report concluded by quoting a statement made by Canada's deputy minister of the interior on this subject: "They [the Germans] do not allow us to work openly but we can work quietly."[61]

Ottawa's "quiet" efforts to circumvent the German prohibition on solicitation were expressed in a variety of ways. Since permanent resident agents were taboo, Canadian government recruiters worked the German field from without. Antwerp and Liverpool had served as recruitment centres since the earliest Canadian attempts at soliciting Continental emigrants, but a German ban on official agents significantly expanded efforts from these centres and elsewhere. Agent John Dyke, for example, who had been arrested for soliciting emigrants in 1873 in Prussian Pomerania, continued to distribute Canada materials from Liverpool in 1894.[62] In 1905, Rudolf Franksen, the German consul in Montreal, reported that a William Hutchinson, formerly an army officer and later an employee of Canada's Ministry of Agriculture, had been soliciting German immigrants from Liège in Belgium while overseeing the Canadian contribution to the International Exhibition there. Among other things, Franksen claimed, Hutchinson had distributed "thousands of publications describing Canada."[63]

In 1912 General Consul Karl Lang, who succeeded Franksen in Montreal, reported another type of "quiet" recruitment procedure, namely the sending of temporary, unofficial (disguised) agents to Germany. According to him, the one-time real estate speculator Anton Tilly of Winnipeg had ingratiated himself enough with Ottawa to be appointed "Canadian Farmer Delegate" with the task of recruiting German immigrants. Tilly's backing included a salary and an allowance to cover his travel between Canada and Germany. When he encountered Tilly in Montreal, Lang asked where he intended to set up his office. Tilly handed the consul his business card, which read "Anton Tilly, Canadian Farmer Delegate to Europe, London, England, 11-12 Charing Cross." Since the Canadian government had apparently given Tilly free reign to conduct his business affairs in his own way, however, Tilly had decided to open an office in Berlin. Lang concluded, "Tilly intends to lead a double life. In London he is a Canadian immigration agent, in Berlin a private real estate broker." In the latter position, Tilly believed, he could not be accused of breaking Germany's rule against Canadian government immigration agents residing in Germany.[64]

Freelance agents like Tilly played a less important role in recruitment than agents working for the shipping firms and transportation companies. Although the Canadian government could no longer have its William Wagners, Ottawa might still rely on employees of the Canadian Pacific Railway to recruit Sifton's desired farmers. Otto Zwarg, a young man who solicited in the decade before the Great War, typified the semi-independent CPR operative. Born the son of a druggist in Eisleben in 1881, Zwarg was only twenty-one when he came to the attention of General Consul Franz Bopp, Franksen's predecessor in Montreal. In 1902, Bopp reported to Germany that Zwarg, who had worked for several months on a western Canadian farm, was being sponsored by the CPR to recruit German immigrants in the Reich. To this end, the CPR had recently sent Zwarg on a three-month fact-finding tour of Canada's North West "to familiarize himself with that area and to inquire into the suitability of settling Germans there." Bopp informed Berlin that Zwarg had also negotiated specifically with the Canadian government to "solicit German immigrants to settle as homesteaders in closed colonies in the Territory of Alberta" and that for any successful solicitation Zwarg had been promised a handsome commission. He intended to conduct his emigration efforts in Germany working out of his former hometown.[65]

Although Bopp registered doubts about Zwarg's effectiveness due to his youth and rather unprepossessing demeanour, his skepticism appears misplaced. In 1905, the Zentral-Auskunftsstelle für Auswanderer (Central Information Office for Emigrants) in Witzenhausen expressed concern about Zwarg after receiving a copy of the agent's correspondence with a prospective emigrant named Schmidt. Allegedly written in response to a request for information about settlement possibilities in Canada, the Zwarg letter painted a particularly rosy picture of Canadian farming opportunities. Not only was superior Canadian farmland still available at prices well below anything in Germany, he described both livestock raising and wheat farming as largely trouble free: "Cattle did not have to be tended but rather could wander freely about their pastures for nearly the entire year. Only during two winter months did the farmer have to provide hay for his herd, and hay was everywhere readily available." Wheat could be grown just as easily, for the land's remarkable fertility rendered fallowing or fertilizing unnecessary. Zwarg claimed personally to know farmers who had cropped the same land for nearly twenty-five years "without ever having had to fertilize, and the crops have been wonderful."[66] Because Zwarg had maintained a low profile, the authorities lacked hard information about his recruitment activities. Thus, the Schmidt letter came as something of a shock. Nevertheless, the German officials responded promptly. First, D. Lehmann, the director of the Zentral-Auskunftsstelle, personally warned Schmidt to cease having anything to do with Zwarg. Second, the local police authorities were notified about Zwarg's activities and ordered to investigate just what he had been doing and how extensive his influence had become. Until the matter had been fully investigated, however, the police were permitted to proceed no further.[67]

Because trying to run temporary agents like Zwarg and Tilly was both troublesome and not very effective, in 1899 the Canadian government decided upon a different approach to immigrant recruitment. In a 1906 letter to Berlin, Consul Franksen reported that Clifford Sifton had decided to stop trying to deal with a large number of agents and instead had opted to establish an anonymous syndicate to take over immigration recruitment and propagandizing in Europe. Besides Germany, the countries covered by this "clandestine network of European shipping agents" ultimately included Russia, Austria, Romania, Switzerland, northern Italy, France, Holland, and Belgium.[68] "Since in Germany," Franksen wrote, "it will be composed of German citizens, it will be more difficult for Germany's officials to control it than if it were a foreign entity." Franksen noted that the original 1899 agreement, which expired in 1902, had been renewed in 1904 and the syndicate named the North Atlantic Trading Company. With its seat in Amsterdam, this company was dedicated to propagandizing on behalf of emigration to Canada "through the daily press, through distribution of pamphlets, through personal influences and in other ways." For every farmer-immigrant eighteen years or older the company recruited, Franksen reported, it was to receive from the Canadian government a premium of one pound sterling.[69]

When it became known that the Laurier government had pledged public funds to the North Atlantic Trading Company, the Conservative opposition in Parliament responded vociferously. Although the syndicate had shed its anonymity in 1904, its directorate membership had remained confidential. When pressed to divulge those involved, the Laurier government refused. Arguing that "the conditions surrounding immigration operations on the continent of Europe have required the making of exceptional arrangements for the promotion of immigration to Canada," Laurier justified not only entering into a contract with the North Atlantic Trading Company but the nondisclosure of its membership as well. A valid contract entered into by "a minister of the Crown," Laurier insisted, was "binding on the Dominion" and therefore would not be breached by his government. Nevertheless, in June 1905, as a sop to the opposition and as a way of fending off further criticism, Sifton and Laurier did have the company reconstituted. At a meeting on the Isle of Guernsey, the company declared itself a public corporation with stock shares available for purchase. In addition it named several standing members, mostly obscure Englishmen. The charter listed three Germans, namely, S. Gluck as general director, H. Pfeifel as business director, and N. Kohan as secretary.

Despite the reworking at Guernsey, skepticism abounded that the persons named in the new constitution represented the company's real directors. Franksen wrote Berlin insisting "the named members of the corporation are only straw men ... one may assume with certainty that the company's belated registration was done to throw sand in the eyes of Parliament." The consul then described one of the businesses on the North Atlantic Trading Company's payroll as "a German firm based in Hamburg."[70] This information raised enough suspicions in Germany to launch an official investigation. The Hamburg company allegedly involved with the suspect corporation turned out to be the Karlsberg Travel Agency. In a letter to the emigration authorities in Hamburg, A. Strom, an employee of the Hamburg-American Line, described the connection between the Karlsberg Agency and the North Atlantic Trading Company: "S. Gluck, N. Kohan, and H. Pfeifel ... are only straw men for the actual boss, the emigration agent Karlsberg of the B. Karlsberg and Company of Hamburg. Karlsberg's son-in-law Kohan, a director of the Anglo-Continental Travel Bureau in Rotterdam, handles [Karlsberg's] affairs in Bremen. Pfeifel was earlier in Hamburg and later in Rotterdam an employee of Karlsberg. Both Gluck and Kohan are still employed by Karlsberg, who has named his employees as nominal directors of the North Atlantic Trading Company because Karlsberg does not wish to appear publicly in that role and thus arouse suspicion." Strom claimed to have verified these assertions with a Canadian government representative stationed in London who had frequent dealings with Karlsberg in Hamburg.[71]

On the basis of such reports Karlsberg himself was subjected to interrogation on his alleged dealings with the North Atlantic Trading Company six months later in December 1906. Although the connection between Karlsberg and the Canadian government's efforts at emigrant recruitment seemed to have been made by Strom and others, Karlsberg emphatically denied ever occupying the role attributed to him. Any emigration work where German-speaking people were solicited, he insisted, had been carried out in Russia or in lands of the Austro-Hungarian Empire. Despite the heavy suspicion Karlsberg was under and the comprehensive nature of his interrogation, the German authorities were never able convincingly to document his involvement with the North Atlantic Trading Company nor prove Karlsberg's recruitment of Reich Germans for emigration to Canada.[72] The German government's willingness to let the matter rest may have related to the negligible number of Germans migrating to Canada in this period, but this remains a subject for speculation.

Besides the shadowy government-sponsored North Atlantic Trading Company, a host of private Canadian ventures emerged in the Laurier years to promote immigration. Although these associations frequently claimed to be immigrant aid societies, they were usually quite different. According to the astute Franksen, most of these promotional groups were composed of land speculators who had adopted the help or aid society labels to dupe the unsophisticated: "Their primary goal was not to provide assistance but to sell land at a profit."[73] For example, the Farmer's Auxiliary Association solicited German farmer-emigrants out of its London office during 1904-5. In answer to requests for information on settlement opportunities in Canada, the association usually responded by trying to convince the inquirer of two things: the benefits of settling in Canada and the advantages of utilizing the assistance of the Farmer's Auxiliary Association in the actual settlement. "Our society," a spokesman asserted in November 1904, "has decided in the spring of next year to guide a group of about 50 German families to Canada. Under our protection and guidance the families will be able to enjoy many advantages during the trip over and to have their settlement in the new land made much easier than otherwise." The association intended to lead its charges "to that most favored land between Winnipeg-Yorkton and Qu'Appelle where bumper crops have recently been harvested." Obviously, the association possessed land to sell in this area.[74]

The Union Trust Company of Canada represented an even better example of a private Canadian association pursuing emigrants for purposes of land speculation. According to John Eagle, between 1902 and 1906 the Union Trust purchased 76,765 acres of land in Manitoba and Saskatchewan from the Canadian Pacific Railway for this purpose.[75] Based in London and Toronto, the Union Trust had its interests in London represented by the agent J.F. Hansen, whose job was to secure German farmers for settlement on its land in western Canada.[76] To realize this goal, Hansen waged a vigorous campaign in Germany during 1908-9. J.F. Wolff, the head of the Zentral-Auskunftsstelle für Auswanderer in Berlin, reported in 1909 that Hansen's campaign involved distributing brochures on Canada, advertisements in German newspapers, and personal efforts to contact potential emigrants.[77] Such procedures were traditional; what rendered Hansen's propaganda so disturbing to Germany's officials was the new approach he took to winning converts for Canadian agriculture.

As other private agencies and Canada's government had done before, Hansen and the Union Trust Company targeted Germany's agricultural workers in their recruitment efforts. Aware of the distinct social rankings within Germany's agriculturists, however, Hansen made a pitch for the group's upper ranks, the class of agricultural overseers and minor administrators who were known as agricultural *Beamter*. Unlike Sifton and the Canadian government, the Union Trust did not solicit bodies to occupy the West as a way to fend off the Americans, nor did it promote settlement to enhance the country's material welfare. Put simply, the company wanted

German farmers with the resources to buy the land and farms it had purchased earlier. In the words of Consul Lang in Montreal, "The Union Trust Company possesses large amounts of farm land in western Canada, for the most part wild land but also some under cultivation and even with buildings. For these partly developed farms [the company] seeks buyers, especially in Germany."[78] These buyers, J.F. Wolff asserted, would then "inspire additional purchases of the company's land by their German friends and acquaintances."[79]

The inducement pitched at the *Beamter* was clever. The Union Trust offered employment contracts that promised a position as supervisor or administrator on a farm in western Canada. These farms were all owned by the company's real estate affiliate, the Canadian Land and Development Company. The contract's provisions required the contracting party to accept the position "as economic manager/administrator *(Beamter)* on a farm in western Canada belonging to the Canadian Land and Development Company and to remain at that position for two years." In return, the immigrant would receive a small salary and free food. In his March 1909 report to the German Foreign Office, Wolff provided the details on several offers made to German farmers. For example, Erich Langhoff, a farmer in Brandenburg, responded to a Hansen newspaper advertisement and was offered employment "as a supervisor on a Canadian Land and Development Company farm with the right to purchase the administered farm at a later date." In addition, Langhoff was to receive free board, a yearly salary of 1,500 marks, and part of the farm's profits. Wolff reported that a second inquiring farmer, H. Dodt of Oppenrode, received a reply from Hansen that the Union Trust specifically sought young German farmers to employ as farm administrators in Canada with a salary of 1,500-2,500 marks, free board, and free travel to the farm. Hansen had also offered the inspector Bruno Romanowski of Dietrichsdorf a farm administration job plus the opportunity to purchase a 600 morgan (40,000 square metre) farm with dwellings and "100 morgan [6,700 square metres] already planted in wheat" for only 20,000 marks total with a 3,000 marks down payment.[80]

In Germany, Hansen's offers came under fire virtually as soon as they became known. Critics considered the proposed salaries for the would-be managers paltry, certainly not appropriate recompense for skilled and knowledgeable agricultural administrators but rather "barely the wage of a qualified farm laborer."[81] Since the alleged managerial positions were basically labourers' jobs, they did not carry the security normally associated with comparable positions in Germany. Wolff warned that the so-called managers would be dismissed from their jobs when it became apparent to the officers of the Canadian Land and Development Company that their "managers" did not possess the funds necessary to purchase outright the land they supposedly managed. If these employees were dismissed in October, Wolff added, they would be hard pressed to survive the winter, for that season in western Canada was traditionally a time of significant unemployment.

Wages and tenure were important shortcomings, but the most significant objection to the Union Trust's *Beamter* scheme was its speciousness. Knowledgeable observers in Germany knew full well that a Canadian counterpart to the traditional German land manager did not really exist. Most Canadian farmers owned and worked their own farms and thus had no need for an overseer or manager. In fact, Wolff claimed that the number of managers in Canada was far fewer than that of self-directing owners or even renters. Clearly, the Canadian *Beamter* promoters knew that what they so unscrupulously hawked was fraudulent. A member of the Bavarian government summed up the official disillusionment with the Union Trust Company on this issue: "This recruiting for agricultural managers is merely an inducement *[Lochmittel]*, since in those regions where these managers are supposed to be employed the vast majority of farms possess owner-managers. The farm manager [as in Germany] is a rarity. Those *Beamter* who decide to migrate [to Canada] will undoubtedly find themselves employed as common farm laborers."[82]

The *Beamter* scam disturbed officials in Germany also because the targets of the Union Trust recruiters appeared to be vulnerable quarry. Significant numbers of Germany's modest agricultural officers had been reduced in status during the agricultural changes of the last half of the nineteenth century. Many of these managers desired to possess their own farms in Germany but lacked the means to do so. Again Wolff sums up the problem cogently:

From the investigations we have conducted here, it appears that a significant number among Germany's agricultural overseers have exhibited interest in emigration. As the large number of inquiries [about emigration] that have originated in this group show, many of these persons do not on the one hand possess enough resources to acquire their own land at home. On the other hand, just as many are disenchanted that the landowners [for whom they work] demand such continuous cooperation and attention to their demands. They [the agricultural *Beamter*] are therefore more inclined to emigration than either the landowners or the common labourers.

This vulnerable group, Wolff continued, knew too little about the actual conditions abroad to be able to make proper decisions about emigration. Although these petty officials had no desire to emigrate only to begin as humble farmers creating their own farms from the wilderness, they did respond to the mention of positions there as agricultural managers. Indeed, Wolff sadly admitted, the title *Beamter* had a ring to it that they could not resist.[83] The German cause for alarm, however, again seems to have been exaggerated because, like other German agriculturalists, the *Beamter* did not respond to Canada's siren call as readily as its promoters had hoped.

Germany's Religious Agencies as Facilitators

Along with the Canadian politicians, agents, and land speculators working to promote German migration to Canada, less mercenary and less political facilitators existed in Germany during the period 1890-1914. This included the philanthropic and religious groups that had arisen over the course of the nineteenth century to succour those leaving the country. As in earlier periods, Germany's two largest Christian denominations, the Evangelical Lutheran Church and the Roman Catholic Church, illustrated this kind of promotion best. As discussed in Chapter 2, each denomination had developed its own emigration oversight, care-giving agencies, and service-rendering personnel during the time of Germany's most intense out-migration in the 1870s and 1880s. These services were still available during the generation directly preceding the Great War.

By 1900 the Lutheran emigration mission in Bremen had grown in size and scope to include many contributing members and provide a wide range of emigration-related services. The centennial report on the Bremen Emigration Mission provides a summary of its work: "The bureau provided information and gave advice, arranged for tickets, looked after travel connections and lodging, sent out informative literature or leaflets, and distributed publications. In addition, the mission advised persons against making bad decisions, warned them of swindlers and often held back their departures. The mission provided help in case of sickness, separation from families, and in many other ways. Finally, the mission provided to each who asked for it the name of the nearest pastor whom they could contact upon their arrival in their new homeland."[84] The Hamburg mission provided similar services for its Lutheran emigrant charges.

The Lutheran institutional efforts that had begun in the Hansa cities during the 1870s expanded significantly in 1897 with the establishment of the Evangelischer Hauptverein für Deutsche Ansiedler und Auswanderer (Main Evangelical Society for German Settlers and Immigrants). Founded by Ernst Albert Fabarius and Gustav Adolf Schlichtendahl in Witzenhausen, this organization defined its basic task as advising and informing German emigrants. It acted as a kind of clearing house and coordinating agency for the several separate Lutheran emigration agencies in the Reich, serving people who might be considering leaving the country, those actually in the process of departing, and those already residing abroad.

Although more nationalistic and xenophobic than earlier reports, the 1914 annual summary nevertheless represents the nature and scale of the society's activities. This document described the society's numerous and varied services and provided information on a number of relevant emigration topics.

For example, it reported on Germany's laws affecting emigration, on the problems and dangers of surreptitious or illegal emigration, on the number of Germans who had actually left the country to settle abroad over the past several years, on the trial of agents accused of illegal solicitation efforts in the Reich, and on the unfair privileges that had been granted the Canadian Pacific Railway in the Austro-Hungarian Empire for transporting emigrants to Canada. The report also published prognostications and analyses of farming opportunities and harvest results for a number of foreign lands in Europe and beyond. It even described colonization opportunities in the Reich itself. Finally, the 1914 report dealt specifically with emigration to Canada, in a rather negative discussion: the German emigrant in Canada could expect to find an acute shortage of money, less available employment than claimed, too many other immigrants competing for too few jobs, and declining wages. As if these shortcomings were not sufficient, the immigrant, the report concluded, must know English to be able to compete successfully in the Canadian job market.[85]

By the end of the nineteenth century, Germany's Catholic Church had developed its emigrant assistance to an even more comprehensive and structured level than the Lutherans had. The most important element in this system, the St. Raphaels-Verein (St. Raphael Society), continued to supply reliable information on conditions in the proposed receiving countries while at the same time providing agents and society officials to assist those emigrating from Germany. The society's quarterly publication, *St. Raphaels-Blatt* (St. Raphael's Paper), informed on both subjects. The first issue of 1913 carried feature stories on conditions in New York, Texas, Argentina, and Canada, and reported on the society's agencies in Bremen, Hamburg, Rotterdam, Antwerp, New York, and Quebec. It also discussed Russian and American immigration laws, as well as emigration to Germany's colony in East Africa.[86]

Although the *St. Raphaels-Blatt* occasionally printed articles critical of Canada, most of those published in the generation directly before 1914 presented the dominion favourably. A 1911 article entitled "Kanada als Kolonizationsland" (Canada as Colonization Land) typified this favourable coverage. The story began with a discussion of how much Canada had trailed behind the United States as an immigration land over the past century, but asserted that things had changed. Quoting the "great Canadian Prime Minister Sir Wilfrid Laurier, a Catholic" the paper claimed that "the 20th Century will be the century of Canada." Developments in Canada over the past thirty years, the paper asserted, were responsible for the country's unification, the building of the transcontinental railroad, the opening of new mines and harvesting of uncut forests, and, most important, the successful settlement of the West's seemingly unlimited prairie lands. Final proof could be seen in the huge number of American farmers who had recently abandoned the United States and migrated to Canada. Aside from these material promises, the article deemed Canada a worthy receiving land because the Catholic Church had played a significant role there ever since the arrival of the first Europeans. Catholics had not only established themselves in Quebec before any other religious group, but French Catholic missionaries had been the first to explore and open up the West. The present status of the Catholic Church in Quebec as well as in Manitoba and the lands to the west was most favourable. Indeed, the *St. Raphaels-Blatt* claimed that "for German Catholics Canada offered the best religious environment of any new land." The reasons for this were several: German Catholics had an established diocese and bishop in St. Boniface, Manitoba; Canada's Prairie Germans had their own German-language newspapers; and German immigrants to western Canada had extant colonies of German Catholics in Saskatchewan with which to identify. In summation, the article claimed that "considering present-day conditions in Canada, one might legitimately consider this extensive English colony a promising place for emigration. Clearly, it is a country where landowners, agricultural workers, and diligent skilled craftsmen engaged in trades related to agriculture are justified in harbouring high hopes for advancement."[87]

By 1900, the St. Raphael Society had appointed advisors in strategic places in both Canada and Germany to provide guidance for German Catholics swayed by such rhetoric. Hamburg and Bremen were staffed with society members ready to render assistance. Discussing its Hamburg representation, the *St. Raphaels-Blatt* provided in January 1908 this rendition of what a society's agent should do for a Catholic emigrant arriving in the Hansa city: "For the emigrant, the Society's representatives should be in all matters a conscientious advisor and true friend. They should be present at the train station to receive the emigrant when he arrives in Hamburg. Moreover, the advisor should help find suitable lodging for the emigrant and assist him with his shopping and in changing his currency. Likewise, the society's representative should arrange for the emigrant's attendance at church and help make it possible for him to receive the sacraments. Finally, the agent should assist the departing brother in boarding the ship that will take him abroad."[88]

The same article listing these duties also described an actual human paragon. Theodor Meynberg, the society's first representative in Hamburg, had served from the founding of the Hamburg office in 1872 until 1907. In this time, the article pointed out, Meynberg had transformed the "sad" situation for Catholic emigrants in Hamburg. In March 1907, "Meynberg sent out 238 letters dealing with emigration matters and personally helped 128 emigrants in leaving [Hamburg]." He rendered service to groups of missionaries from Steyl and Limburg on their way to Togo and Kamerun. Responding to an army officer's request, Meynberg assisted that man's son to migrate to Brazil and, when the son returned to Germany for further education, he again handled all the arrangements for the boy's arrival in Germany as well as his return trip to Brazil. Meynberg had assisted housemaids going to New York, and mothers with children returning to Germany from there. The article concluded its encomium with the following account:

> The housemaid Maria N. from Alsace, in the process of migrating to New York, was scheduled to appear at Meynberg's office at 2 o'clock in the afternoon to have her luggage checked. In the course of the afternoon, she never appeared despite the police having been notified of her non-appearance. Finally at 9 o'clock in the evening the 21-year-old girl showed up at Meynberg's home. Lost in the city and not knowing the address of her lodgings, she had wandered about Hamburg for seven hours. Finally, a policeman checked her papers and noticed the blue St. Raphael's card. Thereupon, he immediately took her to the society's representative [Meynberg]. Naturally, it required much last-minute arranging to prepare the girl to leave with her ship the next morning at 7 o'clock.[89]

The St. Raphael Society duplicated in Canada the advising and assisting system it had created in Germany, appointing persons to fulfill Meynberg-type roles in the Canadian centres for German immigrant reception and settlement. In 1904 the society had positioned its agents for Quebec in Montreal, for Manitoba in Winnipeg, for Assiniboia (Saskatchewan) in Estevan and Regina, and for Alberta in Calgary. The *St. Raphaels-Blatt* described the society's arrangements in Winnipeg in this fashion:

> With the increasing immigration into Canada, the St. Raphael Society has seen fit to ensure that an appropriate number of its representatives are in place to provide arriving Catholics with advice and help. The most worthy bishop of St. Boniface [Manitoba] has designated Reverend Woodcutter in Winnipeg to take under his wing the immigrants arriving in the city. Thus, the society will have a deputy stationed at the train depot to greet the newcomers and to ensure that they have a place to stay. Moreover, the society will make certain that the new immigrants receive sound advice as to the location of the best farmland and that they are informed about what national [ethnic] groups are settled in which regions and where other Catholics are located. Finally, for the immigrant who arrives with insufficient capital, the Reverend Woodcutter, who understands German, will see to it that the newcomer is provided with farm employment to enable him to earn enough money [to be able to buy his own land].[90]

To assist the St. Raphael Society in its Canadian work, an indigenous German-Canadian Catholic organization was established in 1913. Der deutsche katholische Volksverein (The German Catholic People's Society) not only developed a parallel organization with the St. Raphael Society but it also shared members. "With the St. Raphael Society," the *St. Raphaels-Blatt* reported, the German Catholic People's Society "worked hand in hand. In fact, most of the People's Society's executives are at the same time St. Raphael Society members."[91] As the religious agencies in Germany were accustomed to do, the Volksverein described itself as an organization that did not attempt to convert its advisees to emigration. It offered services only to those "Catholic Germans who were 'Europe tired' and thus already resolved to migrate to Canada."[92] Father P. Bour of St. Mary's Church in Regina, the Volksverein's secretary, defended its task in Canada as basically the same as that of the St. Raphael Society. "The People's Society," Father Bour wrote in 1913, "protects the immigrant in all the difficulties he might encounter; it provides him with advice and help in the settlement process, and makes sure that he settles in the best possible districts and in closed German communities that offer regular Catholic Church services and [genuine Catholic] schools."[93] Society spokesmen sincerely believed that the Catholic religion could best be preserved by maintaining the German language and preserving social cohesiveness among the faithful. Through organizational skill and persistence, the society convinced Ottawa to station a special German-speaking Catholic immigration agent in Regina, whose charge included not only coordinating economic and vocational matters for German Catholic settlers but also locating them on land near other Catholic homesteaders, where their religion would be safe.[94]

The Volksverein's structure was impressive in Saskatchewan, "the main collection point for German immigrants." By 1913, the society had developed a pervasive and committed hierarchy under the direction of the Reverend Suffa of St. Mary's Church in Regina. Beneath him served the general secretary, Bour, followed by the local secretaries. According to the *St. Raphaels-Blatt*, Saskatchewan possessed enough of these secretaries to provide "every immigrant with a person to contact by pen or word of mouth" when in need of the services of the society. In addition, Saskatchewan possessed forty-five German-speaking priests to provide for the religious needs of the newly arrived immigrants.[95] Because in Manitoba, Alberta, and British Columbia the German-Catholic immigrant community never developed to the same extent, the Deutsche katholische Volksverein remained essentially a Saskatchewan phenomenon.

German Migration Policies
Despite the considerable assistance and support of the religious orders, the exaggerated claims of the brochure writers, the frenetic activities of the public "return men" and private railway agents, and even the devious schemes of promotional syndicates, Reich German emigration to Canada never reached

the levels the propagandists sought. The Zentral-Auskunftsstelle für Aus-wanderer (Central Information Office for Emigrants) in Witzenhausen kept tabs on any Germans who sought information from it on emigration. Its statistics for the years 1901 to 1903 illustrate just how few German farmers contemplated emigrating and, further, what a small percentage of these considered Canada an option. For example, for the six travel months of April to September 1901 the office recorded 307 out of 2,654, or roughly one in nine, of those seeking emigration information as farmers by occupa-tion. In 1902-3 these low numbers continued, with 501 out of 3,376, or about one in seven, described as agricultural workers or farmers. The re-quests for information on Canada specifically were even fewer: in 1901 only 15 out of 3,211 total potential emigrants, and in 1902 only 62 of 4,173, listed Canada as the land about which they needed to know more.[96] Since potential farmer-emigrants were in such short supply in Germany, Canada's farmer-only policy failed either to create emigration demand or to supply an option for what demand did exist. Indeed, Canada's official prewar policy of seeking immigrant-farmers had become increasingly anachronistic in other European donor lands as well. Most obviously, in Britain those in-clined to migrate in the generation before 1914 did so to find labouring jobs in mining, construction, factories, or other trades rather than farm work.[97] Despite these obvious shortcomings, the reason Canada failed to attract German immigrants in any significant way extends beyond anach-ronistic policy or badly conceived advertising campaigns. Just as obviously it has to do with government posturing – both Canadian and German. Ger-many launched a counter-emigration policy in the decades before the Great War that Ottawa's feckless response could neither defeat nor circumvent.

Throughout the Laurier years, German officials were quite aware of Canada's efforts to solicit Germans to farm its newly acquired western em-pire. In the period 1890-1914, German observers tended to respond nega-tively to the agrarian emphasis of Canada's immigration policy and to the elaborate claims made for Canadian agricultural productivity. This negativ-ity increased as the new century progressed. In 1903, E.A. Fabarius, the head of the Deutsche Kolonialschule (German Colonial School) in Wilhelmshof, filed a representative critical report. Writing to Robert Count von Zedlitz, a high-ranking Hessian minister in Cassel, Fabarius decried the extent of Canada's solicitation efforts not only in eastern Europe but also "within the borders of the Reich." Fabarius saw Canada's recruiting campaign directed at farmers and those suffering from wanderlust as increasingly a threat be-cause of the close cooperation between the CPR and the Canadian govern-ment. Their incessant pitching of readily available free and fertile land in western Canada particularly provoked Fabarius, who insisted that those who took up the CPR's offer usually ended up on mediocre land isolated from other settlers and distant from any railhead. Such location obviated success because the distance from the railroad inflated the price of necessary consumer goods and also made delivery of marketable crops extremely difficult. Furthermore, "In those areas where the settlements are small or the settlers scattered the prospects for European or German homesteaders succeeding are not favourable." Settler scarcity, of course, prevailed in western Canada. Fabarius ended his report with a strongly worded warning against any "unplanned and ill-conceived" emigration to North America. He encouraged those who remained adamant about leaving to seek out fellow Germans already in Canada. Among their own kind, the Kolonialschule head wrote, "for national as well as economic and religious reasons, their possible advance was more promising." In addition, among other Germans "they would be more useful to the fatherland's economy."[98]

Such explicit hostility among German observers of Canada intensified particularly on the eve of the Great War. The reports sent to the Reich chancellor's office by Lang, the German consul in Montreal, typify the growing antagonism. In January 1913, Lang wrote a lengthy memorandum dealing with the related topics of German emigration to Canada and the larger issue of the Canadian economy. Lang argued that Canada was very short on capital, a necessary ingredient for any significant expansion, and noticeably short of labour. In British Columbia, he claimed, fruit had recently rotted on the vines from lack of pickers, and problems were rampant on the prairies as well. Nearly all of the good southern homestead land had already been claimed and the rest lay in the hands of unscrupulous speculators. Thus the only available homestead property existed in the less fertile, remote, wooded lands to the north, an area normally distant from any rail lines, where "every month of the year was not without its frost." Even if one successfully grew wheat there, Lang pointed out, the huge problem of transporting the harvest to a railhead remained. Given the exorbitant freight rates charged by the monopolistic Canadian Pacific Railway, raising wheat in western Canada had become less and less attractive to more and more farmers. These difficulties, Lang asserted, had prompted growing numbers of disgruntled farmers to leave Canada and migrate to the United States.[99]

All these unfavourable conditions facing Canada's German settler-farmers, Lang pointed out, were exacerbated by nativist prejudice and pressures to assimilate. He rejected the propaganda claims that Canada differed from the United States in allowing its Germans to remain culturally German: "Even if the parents want their children to retain the German language, the children have been shamed by their English schoolmates for being 'damned Dutchmen or damned Germans' and consequently want nothing more to do with things German." The combination of material disadvantage, cultural antipathy, and lonely isolation in the West, Lang found simply too much. "The Canadian prairie with its long winters and impermanent rectangular houses," he confessed, "conveys something indescribably sad and depressing." As a result, he believed that Canada's west offered little to would-be German immigrants and he insisted that other knowledgeable Germans shared his view.[100]

To combat the threat of emigration, in 1902 Berlin decided to fund the Zentral-Auskunftsstelle für Auswanderer recently established by the Deutsche Kolonialgesellschaft (German Colonial Society). Located in Berlin, the Zentral-Auskunftsstelle für Auswanderer was made answerable to the Reich's chancellor, who had the power to veto its decisions. The agency had been formed to bring order to emigration policy and its administration, since in 1902 no less than fifteen different agencies in Germany were actively involved with emigration facilitation and advising. Besides the Kolonialgesellschaft and the two religious agencies discussed above, these included the Verein für deutsche Auswandererwohlfahrt (Society for the Welfare of German Emigrants) in Hanover, the Zentralverein für Handelsgeographie und zur Förderung deutscher Interessen im Ausland (Central Society for Commercial Geography and for the Advancement of German Interests Abroad) with offices in Berlin, Leipzig, Jena, and Stuttgart, the Überseeische Verein (Overseas Society) in Munich, the Deutsche Schulverein (German School Society), and the Nachtigallgesellschaft (Nightingale Society). The establishment of the Central Information Office brought these fifteen societies under one umbrella.

All these member societies were directed by the president of the Kolonialgesellschaft in Berlin, who headed the Central Information Office's executive board. Six societies had representatives on this board: the Zentralverein für Handelsgeographie in Berlin, the Evangelischer Hauptverein (Principal Evangelical Society) in Witzenhausen, the St. Raphaels-Verein in Limburg, the Öffentliche Auskunftsstelle für Auswanderer (Public Information Office for Emigrants) in Dresden, the Deutsche-Brasilianische Verein (German-Brazilian Society) in Berlin, and the Weltkorrespondenz (World Correspondence) in Berlin. Former general consul Koser was the first appointee to the presidency. Deemed appropriate because of his twenty-seven years of consular service in both North and South America and extensive knowledge of migration matters, Koser died within a year. He was succeeded by D. Lehmann, another career diplomat who had rendered consular service in South America.[101]

The task of the Zentral-Auskunftsstelle für Auswanderer, which by 1910 had established fifty-five branch offices in cities across the country, was to provide sound advice and information to any German contemplating emigration abroad. This "sound" advice would originate with and be based upon accurate portrayals of conditions in those countries accepting Germany's emigrants. "To this end," Wilhelm Monckmeier wrote, "it [the Zentral-Auskunftsstelle] collected as much news as possible on the economic, cultural, and social conditions in the receiving lands; it sought direct reports from members of the German foreign service [consuls and ambassadors] stationed abroad and from representatives of the Main Evangelical Society and the St. Raphael Society positioned in the chief immigration lands."[102] Supplied by these reliable sources, the Central Information Office provided both oral and written information. Personnel in the agency's branch offices answered the questions of curious would-be emigrants and discussed their hopes and anxieties. Published materials produced by the agency were provided through mailings and distributions from the branch offices. The Central Information Office's publications included pamphlets, flyers, and brochures either providing sober facts or warning about the dangers and risks in emigration. One of the office's brochures dealt with Canada specifically.

The Central Information Office's Canada brochure, an eleven-page pamphlet allegedly written by Koser, the first president, painted an exceedingly bleak picture, one quite different from the typical Canadian propaganda publications and much more critical than most German accounts. The introduction's first two paragraphs warned the reader that "because of its climate, the greatest part of Canada is uninhabitable for Europeans" and that "for those with lung ailments Canada is dangerous ... Respiratory illnesses result from the harsh winters with their sudden and excessive temperature swings." This negativism extended into the second section's discussion of the several provinces. Nowhere in Canada, the pamphlet claimed, was land either cheap or easily available. The brochure's third section, the document's heart, which described alleged opportunities in Canada, was equally unflattering: "As we have seen, Canada is very thinly populated. The central government, the provinces, and the railroads are all trying as hard as possible to win immigrants. They distribute brochures that praise Canada to the heavens. Care, particularly with regard to these publications, is strongly urged." The brochure described Canadian official statistics as unreliable, failing, for example, to record how many unsuccessful German immigrants had abandoned Canada for the United States. Koser also pointed out that German immigrants in Canada quickly lost their German language and culture: "The first generation of German immigrants born in Canada is no longer German." He asserted that "the prospects for immigrants of British stock are better than for foreigners. In most instances, the British job seeker will be successful where the German fails." Koser's polemic ended by reminding those thinking of emigrating that neither towns nor neighbours as in Germany would be available to alleviate the loneliness and isolation of Canadian life.[103]

Like pro-Canada propaganda, Koser's piece on emigration provided German immigrant testimony on living conditions in Canada. This commentary, which included the views of "a most knowledgeable immigrant" who had "lived many years in Canada's northwest," is worth quoting at length.

> The difficulties in getting started here are many and great. Whoever arrives here with 800-1,200 marks can begin something and after a few years establish a comfortable life. If not [i.e., without such funds] it will go poorly when old man winter comes knocking at the door. Everything here is nearly three times more expensive than in Germany. Besides this, there are many other difficulties. Those [immigrants] who arrive at this time are forced to settle at long distances from any railway station. Moreover, they must be able to understand English, for otherwise things can go badly. In the farms of the north nearly every third harvest is ruined by bad weather. In the south, where farms are almost exclusively devoted to raising livestock, one can expect snowstorms that will kill 50-60 animals.[104]

The more organized and systematic emigration policy reflected by the Central Information Office's activities was mirrored as well in the national law that passed the Reichstag in June 1897. Divided into eight sections, the statute covered all facets of the migration process. It regulated just who could provide the means to emigrate; it defined what these contractors and their agents could legally do to secure clients; it provided general rules for protecting emigrants from exploitation; it set out special regulations for transoceanic migrants; it described the duties for Reich officials charged with overseeing migration; it regulated movement through non-German harbours; and finally it established a code of penalties for violations of the law.[105]

The law's provisions illustrate the lawmakers' determination to bring order out of chaos and regularity to a formerly freewheeling area of German life. A licensing system was set up to regulate emigration contractors and their agents. A contractor's licence required the posting of a 50,000 mark bond, while an agent had to come up with 1,500 marks. These licences for contractors or agents were available only to German citizens or associations with residences or home offices in the Reich. Moreover, the licences, which were valid throughout the Reich, were granted only for certain embarkation ports. Controls applied to agents as well. Only specially approved persons received the revocable agent licences. Both contractors and agents were required to conform to rules laid down by the Reichstag and both were under the purview of the Reich officials specifically charged with monitoring the country's emigration. Noncompliance with the rules brought swift punishment. Those soliciting emigrants were specifically prohibited from recruiting or assisting to emigrate those who still owed military service, those wanted by the police, those whose transportation costs were being assumed by foreign governments or colonial societies, and those who had contracted to work off the costs of their transportation after arriving in the new homeland. Facilitator agents or contractors were not permitted to limit the emigrant to certain destinations nor to require them to work at certain vocations upon arrival abroad.

Other provisions of the 1897 law sought to protect the emigrants by requiring the fulfillment of certain conditions by agents, ship owners, hotelkeepers, and others who dealt with the emigrants in passage. These legal provisions, which continued the tradition of legislating care for the emigrants that the Hansa cities had begun fifty years earlier, required providing protections for the migrant during the journey to the embarkation port and punctual consideration upon arrival there to see that the departing were properly informed and looked after. Regulations also covered medical examinations, hygienic conditions on board ship, provisions for the journey, and even means for obtaining legal redress for injuries or damages sustained during emigration.[106]

Although impotent outside the Reich, the new law signalled a major new policy direction in handling the emigration question. It extended the liberalizing of movement that had appeared in the abolition of passport and other documentation requirements in Bismarck's time. But the law's innovative elements relate to its implied interpretation of emigration's significance. Prior to 1897, emigration had either been sanctioned as an effective way to eliminate undesirable or surplus populations, or it had been opposed as a threat to the nation's power, strength, and well-being. Although state officials recognized the right of free movement, they had still considered it their "chief task to hinder secret or illegal emigration in order to protect the country from any possible damage that emigration might cause. In practice this often meant obstructing emigration."[107] Thus the police in the 1870s and 1880s kept tabs on agents and brokers, just waiting for the chance to expel or bring charges against offenders under earlier anti-solicitation laws. The 1897 statute broke decisively with this negative tradition. Not only did the law commit the state and government to accept the citizen's right to move freely within and without the country but it provided measures to safeguard and guarantee this freedom. In Monckmeier's words, "With the new law an end was made to invoking the law as a tool to oppose emigration. The basic right of free movement was not only recognized but also incorporated into the legal system. For those who have decided to leave the country the law will provide the guarantee that their decision can be carried out not only without the danger of suffering exploitation and fraud but also under relatively favourable conditions."[108] After 1897 German emigrants possessed guarantees of noninterference and support for their planned departure unheard of in earlier times. A similar solicitous spirit prompted Italy's government to pass a comparable law shortly thereafter (the Passport Law of 1901), which also provided protection for emigrants from various commercial interests and guidance and assistance in departing.[109]

If the new law confirmed the liberal ideal of free individuals deciding their moves independently of the state, it possessed possibilities for the nationalist cause as well. Certain provisions within the law (sections 6 and 7 particularly) allowed the state to influence where migrants settled. For example, state control over the licensing of agents and contractors represented one way to guide "proper" emigration by licensing only agents for specific lands. The Reich's chancellor also had the authority to waive bonds for those migration societies seeking to promote group settlements in favoured lands. If the law were manipulated correctly, as many imperial promoters hoped, "it would benefit the fatherland both through discouraging emigration to unsuitable places while at the same time encouraging it to those lands that could serve Germany's interests."[110] In the decade before the Great War, when relations between Great Britain and the German Empire had soured, the 1897 law offered Berlin an opportunity to steer emigration to areas of the world, such as Argentina or Brazil, where British influence was slightest. If such a positive emigration policy were pursued and the settlement of Germans in South America cultivated properly by authorities in the Reich, nationalists believed, emigration would cease to represent a national loss.

Canada's Problems in Implementing Its German Policy

After four decades of experience and experiments with migration, both Canada and Germany had by the end of the nineteenth century finally settled on some definite approaches. In both countries, as discussed, the framing of policies and procedures occurred in conjunction with the growth of the national state's power and authority. For both Canada and Germany, the migration issue had become intertwined with not only the state's expanding role but also with the maturation of each country's nationalism. Both state pretensions and national ambitions contributed directly to the impasse that developed between Germany and Canada in the 1890s over migration. This impasse obstructed or prevented Reich farmers from participating as they might have in the settlement of Canada's west.

The origins of the German opposition to emigration to Canada lay in the Macdonald/Bismarck age. Although neither country had followed a clearly defined migration plan in these years, each state nevertheless discovered basically what it did or did not wish to see transpire in the transfer of population between them. Briefly put, the Germans did not wish to lose farmers to Canada; Canada did not want any Germans except farming ones. The rough treatment and incarceration of John Dyke in 1873 for soliciting rural Prussians for Canada's farms presaged ill for the future relations between the two states on this issue. From Dyke's time on, it was obvious that Germany meant to do whatever was necessary to prevent the loss of its agriculturalists to the former British colony. It was equally apparent that without a vigorous effort on Canada's part to have Berlin soften or abandon this opposition, the movement of migrants from the Reich to Canada would be frustrated.

From the 1890s on, Canada's knowledgeable immigration officials knew of Berlin's determined hostility toward Canada's soliciting farmers in the Reich. In July 1891, John Lowe wrote, "The Germans will not permit any representations of any kind to be made by agents to promote the emigration of German subjects." They effectuated this prohibition for Canada, he continued: "No German immigration agents are allowed to book immigrants to Manitoba, on pain of forfeiting their licenses."[111] Four years later, Sir Charles Tupper, Canada's high commissioner, described the same German obstructionism. "The German government policy," he informed T. Mayne Daly of the Immigration Branch in September 1895, "is against emigration, no matter by whom it is encouraged, and the laws in Germany prohibit the dissemination of emigration literature except to persons who ask for it."[112] An occurrence in 1893 dramatized for the dominion's immigration officials the results of attempting to circumvent the German prohibition.

The precipitating event was a challenge by the resident CPR agent in Amsterdam, R.R. Toe Laer, to the German prohibition of overt solicitation. According to John Dyke, who knew about such matters first-hand, the impatient Toe Laer acted from a belief "that things [in Germany] were not being pushed fast enough." On his own initiative, the CPR man "flooded the different army depots in Germany and especially in Hanover with Canadian Pacific Railway printed matter."[113] More precisely, he "broadcast distribution of Manitoba and the Canada Northwest folders and pamphlets."[114] Since Toe Laer resided outside Germany, he could not be held accountable under German law for such defiance, but German agents and steamship personnel working on behalf of Canada within the Reich were legally liable. The Hanoverian government decreed that it was henceforth illegal for any agent working within the Reich specifically to promote any emigration to Canada's west. Defiance of this prohibition would bring an immediate suspension of the agent's licence.

Speculation abounded in Ottawa over what appeared to be a serious German overreaction. It seemed particularly unfair to single out Canada's North West as forbidden territory when the United States, which had removed many more Germans than Canada ever had, faced "no prohibition against booking Germans to Minnesota or Dakota."[115] In a November 1894 letter to the deputy minister of the interior, the former agent William Wagner tried to explain the German position. According to Wagner, the German opposition to Canada's solicitation was due to the dominion's exclusive agrarian recruitment. While the Americans recruited indiscriminately (taking, for example, unwanted, unemployed labourers), Canada focused on precisely that group which the Germans were most concerned in retaining at home, particularly in Prussia during the last two decades of the nineteenth century.

In his letter Wagner described both the historical background to and modern reasons for the Prussian policy. According to him, Prussia's need for peasants had roots that extended back to the partition of Poland during the reign of Frederick the Great in the eighteenth century. At that time the Hohenzollern kingdom acquired extensive lands formerly worked by Polish peasants. The Prussian program of land reform in the early nineteenth century and the abolition of serfdom in 1848 had transformed the social structure of these lands, creating not only a proprietary peasant class but also a rural proletariat out the resident population's less successful elements. These had emigrated during the 1870s and 1880s in significant numbers, leading to a dearth of necessary labourers in Prussia's east. To remedy this situation, the Prussian government passed a bill in 1886 to facilitate the settling of the provinces of Posen and West Prussia with German peasants and labourers. To do this, Berlin had purchased a number of large estates, divided them into smaller farms of 20 to 100 hectares and then offered them to German purchasers at low-interest, government-backed loans. Over the years 1891-4, Wagner claimed, the government had settled on these lands "1,500 families of which at least half would have come to Canada."[116] In short, Canada's solicitation of farmers competed directly with Berlin's settlement policy.

The Canadian response to the impasse that developed in the 1890s in Germany reflected the timidity and lack of forthrightness typical of so much of its past policy. Despite the progressive spirit and more aggressive immigrant proselytizing generally characteristic of the Laurier/Sifton years, Canada's German policy continued to exhibit a traditional ineffectiveness. Awareness was widespread that things were not working out in Germany as well as immigration advocates might have wished. In April 1895, T. Mayne Daly pointed out for Sir Charles Tupper the disappointing realities of Canada's efforts: "We are doing very badly [at recruiting in Germany], so badly that the fear of doing worse need not restrain us from considering adopting new measures."[117] By this, Mayne Daly meant confronting the Germans with a more aggressive representation in Berlin. He urged the appointment of an official Canadian government agent stationed in Germany, both to pursue potential immigrants and to plead the dominion's cause.

Without much apparent agonizing, Canada's immigration officials responded negatively. John Dyke, for one, summarily nixed the idea of appointing a Canadian agent to Germany. In a letter to J.G. Colmer, he wrote, "I do not see how he [an official Canadian agent in Germany] could keep clear of the [charge] of inciting to emigrate, a very elastic term in German official minds. Offers of free grants of land would be certain to bring about punishment."[118] In fact, Dyke urged no present action for fear of making matters worse than they already were. "I feel confident," he wrote three weeks later, "that if any effort is made to remove the restrictions it will result in further orders being issued which will make it almost impossible to promote emigration from any part of the German Empire. We are doing well under the circumstances."[119] Colmer apparently concurred with Dyke's "don't rock the boat" analysis, for several weeks later he wrote Sir Charles Tupper urging the high commissioner to ignore the prohibition against Canadian solicitation efforts because energetic protestations might induce an even more extreme reaction from the Germans: "The game is not worth the candle."[120]

For his part, Tupper agreed with Dyke and Colmer. To start with, he did not believe the German position could be significantly altered, so appointing an agent to soften German opposition seemed futile. "With regards to the appointment of government agents," Tupper wrote Mayne Daly in September 1895, "I do not think ... that officers of the kind, especially in Germany, would do us much good." He recalled Dyke's experiences: "You will remember Mr. Dyke was once imprisoned for engaging in work of this kind, and it would not be good policy in my opinion, to make a parade of any intention on our part in the direction of increased activity." Tupper therefore agreed that in the matter of German immigration, Canada "must let sleeping dogs lie." If the dominion were to act at all, it had to move circumspectly to avoid exacerbating the situation. Instead of official agents, he recommended that steamship companies do the recruiting, but he warned that "the steamship companies have to work quietly."[121]

Tupper's reliance on steamship companies and their agents presented several problems. Canadian agents such as Toe Laer were discriminated against and clearly disadvantaged in Germany. German shipping agents did exist, but they also were clearly controlled, as official German policy disfavouring emigration in general supported out-migration only to places other than Britain's colonies. By the end of the century not only was emigration from within Germany manipulated but emigrants from without the Reich who passed through on their way west were closely controlled as well. Designed allegedly to prevent the spread of cholera, this new German control was exercised through stations established on the Reich's eastern borders, through which any westward-travelling emigrant from Russia or Austria-Hungary was required to pass. Manned by representatives of the German shipping lines North German Lloyd and Hamburg-American (HAPAG), these control stations permitted entry into the Reich only to those who held valid tickets on a ship of these lines departing from Bremen or Hamburg. Emigrants with tickets from another shipping firm were turned away and had to circumvent Germany to reach their Atlantic embarkation port. These controls affected not only Slavs and Jews travelling west but also ethnic Germans from the Russian or Hapsburg Empires. Since a significant number of these Germans were destined for Canada, this control process affected Canada directly. The German ticketing requirement influenced not only the travel arrangements of individual emigrants desiring to reach Canada but also the shipping business of the Canadian Pacific Railway. Throughout the two decades before the outbreak of war in 1914, Canada's immigration officers complained loudly about this German effort to monopolize the Atlantic migration trade.[122]

Travel to Canada

In general, by the end of the nineteenth century overseas travel between Europe and Canada had become both speedier and safer than previously. "The replacement of sails by steam and the consequent shortening of the ocean voyage," a 1909 report announced, "have practically eliminated the problem of a high death rate at sea. Many of the evils of ocean travel still exist but they are not long enough continued to produce death. At present a death on a steamer is the exception and not the rule. Contagious disease may and does sometimes break out and bring death to some passengers. There are also other instances of death from natural causes, but these are rare and call for no special study or alarm."[123] Passage was more comfortable than ever before. Although the slick Canadian propaganda publications that presented flattering pictures of clean, neat, roomy sleeping quarters, smoking rooms with comfortable furniture, and well-lit and nicely furnished dining facilities were exaggerated, arrangements in 1910 for those travelling in steerage or third class greatly exceeded in comfort what the previous generation of immigrants had known.[124] This improvement was attributable to such amenities as fresh running water, electric lighting, steam heat, infirmary facilities, better lavatories, dining halls with seating, more personal space per passenger, and superior service from ship personnel.

Although the vessels of all the major transatlantic shipping firms provided enhanced passenger comfort in the two decades before the Great War, the German ships in particular set the pace. Both the North German Lloyd and the Hamburg-American Line produced "beautiful, dashing," truly remarkable ships at this time. According to the shipping historian Terry Coleman, from 1890 to 1910, "the Germans owned the Atlantic." During this twenty-year span, the North German Lloyd, the more successful of the two firms, "carried almost a quarter of the total of the entire Atlantic passenger trade." This included all classes, from first to steerage. German success, Coleman claims, derived from speed, size, and also significant comfort. North German Lloyd's *Kaiser Wilhelm II*, for example, astonished nearly everyone "with its 14,350 tons, its 22½ knots and its imposing four funnels" but even more so with its amenities. On the North German Lloyd ships, Coleman writes, "the food was good. The ships' bands were famous. Only musicians were employed as second class stewards and they played on deck every morning at eleven. One American passenger said even the seasick were reheartened. Who, he asked, would ever forget the sweet, deep pleasure of being wakened on Sunday morning by the playing of 'Nearer My God to Thee'?"[125]

Despite such coddling, inconveniences still existed for many steerage passengers at this time. Steerage conditions differed significantly among the ships transporting immigrants overseas. On the older vessels, which continued to provide old-style steerage, and on those that had undergone only partial renovation and offered a combination of old and new steerage arrangements, abuses continued.[126] Almost all complaints directed at conditions on these ships involved either overcrowding or the resultant problems with hygiene or morals. Despite the fact that, as a rule, ships carrying immigrants from northern Europe were newer than those transporting persons out of southern Europe, and thus offered old-style steerage less often, the northern route still had its steerage problems. In 1910 German officials had to defend the old-style steerage on the *Kaiser Wilhelm der Grosse* from criticism raised by the Reichstag member and founder of the St. Raphaels-Verein, Peter Paul Cahensly, that the vessel's steerage was too crowded and inadequately equipped to maintain proper moral standards. The doctor who responded to Cahensly's charges insisted that the *Kaiser Wilhelm der Grosse* (and the other North German Lloyd ships) met all the standards for safety and hygiene required by German law. His inspection, he claimed, revealed appropriate dining procedures, cabin sizes, toilet and bathing facilities, and ventilation arrangements. Refuting the accusation of unacceptable hygienic conditions, he described the dishes and cutlery provided the steerage passengers as "brand new." The "sinks providing fresh running water," he insisted were "sufficient in number so passengers could easily wash their dishes."[127] But even if the physical arrangements had been upgraded in the older ships, the traditional complaints about food persisted. The issue was no longer the amount or the condition of the food before cooking, but preparation and serving on board. A captious passenger travelling in steerage to Canada in 1910 apparently captured the sentiment of many when he asserted that "if you abstain from exact analysis, it is possible to get through your meal without getting sick."[128]

Conclusion

In the quarter-century from 1890 to 1914, both Canada and Germany witnessed the maturation of programs and ambitions only partially perceived or incompletely expressed before 1890. In the economic sphere, both states experienced major growth and development. Germany's industry equalled and in some areas overtook the British, particularly in the chemical and electrical industries. "Made in Germany" became a watchword for quality, and engineering students beyond the Reich learned the German language. In Canada, modern industrial take-off occurred in the country's burgeoning eastern urban centres while the volume of agricultural output, the fruits of the rapidly developing western prairies, amazed all observers. King wheat did indeed reign in these halcyon years. Politically, Canadian efforts to assert independence from both the United States and Great Britain made significant progress as Macdonald's empire to the west was populated and tied to both the east and west coasts. Meanwhile, the Reich successfully entered the world stage as a major political player. Thus, in both countries modern nationalism came of age, reaching its highest level of influence thus far. In Germany the country's parts had come together as national sentiment fused with the new imperialism. In Canada the nationalist movement developed a different momentum, since it possessed both a French Canadian expression and an English Canadian version. Although English Canada's attachment to the British Empire made reconciling the two indigenous nationalisms problematic, Ottawa pursued as much as possible a rigorous dominion-first policy.

These several ideological, political, and economic developments all affected migration: as the economic and political context changed, the patterns of migration followed suit. Germany's third major wave of out-migration ended in the early 1890s, and emigration had all but ceased by 1914 as a result of industrialization. As the German industrial base expanded, labour needs and opportunities did also. Available industrial jobs drew agricultural workers off the land to the cities. Farm labour thus became a sought-after commodity, especially in eastern Germany. Across the ocean, the needs of Canada's National Policy promoted almost exclusively agricultural workers or farmers as immigrants. Employing the traditional romantic/civilized image of the Canadian frontier, those soliciting for Canada advertised for settlers to live on newly created western farms. Although positive responses came from Germans living beyond the Reich in Austro-Hungary or Russia, Germany itself provided only a handful of new Canadian farmers between 1890 and 1914. The number of potential German farmer-immigrants for Canada had shrunk dramatically in the two decades before 1914. To make matters worse, Germany's desire to retain what was left of its agriculturalists led to prohibitions against Canada's farmer recruitment policies.

Ultimately, the responses of migration officials in both countries to each other's contradictory policies led to an impasse, and both sets of policies failed. The German government was unable to restrain its peasants from drifting to the cities, and Canada's efforts to secure peasant immigrants from the German Reich as reinforcement for the Arcadian myth of Canadian rural bliss likewise came to naught. Clearly, the Canadian solicitation effort was largely, if not wholly, inappropriate for the newly industrialized, expanding world power Germany. The land whose ships dominated the transatlantic passenger-carrying business between 1890 and 1910 ferried nearly none of its own people to Canada. In large measure this was because of that very industrial success that had produced those ships. Germany, the world industrial power, offered such opportunities at home that the historical transoceanic migration of its people had become passé.

Despite the differing reasons underlying migration policy in the German Empire and the Canadian dominion, similarities also existed in the views and handling of such policies. In both lands, new attitudes toward and appreciation of population migrations emerged in the period 1890-1914, and in both, perceived national needs determined policy. The German central government finally adopted what Wilhelm Monckmeier labelled "positive emigration politics" when it assumed a role in regulating the out-migration of its citizens with the imperial law of 1897. This statute clearly accorded with the increasingly popular view that a stable or expanding population constituted a national asset too valuable to be squandered by inattention or indifference. Berlin's support for agencies to assist if necessary and to dissuade when possible those contemplating emigration illustrates the changed thinking. So also does the effort to influence the direction of the flow abroad and the desire to tie those groups and individuals already settled overseas more closely to the fatherland. The primacy of foreign affairs *(Primat der Aussenpolitik)* influenced emigration policy just as it did so much of Germany's domestic politics in the years before the First World War.

In Canada, the importance of immigration loomed large enough for Ottawa to promote a policy calling for larger-than-ever numbers of immigrants, and to draw on new sources in eastern and southern Europe, thus risking a change in the country's traditional cultural makeup and ethnic balance. In effecting this change, Canadian immigration officials had been obliged to move down the "Great Chain of Race" from the preferred Anglo-Celts to less desirable groups. Although some Canadians considered the importation of non-English-speaking Slavs and Italians a danger to Canada's English and French culture, Ottawa largely ignored the nativist objection. Responding instead to pressures from Canada's business leaders who demanded additional labour regardless of ethnicity, Ottawa did not implement exclusionary measures "in such a manner as to significantly restrict the immigration of central and southern Europeans."[129] The break with tradition was justified as necessary to thwart the threat of possible American expansion onto the prairies. In this instance, political nationalism took precedence over cultural racism.

Finally, the new immigration and naturalization laws passed in the decade before 1914 indicated a major shift in the role of the state. By the eve of the Great War, it had become clear that decisions on the admission or retention of immigrants remained entirely within the purview of the executive branch of the federal government. Ottawa could deport or naturalize at will. With these wide powers, the sovereign, modern Canadian state thus assumed the exclusive position of defining just who might become full-fledged members of the Canadian community. Its role in defining any future German migration to the dominion had been set well before the guns began to fire in 1914.

4
Interwar Migration, 1919-39

The Great War, which began in August 1914, disrupted life in Europe and the world in unimaginable ways. Governments, social conventions, economic traditions, and ideological assumptions were all changed profoundly. The disruption of previous economic and political relations transformed European migratory patterns as well. As Carl Strickwerda writes, "The First World War marks a decisive break in the history of migration as it does in world history. The war destroyed the international regime of the nineteenth century while the nationalism and ideological conflict resulting from the war prevented any new international regime from emerging."[1] Thus, the migration of Germans to Canada during the interwar years could not avoid reflecting the war's impact in manifold ways. Most obviously, as belligerents on opposite sides, intercourse between the two countries ceased during the conflict. When German immigration into Canada recommenced in 1923, it closely mirrored the profound political, social, and economic alterations that had occurred in both states. Then beginning in 1929 the worldwide Depression, itself a direct legacy of the Great War, closed off migration between Canada and Germany nearly as completely as had the war. Since these events are so pivotal, a general consideration of how they affected both countries seems in order before commencing a more detailed discussion of interwar migration.

Impact of the Great War and Depression
As it was in countries on both sides of the conflict, news of the war's outbreak was greeted enthusiastically in English Canada as the country rallied to defend Great Britain, the empire, and civilization against the alleged forces of evil. Most Canadians shared the near-universal view that the war would be short and glorious. The federal government acted promptly and passed the War Measures Act, which granted Ottawa sweeping powers to do whatever it deemed necessary to win the war.[2] This translated into raising an army, providing for its material needs, and seeing that critics of the war

effort were silenced. Under the War Measures Act, enemy aliens including Germans were required to register with the government and carry identity cards, restricted in their movements, and prohibited from owning firearms. German-language newspapers were also suppressed.[3] As the war dragged on, many of the restrictions on property and civil liberties placed on the so-called enemy aliens were extended to include other Canadians, and the role of government expanded accordingly: "By 1918 the governors had become regulators and controllers, the governed regulated and controlled."[4] By the war's end in 1918, Canada had lost its innocence. Beyond the ghastly battlefield casualties and the huge material costs of supporting the war effort, the struggle had altered Canadian life in other important ways. Generational attitudes, political parties, French-English relations, women's rights, and labourers' and farmers' expectations were all profoundly affected. As Canada moved into the 1920s, a new set of political, social, and economic forces had been set in motion.[5]

The war's impact in Germany was even more dramatic. Because Germany lost, the disappointments in general exceeded those experienced by Canadians. But at the conflict's beginning Germans, like Canadians, went off to war enthusiastically, believing it would be both short and beneficial. As the war continued, opposition grew among workers, socialists, and other early skeptics. The announcement in early November 1918 that the war was lost greatly shocked a people who had for over four years heard only of impending victory.[6] By then the war's cost in lives ruined or lost and wealth expended exceeded even the most pessimistic projections. The sufferings at the front and the deprivations experienced at home by noncombatants brought revolution to the streets. The new western-styled liberal government, the Weimar Republic, which survived the chaos, was then saddled with the responsibility of accepting the peace agreement fashioned by the victors in Paris. To the overwhelming majority of Germans, the Versailles Treaty required a *maxima culpa* well beyond reason. Many considered the requirement to pay reparations for the costs of a war forced upon them egregiously unfair. Germany began the new decade under a terrible weight. Squandered resources, ruined markets, inflated prices, food shortages, dead sons, brutalized veterans, disgruntled nationalists, disillusioned liberals, and impoverished middle-class folk all boded ill for the country's future. Germany entered the 1920s in what appeared to many as a genuinely hopeless state.[7]

Although in the immediate postwar years, Canada experienced unemployment, dislocation, and deflation due to readjustment from the wartime economy, these problems did not last. The dominion's economy gradually improved as the decade progressed, thereby creating considerable prosperity, especially toward the end of the 1920s.[8] Industrial expansion occurred in such traditional sectors as furniture manufacturing but also in new areas such as the automobile industry in Ontario. In the near north, pulp and paper mills appeared for the first time in many places, new mines were sunk, and hydroelectric plants sprang up to provide for the escalating energy demands associated with these advances. For prairie farmers, the price of wheat rose enough in the last half of the decade to inspire both widespread hope for the future and practical plans for expansion. Immigration from Europe resumed, and the West once more absorbed the majority of the newcomers. When Wall Street crashed in October 1929, signalling the end of the good times, neither Ottawa nor the country were prepared for the economic disaster which soon befell the dominion.

Germany experienced economic catastrophe rather sooner. The war's losses in manpower and productive capacity, the revolutionary chaos of the immediate postwar years, and the disastrous influence of substantial war reparations were readily apparent in the early 1920s. The classic hyperinflation that swept Germany in 1923 not only destroyed the life savings of much of the country's dependable middle and working classes but it left psychological scars as well. In Peter Pulzer's words, it "created a climate of profound insecurity, the after effects of which lasted a generation or more."[9] After the war German agriculture entered a period of extended crisis.[10] Because of the severity of the agricultural problem, the Weimar government remained adamantly opposed to German farmers emigrating throughout the 1920s. Despite the restoration of the country's currency, and the political stability and rising industrial production from 1924 to 1929, the country's economic system had not recovered enough to withstand the economic crisis that befell Germany as it did Canada in the fall of 1929. The economic catastrophe undermined the fragile political order as well. The Weimar Republic, Germany's first real attempt at a liberal, democratic order, collapsed, and the resulting political void was soon filled by a once obscure Austrian, Adolf Hitler.[11]

Although the Depression severely strained Canada's liberal traditions and institutions, its parliamentary system remained intact.[12] By 1930, however, the Depression's burden had grown more and more onerous and the inability or unwillingness of the Liberal government to act decisively to combat it became more and more apparent. In the fall of that year, Canadians elected a Conservative government, but Conservative efforts to cope made little headway and the economic crisis continued. Canada's basic problem during the Depression, the country's dependency on exports in a contracting world market, could not be solved cosmetically.[13] Demand for Canada's wheat, minerals, and wood pulp had dropped off precipitously after 1929. In the West, the wheat economy nearly died as grain prices dropped from $1.60 per bushel in 1929 to $0.38 in 1930. Although central Canada began to pull out of its slide as early as 1935 and was followed by much of the rest of the country soon thereafter, the West remained depressed until the outbreak of war in the fall of 1939.[14]

The German economy suffered business failures and unemployment after 1929 just as Canada did, but with a much more severe scope and scale. In 1932 German industrial production was half of what it had been in 1928. Unemployment had ballooned to 30 percent, not including many women who had been employed part-time before 1929 and lost their jobs thereafter. Germany's governors tried at first to deal with the crisis by adopting a deflationary policy of cutting government expenditures while raising taxes. This only exacerbated the crisis and paved the way for the triumph of the National Socialists in January 1933.[15] Shortly thereafter, Hitler and his party moved to consolidate power. After destroying his political opponents, the socialists, democrats, liberals, and any other potential threats, Hitler turned his attention to bringing the other facets of German society under control. By 1935 the domestic Nazi revolution was largely complete: Germany had been turned into a model totalitarian state run exclusively by Hitler and his Nazi Party.[16] Germany began a crash program of military expansion that included huge public works projects and armament production, both of which required workers. Within a year, Germany's unemployment had disappeared and economic expansion had begun.[17] In Hitler's Reich, the Depression, which continued to plague other industrialized nations including Canada, was over.

Although the liberal Canadian and totalitarian German approaches to controlling their populations differed fundamentally during the 1930s, both states did share in the general postwar trend to increased documentary control. Initially, those who supported the reintroduction of passports and other documentary devices to register population had intended the move to be temporary, but many of the controls introduced during the conflict remained after the guns fell silent. The crucible of war had induced European states to tighten their border controls. Believing documentary requirements would permit the nation-state's functionaries to distinguish more efficiently between "us" and "them," many considered the new passport regimes necessary to cope with mass postwar migrations of refugees and forced transfers of allegedly "undesirable" nonnationals.[18]

Both Canada's and Germany's participation in the new passport regime developed in step with most other western states. The Canadian passport, which had existed since 1862 but was only sparingly utilized before the Great War, evolved rapidly once hostilities began. In 1915 Canada abandoned its single-sheet form stamped with an official Canadian seal, and adopted a more complex British-styled document with ten sections folded together. In the 1920s, the dominion initiated additional changes. In 1921 it adopted the booklet-type passport, and in 1926 it began issuing its document in both French and English. From 1930, Canada provided passport services abroad at Canadian consular centres rather than, as previously, at British consular offices. In the interwar period, Germany's extension of the passport regime was even more comprehensive. Not only were passport usages extended and services provided for Germans travelling abroad, but documentary control was extended over nontravellers residing at home. In 1935, following the Soviet precedent, the National Socialists introduced an internal passport, the so-called "work book." Recording residence and employment information, this document monitored Germany's labour pool and assisted in allocating the country's work force as well. Other documentary controls followed, even ones designed to track beggars and vagabonds. The climax came with the 1937 Law on Passports, the Foreigner Police, and Residential Registration, As Well As on Personal Identity Documents, which combined "internal and external types of registration and documentary controls on movement" for all Germans. This comprehensive, "embracing" system could be employed against both "good" Germans and alleged enemies of the Volk, such as Jews.[19] This documentation, combined with the Nazi coordination *(Gleischaltung)* policy, decreed that the German people would now be controlled more completely than any eighteenth-century German would-be-absolutist-prince imitator of Louis XIV could have dreamed.

Immigration Policy and Migration Controls in Canada

By the time of Hitler's takeover in 1933, both the pool of German immigrants available for Canada and the Canadian desire for them had largely dried up. Nearly all Germans who emigrated to Canada in the interwar period made their moves between 1923, the year Canada's prohibition against admitting Germans was raised, and the full onslaught of the Depression in 1930. At its peak levels, the 1920s migration resembled the preceding century's waves of emigration. The available statistics show how dramatically this fourth wave of German emigrants swelled and then receded in the twenty years after the war. According to Hartmut Bickelmann, Germany's postwar migration went through several distinct phases. Directly after 1918 emigration was modest. Then it picked up momentum, reaching a climax in 1923, when over 115,000 Germans departed. This figure compared favourably with the yearly totals from the last great wave of emigrants, during the years 1881-4. After 1924 the numbers leaving the country levelled off for several years at between 50,000 and 60,000 per year, twice as many as in the years immediately preceding 1914. In 1930 the numbers dropped again, remaining just over 10,000 annually until the beginning of the Second World War in 1939. Overall, Bickelmann concludes, Weimar Germany and Hitler's Reich lost about 600,000 people to emigration. This figure does not include the estimated 70,000 German Jews who fled the country between 1933 and 1939.[20]

As in the past, only a small percentage of Germany's emigrants selected Canada as their future homeland. Again, part of the explanation for this lay in Canada's approach to immigration. During the interwar period, Canada's immigration policy underwent a major transition from the generously liberal prewar policy to being much more restrictive after the onslaught of the Depression in 1929. This transformation was caused not only by economic forces but also by administrative and legal changes. The most important administrative development was the extrication of immigration from the Department of the Interior with the establishment in 1917 of an independent Department of Immigration and Colonization. From there, it was believed, the increasingly complicated and vital immigration matters could be more thoroughly managed and controlled. With the Immigration Act of 1919 and the Naturalization Act of 1920, Canada's lawmakers amended the country's immigration statutes to effect the desired more thorough oversight and control.

The dominion's immigration officers exercised their greater control by following a two-pronged approach: they became more selective in who was permitted to enter Canada, while applying the law's deportation sections more vigorously to rid the country of undesirables. Although the harsh provisions that had been instituted during the Great War were temporarily abandoned in the early 1920s and replaced by a much more receptive policy, Canada's door stood open only from 1923 to 1929. In that period, the Immigration Department tried various schemes to increase immigration. The preferred immigrants were still British, the idea being to "purify the immigration stream" by attracting as many of these as possible.[21] Ottawa first tried to recruit British immigrants by sweetening the pot. In 1922 the Canadian government instituted the Empire Settlement Agreement, which, among other things, provided transportation assistance. Likewise, the Farm Settlement Act sought to recruit British farm families for Canada's west by assisting with travel expenses, credit for land purchases, and instruction in farming techniques.

Despite the encouragement and support of the British government, which sought to use these agreements as a way of reducing the number of its own welfare recipients, the Empire Settlement and Farm Settlement schemes failed to lure the desired numbers of British citizens to Canada.[22] As a result, Ottawa was forced to increase its recruiting efforts beyond Great Britain. It did this by facilitating and encouraging the two main Canadian railways, the CPR and CNR (Canadian National Railways), to step up their recruitment efforts on the Continent. The so-called Railways Agreements, which existed from 1924 to 1929, provided the railways with freedom to recruit "bona fide" farmers and agricultural workers at will in southern and eastern Europe. In 1926 Ottawa loosened up its immigration requirements even further by introducing the permit system, which allowed into the country any immigrant whose labour Canada needed. The railway agreements and the permit system allowed thousands of non-British Europeans, including Weimar Germans, into the dominion between 1923 and 1929.[23]

The readmission of Reich Germans necessitated another significant transformation in Canadian immigration policy. For over two decades before 1914, ethnic Germans from the Reich and beyond had been welcomed as part of the grand immigration expansion associated with the age of Laurier. The war immediately changed this. As enemy combatants, Germans became *personae non gratae* and were prohibited from entering the country. The prohibition continued after the war, since policy makers and politicians alike agreed the dominion could do without any more "Huns." Nevertheless, the basic reasons supporting a liberal German immigration policy before 1914 remained in 1920. Canada still needed bodies to fill and then till its undeveloped western lands. The failure of the pro-British recruitment efforts thus paved the way for Germans not only to seek admission but to be heard as well.

Between 1919 and 1922 Ottawa received frequent requests from German nationals seeking permission to immigrate.[24] All but a few were rejected, the exceptions being those seeking to join husbands, wives, or parents already in Canada with the special permission of the minister of immigration. As the anti-German mood of the country waned in the early 1920s and the sought-after British farmers never appeared, Canadian officials began to respond more favourably to German petitioning. Soon immigration officials in Ottawa were advising German supplicants to have patience, for a change in the exclusionary policy seemed imminent. In December 1922, F.C. Blair, secretary of immigration, wrote one German petitioner these encouraging words: "The greatest opportunities here are for agricultural and domestic servant classes ... There is a great deal of cheap land in Canada and still more free homesteads left in Manitoba, Saskatchewan, and Alberta ... If you are still interested in Canada, I wish you would write me again in the course of six months."[25]

As Blair had implied, in April 1923 the enemy alien restriction in effect since 1914 was abolished by Order-in-Council. Although Germany remained on the list of "nonpreferred" countries, the official restrictions on German immigration were lifted, and any bona fide German farmer, farm labourer, or female domestic could now be admitted into the dominion at the discretion of the Immigration Department.[26] The nonpreferred label itself, after being increasingly ignored, was abolished in January 1927. Germans were reclassified as "preferred" immigrants and subject to the normal immigration procedures that, besides acceptable health and a noncriminal past, required only proof of work after arrival in the dominion or enough financial resources to tide a newcomer over until work became available.[27] This liberal policy, which resembled that under which Germans had entered Canada in the age of Laurier, lasted until August 1930, when Ottawa reversed itself again.

As the full force of the Depression struck, the permissive system promoted so vigorously since 1927 was abruptly discontinued. Misgivings about Canada's new immigrants, who were increasingly viewed as threatening the jobs of native Canadians or as undermining the purity of Canada's British-style institutions and culture, contributed directly to this change.[28] The victory of the Conservatives under R.B. Bennett in 1930 signalled a radical shift in immigration policy, as the government imposed a series of limits that produced the most restrictive admissions policy in the country's history. After 1931 essentially the only acceptable immigrants were Americans or British who brought enough support with them to tide them over until work could be found, farmers with similar assets, and the wives and children of Canadian residents. With such a pared-down list, Ottawa no longer needed nor desired to promote immigration. With the country facing the economic and social crisis of the Depression, immigration and immigration policy ceased to be a major concern for either government or citizens. The Department of Immigration and Colonization lost its independent position in 1936, demoted to branch status in the Department of Mines and Resources. Immigration policy was "reduced to an essentially explicit concept of exclusion" as it became a matter of selecting only the most economically viable candidates from those expressing an interest in the dominion. Canada's immigrant numbers dropped from 88,000 in 1931 to 11,000 in 1936.[29]

The opposite side of the migration phenomenon, the deportation of immigrants, increased almost as dramatically as incoming totals declined. In an effort to deal with widespread unemployment and overburdened welfare rolls, Canada's government consistently employed the restrictive immigration laws and the criminal code to expel immigrants considered serious risks or burdens to the state. Again, the figures reveal Ottawa's new priorities. Between 1902 and 1928 deportations had averaged about 1,000 per year; from 1930 to 1935, the worst of the Depression years, the yearly average increased to 5,700. Although deportees included a number of those accused of antigovernment agitation or of various criminal acts, most were expelled for being unemployed and without means of support.[30] German immigrants were among those deported for being public charges. According to Henry Drystek, between 1932 and 1935, the Canadian government deported more than 5,300 persons for being public charges. Over 60 percent of these were British, but 260 Reich Germans were expelled on the same grounds. Of the 260, 113, or 44 percent, had applied to be deported.

Three-quarters of the remaining 147 were forcibly removed because they allegedly refused employment, were too ill to work, demanded impossibly high wages, or believed they had a better chance for employment back in Germany.[31]

Three examples from among the Lutheran Church's emigrant advisees illustrate how the process worked. All three were young men, victims of the Depression; all three had no appeals in their deportation processes. The first, Gerhard Einstmann, had come to Canada in the spring of 1929. After working as a farm apprentice, he joined up with another young German immigrant to try trapping in northern Saskatchewan. In 1930 he abandoned trapping and moved to Prince Albert, where he worked at various jobs including farming, lumberjacking, and relief road work. He eventually married the daughter of a local farmer and moved in with his wife's parents. A threshing injury necessitated a lengthy hospital stay and a $150 medical bill. Unable to pay this, he was deported back to Germany in 1934.[32] Gustav Kiessling, the second deportee, the twenty-three-year-old son of a military officer, had immigrated to Canada from Saxony in 1927. Settling in Galahad, Alberta, Kiessling tried farming, but was also injured on the job and hospitalized. Unemployed, sick, and unable to pay either his medical bills or his daily expenses, he quickly became a charge of the Galahad municipality. Unsuccessful at finding work, Kiessling could not pay what he owed the municipality. When his bill reached $150, the local authorities sent him back to the immigration officers in Edmonton, from where his deportation was launched. Third, Helmut Balser, the seventeen-year-old son of a deceased soldier, had emigrated from Germany in May 1930. Shortly after his arrival in Canada, he took over a farm on his own, paying $100 of the total $450 asking price. Predictably, the farm failed and Balser quickly became a public charge. Moving to Winnipeg to find work, he failed at this as well. Destitute and desperate, the youth robbed a local candy store and was forthwith apprehended, tried, convicted, and imprisoned in Manitoba's Stony Mountain jail. After he served his sentence, the Canadian government deported him back to Germany in July 1936.[33]

German Migrants to Canada

Although the ranks of the deported and those who entered Canada to settle during the interwar period included Weimar Germans, they represented a relatively small portion of the total number of Germans immigrating to Canada. When Heinz Lehmann studied Canada's German community in the 1930s, he estimated that slightly over 100,000 German-speaking people migrated to the dominion during the interwar years, about 20,000 being natives of Germany proper. The other four-fifths came from eastern Europe or the United States.[34] Another migration scholar, Hartmut Bickelmann, researching the receiving lands during the period 1919-39, found the United States, Canada, Argentina, and Brazil to be the preferred places for settlement. The United States always ranked above the others in popularity, normally receiving at least three-quarters of the total migration. Canada trailed Argentina and Brazil for thirteen of the seventeen years between 1923 and 1939. Only from 1927 to 1930 did Canada rank as the second-most preferred destination. In 1930 the country took in 12.4 percent of the total Reich emigrants, compared to 3.1 percent for Brazil, 7.8 for Argentina, and 68 percent for the United States.[35] According to Canadian government estimates for the years 1927 through 1930, the actual number of Reich Germans immigrating to Canada averaged 4,476 per year.[36]

As one might expect, a profile of the 20,000 new Reich Germans who settled in Canada between the wars reveals some continuities with the past but also some new trends. Those who came were, as they had been from the end of the previous century, mostly of working age. The number of children in the group remained low compared to earlier periods when family migration predominated. From 1923 to 1937, the majority of the newcomers were between the ages of twenty-one to fifty years old. In fact, for five of these years this age cohort made up over 70 percent of the total and for only three years did it fall below 60 percent. Those under fourteen composed less than 15 percent of the group for all years except 1924 when the figure reached 17 percent; for six years children made up less than 10 percent of the total. Likewise, those over fifty were usually less than 10 percent, and from 1923 to 1930, they totalled less than 5 percent.[37]

What age data suggest, marital data confirm: from 1923 to 1934, twice as many single Germans as married persons immigrated to Canada. For eleven of those twelve years over 65 percent of the total were unmarried, and for five of those years single people exceeded 70 percent of the total.[38] Gender percentages also reflect the nonfamily nature of the immigration. Although for all German emigrants between 1923 and 1938 the gender ratios reveal a significant disparity between males and females, this disparity reversed itself during the period. In the 1920s males exceeded females by as much as 21 percent and as little as 7 percent. From 1931 on, the ratios were reversed, with females outnumbering males by between 3 and 20 percent. Nevertheless, during the height of the migration, the gender statistics favoured the males. Each year from 1926 to 1930, two to three times as many young men as women emigrated to the dominion.[39] Thus, the age, gender, and family status statistics describe Canada's interwar German immigrants as a group of youthful, working-aged, unmarried males.

Vocationally, interwar migration from Germany reflects prewar patterns. To begin with, the decline in the number of farmers and farm workers among those departing continued. From 1925 to 1930, for example, they normally composed about a fifth of the emigrant total, which reflected closely the proportion of Germans actually engaged in agricultural work. The proportion of interwar emigrants previously employed in industry ranged normally between 35 and 39 percent while those previously employed in trade registered at 15 to 17 percent. These proportions also continued prewar trends that had seen occupations other than farming and the skilled crafts increase in importance. Female domestic servants, the last major vocational category from the interwar period, became more numerous in the 1920s, as at the end of the nineteenth century. In the interwar period they represented between 16 and 22 percent of the total emigrant pool.

The *Reichsdeutsche* who migrated to Canada between the wars differed significantly from the overall picture of German-speaking migrants, nearly 80 percent of whom came from eastern Europe or the United States. According to Lehmann, the majority of ethnic Germans who immigrated to Canada between the wars were farmers or farm labourers. Whether from the Reich or elsewhere, 80 to 85 percent of all Germans settled on the land in western Canada.[40] But those Germans migrating to Canada from Germany itself, Lehmann contends, exhibited less homogeneity, being merchants, industrial workers, and other nonfarmers. Moreover, he claims they settled in other parts of the country more often. Despite the greater vocational variation in the Reich German sample, Lehmann's contention that the majority of Reich Germans did not pursue agriculture in Canada is not accurate. According to Bickelmann, emigrants from the agrarian areas of eastern Germany such as East Prussia, Brandenburg, and the Grenzmark constituted an unusually "high portion of the emigration to Canada."[41] Ottawa calculated the proportion to be as high as two-thirds.[42] Much impressionistic evidence supports the contention that even among the *Reichsdeutsche* the majority took up farming in the West after their arrival in Canada.

In the main, evidence indicating a preponderance of farmers or professed farmers among Canada's Reich German immigrants between the wars conforms closely to Canada's traditional policy of soliciting Germany's agriculturists rather than its industrial workers, merchants, or professionals. An Order-in-Council of 31 January 1923 specifically urged the recruitment of "bona fide" farmers and farm workers. A Canadian Pacific Railway memorandum from February 1929 to its agents in Germany also showed this agrarian bias by emphasizing the desirability of soliciting German nationals "who intend to occupy themselves exclusively with farming."[43]

That such a policy was implemented in Germany seems beyond doubt given abundant evidence of Reich Germans both migrating to Canada as professed farmers and then actually farming. The extant passenger lists of ships departing Bremen for Canada in the late 1920s show a heavy incidence of farmers and farm labourers among those with indicated vocations.

The North German Lloyd ship *Crefeld,* which made three trips to Canada from Bremen between June and October 1928, was representative. On these three voyages it delivered 256 passengers at Montreal, 190 of whom were Reich Germans. Of those listing occupations, 52 claimed to be farmers or farm workers, while 22 others categorized themselves as carpenters, apprentice merchants, tailors, locksmiths, chauffeurs, and the like. The remaining 116 Germans were described as either housewives or minor children. Of the 74 employable, then, better than 70 percent were agriculturalists. Other North German Lloyd ships such as the *Köln, Sedlitz, Trier, Derflinger, Yorck,* and *Stuttgart* that ferried passengers to Canada during the late 1920s also transported significant numbers of Reich German migrants intent on farming in Canada.

The high number of farmers in the *Crefeld's* passenger lists recurs in the statistics that the Lutheran Church in Canada kept on those it assisted in immigrating. From January until mid-October 1927, for example, the Lutheran Immigration Board reported assisting 924 German emigrants headed for Canada, 524 of whom were *Reichsdeutsche.* Of the 524, the Lutheran Immigration Board reported 389 claiming farmer status broken down further as follows: 184 single men, 38 single women, and 50 families with 167 members, of which 19 were men travelling alone and 5 were wives with children journeying to join their farmer husbands in Canada.[44] The church required those it sponsored to Canada to fill out questionnaires, and a small surviving collection of these shows a similar pattern of professed intention to farm upon arrival in Canada. The sample includes forty-nine questionnaires completed in the period 1925-9, most of them (80 percent) by young men under the age of thirty. Occupationally, the surveys reveal a majority (thirty-four out of forty-nine, or 69 percent) of farmers or agricultural workers among the aspiring emigrants. Many of those who hailed from nonfarm families in Germany did fulfill their avowed intention of settling on the land. Of the forty-seven whose fates in Canada are known, a majority did attempt to farm, at least at the beginning.[45]

Other nonagriculturist Reich Germans who took up farming in Canada in the interwar years are not difficult to find. For example, the twenty families who settled Loon River, Saskatchewan, in 1929 mostly had no prior farming experience. Although some hailed from Holstein, Mecklenburg, Westphalia, and even the Baltic coast, most of the group emigrated from Thuringia in eastern Germany. These would-be homesteaders had had the following vocations in Germany: eight farmers, one typesetter, one shoemaker, one tailor, two cabinetmakers, one bank employee, one sailor, two engineers, one painter, one health-spa director, and one vegetable dealer. From this list it is readily apparent that the majority were not well equipped for farming in the Canadian bush.[46]

The thousand Sudeten Germans who fled to Canada as political refugees in 1939 after the German annexation of Czechoslovakia represent an even better example of nonagriculturist Germans settling on the land. Although these *Volksdeutsche* lived beyond the Reich's borders, they resembled Reich Germans more closely than did the Mennonite farmers from Russia or the German peasants from the Austro-Hungarian Empire who had migrated in such numbers to Canada in the age of Laurier. As refugees, these former socialist party functionaries and union leaders had little choice in determining where in Canada they would end up. That decision was made by Ottawa and its agencies for settlement, the Canadian Pacific and Canadian National Railways. The two railroads divided the refugees nearly equally, with the CPR looking after 152 families and thirty-seven single men and the CNR 148 families and thirty-four unmarried men. The CPR settled its group on land in northern British Columbia's Peace River district near Tupper, where they were to develop farms on virgin land provided for them. The CNR located its charges on previously farmed land in and around St. Walburg, Saskatchewan. As might have been expected, both settlements experienced hard times and much deprivation at the beginning, for the simple reason that few had any farming experience. For the Saskatchewan group, the Immigration Branch of the CNR listed sixty-six different occupations for the 168 employable men, only 14 of whom qualified as farmers. The overwhelming majority of Saskatchewan's Sudeten German refugees were artisans (electricians, locksmiths, bakers, tailors, etc.), factory workers (glass, iron, and textile workers), or other kinds of labourers such as miners, railroad men, and truck drivers. In the Sudetenland they had been urban dwellers who had little association with farmers and less contact with farm work. Essentially the same was true of the British Columbia group.[47]

Although political asylum was the reason these Sudeten socialists immigrated to Canada, the majority of Reich German emigrants between the wars had nonpolitical reasons. As was true so often in the past, a complex mixture of push and pull factors affected their decisions. This was particularly evident during the years 1923-9, when Reich German emigration to Canada was most extensive. This seven-year stretch included the catastrophic German hyperinflation of 1923. For many of those who had seen their fortunes ruined, the improved economy in the middle of the decade could not restore their faith in the fatherland's ability to recover. Emigrants frequently appeared to be fleeing before more ill fortune befell them. Economic woes, social uncertainty, and political instability all contributed to a sense of helplessness. A contemporary, Otto Preusse-Sperber, who attributed Germany's plight more to overpopulation than the war's devastation, argued that the absence of future material possibilities drove his fellow Germans out. "It is," he wrote in 1924, "the lack of land, of raw materials, of the freedom to move which forces Germany's people to leave." In such circumstances, he continued, "Germany cannot offer a significant proportion of its people an adequate livelihood."[48] Poor employment opportunities, the absence of real prospects for advancement, and inadequate housing all played a role in emigration. In this sense, Germany's emigrants resembled the masses of southern Italians who immigrated to the United States between 1880 and 1914; that is, they left due to the "low ... substandard conditions in the zone of origin."[49] Finally, as Bickelmann points out, the desire to emigrate spread well beyond those actually experiencing economic deprivation: "It was frequently less direct suffering and unemployment, but rather the fear for the future, the prospect of possible suffering and unemployment which prompted the desire to emigrate."[50] As a contemporary German observer put it, significant numbers viewed "flight abroad ... as the only way to be saved."[51]

Bickelmann's observation about Germany's emigrants in general applied to those who ended up in Canada. D. Gleiss, a Lutheran Church observer who travelled through the German communities in Ontario, Manitoba, Saskatchewan, and Alberta in 1924, reported to the German general consul in Montreal, Ludwig Kempff, that "we Germans do not approve of emigration from Germany. However, it cannot be prevented. These emigrants leave because they see no possibility in Germany of becoming self-sufficient, of being able to start a family or of establishing themselves as independent farmers. They want to have a future but they see none in Germany."[52] Writing in the paper of the Deutsche Ausland-Institut (German Foreign Institute), Edith von Schilling, one of the settlers in Loon River, agreed. Because the "massive unemployment in Germany seemed unbearable," she wrote, the Loon River homesteaders had "sold their earthly possessions and emigrated [to Canada] with much hope in their hearts."[53] Such explanations clearly expressed what Kerby Miller in his analysis of Irish immigration to America labelled an "exile" mentality; that is, emigration appeared to be "an involuntary expatriation obliged by forces beyond individual choice or control."[54]

The Lutheran exit surveys mentioned above also support the views of Gleiss and von Schilling. The questionnaires provided space for the surveyed to describe their thoughts in their own words and specifically asked about reasons for leaving Germany. Of the forty-seven surveys still in existence, twenty-five answered that question. Seventeen emigrants indicated they were leaving for a better existence abroad; seven described a lack of opportunity for advancement at home; and one cited unemployment. Likewise, many of the letters written home by these same Lutheran-sponsored immigrants cited discouragement over their futures in Germany as basic to their decision to emigrate. For example, the married, twenty-seven-year-old Manfred von Bresler left Germany alone in April 1927 intending to establish himself in Canada before bringing his spouse to join him. His reasons for leaving Germany he described in a letter to his parents: "Our fatherland has become too crowded to provide its young people with an opportunity to advance themselves. This left no option for me, an aspiring farmer, than to venture into the world beyond Germany and seek my existence abroad. I decided to go to Canada since its borders were again open for Germans."[55] Writing home from northern Alberta in the same year, Julius Soriba, another young Lutheran advisee, described for his family both his own and a fellow immigrant's disillusionment with Germany: "My friend and companion in trouble Georg Fischer from Hildesheim is about a year and a half younger than I. His father, who died from complications following an appendectomy in October 1926, had been an estate manager. Because the prospects in Germany were so poor, his son abandoned his intention to become a real estate official and went to Canada. Thus he and I share the same reasons for emigrating."[56]

Such disappointments were echoed by older emigrants as well. A letter from Hermann Merkens, sent in January 1935 from Northmark, Alberta, to the Lutheran emigrant's mission in Hamburg is worth quoting at length.

> From 1910 to the end of July 1920, I served in the German military. Initially I was attached to the navy's torpedo and submarine section where I attained the rank of deck officer. From 1916 until the summer of 1918, I worked in the navy's air force department ... After the war, I fought against the Bolsheviks in the Baltic. From the summer of 1919 until July 1921, I was in Berlin employed in the navy's technical division ... I did all this out of devotion to the fatherland. But what kind of thanks did I receive? The government did not keep its promises. Then came that terrible inflation in which I lost everything. After that, I found a job working for a salvage business. Here I thought I had finally found permanent employment. But because the business suffered from lack of work, I lost this position as well. Having experienced one disappointment after another and not liking the idea of receiving unemployment relief, I decided to emigrate.[57]

Aside from the negative forces pushing Merkens and other disgruntled Germans out of their homeland, opposing energies pulled emigrants to Canada or elsewhere abroad. Normally, these were positive, alluring, and hopeful. Yet these pull factors often reflected wishful thoughts rather than realities. As Peter Marschalck has noted, migration is frequently determined not by awareness of actual conditions in the receiving lands but rather by what the would-be emigrant thinks these conditions are. Writing in 1924, Otto Preusse-Sperber, the head of the Reichsverband deutscher Auswanderer (Reich League of German Emigrants) complained bitterly that "The majority of [Germany's] emigrants are completely ignorant here at home and discover for the first time when they are abroad how stupid and un-worldly-wise they really are in all things having to do with emigration matters."[58]

The 1929 annual report of the Organization for Lutheran Emigrant Aid described precisely this issue when it asserted that of the 1,300 potential emigrants advised during the year by the organization's representatives, "It appeared time and again that in most cases those interviewed did not have the slightest understanding of conditions prevailing abroad but still clung to the belief that by emigrating they would be able to rid themselves of all their economic woes."[59]

Canada's Image in Germany

Perceptions come from images, and the emigrants' perceptions of Canada reflected the prevailing Canadian image in postwar Germany. Directly after the war, the indifference or ignorance among Reich Germans that had existed for so much of the preceding century was again pervasive. Writing in 1926, the German general consul in Montreal, Ludwig Kempff, claimed, "Canada for most Germans, including the educated ones, remained little more than a geographic expression synonymous with huge stretches of forest, wilderness, and the absence of culture."[60] Dr. F. Roth, another first-hand Canada observer, asserted in 1930 that "the broad public in Germany knows the 'Canadian only as one unfamiliar with European manners';[61] the commercial classes know of the land because of its wealth in fur; and the commodities traders are familiar with Manitoba I or II as a superior grade of wheat." This ignorance, Roth continued, existed basically because Canada had been unavailable for German immigration from 1914 to 1923. After the dominion had reopened its doors in the mid-1920s, interest in Canada had revived and a less vague image emerged.[62] This revitalized interwar image mirrored earlier themes but also revealed new permutations effected by the unique forces at work in that stressful period.

In the postwar years Canada still possessed a special fascination because of its huge size, its rich abundance of natural resources, and its sparse population. Because Germans were so often concerned with the problem of living space in the interwar period, Canada appeared as Germany's antithesis. Many shared the envious view expressed by C.R. Hennings, that if one considered Germany "a people without space, then Canada could be called a land without people."[63] Most commentators agreed that Canada was "a country which contains within its limits unbounded natural resources" and that these resources simply awaited the people who would exploit them.[64] Because opportunities for emigration to the United States had been curtailed in the 1920s, those who favoured emigration to Canada frequently argued that it represented "the last great piece of our earth where climate and customs were suitable for the mass settlement of the Nordic races."[65]

In general, supporters of migration to Canada emphasized two particularly positive features. First, Canada was a land of individual freedom, offering, in the words of one enthusiast, "sweet freedom, freedom in the truest sense of the word."[66] Among other things, this meant that Germans could remain culturally German if they so chose. As Reichstag member Erich Koch optimistically asserted in 1927, "the danger of forced denationalization [of Germans] did not exist in Canada."[67] In practical terms, German immigrants believed they would be allowed to have their own churches, German-language newspapers, and even some educational opportunities in Canada. This being the case, particularly in the Canadian west where most immigrants headed, they assumed that they would be able to maintain close ties to the fatherland. Second, Canada offered material advancement for those willing to work. Canadian apologists nearly always emphasized that advancement in Canada would not come without solid effort. Thus, the country needed people who were *fleissig,* or hard-working, a characteristic Germans normally prided themselves upon. Berlin's *Nordische Volkszeitung* editorialized: "What the land [Canada] lacks are people who can make the land fruitful. But not every person is suitable for or capable of doing what is required. One needs hard-working, tough, persevering types, people who can acclimatize themselves to new and unusual circumstances. If an immigrant came to Canada without illusions about having to toil, if he or she deferred seeking to own land or property until after learning the ropes, if the would-be farmer spent the first several years as a farm labourer working on someone else's land, then the individual immigrant would advance."[68] If one were both patient and hard-working, success would come.

The letters sent home by the Lutheran charges mentioned above illustrate how receptive some Germans could be to this kind of image. The romantic vision of wild, untamed Canada is exemplified by the passage from Manfred von Bresler cited in the introduction to this book and was repeated many times by other enthusiasts. One of these described the train trip from Montreal west through the great Precambrian Shield: "On Tuesday morning we entered the region around Lake Ontario. It was a fantastic trip. You can't imagine how beautiful it was. The entire day we saw nothing but rocks and water. On our left the largest lake [Lake Ontario], the other side of which you could not see. On the right huge granite rock formations, often with nothing growing on them, frequently covered by snow and ice."[69] These young Germans also expressed in their letters the belief that Canada offered peace and freedom. In Canada, for example, one could remain German and retain independence on one's own land. To understand just what this meant, one youth wrote, a person had to experience Canada first-hand: "Even if one returns to the fatherland and works there, either in the cities or on the land, he will never forget Canada. He cannot stay away. Many have gone home [to Germany] and then after two years returned. In the beginning I found it lonely here. The usual pleasures such as the theater do not exist, and yet I am better off and I feel freer here than many great men in Germany." In addition to being freer, the author continued, he felt safer in

Canada, for "in Germany one can expect only class hatred and civil war. Indeed, poor Germany! Oh, how glad I am to be out of that mess. Here the most beautiful peace reigns."[70]

Finally, the idea that Canada was a place where one could advance materially also appeared frequently in the writings of the Lutheran advisees. One young man even referred to Canada as "a land where milk and honey flows."[71] In Canada, one could both live more cheaply and acquire more wealth. In an April 1929 letter to his family in Germany, the young Gerhard Einstmann exhibited the optimism so characteristic of new arrivals who had accepted the image of Canadian material promise: "All in all, the conditions and prospects here in Canada are positive. Surely, one is better off here than in Germany when it comes to farming. For farmers living conditions here are very good. At least 100 percent better than is the case for Germany's farmers. Here one can eat as much as he wants ... Here everything is much cheaper than there."[72] Sadly, as we have seen, he was deported as an indigent in 1934.

The Volkish Movement and the Image of Canada

Such enthusiasm for Canada began to decrease rapidly after 1930, and not only because of the worldwide Depression. The spread of volkish ideology in Germany provided a new set of loyalties for Germans, whether living within the Reich or residing elsewhere. Twentieth-century volkish ideology is rooted in the romantic era of the previous century, when Germans had begun to look upon their own people, their Volk, as something special, unique, and valuable. In the course of the nineteenth century, the concept of the Volk as "a unique potency ... as something great *sui generis* alongside the state and society" evolved steadily.[73] Viewing the Volk as an independent and unique force, volkish thinkers eventually came to see in the Volk the only valid determinant of social institutions. The state and its institutions were important only insofar as they served that unique potency, the Volk.

The uniqueness of the Volk could not be defined in rational terms. Volkish greatness lay in depth of soul, in the possession of deep, subjective qualities. Each separate Volk was defined by nature and history. The authenticity of a Volk was judged on the basis of its closeness to nature, to the landscape in which it had grown and matured. Likewise, a Volk was defined by its past, by those special traditions, customs, and manners it had evolved over the centuries. Thus each Volk remained culturally distinct, unique in thought and feelings, because its soul had a history of its own. The closeness of the Volk to nature, the Volk's possession of a tradition, of a history, meant that the Volk had roots. All true Volk groups were rooted firmly, secure in the belief that they had a permanent place in nature and history. This rootedness also gave the Volk a claim to a role in the future; it made the Volk not only a unique creation but one capable of creating in turn.[74]

Originally the volkish movement insisted upon the distinctiveness, but not necessarily the superiority, of the German Volk. As the movement evolved, however, volkish thought developed in the direction of an exclusive racism. By the twentieth century, it was elitist. The special qualities that set Germans off from other ethnic groups and nationalities had become superior qualities. A volkish definition of race (i.e., the possession of certain mystical, spiritual qualities as well as physical attributes) led not only to German discrimination against other people but also to a greater sense of ethnic solidarity among members of the Volk. The astute Canadian immigration official F.C. Blair captured this volkish identity in his reflections on his 1928 German trip. "The [Weimar] government," he pointed out, "is particularly anxious to retain their German people in the border regions, such as East Prussia, Silesia, Schleswig-Holstein and others. They even went so far as to tell us that they would not favor the bringing of Germans out of neighboring states. German people, in whatever state of Europe they might reside, are regarded of much value to the interest of Germany."[75]

The volkish ideology, which spread widely in the Weimar period, was even more suited to the cultural-political revolution that succeeded in Germany in 1933. The extreme nationalism of the Nazis, their pervasive social Darwinist ideas, their glorification of the mystical-historical roots of the German people, their emphasis upon the necessity for a spiritual rather than a materialist revolution, and their intense anti-Semitism all accorded with the basic thrust of the mythical, romantic, volkish ideology. Because the volkish system suited the National Socialists so well, the triumph of Hitler greatly stimulated the volkish movement. The Nazis strongly opposed emigration of Germans, that is, genuine members of the volkish racial community leaving the fatherland. As a corollary, they favoured the return to the Reich of all members of the Volk residing outside Germany. If this were not possible, they nevertheless sought to proselytize among their far-flung racial brothers and sisters and transform them into National Socialist supporters abroad.

This being the case, German apologists for Hitler could not view Canada with anything but jaundiced eyes. Under the influence of spreading volkish ideas, a revised image of Canada appeared in Germany. The traditional romantic image of Canada as a wild, uncorrupted land of astonishing natural beauty faded, and Canada's wilderness became foreign, inhospitable, and estranging. The pro-Nazi, volkish author Karl Götz summed up this attitude in his 1938 comparison of Germany's Alps with Canada's Rocky Mountains: "How beautiful your mountains are, Germany. In the green meadows of their valleys cottages can be seen, and as one climbs higher sparkling lakes appear. Children play near these lakes." The Rockies, on the other hand, "are as cold and hard as their name. The peaks are hostile and shrouded in storm clouds. They are dark; their forests filled with oppressive gloom, their rock formations weird and lonely. Through their dreadful canyons wild rivers rush; their lakes are silent. No trace of man can be found." For Götz, who believed the German Volk could survive only on German soil amid its own race of shared blood, emigration to Canada was tantamount to racial suicide.[76]

Volkish apologists rejected not only the Canadian landscape but also its British-style liberal government and Americanized consumer society. Colin Ross, a German journalist born in Vienna to British parents, provided the most complete expression of this negative opinion in his 1934 travelogue account of Canada entitled *Zwischen USA und dem Pol* (Between the USA and the Pole). To the pro-Nazi, volkish Ross, Canada seemed artificial because the society was composed of too many different, unrelated parts; it was not united by blood nor tied together by long-standing traditions. "The difficulty," he asserted, "is that there is not yet a Canada, at least not in the sense of a nation and a Volk."[77] He cited the differences and animosities that existed between the French and the English, a division within the country that had become only too evident during the last war, when the French had opposed the Anglo-Celtic effort to defend Great Britain. "It is no accident," Ross wrote, "that monuments commemorating the World War exist only in British Ontario. In French Quebec, on the other hand, the war memorials consist of [eighteenth-century] cannons left there to remind the people of the conflict with the English."[78] In discussing Ottawa, he employed a favourite volkish metaphor: Was the capital like a heart to Canada or was it simply a watch? Was it a genuine organ, the mysterious centre of life for the living body of the Canadian nation, or only a mechanical gadget put together step by step after the designs of human technicians? Unfortunately, Ross concluded, the Canadian political system was mechanical and nonorganic.[79] Having been alienated from themselves by their artificial society and political system, Canadians were incapable of understanding true culture. Their wholehearted embracing of the materialistic and mechanical fetishes of modernity showed this. According to Ross, no significant distinction existed between America and Canada in this regard: "America has up to this point led in the mechanization of life. It bears the chief responsibility for the present crisis of the white man. Yet the huge land which extends from the United States to the North Pole is also America."[80]

In the 1930s the critical sentiments voiced by volkish ideologues were increasingly echoed in the traditional travel literature on Canada as well. The country was no longer depicted as a better version of America, that is, as a land of boundless opportunities, immigrant-friendly institutions, and ubiquitous freedom. Fritz Könekamp's travel account of Canada, which appeared in 1930, warned his readers to be wary of accounts describing Canada as the land of "milk and honey," for the opposite held sway. Similarly, Lothar

Mattheis, who travelled across the dominion in the Depression as a hobo, described in his travelogue *Irgendwo drüben in Kanada* (Somewhere over There in Canada) the reality of Canada's unemployment, deprivation, and disillusionment. Even those travel accounts that normally depicted Canada's romantic landscape and wilderness or its hunting and fishing opportunities with so much enthusiasm had cooled off. In 1931, Armin Otto Huber summed up the new disapproval when he wrote, "The romantic fire burned somewhat weaker in this environment of snow, ice, and pigsty-like trappers huts." More and more often the reports described failure and disillusionment among German migrants who had tried their luck at settling in Canada.[81]

Whether from volkish prejudice or personal disillusionment, those critics who ascribed to Canada artificiality, materialism, and alienation now also increasingly believed that German immigration to Canada was a mistake. Many felt a sense of tragedy when they considered how Canada's Germans were forced to live in an inferior "empty civilization."[82] They sympathized with the regrets of the Canadian from Thuringia whom Karl Götz quoted: "Really we have left too much behind; the fields, the fruit trees, the forested mountains, the castles ... the singing, the talking ... the Tannhäuser, the Rudelsburg, the Wartburg, the Naumburg Cathedral, Erfurt, Jena, Halle ... All this is too much."[83]

Again, the Lutheran advisees offer evidence in their letters home of this spreading general belief that emigration abroad and to Canada in particular had been a mistake. In a 1935 letter from Northmark, Alberta, a homesteader chronicled for the Hamburg mission his failures in Canada and his intense desire to return to Germany. Describing his decision to immigrate to Canada as "the greatest mistake of my entire life" and one that he "rued to this very day," he wrote, "I want very much to return to Germany but unfortunately lack the means to do so ... Most people have no idea how terrible it is here. I keep trying to sell my homestead but nobody has any money ... Perhaps you could arrange for me to work [as a ship's hand] for my passage home and then arrange a job for me when I get home?"[84] In answer, Hamburg recommended he first try to find his way to Montreal (perhaps on a cattle train as two others had done) and then turn to the German consulate there for further advice.

Another exchange of letters, this time from 1939, between Hamburg's Lutheran mission and a young former mechanic named Gotthold Roth discussed the same concerns. Roth, who described himself as "unemployed ... and living in his small block house on his homestead while enduring the extreme Canadian cold," sought the mission's help in returning home. He explained his three major concerns. First, because he could not sell his homestead, he lacked the money to pay his way home. Second, he wondered whether he could find employment upon his return to Germany. Third, since he had become a naturalized Canadian, he was unsure of his citizenship status in the new Germany. Hamburg replied that none of these concerns should deter him from returning. Roth was assured by Heinrich Brakelmann, the mission's spokesperson, that the cost of his return would be covered by Roth's sister. Brakelmann continued:

> As far as finding work in Germany, do not worry. Mechanics are in great demand here. Since you are a *Volksdeutscher* and have Canadian citizenship, before your departure for Germany you should contact the German consulate. To ensure reinstatement of your German citizenship, you must bring with you a document indicating that after the five-year required residency period you took out Canadian citizenship because otherwise you could not have owned your homestead. It is very important that you bring this document with you because it will prove that you did not view your German citizenship indifferently but were forced by circumstances to become a naturalized Canadian. With this paper, it will be possible for you to regain your German citizenship quickly.[85]

Such exchanges exhibited not only the disillusionment of the émigrés but also the inherent dualism of volkish migration policy, which campaigned to return the scattered Volk to the homeland while at the same time developing intensified volkish sympathy among Germans living permanently abroad.

Canadian Agents and Agencies to Assist Migration

Although recruiting settlers in Germany became impossible after Hitler's accession, this had not been the case in the years from 1923 to 1929. In that period, both Canadian and German emigration agents and agencies sought to promote migration out of the Reich to the North American dominion in new and more effective ways. These agents and agencies resembled earlier promoters in including both secular and religious groups, private persons and public officials, and Canadian and German participants. In fact, much interwar proselytizing and facilitating was carried out by agencies and organizations that had existed before 1914 and then re-emerged in the 1920s in response to the stressful conditions in Germany and the apparent opportunities in Canada. Although recruiters enjoyed new opportunities, they also faced different controls and state organizations than before the war.

Because of the greater degree of official control and organization, the lone-eagle, freelancing agent of the past largely disappeared in the interwar period. The extraordinary case of Alfred Schwarz illustrates the kind of opposition independent soliciting could produce in Weimar Germany. In 1927 the former Danzig resident, who had emigrated to Canada, sought to return to Germany to recruit settlers to homestead on land he owned in western Manitoba. As a boarding-house proprietor in Winnipeg, Schwarz had become familiar with the German immigrants flowing into Canada after 1923 and had decided to take advantage of the resulting opportunities in real estate. Thus Schwarz purchased a sizable parcel of land in western Manitoba near Portage la Prairie, which he hoped to sell as 160-acre (147.5 square kilometres) homesteads to incoming German immigrants. To this end, he advertised in Germany for thirty-five to forty farm families willing to accept his offer, describing the land as fertile and suitable for both grain and dairy farming. Furthermore, he offered to help his settlers through the initial period of adjustment by providing communal housing, central dining facilities, and shared farm machinery. Whatever the community produced initially would be pooled and marketed for the group as a whole. Schwarz's intentions came to the attention of the German authorities even before the promoter arrived in Germany. They deemed Schwarz a swindler, his land unsuitable for wheat growing and subject to flooding, his background as a butcher and horse trader inadequate for supervising homesteaders, and his utopian plans for group settlement as "impossible of being carried through in Canada." When the promoter reached Danzig, the authorities flatly refused to grant the "unreliable and self-seeking" Schwarz permission to recruit.[86]

Although Schwarz and his kind were disadvantaged in postwar recruitment, the Canadian government's agents generally were not, because of a fundamental shift in its recruiting tactics. The new policy, which replaced the disorganized and inefficient past procedures, resulted from Ottawa's decision to entrust the government's immigrant solicitation and recruitment to the two main railways, the Canadian Pacific Railway and the Canadian National Railways. In the Railways Agreement of 1925, the Department of Immigration and Colonization largely bowed out of the European recruitment campaign, marking, as Reg Whitaker puts it, "the high water mark of private sector participation in immigration policy."[87] Under the Railways Agreement, the railway employees involved in immigration operated as Canadian government agents. From this point on, the federal government concerned itself basically with medical examinations and visa matters, leaving the search for and winning over of immigrants to railroad agents. Ludwig Kempff, the German consul in Montreal, reported the details of this relationship to Berlin in November 1925, based upon the report he had received from W.J. Egan, a deputy minister in the Department of Immigration and Colonization.[88] Egan informed Kempff that those working for the Canadian railways in recruiting immigrants would be acting "as our agents for advising migrants" and would issue "a certificate containing information as to the occupational fitness of the migrant for Canada." Once again, the occupations Ottawa instructed the CPR and CNR to recruit were exclusively limited to "agricultural and female domestic classes and their children."

Whether the aspiring immigrant fulfilled the desired criteria of "bona fide" agriculturalist or domestic remained at the discretion of the railway agent. If the would-be immigrant appeared acceptable, the agent would issue a certificate to the migrant, who in turn would present this to the Canadian immigrant inspectors in Germany. The certificate "signed by one of these accredited agents would be regarded as binding upon the company" and "embody a guarantee of placement [in Canada on the land]." The railway agents, Egan assured Kempff, had been appointed "on account of their trustworthiness, their knowledge of Canada and their general ability to properly represent the company." The agents would "carry on their work ... without contravening the laws of the countries from which migrants come to Canada."[89]

In the recruitment efforts of the Canadian Pacific agents, the Weimar government – having abandoned the prewar ban on Canadian agents but retaining many agent restrictions – expected no deviation from past procedures. Thus, it frequently reminded the CPR chief representative in Hamburg what was permissible and what was not. In September 1924 the Reich's interior minister sent out a circular to the various shipping firms, the CPR included, warning them to avoid advertising or soliciting activities that might create "an artificial increase in the desire to emigrate." Examples of such improper stimulation had recently appeared in several of Germany's daily newspapers, in the form of advertisements requesting readers wishing to emigrate to provide names of relatives living abroad, to whom the transportation company could appeal to buy prepaid tickets for them.[90] The CPR agents were on occasion chided for their sins of commission as well. A December 1927 letter to Dr. Schroder, the CPR's chief in Hamburg, specifically cited the September 1924 circular in requesting that the CPR's problematic behaviour cease: "There appeared the following advertisement in the November 26 edition of a Königsberg daily: 'Canada! We have recently been appointed representative for the Canadian Pacific Railway in East Prussia. The CPR is the only Canadian [shipping] line that owns a railroad, hotels, and the best land for settlement. Information on tickets and other matters can be had free of charge from Herr von Keyserlink of the Travel Bureau Unitas.'" According to the minister, this type of advertising was exactly what he had described as unacceptable in his September circular, that is, the CPR was offering special advantages in Canada after the immigrant's arrival there: "It was suited to cause an artificial increase in the desire to emigrate and publications of this sort must be stopped immediately."[91]

Despite such reprimands and the German government's continued dissatisfaction with the CPR's activities, the railway retained its recruitment privileges in the Reich. As the decade progressed, the scale and scope of the CPR's involvement in German recruitment increased dramatically, as did the number of its agents working the Reich. In 1925 there were only two

CPR agents for the whole of Germany, but by 1929 there were fifty-one. Fully two-thirds of them resided and worked in either Prussia (thirteen) or Baden/Württemberg (twenty-one), areas from which Canada's Germans had traditionally originated.[92] As the agent numbers increased, so did the CPR's concern that its business interests continue successful. An interdepartmental memo from February 1929 described the CPR's escalating ambitions for "the immigration of persons to Canada who intend to engage in farm work exclusively." The Hamburg CPR office received from the Canadian government instructions on the number of farmers and female domestic servants desired as well as the dates they should arrive in Canada and where they were to be sent. For example, in the period 15 March to 15 August 1929, Toronto should receive eighty-five farmers and female servants and Montreal sixty-five. The same memo announced that the Canadian government would like to see 665 Reich German immigrants arriving in Winnipeg in that period. The 665 total included, among others, 50 male farmers nominally Christian, 250 Lutheran farmers, 250 Catholic farmers, 50 Lutheran female domestics, and 25 Catholic ones.[93]

Rivalling the CPR in immigration recruitment efforts, the Canadian National Railways also developed staffing and policies in the late 1920s designed to tap into the German immigrant pool. Because the CNR lacked the CPR's shipping capacity, in 1925 it worked out an agreement with Bremen's North German Lloyd shipping firm to transport its recruits to Canada. From its centre in Rotterdam, the CNR coordinated agents in Germany who pushed Canada on potential migrants as vigorously as the rival CPR. In making exaggeratedly positive claims for Canada, CNR representatives irritated the German authorities every bit as much as the CPR officials did.[94] In its recruitment efforts, the CNR also utilized German and Canadian religious agencies as affiliates, founding both a Catholic Immigration Aid Society and a Canadian Lutheran Immigration Society specifically for recruitment purposes. A November 1928 memorandum from F.C. Blair's office in the Department of Immigration described these two agencies as "designed to co-operate with the Canadian National Railway in handling immigration from the Continent."[95] Both affiliates enjoyed considerable success. In 1929, for example, the CNR's Catholic society assisted 928 Catholic Germans to Canada, and the following year, the railway's Lutheran organization moved 567 immigrants to the dominion, with "399 coming directly from Germany." Of the 567 total, "360 came to pursue agricultural work."[96]

Germany's Laws and Efforts to Combat Emigration

When the Great War ended, emigration from Germany was still governed by the Reich's law of 1897. Because the nation's defeat had changed the circumstances of German life so drastically and prompted, among other things, massive out-migration, a new debate over emigration arose almost immediately. The war's destruction of so many young men and so much of the country's productive forces, the confiscation of Germany's former colonies, and the burden of war reparations forced the Germans to rethink their emigration policy. The opposition to emigration that had long existed in one form or another now intensified. In an April 1919 lecture delivered in Hamburg to the Deutsche Auslandsarbeitsgemeinschaft (German Foreign Lands Study Group), Dr. W. Jung spoke for many when he asserted, "After the terrible damages caused by the war and the hunger blockade, we need everyone here in Germany. There is enough work for all; a massive emigration would be a national disaster ... Those who emigrate are irreplaceable. Among the emigrants, persons between the ages twenty to thirty compose between 60 to 70 percent of the total. Those are exactly the strong people we need."[97] From such concerns, a demand arose in Germany during the 1920s for a more positive emigration policy, meaning a policy based on new restrictions and more extensive planning. To avoid the threatening "national disaster," increasing numbers came to believe that the fundamental right of Germans to migrate, a right explicitly guaranteed in the Weimar Republic's constitution, should be amended. Moreover, the called-for "more positive policy" should include a central planning agency that would channel necessary emigration abroad to closed settlements so as to strengthen the nation rather than debilitate it. Despite the debate's intensity and the numerous proposals which emerged from it, an updated comprehensive emigration law to replace the 1897 statute never appeared. As Karl Thalheim noted in 1926, the German government was caught in the midst of economic collapse and demands for reparations, and lacked the resources to introduce and fund the changes that such a new law would require.[98]

Even though the efforts to create a new blanket law failed, the Reichstag nevertheless passed two ordinances to deal with problems that had arisen since 1897 and were thus not covered by the earlier law. A belief in the need for a system of comprehensive licensing for all those involved with emigration inspired the new legislation. The first ordinance, passed in October 1923, dealt with the recruiting of workers in Germany for placement abroad. For those who sought labourers in Germany, the law now required a solicitation licence, to be issued only with approval of the Reichsarbeitverwaltung (Reich Labour Administration). Permission would be granted only if such recruitment did not negatively affect Germany's larger economy. And as Thalheim remarked, "Germany's interests will be considered not negatively served only if existing unemployment makes an out-migration of such labourers appear worthwhile."[99]

Since this law applied only to workers being recruited for specific jobs abroad, another ordinance to limit more general solicitation was deemed necessary. This second ordinance was directed against "abuses in emigration matters," namely seductive advertising and propagandizing, and also expanded licensing. The February 1924 law was explicit: "The providing of information or advice on the prospects for emigration including details on living conditions, work opportunities, and settlement options in foreign lands was prohibited." More general, non-emigration-inducing information could be provided but only by licensed agencies and agents. The agencies, societies, and agents involved with emigration would be monitored to prevent them from "damaging the commonweal, especially by exerting a deleterious influence on German emigration or by misleading and exploiting those wishing to emigrate." To this end, the state authorities were called upon to investigate closely what and who were involved in solicitation, to attend their meetings and conventions, to scrutinize their publications, and to require appropriate bonds as insurance. Although the emphasis in the ordinance on the role of Germany's separate states failed to satisfy those who wished to see a stronger central agency controlling emigration, this new ordinance apparently did remedy the worst deficiencies of the 1897 statute.[100]

The Reichswanderungsamt and the Reichsstelle für das Auswanderungswesen

In the Weimar period the application of the laws restricting emigration largely rested with a governmental agency in Berlin created at the end of the Great War. This central office for controlling Germany's emigration was intended to supersede that long, fluctuating tradition of regional and state control described in earlier chapters.[101] Formally established in May 1919, the office bore the title Reichsamt für deutsche Einwanderung, Rückwanderung und Auswanderung (Reich Office for German Immigration, Return Migration, and Emigration), or Reichswanderungsamt (RWA) for short. Conceived during the war in preparation for victory, the RWA was originally designed to fulfill a variety of imperialist functions in directing the migrations of Germans within Europe and beyond to Germany's colonies. As a result, the RWA established branch offices throughout the country, numbering at one point as many as 120.[102] The harsh reality of postwar Germany substantially reduced its activities to just three issues: collecting reliable information on those lands where Germans might settle, providing accurate advice and information to those contemplating emigration, and protecting migrants from exploitation. It carried out its mission in several ways. It published materials on its own and in the German daily press; it developed extensive contacts with nongovernmental, private agencies in Germany involved in facilitating emigration; and it maintained close ties to government labour exchanges and passport offices. The RWA also exercised broad authority over the granting or withholding of licences for those promoting emigration. In essence, as Bickelmann puts it, the RWA saw itself charged not only "to provide protection and care for those emigrating but also to prevent any artificial effort to increase the desire to emigrate." The agency's guidelines went further, allowing it "to dissuade those considering leaving from doing so by providing employment at home." This would "secure the country's agricultural and food producing ability while at the same time helping to rebuild the people's economy."[103] In tenor and tone, the RWA resembled Italy's General Emigration Commission, which at the height of Italian emigration in 1901 sought to look after the affairs of the outward bound as well as prevent migration agents and agencies from promoting emigration positively.[104]

Since Canada prohibited German immigration until 1923, Reichswanderungsamt activities involving Canada in the early 1920s were minimal. Nevertheless, RWA officials kept tabs on events in the dominion in case the prohibition on German immigration should be lifted. For information on Canadian conditions, the RWA relied upon external sources, usually the diplomatic corps stationed there. The general consul Ludwig Kempff was posted to Montreal in December 1920, and his early reports to Berlin described attitudes in Canada toward Germany and Germans as very negative. In April 1921 he claimed that the vocal wartime anti-German sentiment still pervaded much of the dominion, which was therefore not an appropriate place to send Germany's sons and daughters.[105] Kempff's negative reports confirmed RWA prejudices, and the agency made sure such unfavourable views received wide circulation. Even after Canada removed Germans from the enemy alien list and offered admission in 1923, the RWA strongly opposed any German emigration to the dominion. In fact, the RWA fabricated horror stories about Germans being misused in Canada to dissuade potential migrants from heading there.[106]

Because the German economic situation deteriorated so dramatically in 1923, the original plans for the RWA, as noted, had to be abandoned. Reduced in size and resources, it was made a branch of the Interior Ministry. Nevertheless, the new Reichsstelle für das Auswanderungswesen (RA; Reich Office for Emigration Affairs) continued its predecessor's anti-Canadian policies. The significant German migration to Canada that occurred between 1923 and 1930 meant the RA became more engaged with Canadian matters than the RWA had been. The new head of the RA, Oskar Hintrager, an experienced administrator with a background in foreign service and emigration work, brought to the office a strong commitment to keeping Germans in Germany. Moreover, he firmly opposed emigration to Canada.[107] In a memo to the Reichswirtschaftministerium (Reich Economics Ministry), he stated flatly that "Canada was without a doubt an unsuitable land for German emigration ... if one considers working conditions and possibilities for agriculturalists within Germany, emigration to Canada of those engaged in agriculture should be prohibited."[108]

Consequently, Hintrager acted aggressively to combat Canada's efforts at recruiting immigrants in Germany: he hassled agents, interfered with agencies, and lobbied political leaders, proceeding against whomever and whatever he perceived as a threat. His suppression of the pro-emigration film, *Canada: seine Bodenschatz und landwirtschaftlichen Möglichkeiten* (Canada: Its Mineral Resources and Agricultural Possibilities) symbolized his determination to frustrate Canadian immigrant solicitation. Produced in 1926 by the CNR, the film described the success of a young German immigrant, who, starting out from Winnipeg in the depths of winter, managed in record time not only to find work and learn farming but also to purchase his own farm. Such easy success, Hintrager objected, clearly belied the harsh realities of western Canadian settlement. He labelled the film an egregious misrepresentation, a bogus presentation meant to seduce innocent Germans into migrating, and a flagrant violation of German law.[109]

Hintrager's opposition to Canada involved journalistic efforts as well. He voiced his disfavour most often in the RA's *Nachrichtenblatt* (News Sheet). This information source on such matters as immigrant-receiving lands, laws affecting emigration, passport and money requirements, settlement assistance societies at home and abroad, and other subjects of interest to potential migrants appeared in all the Reichsstelle's branch offices and advisory centres. Although supporters claimed that the periodical presented unbiased, objective accounts on emigration, this was not the case. As it did for all the major receiving lands, the *Nachrichtenblatt* regularly discussed and made recommendations on emigration to Canada throughout the interwar period. The Canadian image presented in the *Nachrichtenblatt* in the 1920s differed significantly from the traditional positive one broadcast by Canadian apologists. As with the volkish spokesmen, the alluring, romantic version of the dominion faded from view and the harsh criticisms of Canada that had appeared in earlier times reappeared. For example, Canadian weather ceased to be salubrious and became instead a threat to economic survival. "The [immigrant farmer's] main income," a January 1926 article on Canada reported, "comes from the sale of wheat. Unfortunately in many years the nights in August in those areas of Saskatchewan where immigrants settle are so cold that the wheat freezes. In the climatically milder Alberta the absence of sufficient rainfall frequently destroys all hope of harvesting a wheat crop. In both provinces the incessant, dry winds withdraw necessary moisture from the soil. Failed harvests in succeeding years continue to threaten the settler's existence."[110]

Worse than parching winds and early frosts, the *Nachrichtenblatt* repeatedly pointed out, were Canada's ungodly winters: "Any consideration of life in Canada must factor in the country's long winter, which more or less turns the land into a frozen desert." Quoting a German trapper who had resided in Canada for nine years, a 1930 article concluded by describing

Canada as the land of "eternal ice."[111] As the healthy, bracing winter climate that produced long life, rosy cheeks, and romantic sleigh rides disappeared, so also did the picture of Canada as the starkly beautiful, pristine land where one could relate closely with nature. The wild, romantic Canada that had nearly always been depicted in sympathetic accounts as a fishing and hunting paradise no longer offered even these opportunities. "Who ever thinks," the *Nachrichtenblatt* asserted in 1930, "that as a farmer he will be able to supplement his food supply by hunting and fishing is deluded. To begin with, the farmer never has enough free time to hunt or fish. Secondly, wild game is scarce in the inhabited areas of the country."[112]

As it denied the romantic image, the *Nachrichtenblatt* also refuted the civilized version of Canada. A land whose government, schools, method of taxation, criminal justice system, recognition of and tolerance for ethnic differences, and social intercourse had been so often celebrated in the past now became a country characterized by inadequate schools, national bigotry, brutal laws, and primitive living conditions. The *Nachrichtenblatt* claimed that the isolation of rural Canada condemned German immigrant children to economic stagnation because it was "extremely difficult if not impossible for the children to acquire a good education."[113] Throughout the 1920s, the RA's publication emphasized the hostility Canadians expressed toward German immigrants, their language, and customs. The resulting discrimination, it was claimed, even led to efforts to dissuade or prevent German young people from marrying.[114]

If by chance immigrants should be admitted to Canada, their expectations about civilization there would be, the *Nachrichtenblatt* pointed out, quickly disappointed. The Reichsstelle's organ repeatedly warned readers that "whoever cannot imagine living without the comforts of civilization and culture should stay home."[115] Canadian primitiveness could be shocking, as a letter from a Danish immigrant living in Canada's west in 1925 revealed. Because the author, a bookbinder by trade, could not find work in his specialty, he was forced to work as a farmhand. He found farming disastrous: he had to work from four in the morning until nine at night for slave wages, slept in a stall with the horses, and had to "wage an unending and futile war against hordes of mosquitoes." If the poor hired hand was lucky enough to escape the farm and make it to a city, the author warned about what to expect: "After arriving in town, one goes to a hotel or boarding house and pays too much for the chance to spend a night in a clean bed and feel human again. However, as soon as the lights go out [after going to bed], all hell breaks loose in the room. I would rather do battle with wild animals than with the battalions of bed bugs, fleas, and cockroaches which reside in all the wooden houses [in Canada's west]."[116]

Finally, the Reichsstelle's publication attacked Canada's image as a land of unlimited opportunities. Instead of a place of likely advancement, it was a dead end, a place of ruination. Long before the onslaught of the Depression, the *Nachrichtenblatt* described a weak Canadian economy and shrinking employment opportunities. For example, an August 1925 article on North America warned readers that the available Canadian jobs advertised in Germany were nothing more than temporary positions which native Canadians refused to fill. Since Canada offered only work without future promise, the *Nachrichtenblatt* advised its "German brothers to remain at home or to emigrate to other places but to avoid Canada."[117] The basic problem for Canada lay in its undeveloped economy, which was unable to absorb the large numbers of immigrants pouring into the country after the war: "The surplus of emigrants to job opportunities is so great that even those from the motherland [England] cannot find employment." In the event of a job opening, the unemployed English who know the language "will always enjoy the possibility of employment. Such an advantage is completely absent for Germans."[118]

After 1929, as the employment picture worsened, the *Nachrichtenblatt* reflected the crisis in Canada faithfully. Now, as job opportunities shrank further, the advice became even more ominous. Long the object of contempt and hostility, Germans now faced, the periodical pointed out with relish, possible nativist violence from unemployed Canadian workers. In a *Nachrichtenblatt* report from early 1930, an anonymous German who had resided in Canada for nearly fifty years described this new tension: "I can tell you that throughout Canada but especially in the great cities there is massive unemployment. In centres such as Montreal, Toronto, and Winnipeg, the newspapers have reported demonstrations by the unemployed. I would not recommend that German immigrants come to Canada because not only does great prejudice against everything German exist but one never knows when this will break out into violence."[119] The one-time land of milk and honey had become, as another *Nachrichtenblatt* article from 1930 put it, "a land of privation [*Entbehrung*]."[120]

Despite the negativism of Hintrager and his *Nachrichtenblatt*, the Reichsstelle could not stem the tide of Germans migrating to Canada in the 1920s. Although the RA did indeed represent the Weimar government's official disapproval of emigration, it could not effectuate its opposition for four basic reasons. First, the RA's resources and powers were limited by the general crisis affecting all of Weimar's governmental agencies. Second, the policy of obstruction contradicted the right to free movement guaranteed by Weimar's liberal constitution. Third, the Weimar government never prosecuted what it clearly considered violations of German law because it apparently did not wish to precipitate a conflict with either Ottawa or London, a conflict that might have had serious repercussions on Germany's economic and political future.[121] Fourth, the various negative material conditions in Germany (inflation, reparations, and slow economic recovery) exerted such pressure on so many to leave that the best intentions and efforts of the RA and its supporters came to naught. The Weimar Republic's inability to control emigration agents and thus obstruct emigration to Canada contrasted dramatically with Germany's smothering prewar opposition. Hence, the CPR and CNR functionaries recruiting Germans in the 1920s enjoyed much greater success than their prewar predecessors.

German Private Secular Agencies Assisting Emigration

The Weimar government was likewise impotent to prevent private associations from assisting emigrants. A large number of such agencies appeared in response to the emigration fever that swept Germany after the war. According to Bickelmann, during the 1920s, hundreds of such associations had "sprung up like mushrooms after a rain."[122] Since the Weimar government provided no material or monetary help to prospective emigrants, the actual granting of such assistance (*Fürsorge*) devolved upon nongovernmental agencies. These societies, which could be fraudulent or honest, secular or religious, assumed two forms: emigration associations committed to assist emigrants in their migrations, and settlement societies that aimed at founding settlements abroad to receive emigrants as members. In the 1920s both types most often sought to direct their charges to South America. The Deutscher Bund sudamerikanischer Auswanderer (German Alliance of South American Emigrants) in Leipzig was representative. This society's program included the usual information office, plus a support centre for negotiating on behalf of the emigrants for jobs and property abroad, an office to prepare the emigrants for their new lives with language courses and lectures, an insurance and banking department to assist with financial matters, and a travel bureau to arrange transport and help with documents and other travel issues.[123]

Generally the agencies that looked after the material and spiritual well-being of Germany's emigrants in this period did so for several reasons. Besides pursuing the usual humanitarian goals, agencies sought to assist emigrants to maintain their German culture and language in the new homeland and thus to continue their connection with Germany and things German. Both the Catholic and Lutheran emigrant aid societies supported the maintenance of the German language among their charges, as the best way to guarantee the survival of the emigrants' religion. Emigrant aid societies often provided support in the hope of creating German communities abroad that could be used to support the political and economic needs and goals of the fatherland. In the tradition of Friedrich Fabri, they saw in the *Volksdeutsche* an opportunity to increase Germany's international prestige, world trade, and ultimately its domestic economy. If tied properly to the Reich, the Germans living abroad would act as surrogate colonies for those lost during the war.

During the 1920s, the Reichsverband deutscher Auswanderer (Reich League of German Emigrants) represented one of the most prominent secular societies advocating strong ties with emigrants after their settlement abroad. Founded in 1920 in Hamburg, this organization claimed 3,000 members in twenty-seven local branches by mid-decade. Through its newspaper, the *Allgemeine Deutsche Auswanderer Zeitung* (General German Emigrant's Newspaper), and its advising centres, the society sought to explain the significance of emigration for Germany and justify support for it. In the mid-1920s the Reichsverband was headed by Otto Preusse-Sperber, the nationally recognized emigration authority and former emigrant to Brazil. Besides editing the organization's paper, Preusse-Sperber assiduously developed an elaborate plan for financing, administering, and utilizing immigrant communities abroad. He insisted that Germany's emigrants should have their moves paid for and receive free land abroad in healthy locations near other Germans; he called for a guarantee that Germany's emigrants be granted equal access to all opportunities afforded others in the receiving lands and that nothing interfere with their naturalization in their new countries; he urged that Germans remaining at home consider their departed brothers and sisters valuable members of Germany's society, who continued to contribute both directly and indirectly in the fatherland's economic life. Finally, Preusse-Sperber demanded that the present laws discouraging emigration be changed.[124]

Preusse-Sperber not only rationalized and supported German emigration but also attempted to advance it through his own acts on behalf of individual members of the Reichsverband. In lands where Germans intended to settle, he tried to recruit wealthy individuals who would guarantee jobs and provide funds to defray transportation costs. To this end, he made recruitment trips to both Canada and Brazil, though his efforts were largely unsuccessful.[125] In Brazil he found no backers, and in Canada during 1923-4 he obtained support for only 14 of the 200 persons for whom he requested aid. Although the attempts of Preusse-Sperber and other private individuals yielded little, they illustrate the lengths to which some would go to influence emigrants for the fatherland's benefit. In an age when Germany's economy suffered so severely, the importance of not only securing safe havens for fellow Germans but also of cultivating sympathetic Germans living abroad seemed obvious.

German Religious Agencies Assisting Migration
In marshalling support among fellow Germans in the receiving lands, the religious emigration assistance organizations at work in the 1920s showed much greater returns for their efforts than the secular ones. Although Jewish agencies to assist the emigration of both German and eastern European Jews existed in the Weimar period, the most extensive efforts by religious

organizations were made by Germany's two main Christian denominations: the Roman Catholic and Evangelical Lutheran churches. For Catholics, the work of the St. Raphaels-Verein again ranked foremost in importance. Although dormant during the Great War, the society re-emerged at the war's end committed to serving the needs of emigrating German Catholics. With Cahensly dead, the society's leadership was turned over to his friend Lorenz Werthmann, former president of the Deutscher Charitasverband (German Charity League), and its administrative centre was transferred from Limburg to Freiburg im Breisgau. Having the branch offices of the Charitasverband functioning at the same time as St. Raphaels-Verein advising centres, Werthmann greatly expanded the society's capacity to advise and assist. The society's offices in Bremen and Hamburg were reactivated as well. Thus, by the end of 1918, twenty St. Raphael service centres existed in the Weimar Republic ready to deal with the flood of refugees and emigrants. By 1923 this number had increased further and the *St. Raphaels-Blatt* had been re-activated as well. As the society's eightieth anniversary publication reported in 1951, in the mid-1920s the St. Raphael Society operated sixty-six emigration assistance offices throughout Germany, maintained a centre for spiritual and material assistance in Hamburg, and actively mediated or arranged for settlers in their new lands, including Canada.[126]

The St. Raphael Society activities in the dominion during the interwar period included allying with the Verein für Deutsch Canadier Katholiken (VDCK; Society for German Canadian Catholics). Established in 1909 to promote both Catholicism and the German language, this indigenous association extended its mission after 1920 to include working with immigrants, collaborating with the Canadian Pacific Railway in Canada and the St. Raphael Society in Germany.[127] The VDCK developed its immigrant assistance connection initially through Hamburg. The process was straightforward. The intended emigrant would be referred to the St. Raphael representative in Hamburg by his or her parish priest. This representative would provide for the emigrant's immediate needs and then pass the migrant on to the VDCK's network in Canada. Although the VDCK assisted the new immigrant in a variety of ways, including the usual reception help in securing train tickets, arranging temporary housing, and exchanging money, the most important task for the VDCK remained farm work placement. The Verein für Deutsch Canadier Katholiken sought to guarantee each newly arrived coreligionist not only a farm job but a German Catholic environment as well. And these efforts succeeded. By 1927, the VDCK's collaboration with the St. Raphaels-Verein had become so successful at generating emigrants in Europe that the VDCK had "to appoint seven representatives in Saskatchewan alone to look after immigrant and settlement needs."[128]

Much of the VDCK success derived from the inspired leadership of Father Christian Kierdorf, the society's general secretary. Originally sent to Canada in 1920, Kierdorf quickly became the leading spokesperson for Canada's western German Catholic immigrant community. Priest, teacher, advisor, and enthusiast of German language and culture, Kierdorf dedicated himself wholeheartedly to organizing efficiently the admission and settlement of German immigrants in Canada. To better inform himself on conditions in Germany, to reinforce his connections with the St. Raphael Society administrators, and to improve his ability to facilitate German immigration to Canada, Kierdorf made two trips to Germany between 1925 and 1930. His commitment paid off in increased immigrant numbers. Although most of the 10,000 to 12,000 German-speaking immigrants Kierdorf and the VDCK assisted to Canada were not from Germany, reasonable estimates have nevertheless allowed that at least 10 to 15 percent were.[129]

Although the 10,000 Reich Germans Kierdorf and the VDCK assisted to Canada represented a success, not all their projects turned out so well. An example of failure was the so-called Schneider Colony.[130] The brainchild of the Freiburg lawyer Fritz Schneider, the colony was established twenty kilometres from Winnipeg in the spring of 1927 with thirty farm families. They had been recruited in south Germany by Schneider with the help of the St. Raphael Society and the VDCK. The colony's founders envisaged a closed settlement of German Catholic families living in their own houses and working assigned segments of the colony's land while sharing common social and religious experiences. The location near Winnipeg appeared to promise a ready and convenient market for the fruits of the colony's labour. Initially, the group seemed to be succeeding, but poor crops and failure to penetrate the Winnipeg dairy market as expected boded trouble. Then financing difficulties arose, with loans being held up and creditors demanding to be paid. These early cash flow problems delayed the promised individualization of family units by preventing the construction of private family houses. Discontent grew from these issues as well as from dissatisfaction with Schneider's role as leader. At this point the Depression descended, and the poor initial returns from the colony's limited agricultural success became suddenly much worse. By 1930, according to Grant Grams, "the Schneider colony was in shambles."[131] Group solidarity had evaporated, and those who did not leave the colony outright were forced to try to exist entirely on their own.

Germany's Lutherans did not attempt comparable group settlements in Canada during the 1920s, but the Lutheran Church did revive the tradition of support for individual immigrants that had been rudely interrupted by the Great War. Since the nineteenth century, Lutheran assistance work had grown in scope and scale to include "mission, bible, and negotiation societies, youth groups, and women's societies for the care of the poor and sick."[132] Although Lutheran assistance offices and bureaus appeared in many places in Germany, the main centres remained in Hamburg and Bremen. As the tradition of helping emigrants developed, the prevailing attitude expressed toward those who emigrated was summed up by the church's Central-Ausschuss für die Innere Mission (Central Committee for the Interior Mission) with these words: "The emigrants are not excommunicants but pilgrims, and even if they leave us, they still remain with us."[133]

The postwar period saw the several Lutheran affiliates concerned with emigration expand rapidly in response to the surge of interest in emigration. By the 1920s the whole matter of aiding emigration had been both defined and organized more efficiently. A 1930 statement from the president of the German Evangelical Church Association in Berlin summed up the church's emigration organization and mission:

> The Verband für Evangelische Auswandererfürsorge [Organization for Lutheran Emigrant Aid] in Berlin has brought together the work of the following organizations: the Evangelical Emigration Mission in Hamburg, the Evangelical Mission in Bremen, and the Central Evangelical Society for German Settlers and Immigrants in Witzenhausen. The task of the Berlin Verband is to provide for all emigration concerns in an ordered and spiritual fashion. Such concerns include advising intended emigrants in Germany about conditions in the receiving lands regarding religious, economic, and cultural matters, providing religious care and concern for the emigrants, assigning immigrants to trusted persons in the new colonies, and finally assisting those migrants who return to Germany.[134]

Even though the Lutheran Church's emigration work remained generally consistent throughout the period 1920-33, the details of the work varied significantly. The annual reports of the Verband für Evangelische Auswandererfürsorge depict the changes and alterations in policy that occurred in response to the changing nature and needs of the emigrant community. Church leaders had to adjust to conditions in both the receiving and sending lands and within the ranks of Germany's migrants. The Lutheran assistance centres responded initially to the rising enthusiasm for emigration "by providing information about the emigration process."[135] Echoing the ideas expounded earlier by Preusse-Sperber for his Reichsverband deutscher Auswanderer, the Lutheran Verband's year-end report for 1927 described these services and goals as threefold. First, the organization committed itself to gathering and providing more extensive and reliable information on the various receiving lands. Second, the agency pledged itself to increase the efficacy of its service capacities for emigrants, not only by making information readily available but also by expanding the scope and scale of its assistance to emigrants at all stages of their odyssey, including the embarkation port, on board ship, and once they were settled at their destination. Third, to prove to these lost brothers and sisters that the German state and its people still cared about them, the Verband promised to maintain through correspondence and visitation much closer contact with the departed than ever before.[136]

The mission of Lutheran emigration aid efforts changed substantially with the onslaught of the Depression in 1929. Most obviously, the total number of Germans emigrating anywhere fell off dramatically, decreasing the need for many traditional services. The Hamburg mission's 1930-1 report indicated that the volume of visitors had fallen off from 5,044 to 1,007, advising sessions from 2,493 to 369, church services from 90 to 59, and shipside farewells from 266 to 194.[137] This severe drop-off in numbers of those interested in or actually involved in emigration, however, did not mean a decline in emigration aid work. Efforts now shifted to solving new problems. Both missions had to assist needy family members of earlier emigrants now stranded in Germany, and those who had tried unsuccessfully to emigrate and had returned. The *Rückwanderer,* or returnees, some of whom had been deported back to Germany, needed extensive help. The Hamburg report for 1931-2 asserted that they were "often entirely without means and very often sick as well."[138] Attempting to reintegrate these persons placed a heavy burden on Hamburg's Lutheran aid sources. The same held true for Bremen, where the mission's activity reports for 1930 asserted that work had "expanded considerably" because, among other things, "increased numbers of deportations from Canada and the United States have had to be dealt with."[139]

Although correspondence with immigrants abroad had been widely practised throughout the 1920s, at the end of the decade the Lutheran missions expanded their efforts at developing contacts with those who had departed. This involved writing letters to the relatives of emigrants. The Hamburg mission's report for 1929 claimed that recently "an entirely new form of assistance was developed. In the fall a circular seeking information about their family members abroad was sent out to the relatives of our immigrants." The results of this effort had led to "contact with hundreds of immigrants."[140] As it turned out, letter writing and contact follow-up became a particularly useful tool for developing relations with German immigrants in Canada.

Efforts to foster relations with Canada's Germans had begun well before the troubles of the late 1920s. The nurture of Canada's Germans had received church sanction with the founding in 1923 of the Canadian Lutheran Immigration Board (LIB). Established to serve the needs of the new wave of postwar German immigrants, the LIB set up offices in Montreal and Winnipeg. Manned by German Lutheran pastors who were permanent residents of Canada, the LIB centres offered a variety of services, and worked closely with the emigration missions in Germany to secure appropriate immigrants. Once the immigrants arrived in Canada, the LIB pastors met them at the train stations, visited them in the immigrant reception centres, and even "traveled out into the countryside to look after the immigrant's spiritual and economic well being."[141]

The Lutheran Immigration Board became such an influential force in the immigration process because it formed a partnership with the Canadian authorities in facilitating German immigration. A memo from 1926 described the special arrangements with Ottawa: "The LIB pledged to the Canadian government to find a year's work for those immigrants in its charge among the Lutheran communities in Canada. In exchange, the LIB received permission from the government to bring to Canada the approved categories of immigrants [farm workers and domestic servants]. Moreover, these approved persons were not required to secure the special sponsorship of a Canadian citizen."[142] Since the German Lutheran communities in Canada did not have the wherewithal to fulfill their immigration plans independently, they turned to the major Canadian transportation companies, particularly the Canadian Pacific Railway.

The LIB's close relationship with the CPR is easily explained: the CPR not only ran trains across Canada but also possessed its own line of ships for ferrying persons out of Europe to North America. Thus, the LIB's representatives could negotiate for the transportation of its immigrant charges from Europe directly to the places of settlement in western Canada exclusively through the CPR. The LIB preferred the CPR over the Canadian National Railways because of the CPR's special influence with the Canadian government and its position in the country's financial infrastructure. The 1926 memo cited above also pointed out that the CPR possessed "a large number of fully prepared farms ready and available for immigrants and settlers" and that these were being made available on very favourable credit terms. Furthermore, the memo described the CPR as having "its own department, the Canadian Colonization Association, for assisting the settlement of immigrants after arrival in Canada." In short, as Pastor Schmok, a prominent member of the LIB, put it, "the benefits to be had from doing business with the CPR appeared so significant to the LIB that the Board resolved to deal only with it."[143]

The specifics of how the LIB and its agents in Germany recruited immigrants, organized them for travel, and ultimately settled their charges in Canada reveal how closely the LIB and the emigration missions worked together. One indication is that the Lutheran missions in Germany claimed to promote for emigration to Canada only "farmers and female domestic help," since these were the occupations approved for admission. Although the Canadian government waived for the LIB the usual requirements that emigrants possess $1,500 at the time of departure, the LIB nevertheless only "took under its protection immigrants who could pay their own way" from Europe to Winnipeg. In addition to financial independence and a clean bill of health, would-be immigrant farmers normally had to prove by reliable witnesses that they had been employed in agriculture. As well, to be supported by the Lutheran agencies in Germany and Canada, the immigrants had to provide evidence "through certification by a pastor that they had been active church members in Germany and that they intended to participate in Lutheran religious life in Canada."[144]

Once the emigrant received approval in Germany for settlement in Canada, the mission referred the person to the LIB authorities, who sought to find a suitable farm for the men or an appropriate home for the female domestic servants. Since the majority of LIB immigrants were young men, finding farm work consumed most of the LIB's energies. The leader of the Hamburg mission described for a prospective farmer-immigrant the contract between the LIB and its charges: "Obtaining a position is exclusively in the hands of the LIB. You on your side must trust the LIB that it will find suitable work for you ... The LIB can assure you that the job will provide a minimum earning of $300 per year. To make this sum, you must remain for an entire year on the farm of your Lutheran employer." The same letter also informed the emigrant of the burdens and benefits of settling in Canada. Before all else, any migrant had to be prepared for very strenuous work during Canada's short summer season; the new settler must be prepared to do all "the simple and complicated farm tasks himself." Moreover, all prospective immigrants needed to be fully aware of the terribly cold winters, in which "the farms are often completely snowed in." Aspiring immigrants must therefore seriously reflect on whether they "can bear such cold temperatures and such long absences of social interaction." For those who could overcome or cope with these negatives, the chances of success were great: "Whoever can gain the trust of his employer and the community, can in a relatively short time secure his own farm."[145]

In assisting the settlement in Canada of needy or desperate Germans bent on leaving home, both the LIB and the Lutheran missions in Hamburg and Bremen always professed to be acting from lofty motives. Emigrants not given reliable and compassionate assistance, it was firmly believed, would be exploited and misused mercilessly. Thus Christian concern called for intervention on their behalf. But volkish and nationalist reasons also justified the work of the LIB and the missions: one supporter claimed that "the work of the LIB" represented "work by Germans for Germans."[146] Emigration not only relieved distress in the fatherland by providing outlets for the disgruntled and surplus, but also "strengthened Canada's German community by adding new Germans to it."[147] As a result, Canada's German community would be more likely to retain and preserve its culture and heritage, which would advance the cause of Germany and its Volk in the world. More precisely, in the words of the chairman of the LIB in Canada, H.W. Harms, its work should serve "not only German communities in Canada but also the German fatherland."[148]

The combined work of the missions, the LIB, and the CPR raised fears among Germany's officialdom of inordinate success. In particular, the Reichsstelle für das Auswanderungswesen viewed these cooperative efforts as subversive and threatening. In September 1925 the Reichsstelle's Oskar Hintrager circulated a report from an informant in Canada stating that "the Lutheran Immigration Board is an association of Canadian pastors under the clandestine control and guidance of the Canadian Pacific Railway. The LIB is a secret immigration agent for this railway and is financed by it."[149] On the basis of this view, Reichsstelle authorities committed the agency to opposing vigorously the LIB and its representatives in Germany. Dr. Hermann Wagner, the head of the Lutheran Church's Hamburg mission and the chief LIB representative for Germany, drew most attention from the Reichsstelle.

Hermann Wagner's Role in Migration Assistance

Born the son of a Lutheran pastor in 1891, Hermann Paul Johann Wagner grew up in Luther's city, Wittenberg. Beginning university in 1909, he studied first at Tübingen, then at Halle, and finally at the Lutheran seminary in Bethel. Interrupted in 1914 for military service, Wagner's studies resumed upon the war's end. By 1920 he had earned a doctorate in theology and passed his theological exams. Ordained in the Lutheran Church that summer, he returned to Bethel to work as an assistant pastor with Fritz von Bodelschwingh, the well-known author and instructor at the seminary. Wagner remained in Bethel until August 1925 when he accepted a position as pastor in Hamburg's Auswanderermission. Within a few days, he became the mission's director, and he stayed in Hamburg working for and representing the mission until 1931. In this period he edited the Christian periodical *Die Christliche Volkswacht*, which became "a much respected and highly learned publication."[150] After resigning from the mission, Wagner fulfilled pastoral roles in Kotzschar and at the Moritzkirche in Naumburg from 1940 until he retired in 1958. He died in Naumburg in 1970.

From his appointment as head of the Hamburg emigration mission, Wagner claimed to be aware of the sensitive nature of his new position. He understood he should not recruit immigrants for Canada, as he readily confessed that he sincerely wished to avoid conflict with the authorities.[151] Rather, he interpreted his job as an advisory and facilitating one for those who had already decided to abandon the fatherland. In a September 1925 letter to the Reichsstelle für das Auswanderungswesen, Wagner described his obligations to the LIB, the Lutheran Church, and his native land. According to Wagner, his job for the LIB required fulfilling five tasks. First, he must try to dissuade would-be emigrants who might be able to survive in Germany from leaving. Second, he must see that all possibilities for gainful employment or resettlement in Germany had been fully pursued, inducing aspiring emigrants to direct themselves toward "any opportunities that

offer colonization within Germany." Third, if emigrants could not be dis-
suaded from leaving, they should be directed to settle abroad "in closed
German settlements where the guarantee exists that they will not be lost to
the German Volk even if they cannot be saved for the German state." Fourth,
emigrants should be induced to settle in places where "the connection to
their native [Lutheran] church can be maintained." Fifth, Wagner pledged
to stay in touch with all those he had advised to settle in Canada: "I shall
remain in contact with all immigrants to Canada who migrate to areas designated by the LIB to see that they keep up their Lutheran religion."[152] In
fulfilling his several tasks as Germany's LIB chief, Wagner thus claimed that
he served both his faith and his fatherland. The interests of Canada came in
a weak third.

This explanation of his patriotism and intentions regarding Germany's
emigrants did not settle his problems with the Reichsstelle. Director Hintrager
remained convinced that Wagner propagandized for Canada and was violating the law. On numerous occasions Hintrager pointed out to Wagner
that as both the German representative of the LIB and alleged Lutheran
Church impartial advisor he was caught in a conflict of interests. Hintrager
strongly urged Wagner to resign his LIB post. Wagner, however, refused to
do so, bravely insisting that he never convinced anyone to leave Germany
and emphasizing that by the time the would-be emigrants reached him
they had already decided to leave. Therefore he only helped to Canada those
who could not be saved for Germany. In a letter of February 1926, Wagner
wrote to Hintrager: "I emphasize again that I have been duty bound to
adhere to the national position in dealing with emigration. In all my activities I have only helped people in dire straits to whom the fatherland could
no longer offer satisfaction."[153]

Despite the ongoing conflict with the Reichsstelle, Wagner performed his
duties from 1925 to 1932 as the LIB's main official in Germany with great
energy and enthusiasm. Taking his role as advisor on Canada particularly
seriously, he informed himself as best he could on what emigration to Canada
and settlement there entailed. To do this, he felt obliged to learn about the
country first-hand. That meant travelling to Canada and becoming familiar
with the places he was sending immigrants and with the Canadian Germans who were looking after them. Thus, from 5 May to 21 August 1928,
Wagner journeyed to Canada. From this visit he learned a surprising amount,
publishing his findings in a pamphlet entitled *Von Küste zu Küste: Bei deutschen
Auswanderern in Kanada* (From Coast to Coast: With German Emigrants in
Canada).[154]

In his short article "Eine Reise durch Kanada" (A Journey through Canada),
written in 1928 for the Lutheran periodical *Der Deutsche Auswanderer* (The
German Emigrant) Wagner summarized the Canadian experiences and im-

pressions he later described in *Von Küste zu Küste*. Endorsed and financed by the Lutheran Church and its emigration missions in Germany, Wagner's visit was also underwritten by the CNR and CPR, which provided "free rail passes for the entire country so that I had the opportunity to travel where I wanted." After landing in Halifax on 16 May, Wagner travelled by train to Montreal to meet Dr. Klaehn, the LIB representative there. Klaehn, who assumed responsibility for making the first contact with the new immigrants from Germany and for sending them on their way west, provided Wagner with details on the initial leg of the immigrants' North American odyssey. Wagner then travelled to Ottawa for a round of official meetings, followed by ten days visiting German communities in eastern Ontario. He found "settlement possibilities for German immigrants in Ontario and the eastern provinces to be limited."[155]

After Ontario, Wagner headed west "to inspect the two prairie provinces, Saskatchewan and Alberta, which at the moment most concern German immigrants."[156] By inspection, he meant personal observation of the material conditions affecting both recent German immigrants and those Canadians involved in assisting the new arrivals. He described his intentions thus: "My journey was inspired by two thoughts or goals. First, I wanted to visit as many immigrants as I could who were under the protection of the Lutheran missions and with whom we in Hamburg had corresponded, and second, I wished to obtain as accurate a picture as possible of living and settlement conditions in these provinces." For the next several weeks, Wagner conducted a whirlwind tour of Saskatchewan and Alberta, visiting Yorkton, Regina, Saskatoon, Prince Albert, Edmonton, and Calgary. In addition, he ventured into the countryside: "If both Lutheran pastors and farmers had not been willing to make available their automobiles for my use, I would not have been able to make so many individual visits ... I came to know farmers who for years had lived on the land; I met both unsophisticated and educated farm workers; I visited pure prairie districts and areas of bush land; I saw land that had been under cultivation for years and land of the most recent settlement."[157]

In his travels and correspondence, Wagner formed a favourable opinion of Canada as a haven for German settlement. Although he found the Canadian state to be "artificial" in a volkish sense, he approved of its political, educational, economic, and religious opportunities. He even described the climate as "not only bearable but favourable for north Europeans." Moreover, he strongly approved of the LIB for its service to the entire process of German migration to Canada. From his experiences in western Canada, Wagner thought he had learned the key to settlement in Canada: hard work, frugality, perseverance, and patience. For those who first learned how to farm as agricultural labourers and then moved on to acquire their own farms,

Wagner believed success was highly probable. He concluded, "My journey has strengthened me in the conviction that Canada represents a suitable land for German immigration."[158]

When Wagner returned to Germany at summer's end in 1928, he applied his expanded knowledge to his Canada work. He wrote about his experiences in Canada, he travelled around Germany giving lectures, and he continued to advise those hoping to emigrate. His renewed activity brought new protests from the Reichsstelle's Hintrager. In January 1929 Hintrager wrote Wagner complaining that his recent lecture in Dortmund, entitled "Kanada, das Land der eigenen Scholle" (Canada, the Land of Self-Owned Farms), constituted "emigration propaganda in the truest sense."[159] Although writing and lecturing formed a major part of Wagner's LIB work after his return from Canada, his Canada-related correspondence became even more significant. He remained dedicated to soliciting and answering letters from emigrants until his resignation from the mission.

After Wagner left Hamburg in 1932, the task of continuing contact with the Canadian immigrants was assigned to Heinrich Brakelmann, a native of Hamburg who had served as deacon in the church. Born in 1883, Brakelmann had understudied Wagner for several years before the latter's resignation. As his letters reveal, Brakelmann's role in the mission differed markedly from Wagner's. The advising of would-be Canadian emigrants, which had consumed so much of Wagner's time in the period 1925-9, had by 1933 all but ceased. Instead, Brakelmann dealt with solving problems for immigrants in Canada, counselling returnees, and proselytizing on behalf of the "New Germany." From the time of National Socialism's accession to power in 1933, Brakelmann identified publicly with the Hitler movement, and in June 1937 he joined the Nazi Party. In his mission work from 1933 to the outbreak of war in September 1939, Brakelmann remained a strong apologist for the Nazi cause, giving frequent testimonials to the *Volksgenossen* (members of the Volk) in Canada on the virtues and accomplishments of the NSDAP (National Socialist Democratic Workers' Party) and Hitler.

A letter from March 1935 to one of the mission's emigrants then weathering the Depression in Wolf Creek, Alberta, illustrates Brakelmann's enthusiasm for the Hitler movement. The earlier westward migration of Germans had been reversed, Brakelmann proudly asserted:

> Canada no longer offers opportunities for immigrants. Our farmers have better prospects here in Germany ... It is indeed fortunate that our people remain at home and no longer turn foreign wildernesses into fruitful places through their sweat. We Christians have been blessed that God has given us our leader Adolf Hitler, who has brought the country back from the abyss of Bolshevism. If you had been here to experience the great transformation, you would understand. Order has returned to our economy; the streets are

clean again ... God bless the efforts our Führer has made to restore our economy, to heal the interior and exterior sickness of our country, and to restore our living space in the world.[160]

Wagner, by contrast, had judged the Hitler phenomenon very differently. To an Alberta farmer who wrote him in January 1931 praising Hitler "for his efforts to save our Volk from international enslavement and jewification,"[161] Wagner responded at length with skepticism:

It appears especially significant to me that in the denial of the purely technical and rational, which has characterized our times, the National Socialist movement has turned to the natural origins of our people by emphasizing race and homeland. I consider the National Socialist movement analogous to the Romantic reaction which 100 years ago also rejected the Enlightenment and rationalism. But if truth be known, I cannot identify with this movement since it places too much emphasis upon Germanness and German power, it exhibits an arrogance in its harsh anti-Semitism ... Therefore, I have little hope that this movement can lead to any real solution for the problems of our people or for those of the entire European continent. On the contrary, I see this movement with its elemental emphasis upon the basest part of human nature as a threat to Europe's social order.[162]

Secular Volkish Agencies

Although Germany's religious organizations reflected the political upheavals then plaguing interwar Germany, they did so far less than the country's secular agencies. Two such organizations, the Deutsche Ausland-Institut, or DAI (German Foreign Institute), in Stuttgart and the Volksbund für das Deutschtum im Ausland, or VDA (Volk Alliance for Germans and German Matters Abroad), in Berlin, illustrate this politicizing trend. They shared Brakelmann's assumptions about the necessity to mobilize the *Volksdeutsche* for the fatherland's benefit. Both the DAI, founded in 1917, and the VDA, established in 1908, represented a new kind of emigration aid organization. Unlike the St. Raphael Society or the Lutheran Church's missions, the DAI and VDA were conceived as agencies to serve Germans who had left Germany rather than those in the process of leaving. The DAI's description of its mission reflects this shift:

The DAI seeks not only to maintain but also to develop more closely the relations between the German communities abroad and the motherland ... To this end, the institution intends to spread awareness of the culture and material conditions prevailing among the foreign Germans, to exhibit the relations of the foreign Germans to their old as well as the new homeland, and most importantly to describe the contributions which the

German pioneers have made in their adopted lands. At the same time, the DAI offers advice and assistance to all Germans wishing to emigrate as well as to those living abroad needing a helping hand ... All Germans regardless of citizenship should be made aware that they belong to the great German cultural community.[163]

To accomplish this consciousness-raising task, the DAI made threefold efforts. Its resource and information division consisted of a library, an archive, and an extensive collection of photographs and maps at its centre in Stuttgart. Another section publicized its programs and spread its propaganda through press releases, exhibits, public lectures, and the periodical *Der Auslands-deutsche* (The German Living Abroad). And the DAI's service department dispensed – in person and via correspondence – advice and information on such matters as emigration procedures and laws, desirable receiving lands, and employment opportunities abroad. The year-end report for 1928 de-scribed how active the institute had been during the 1920s. Between 1921 and 1928 the service department had advised over 70,000 persons seeking information on emigration, and it had located positions abroad for over 4,000 unemployed. The archive had increased its holdings of foreign German-language newspapers from 132 in 1921 to 314 in 1928; it had augmented the number of foreign German societies and organizations registered with it from 10,324 in 1921 to 29,534 in 1928. Over the same period, the library had expanded its holdings of books from 10,378 to 31,995, of maps from 5,923 to 8,190, and of pictures from 12,123 to 27,322.[164]

In addition to acting as an information source on Canada and to provid-ing programs for propagandizing the *Volksdeutsche* on behalf of Germany and German culture, the DAI involved itself in German emigration during the 1920s. The tour of Canada undertaken by the DAI's head, Manfred Grisebach, in the summer of 1929 illustrates how serious this involvement could become. Grisebach, who had visited Canada in 1911, admitted in 1929 that he intended his current trip to learn about the "possibilities for the settlement of German people in Canada." Arriving in eastern Canada in early July, he headed quickly for the prairies, where he knew most future German immigrants would ultimately settle. Canada's immigration officials, both in the Department of Immigration and in the management circles of the Canadian National Railways, enthusiastically supported Grisebach's tour. Believing he and his agency were crucial for future German immigration, they were, as one CNR official put it, "anxious that he should be favorably impressed with conditions in Canada."[165] The Canadian National Railways acted as Grisebach's official host, providing free transportation, guides, and a carefully scripted itinerary. The CNR officers charged with looking after him conducted him about the West carefully, trying their best to make his tour both comfortable and properly informative. Travelling through the

Prairie provinces and British Columbia, Grisebach visited major centres such as Winnipeg and Edmonton, smaller ones like Prince Albert, Saskatoon, St. Walberg, Grand Prairie, Swan River, Pouce Coupe, and Prince George, and many even smaller settlements along the CNR lines.[166] Throughout the tour, railway guides exposed the DAI leader to some of the best agricultural areas in western Canada and stopped off at well-established and successful German settlements. Hoping to create a favourable yet plausible impression, guides tried to make "all contacts to Canada's Germans appear casual and normal with the Germans being able to demonstrate some measure of success."[167]

CNR officials prepared letters of introduction for Grisebach to the German centres he would visit, the idea being to facilitate not only his information gathering but to impress upon him the sincere approval of Canada's officials for future German immigration.[168] Apparently their efforts succeeded, because when Grisebach returned to Germany at the end of August 1929, he expressed very favourable impressions of Canada, its people, and its governors. A letter from a DAI staff member to the CNR summed up the German satisfaction: "The trip," Herr Wanner wrote, "has greatly increased our personal friends and acquaintances. They [the CNR officials] made it possible to visit all destinations that we wanted. These contacts provided us with detailed reports ... The many and various impressions which Mr. Grisebach gained during his trip will be used to good advantage in connection with our emigration activities."[169] The DAI officials knew that the obliging CNR guides on Grisebach's tour had acted not simply as businesspeople pushing the railway's interests but also as representatives of official Canadian immigration policy, and that such policy clearly favoured Germans migrating to the dominion.

Although the Grisebach tour appeared to have been a success, DAI participation in emigration activities ceased once the Depression began. After the success of the National Socialists in 1933, however, the DAI's role in Germany and beyond increased in importance. In 1934 a leadership shake-up, which resulted in the appointment of Dr. Karl Strölin as president, brought the agency more closely into line with Nazi intentions. "A thoroughly convinced National Socialist type who was nevertheless temperamentally inclined to be compromising and pragmatic,"[170] Strölin sought to project an image to the outside world of DAI cultural rather than political concern. Yet the close ties between the volkish movement and National Socialist ideology decreed that the DAI's volkish-cultural activity nearly always supported National Socialist political goals. In the Hitler period, the DAI continued gathering information on Germans abroad, publishing accounts of Germans living outside the Reich, and distributing its information at home and abroad. In all three of these areas, the DAI's accomplishments were considerable. The collections on foreign Germans in the DAI's archive and library grew substantially, and DAI publications in periodicals, yearbooks, and monographs were extensive and widely distributed throughout the 1930s. In addition, the effort to inform Germans at home about *Volksdeutsche* and the *Volksdeutsche* about Germany was conducted skilfully. A number of different techniques were devised, from elaborate school programs to the so-called *Lesepaten*. The latter was a kind of pen-pal scheme whereby individuals in Germany sent propaganda materials to Germans living abroad, thus personalizing the effort to win them over to the volkish cause.[171]

Although in carrying out these programs the DAI expended more energy on Germans living elsewhere in Europe, those in South America, Africa, Asia, and particularly North America were not neglected. In the United States the DAI effort assumed major significance. The hostile posture of the American government to pro-Nazi political groups made the DAI's cultural approach ideal. In Canada, the DAI leaders believed that the example of the unassimilated French minority offered unique opportunities for the development of volkish consciousness among Canada's Germans.[172] In collecting information on them, the DAI employed a variety of techniques. Canadian contacts circulated questionnaires soliciting general information from members of the Volk on their age, religion, occupation, residence, family members, place of emigration to Canada, German *(Reichsdeutsche)* relatives, reading habits, club membership, and the sort of reading material they would like to receive from Germany.[173] Another tactic requested information from known leaders of the German Canadian community. In 1936, the DAI asked Karl Gerhardt, the head of the Deutscher Bund Kanada (Canadian German League) in Montreal, to forward a list of names complete with character sketches and an indication of "what sort of reading material would be most useful for the personalities involved."[174]

Sending DAI representatives to Canada to report directly to Stuttgart also remained a viable option for gathering data on the *Volksdeutsche*. During the Depression years, the best-known and most useful mission for dispensing propaganda and gathering facts was Karl Götz's trip to western Canada. A Swabian school teacher, Götz had made a name for himself as a writer before associating with the DAI. Strongly volkish in his commitments and equally a believer in the National Socialist cause, Götz fit in well with the DAI's general program.[175] In fact, the DAI appointed Götz to head the agency's department responsible for Swabians in the world. In 1936 he was entrusted with the task of contacting Swabians dispersed throughout North and South America and of bringing the DAI's greetings to them. His mission, it was hoped, would re-establish the bonds of these long-removed cousins to the German Volk and the New Germany.

Entering Manitoba from North Dakota in early September 1936, Götz began a two-month tour of western Canada that took him into such German settlements as Steinbach and Altona in Manitoba, Saskatoon, Loon

River, and Paradise Hill in Saskatchewan, and Edmonton, Stony Plain, and Dapp in Alberta. Throughout his tight schedule, Götz sought to meet as many Swabians and other Germans as possible.[176] His meetings followed a standard pattern. He began with an illustrated lecture, which frequently included not only slides of Germany and Swabia but also, in some cases, pictures of the very villages from which the Canadian Germans he was addressing had emigrated. After this indulgence in nostalgia, the DAI's representative would elaborate on the New Germany. In his commission he was fully aware that he was "to lead the distant cousins back to an appreciation of their Volk via the path of party ideology."[177]

Götz left no gathering without clarifying several vital points for his listeners. First, he always stressed how Germans of the Third Reich, awakened by the volkish movement, were proud of the *Auslandsdeutsche* and their achievements and how the *Reichsdeutsche* looked upon them as brothers beyond the sea. In the same language that other volkish representatives employed in Canada, he informed his audience "that blood was stronger than citizenship papers."[178] He urged them to cultivate their German essence and to reject the efforts being made to assimilate them into the Anglo-Celtic Canadian nation, for the Canadian melting-pot *(Schmelztiegel)*, he insisted, would destroy that which was most eternal and most positive about them. He emphasized that identification with Hitler's Germany represented the only way to avoid the melting-pot disaster.[179] Götz discouraged assimilation not simply for volkish ideological reasons but for material ones as well. Due to his experience, he believed Germans outside the Reich were being cruelly exploited by the majority groups among whom they lived and toiled. He saw their considerable contributions to the building up of their non-German lands going unrecognized and their only possibility for economic or social advancement lying in the abandonment of their German heritage and a rapid assimilation into the majority group.[180] This, of course, was unacceptable. Like Colin Ross, Götz considered the liberal sociopolitical order in Canada a dying system. The real solution to the problems of Canada's Germans, he argued, lay in return *(Rückwanderung)* to Hitler's Germany.[181]

Götz, whose simplicity of manner and warm, outgoing personality enhanced his natural speaking talents, made a favourable impression in almost all his appearances. The rural people and peasants who composed the majority of the Germans he encountered identified closely with the lecturer, himself of peasant stock. This popularity enabled him to gather extensive information on the Germans in Canada's west and to exploit this for propaganda purposes. The fact-gathering procedure was standardized. From the places where he appeared, he would write Strölin a letter describing his activities. The letter would be signed by those Germans who had gathered at the reception after the lecture to meet him. Once Strölin had received Götz's report, Stuttgart would seek to contact the Canadians listed.[182] For example, on 9 September 1936, Götz submitted a report from Steinbach, Manitoba. Writing on the stationery of H.H. Reimer, a Steinbach merchant, Götz described his activities in and impressions of Steinbach and nearby Gruenthal. Thirteen Steinbach Mennonites signed his report.[183] In a December 1936 letter to Reimer, the DAI's Grisebach, responding for Strölin, announced how happy he was with the friendly reception afforded Götz and expressed the DAI's desire to remain in contact with Steinbach's Germans.[184]

Like the DAI, the Volksbund für das Deutschtum im Ausland arose from a concern that Germans outside the Reich were pressured by the growing national consciousness of other non-German peoples. The VDA had evolved out of the Allgemeiner Deutscher Schulverein (General German School Society), founded in 1881, which changed its name to the Verein für das Deutschtum im Ausland (Society for Germans Abroad) in 1908. During the Great War and the Weimar Republic, the VDA developed into the leading institution for dealing with the cultural concerns of the *Auslandsdeutsche*. From its inception, the VDA had manifested a particular interest in German schools abroad and German language instruction. Throughout the 1920s it devoted much energy and resources to providing free German books for the scattered foreign German communities. Like the DAI, the VDA also provided consultation and advice to intended emigrants seeking information on opportunities in receiving lands abroad. Unlike the DAI, however, the VDA leadership disapproved of emigration and on this issue followed the RWA and RA rather closely. Thus when VDA publications dealt with Canada, they presented an unflattering version similar to that found in Hintrager's *Nachrichtenblatt*.[185]

With Hitler's triumph in 1933, the meaning and status of the Verein für das Deutschtum im Ausland were, momentarily at least, enhanced. The change in title to Volksbund für das Deutschtum im Ausland in 1933 and the appointment of the dynamic Austrian R. Hans Steinacher as leader symbolized the VDA's heightened stature.[186] The VDA's new head reflected the volkish mood of the times. Steinacher believed that "in addition to the obligations of state citizenship each German in the world had duties to his Volk."[187] For him, the demands of the state could be limited by political necessities, but the requirements of the Volk could not be compromised.[188] Volk unity was not something crass, finite, or material: "*Volkstum* is genuine community; the unity of the single individuals and parts with the whole is created ... through bonds of emotion and spiritual ties."[189] Steinacher supported the Nazi cause because it represented a "movement which arose out of the entire Volk's experience and because it brought state into harmony with Volk in a way Germany had not known since the wars of liberation in the early nineteenth century."[190]

The "general and most important goal for the VDA," Steinacher wrote shortly after his appointment as leader in 1933, "is the retention, confirmation, and strengthening of the German Volk groups outside the borders of Germany."[191] Thus, even more than the DAI, the VDA did not concern itself with Germans leaving Germany but rather with those already living abroad. In Steinacher's opinion the German obligation toward the *Auslandsdeutsche* could best be served by his agency, because the VDA represented "the only general, comprehensive conveyer of that far-reaching volkish ideology." To him the National Socialist victory in 1933 was crucial for the VDA, because "the new Reich, which justifies itself ... on its relationship to the Volk, and which no longer equates German [identity] with citizenship status [in Germany], had secured for the VDA the broadest and freest room to educate and unite the Volk."[192]

To realize Steinacher's ambitions, the VDA committed itself to several tasks. After 1933 its most important commission remained support for the *Auslandsdeutsche* in cultural affairs and German schools.[193] In addition, the VDA propagandized Germans abroad through the distribution of its own publications, such as *Der Volksdeutsche*. The VDA also gathered information through its agents in the various German colonies.[194] All these activities were carried out in North America, as evidenced by the sending of blue candles at Christmas to the *Volksgenossen,* the widespread campaign to distribute VDA publications, and the substantial support for German school programs. Because the VDA was conducting such an aggressive and extensive effort in Canada, the leader of the Deutsch-Canadischer Verband von Saskatchewan (German-Canadian Society of Saskatchewan) could conclude happily in his report for 1934 that "the *Auslandsdeutsche* were no longer looked upon as unwanted stepchildren" because in the Reich of that "great German Adolf Hitler" there was "the Volksbund für das Deutschtum im Ausland to listen to our needs."[195]

The VDA's school program in Canada consisted basically of supplying textbooks. The head of the German school program in Ontario reported in 1935 that his organization received from the VDA "free of charge ... school books for teachers and children."[196] VDA assistance to the various German libraries in Canada was equally generous. Its books and other reading materials enabled new book centres to be established and existing libraries to expand their holdings.[197] According to the minutes of the seventh convention of Mennonite settlers of Alberta, held in Gem during mid-July 1937, the Coaldale Library had received 165 books from the VDA in 1936-7. And more good deeds were to be expected: "The VDA has contributed many good books to our Coaldale Library, and wishes further to extend its energetic support to our German school. It also offers to assist the Provincial Committee in establishing a circulating library and to provide our largest settlements in the province with stationary libraries and school materials."[198]

The VDA made its presence felt in Canada not only with libraries and schoolbooks but also through its own publications. The bimonthly *Der*

Volksdeutsche was one of its typical and most successful periodicals. In it Canadian Germans could follow the progress of the Volk movement in the world and could learn how to advance it in Canada.[199] For example, in 1934, seeking to advance nonassimilation, *Der Volksdeutsche* pointed out that "the French in Canada enjoy rights which the Germans could seek to emulate. Clearly, the leadership of the Canadian German community will attempt to win for the *Volksdeutsche* of Canada the same conditions for survival as those which the French enjoy."[200]

The Volksbund für das Deutschtum im Ausland also involved itself in Canadian affairs through its agents. In late 1934, the VDA selected Bernhard Bott as its chief representative for Canada. An immigrant from Bavaria who had settled in Regina after the war, by 1930 Bott had become the leading spokesman for German culture in western Canada.[201] His appointment was prompted not simply by his record of distinguished service to the cause of German affairs, but also his urgent personal desire to serve the VDA.[202] In his capacity as representative *(Vertrauensmann)*, Bott, who received a monthly financial allowance from the VDA, laboured to further German schools and to advance German culture.[203] In addition, he gathered information for the VDA by circulating among Canada's Germans questionnaires asking for details on their work, their habits, and the nature of their communities.[204] After 1935, Bott became the most outspoken propagandist in Canada for Hitler and the National Socialist movement.[205]

The propaganda that Bott and the National Socialists directed at Canada's German community differed from the propaganda disseminated during the Weimar Republic. In the Weimar period, those charged with looking after Germans living abroad had sought simply to raise awareness or consciousness among these far-flung blood brothers and sisters of their membership in a worldwide pan-German Volk community. The VDA and DAI representatives wanted to bind the Germans outside the Reich to the Volk in Germany by developing cultural ties; they did not try to induce Germans living beyond Germany to return to the fatherland.[206] After 1933, the Nazis reversed this policy. Following Hitler's accession to power, the siren call of "Heim ins Reich" (Home to the Reich) was pitched successfully first at Austria's Germans, then at the Sudeten Germans in Czechoslovakia, and finally beyond Europe. Well before the war, Nazi ideologues believed the German diaspora of the preceding two centuries could be reversed. After 1939 this fantasy grew, and Canada's Germans were included in it.

Travel out of Germany to Canada

The journey from Germany to Canada during the interwar period compared most favourably with past conditions. In general, it was much safer and more comfortable, as well as bureaucratically more organized. A 1928 pamphlet published by the Hamburg-American Line for its German-speaking clientele described the new services, conveniences, and organization in detail. The shipping firm dispatched easily recognizable representatives wearing "caps emblazoned in gold lettering with 'Hamburg-Amerika Linie'" to the Hamburg train station to receive all incoming emigrant trains. These agents were to assist with advice and help in transporting baggage. Since all passengers were required to be present in Hamburg two days before departure, the shipping firm now provided facilities for their room and board in the firm's Overseas Home *(Überseeheim-Hapag)*. There a traveller could stay without cost for up to five days. The firm's ticket to Canada included this stay plus the medical examination the emigrant was required to undergo before sailing.

To be certified to board ship, the emigrant to Canada had to have his papers in order, a process that illustrated two developments of the interwar period: just how far the liberal nineteenth century's open system of migration had receded into the past, and as a corollary, just how far the modern state's "embrace" of its subjects had progressed. As a first step in the paper ordering, German citizens had to possess a valid German passport and a Canadian visa secured from one of the Canadian immigration offices in Europe. Before granting this visa, the Canadian authorities required from the emigrant the following documents: a valid permit to travel to Canada secured from German authorities within the past twelve months; a police certificate, no older than a month, attesting to the emigrant's good conduct; an official birth certificate; and, if married, a marriage licence. From its future farmers, Canadian immigration officials required a document from the authorities in their home district confirming that they had indeed farmed in Germany. Canada also required, as a bare minimum, that those disembarking in the dominion bring enough funds to reach the place of their intended settlement. From the different categories of immigrants, the Canadian officials required different sums. A single nondenominational farmer was required to bring enough for train fare from Halifax to Winnipeg, normally $25, and an additional $25 for other expenses; a single Lutheran or Catholic farmer needed only $10 to $15; a nondenominational farmer with a family needed between $500 and $1,000; a Lutheran or Catholic farmer and his family needed only $100; a female domestic servant needed $150 to $200; and the wife and family of a German farmer already settled in Canada needed $5 to $10 per person. The active assistance to immigrants provided by Catholic and Lutheran aid organizations in Canada accounts for the significant differences in monetary requirements between those professing religious affiliation and the nondenominational.[207] Finally, in addition to supplying evidence of financial resources, emigrants had to prove good health and, for males over fifteen, literacy.

Once checked in and allowed to board ship, the future resident of Canada was free to enjoy the conveniences of modern travel. The HAPAG publication described in detail the ships it offered for passengers to Canada. In 1927 there were two, both less than five years old and fitted out in modern fashion. The *Thuringia* and the *Westphalia* each had a capacity of 570 (170 first-class and 400 third-class passengers). Although first-class amenities exceeded those available for the third, the distinction was far less than that which had existed between steerage passengers and those travelling above deck in the preceding generations. First class offered separate cabins for families of two to four members and single cabins for those travelling alone, a large dining room with individual tables, a comfortable smoking room, and an elegant ladies' room. Third class, the pamphlet emphasized, was not far behind: "The traveller has available to him or her large, airy rooms with two to six beds. These beds have mattresses and soft pillows and are made up with white sheets. In each room there is a modern sink for washing up; toilets and showers are located nearby. For the third-class traveller, the dining hall provides well-prepared and appropriate meals at designated times. The food is served by stewards on tables with white tablecloths." To back this up, the pamphlet published a typical day's menu. The eight o'clock breakfast included scrambled eggs, sausage, fried potatoes, bread, and coffee; the noon dinner featured soup, baked pork roast, Bavarian sauerkraut, parsley potatoes, and ice cream; and the six o'clock supper was beef stew, mashed potatoes, cold cuts, bread, and tea. In addition, coffee and cake were served in the dining hall at three in the afternoon.[208] When not sleeping or eating, the traveller could make use of the ship's socializing space: a large room for general gatherings, a smoking room, and a special room for the ladies. "Naturally," the pamphlet boasted, "a promenade deck is available for all passengers."[209] The services that accompanied these comfortable arrangements likewise represented a vast improvement over earlier times. The ships each had a physician to look after the sick during the voyage, offered facilities for locking up and safekeeping valuables, and provided Lutheran and Catholic church services.

Thus, compared with the characteristic hardships of nineteenth-century transoceanic travel, conditions for the emigrant in the interwar period had greatly improved. Basically, these improvements resulted from greater speed, more comfort, and more efficient organization of the whole migration process. Travel time, which had been reduced so dramatically by the substitution of steam for wind power over the course of the second half of the nineteenth century, experienced least change during the interwar period. The increasingly efficient propellers introduced in the 1880s and 1890s required little improvement. The length of the voyages in the 1920s and 1930s remained about the same as before the war, that is, between seven and ten days from Europe to New York or Halifax.

Conclusion

Between the wars, German migration to Canada swung from one extreme to another: during the 1920s relatively large numbers of Reich Germans settled in the dominion, and then during the 1930s German emigration all but ceased. The period's economic, social, and political chaos caused these variations and also affected the migration policies of the two states. Generally before 1930, prewar approaches applied in both states. The dominion's immigration officers and policy setters followed, really for the last time, the policy that had been in place since the beginnings of serious recruitment in the 1870s and 1880s, namely, of seeking only female domestic servants and male farmers among Germany's emigrants. To win such converts in disoriented postwar Germany, the Canadian government ran out the old, time-worn romantic/civilized image and Canada was once again presented as a huge land without enough people, rich in natural resources, pristine and unspoiled, yet free, progressive, and peaceful. In Canada, it was claimed, opportunity abounded, and land on which to establish one's own farm was still free or dirt cheap. Although the Canadian policy of recruiting farmer-immigrants appeared even more inappropriate in postwar Germany than it had before 1914, it succeeded rather remarkably in the late 1920s. The Reich Germans who came to Canada during the 1920s emigrated because conditions at home were so inauspicious and Canada appeared to offer hope for the future. For recruiting Reich Germans, the Canadian government expanded its use of agents and agencies, relying basically on the two national railways, the CPR and CNR. Left largely on their own, these quasi-state or semiprivate agencies not only implemented but also shaped the dominion's immigration policies.

In Weimar Germany, meanwhile, emigration to Canada was not viewed sympathetically. Although negative reaction to the positive view of Canada and disapproval of emigration there was expressed often enough in the immediate postwar years, in the late 1920s this disfavour grew in strength. Part of the reason for this lay in the intensification of volkish, nationalist ideas, as reflected in the growth and increasing influence of agencies such as the Deutsche Ausland-Institut and the Volksbund für das Deutschtum im Ausland. Despite the spread of more negative views of Canada, the Weimar government lacked the resources that Germany's prewar governments had possessed to obstruct effectively Canada's enthusiastic propagandizing and recruitment. Throughout the 1920s, the Reichsstelle für das Auswanderungswesen in Berlin waged a largely unsuccessful rearguard action against Canadian solicitation. The forces pushing Germans, particularly the young, out of the country at that time were so great that Weimar's officials could do little to stop those bent on leaving. To look after the welfare of the large number of emigrants, private charity groups, and especially Germany's main Christian denominations, provided the help the impoverished state could not or would not advance. The Lutheran and Catholic Churches developed broad networks of representatives in Germany and Canada charged with seeing that their coreligionists had support enough for successful settlement. With such advanced facilitation networks and the advantage of modern steamship and railway transportation, the emigrants of the 1920s, despite the huge increase in modern bureaucratic paperwork, had it much easier than those who had departed for the promise of romantic Canada seventy years before.

After 1930 radically new programs that drastically restricted migration emerged in both Canada and Germany. In Canada, the Depression forced the restructuring of policy; in Germany, the triumph of Hitler's movement ended the attraction of emigration for traditional German migrants. The flow of Reich Germans to Canada ceased after 1930 because Ottawa, faced with escalating unemployment, closed down further immigration. Even desperate political refugees, with but a few exceptions, were not offered asylum; Germany's persecuted Jews, especially, were not admitted. The type of movement that did increase was deportation, and Germans were included among those sent back to Europe by Canada's anxious immigration authorities. At the same time, in Hitler's Third Reich a number of factors made emigration for "acceptable Germans" neither feasible nor possible. The new National Socialist government possessed both the resources and the will to halt the out-migration of "worthy" members of the Volk that had plagued the Weimar years. Although the repression and intimidation used so often to force out those the Nazis opposed was clearly available, such force did not normally have to be employed to prevent "good" Germans from leaving. In Hitler's Germany, the reasons for emigration that had existed during the 1920s had seemingly disappeared. By 1934 Hitler's public works and armaments programs had apparently ended Germany's depression, and jobs appeared to be available for all those who sought work. Moreover, a new twist developed in the history of German migration abroad: after 1933 the energies expended on migration involved returning Germans to Germany rather than sending the Volk abroad. Economically, Canada presented a much different picture. The Depression's hold had not been broken in 1935 but lasted in portions of Canada, and especially the prairie West, right up to the decade's end. Thus, although in 1935 the technology for travel and the conditions aboard ship were at their highest stage of development since transoceanic travel had begun, German desire or opportunity to utilize these advantages had evaporated. Not until after 1945 and another major alteration in the political, economic, and social conditions in both countries would a new immigration policy be instituted and large numbers of Germany's migrants again head for Canada.

Conclusion

The history of German-Canadian migration over the period 1850-1939 represents more than just the story of members of one national group travelling to live in the lands of another, or the story of Canada soliciting citizens and subjects from Germany. Because migration is by nature such a comprehensive social phenomenon, the history of German migration to Canada describes in microcosm many of the fundamental changes that occurred in both countries in technology, political arrangement, economic organization, and social structure. In all of these interconnected spheres, tensions arose and subsided as developments spawned by the Industrial Revolution forced older accepted traditions and presumptions to give way. Such tensions inspired and fostered the ideological assumptions that sought to drive or impede these political, economic, social, and technological mutations. Romantic, liberal, nationalist, and imperialist beliefs all coloured the debates that in turn influenced the people involved.

Political Arrangements

When Germany's 1848 revolution fizzled out in the spring of 1849, the returning conservatives attempted to restore the status quo ante revolution. Although they could not recreate the *Kleinstaaterei* of the eighteenth century, particularism still reigned. The states composing the German Confederation remained sovereign within their own boundaries, and those who had wielded power before 1848 did so again in the 1850s. These conservative state governments continued to have the last word regarding the movement of their subjects. That word could be encouraging, as in Baden, or discouraging, as in Prussia. In both cases, the mercantilist belief that the state might use its subjects as it saw fit held sway. But this official policy did not represent the only option. The liberal credo, which held that the state existed foremost to serve the individual citizen by guaranteeing civic freedom and property rights, interpreted the state's obligations toward those who wanted to emigrate quite differently. To liberals, the right of movement had become basic. Although the 1848 revolution had supposedly abolished the last vestiges of feudal obligation, the states' practice of interfering with their subjects' free movement continued well after 1850. The slow abolition of passport requirements and reluctant decriminalization of undocumented movement illustrates this. Although greater freedom of movement was ultimately recognized, in the 1860s and 1870s several efforts to redefine explicitly the state's role in emigration were aborted. Not until 1897 did the Reichstag pass a statute applicable to the Reich, which endorsed the absolute constitutional right to free movement while accepting the Reich's obligation to protect would-be emigrants from exploitation in Germany. This latter move represented a significant extension of state involvement in the process of migration.

In Canada, meanwhile, the national government's role in managing the movement of people into the country began in earnest with Confederation. In British North America no clear immigration policy had existed. The separate provinces competed with each other as best they could to influence immigration. For example, before 1870 free land was distributed to would-be immigrants at the discretion of the provinces. London provided little direction. In England the liberal philosophy of minimizing the role of the state prevailed, and this philosophy permeated British North America as well. The Dominion Lands Act of 1872 changed this by placing exclusive control of the newly acquired western lands in the hands of the new federal government. Designed to lure settlers to the West and thus ensure the continued existence of the Canadian federation, this act made the federal government pivotal to the nation's survival. The implementation of Macdonald's National Policy and the completion of the transcontinental railway extended Ottawa's sphere of influence even further. As the National Policy was implemented, a new dominion immigration plan took shape. Thus, by the time of Laurier and Sifton, a more aggressive role for securing immigrants had been established for the dominion's government. The increasingly liberal laws that had progressively decriminalized population movement in Europe benefited this new, expansive Canadian immigration program.

In the first decade of the twentieth century, the Immigration Acts of 1906 and 1910 provided additional evidence of the Canadian state's growing activism. They gave Ottawa additional powers for screening immigrants to prevent undesirables from entering the country. The loose admission procedures of the previous century were replaced by more efficient and systematic ones, not only at the reception centres in Canada but also in the European embarkation ports. These developments signalled the emergence in Canada of a modern state policy extending state sovereignty over both the admission and exclusion of migrants. Thus, the involvement of both the Canadian and German governments in the movement of peoples into and out of their respective lands appeared increasingly similar. Although on the eve of the Great War much tentativeness still characterized policies and their execution, both states had assumed responsibilities and duties toward their migrating subjects long avoided by earlier regimes.

After the Great War, the German federal policy continued to endorse the citizen's right to move freely. In the liberal Weimar Republic this seemed entirely appropriate, and in the chaotic postwar years, many thousands took advantage of this status and left Germany. Although increasing numbers of concerned Germans protested this out-migration as a serious loss for the nation, the policy was not changed, because of lack of federal resources to intervene successfully, devotion to liberal ideals, and the widespread belief that Germany had too many poor and unemployed. After 1933, however, things were different. Embracing the mercantilist traditions of the past, or more accurately, grafting these statist policies onto its own modern totalitarian theories, the National Socialist government denied the individual's freedom of movement. Use of documentary controls extended well beyond the ubiquitous postwar passport requirements. Not only military service but residence, currency regulations, political reliability, vocational usefulness, and a host of other reasons could be and were invoked to restrict or to force emigration. In Hitler's Germany, the individual German appeared not as a citizen but as a subject member of the Volk community. Individual rights in the traditional sense were incompatible with National Socialism and the demands of the New Germany. Remaining at home serving the German Volk made emigration unthinkable.

Migration policy in Canada during the interwar years likewise fluctuated dramatically. In the 1920s Ottawa continued to support immigration, hoping to increase population and thus the viability of the Canadian national ideal. As in the several decades before 1914, western Canada continued to receive most of the country's newcomers, and the preferred immigrants remained tillers of the soil. From 1923 to the end of the decade, even Germans, if they could farm, were welcomed into the dominion. Ottawa's preference for farmers in the years shortly after the Winnipeg General Strike accorded well with the government's more general efforts at controlling labour agitators and political radicalism. This liberal admission policy disappeared with the Depression's onslaught. Widespread unemployment and economic distress, which were particularly severe in Canada's west, made the previous policy supporting the reception of new workers and farmers both politically unpopular and economically untenable.

To effect policy, the modernizing state required tools and powers. As had been true since the modern state emerged in western Europe at the end of the middle ages, the best tools remained bureaucrats pledged to do the state's bidding. The evolution of migration policy in both Canada and Germany therefore occurred in conjunction with the expansion of the state's control of or influence on those actually engaged in migration work. By later standards, both the German states and British North America functioned from 1850 until their unifications with only skeleton civil services. The dearth of bureaucrats was evident in their handling of internal population movements, and even more so in external or transoceanic migrations. In the 1850s what immigrant recruitment occurred for British North America took place overwhelmingly in Great Britain or the United States and was conducted by private individuals rather than salaried state officials. Although early in the 1850s Canada had assigned personnel stationed as domestic agents to guide homesteaders onto the land, only at the end of the decade did the province of Ontario send permanent representatives to reside in Europe and recruit. William Wagner, Canada's first agent charged with soliciting immigrants in Germany proper, assumed his Berlin post in 1860.

During the same period in the German Confederation, where indifference had replaced mercantilist interference, neglect of migration matters was even more apparent. Although huge numbers of Germans abandoned their homeland in the period from 1850 to 1870, no civil service evolved to deal with the problem. Only in a few states, such as Baden, Württemberg, and Hesse, where government personnel and local officials assisted in exporting paupers and other undesirables, did the state become involved significantly. Otherwise, the emigration field was left to private or local philanthropic groups, the churches, or in the case of Bremen and Hamburg, city officials representing business interests. The lack of a coherent emigration policy in Germany, plus the consequent absence of officials assigned to monitor and direct those migrating, helps explain the prevalent abuses travellers experienced in this period not only on their voyages to North America but also as they prepared to leave Germany. The abuses endured before embarkation ranged from fraudulent ticketing procedures to price gouging at hotels or restaurants to being robbed or swindled in the street. Once aboard ship, travellers suffered most often from inadequate food, overly cramped sleeping quarters, and dangerously deficient hygiene.

From 1870 to the Great War, the number of bureaucrats and state officials assigned to and engaged in migration matters gradually grew in both Canada and Germany as in-migration and out-migration respectively increased in importance. In both lands apparent national needs and concerns influenced this expansion of the federal state's role. In Canada the federal government had begun to commit more resources to immigrant solicitation during the Macdonald period. In Laurier's time additional moves were made: a federal department, the Immigration Branch of the Department of the Interior, was created and staffed; the network of agents involved in recruitment expanded, including directly sponsored ones and those working for the subcontracted Canadian Pacific Railway; personnel were hired to produce and distribute a greatly expanded volume of immigration propaganda in the form of pamphlets, flyers, books, and maps; and new statutes requiring officials to monitor compliance were passed to control more tightly the immigrants entering the dominion.

Concurrently in the Reich, similar developments transpired. During the Bismarckian and Wilhelmian ages, both pundits and state officials perceived emigration as a threat to the new Reich. Besides stepped-up surveillance of Canada's agents by German consuls in the dominion and by local police and interior ministry personnel in Germany, the most dramatic expression of a new approach was the 1897 statute aimed at providing a national blue-print for controlling emigration. The staff charged with exercising this control included the Reich chancellor, Bundesrat members, consular officers abroad, and numerous lesser government servants. Five years later, the establishment of the Zentral-Auskunftsstelle für Auswanderer in Berlin, funded and supported by the Reich, continued the effort to expand the number of state-influenced officials engaged in emigration control. By 1914 in both Canada and Germany expanded numbers of elected or appointed officials in government, newly created departments assigned to monitor or regulate migrants, and private migration assistance agencies answerable to state regulators all functioned as agents of the state's modernizing policies.

After the First World War the centralizing tendencies of wartime migration control were retained, such as passport restrictions. Indeed, as a result of the war, the influence of national governments grew much more pervasive and increasingly less questioned. In Germany, the early years of the Weimar Republic represented something of an exception. Although a new central agency, the Reichswanderungsamt, had been created to control Germany's emigration, it could do little more than scold those guilty of violating the laws prohibiting emigrant solicitation; the Weimar government lacked adequate funding and staffing, and the victorious allies frequently exerted pressure to prevent Germany's government from assuming a more aggressive role. By 1930 this impotence had begun to disappear, but after Hitler's accession to power, state and party functionaries abounded who interfered with or prohibited old-style emigration. During the Third Reich emigration became basically an option utilized by the persecuted to avoid the repressive regime.

In the postwar period, the Canadian state's control of immigration also appeared increasingly modern. In the 1920s the government once again took the lead in encouraging in-migration. Agents of the Canadian railways, foreign office representatives abroad, and the Interior Ministry in Ottawa were all engaged. Canada's heavy reliance upon semiprivate agencies such as the Canadian Pacific Railway rather than state-appointed recruiting agents to solicit immigrants remained anomalous, but in other ways modernization progressed. The individual immigrant experienced this change in the plethora of bureaucratic forms to be filled out and references to be secured. During and after the war, expanded laws were passed to control entry to and exit from Canada more closely, including more comprehensive statutes regulating the expulsion or extradition of undesirable immigrants. Although Ottawa pursued an open-door policy from 1923 to 1929, after 1930 the dominion government abruptly halted the flow of Germans and many other nationalities into the country.

As was true in Hitler's Germany, Ottawa's politicians considered immigration a crucial national issue requiring increased direction from the central government. To manage this, the staffs charged with exercising control over immigration had to be more extensive than ever before to perform the numerous and varied tasks expected of them. Consequently, by 1939 in both Germany and Canada the modernizing state had increasingly expropriated from individuals and private entities the means of movement. Although in Canada the railways were charged with the actual recruitment, officials in Ottawa nevertheless defined who and where they could recruit. State regulations and the state bureaucrats involved with migration now "embraced" moving Germans and Canadians as never before. As John Torpey puts it, such regulation of the movement of citizens/subjects had become yet another way to constitute "the state-ness" of the state.[1]

Economic Organization

If changing political forms and procedures between 1850 and 1939 affected the policies and patterns of German migration to Canada, so did the alterations that occurred in the objective, material contexts of each country. In 1850 the economic systems in place in the provinces of British North America and the multiple German states were overwhelmingly characterized in agriculture by small-scale farms and customary farming methods, in industry by artisanal production, and in commerce by local or limited markets. Neither economy remained stagnant, however, because the Industrial Revolution that had already greatly transformed Great Britain by midcentury had spread eastward as far as Germany and westward to England's North American empire. In both Germany and Canada, the railroad, which symbolized the dawning industrial age, had appeared.

Although both economies were changing, they progressed at different rates; Germany's economic growth far outstripped that of the British North American provinces. Besides enjoying a significantly larger population and greater cultural homogeneity, the German economy did not suffer from the geographic problem of distance. Several other major developments facilitated German economic progress. Tariff policies since the founding of the Zollverein (Customs Union) in the 1830s had facilitated the movement of Germany's goods by extending market possibilities well beyond the traditional local ones. German agriculture underwent major innovations in land control and how and what was produced. And consolidation of agricultural units occurred with ever greater frequency as small peasant plots became increasingly untenable. In the period 1850-70, this applied particularly to the country's west and southwest, in areas like Baden and Württemberg, where flight from the land created the basis for mass emigration. As we have seen, some of these displaced persons ended up in Canada. In industry, Germany also experienced rapid growth between 1850 and Bismarck's unification. In the two decades after midcentury, Germany's railway system grew spectacularly, stimulating a surge in capital and consumer goods production. The markets for many of these products extended well beyond Germany proper. The numerous new factories producing such goods required labourers, encouraging migration from the land to the new industrial cities, and Germany's modern urbanization began to take shape. All these agricultural, industrial, and urban developments occurred in the context of a rapidly expanding population. As well, these innovations caused dislocations that prompted many of the displaced to emigrate.

In British North America in the twenty years after 1850, the entrenched system of small family farms and artisan production suffered little of the dislocation experienced in Germany. Some industrial innovation did develop in Canada, but most manufacturers produced traditional goods in customary ways. The most significant Canadian advances occurred largely in transportation, with the railway leading the way. The building of roads into the forest and the clearing of land provided the basis for continued expansion of Canada's traditional agricultural, mining, and lumbering activities. Since the Canadian economy offered potential openings for preindustrial or proto-industrial labourers, it represented an appropriate or at least feasible destination for Germany's surplus of dislocated farmers and artisans. But the disparate provinces of British North America could not produce a coherent migration policy. Thus, in the 1850s and 1860s immigration promotion remained essentially sporadic, limited, and directed almost exclusively at potential recruits from the British Isles.

Between 1870 and 1914, Canada's perceived labour needs changed dramatically, spurring an effort to satisfy the country's rapidly expanding demand by seeking farm labourers in lands beyond the British Isles such as the recently united German states. The opening of the Canadian west also created a huge potential demand for new immigrants. For almost half a century following Macdonald's National Policy, Canada's governors sought to settle the West to ensure the survival of the Canadian nation-state. Those whom they settled had to be farmers, because the unoccupied prairies seemed best suited for agricultural exploitation. In addition, farmers fit the myth of the future western Canadian agricultural empire so zealously promulgated by the Eastern expansionists. Under the dominion's partial industrialization policy, which emphasized the primacy of exporting wheat and natural resources at the cost of consistent industrialization, there appeared to be no pressing need for industrial folk, whether artisans or factory workers. What manufactured goods the Western farmer required could be easily obtained from Canada's protected domestic industry, and luxury items could be secured in Europe or the United States. Ottawa therefore set out to find the necessary number of agriculturists to make successful western farming a reality. This emphasis upon agriculturists accorded with the widespread popular definition of Canada as a country whose people farmed or lived off the land by trapping, mining, or lumbering. In the decades immediately preceding the Great War, the decision to seek only farmers for the newly opening West turned out to be both fortuitous and paradoxical. The ongoing development of Canada's rail system made possible the exploitation of new, greatly expanded markets. Railroads and steamships allowed western Canadian farmers to grow specialized crops that could be marketed far beyond Manitoba or Saskatchewan. Thus, by the end of the nineteenth century, wheat was king in Canada's west, and the farmer who grew and marketed that wheat resembled less and less the independent, self-reliant smallholder whose image had dominated Canadian society for so long.

In Germany, meanwhile, the four decades after 1870 saw agriculture decline in relative importance as industry made increasingly impressive gains. In these years the mixed German economy of midcentury was transformed into an essentially modern industrial one. Indeed, by 1900 the German Empire had advanced far enough to rival the industrial might of Great Britain. Most Germans now lived in cities and pursued livelihoods in industry or other vocations closely related to or dependent on industry, and the hearty peasant of the past had become something of an anachronism in large sections of the German Empire. Peasant numbers had declined so precipitously, in fact, that foreign agricultural workers had become a prominent part of the German landscape. Agriculture's decline at the end of the century was reflected further by Germany's increasing import of foodstuffs. The German experience appeared distinctly different from trends in Canada, where the number of farmers and the amount of land under cultivation were increasing.

In Canada the western expansion maintained its pace right up to 1914. For the Western farmer and his Eastern industrial counterpart, the Great War was a boon, as the Canadian economy expanded even further between 1914 and 1918. Despite some dislocations in the immediate postwar years, this growth did not cease. In the war's aftermath, the country's economy progressed further along the road toward urban and industrial domination. While the heart of the dominion's modern industrial expansion lay in eastern Ontario and Quebec, the Maritimes and west coast did not remain entirely unaffected by these developments. The Prairie provinces, however, continued to be overwhelmingly agricultural and traditional, and the West's wheat economy during the 1920s experienced enough prosperity to make that area's economic future also appear bright. In 1923 this prosperity justified reopening the West to German immigration. Because the dominion's western wheat economy required only farm labourers, emigration from the farmer-poor Reich to Canada's people-poor prairies remained modest, even during Germany's ruinous inflation. When Canada's wheat economy collapsed in 1929, even this small stream dried up.

The disastrous collapse of Canada's western economy in the Depression occurred because that economy relied almost entirely on producing and exporting its produce abroad. By the 1920s the Canadian wheat economy had become modern in the scale of its production and in the scope of its distribution. The huge demand for wheat and its successful movement abroad, which dated from the late nineteenth century, had become by the 1920s an established fact. The transformation of Canadian agriculture from serving local markets to supplying international ones, which had occurred in response to the needs of industrializing foreign markets, was bound to suffer when those wheat-importing industrial systems began to weaken. Precisely this happened beginning in 1929, as the previous international system of interdependent trade and production atrophied.

In Germany, economic developments during the National Socialist reign made the Canadian decision to halt recruiting German farmers in the Reich irrelevant. With its armament production and public works programs in gear by 1935, demand for workers within Germany escalated. For those who previously had emigrated to Canada or elsewhere, Hitler's Germany now provided what had been lacking in 1850, 1880, or 1923, namely, a job at home. Now that Germany needed workers, the push factor that had forced so many in the past to abandon the fatherland did not apply. Hitler's autarchy policy obviated emigration as well: since Germany sought to become self-reliant and self-sufficient, its labour force had to remain within the country making that self-reliance and self-sufficiency possible. This German autarchy accorded nicely with the labour market realities in Canada as well, for in North America, the Depression that decimated Canada's industrial and agricultural spheres made the entry of more workers into the dominion appear both superfluous and socially dangerous.

Social Structure

While changing politics and economies affected the course of German-Canadian migration, so too did the fundamental social alterations between 1850 and 1939. In both societies the social context for the migrations appeared crucial, and the social changes influencing movement were tied to the transition to more modern social arrangements. At the base of this social restructuring lay the broader demographic developments that marked the four generations from 1850 to 1939. In both societies the demographic trends showed significant expansion. On one hand, Germany, like Europe in general, experienced very rapid and extensive population growth, especially between 1850 and 1914. On the other hand, the population of Canada appeared to grow less dramatically, despite the fact that the data for both lands show similar overall growth rates. In 1850 the population of British North America totalled only 2.4 million. By 1870 it had increased to 3.6 million, by 1890 to 4.8 million, and by 1910 to 7.2 million. Thus in sixty years the population of Canada tripled. In the German states the impressive totals occurred even earlier: at the beginning of the nineteenth century, the population of the area of the German states equivalent to Bismarck's Reich numbered about 24 million. By 1914 that total had increased to 68 million, an increase of just under Canada's 300 percent. Although both states experienced dramatic population growth, this similarity is overshadowed by the huge difference between the sizes of the two lands.

Canada's large size, combined with its modest initial population, determined that the dominion's population density would be far less than Germany's. In Germany's Rhineland district, for example, in 1800 there were 70 people per square kilometre; in 1910 there were 264. Further to the east in Saxony density grew from 78 per square kilometre in 1800 to 321 in 1910. Meanwhile, in Canada matters were quite different. In 1911, Canada's nine provinces contained 7.2 million persons in an area exceeding 9.5 million square kilometres. This resulted in a population density of approximately 0.75 persons per square kilometre. Thirty years later, with the number of Canadians at about 11 million, the dominion's population density had increased marginally to just 1.2 persons per square kilometre. Such figures indicate why fear of overpopulation never became the pressing issue in Canada it did in other Western lands. Although nativists in Canada frequently railed that too many foreigners lived among them, these complaints were prompted more by cultural anxieties than by Malthusian ones. Both French and English Canadians periodically voiced concern that their culture, traditions, or languages would somehow be undermined by the increasing numbers of Slavs, Jews, and Orientals who entered Canada after Confederation. In Canada, however, the issue was race, not space.

Germany experienced a different anxiety. Concern over too many Germans straining existing resources had arisen well before the 1848 revolution. After Bismarck's unification, fears about overpopulation persisted. For many Germans, the number of poor and unemployed represented "the social problem" at the end of the nineteenth century, threatening livelihoods, property, and social order. Emigration proponents consistently paraded out such warnings even after 1918. Interwar German expansionists differentiated between Canada and Germany simply by labelling Canada "a land without people," and Germany "a Volk without land."[2] The "too many people in Germany" theme appeared in the Third Reich as well, but the

Nazis did not propose to solve it by inducing emigration but rather by conquering space for Germans in eastern Europe.

If demography and geography combined to influence migration patterns and policies in both states, so also did changing social structure. In Germany, where the traditional hierarchical society of landed aristocrats, peasants, and artisans had been declining since the eighteenth century, the industrial innovations and capitalistic policies that took off after 1850 greatly hastened this disintegration. The recently emancipated peasantry underwent major changes as its bottom elements – the smallholders and landless labourers – were forced off the land. Likewise, Germany's artisan class found itself increasingly out of employment as new machines and new capitalistic attitudes made the previous ways of producing and socializing obsolete. Contemporaneously, factory labourers drawn from the displaced peasantry and artisan groups and residing in the new urban centres emerged as a distinctly new working class. All this social change, as earlier forms gave way to new ones under the pressure of modernization, directly affected German-Canadian migration.

The social makeup of those who left Germany for Canada between 1850 and 1939 closely reflected these social movements. In the first two decades after 1850, most Germans migrating to Canada were ruined or marginalized smallholder or artisan families, who hoped to restore a social status suffering attrition in Germany. From the 1870s on artisan and peasant families appeared less often among those moving out. In the last decades before 1914, the few Reich emigrants heading for Canada hailed from those new social groups that had emerged to replace the preceding migrants: single industrial workers, other urban labourers, and elements of the rural proletariat who chose to reside and work in Canada instead of in the Reich's cities.

Although the social structure of Canada also changed over the period covered by this book, the alterations were less dramatic than in Germany. The most intense emigration of Germans to Canada occurred when the preponderance of those migrating were custom-bound peasants and artisans, those, in short, who would be most comfortable in Canada's conservative society. Emigration from the Reich to Canada fell off at the end of the nineteenth century when Canada deliberately opted to recruit immigrants who were and would remain peasants. Since in the industrializing Reich this social class had already declined, few marginal peasant families remained to be lured out of Germany for settlement in Canada. Incidentally, this occurred at a time of increased migration to the United States of nonagricultural immigrants seeking work in America's cities. Canadian efforts in the Reich at recruiting farmer-immigrants therefore appeared particularly futile, although they succeeded nicely in eastern Europe, where large communities of traditional German peasants still existed. After 1923, more substantial migration of Reich Germans to Canada did occur in spite of the Canadian government's continued efforts to recruit farmers exclusively. Many of those who opted for Canada at this time did not have agricultural backgrounds, but in the chaotic, socially unstable postwar Weimar Republic they were willing to take the gamble of homesteading in Canada's west out of sheer desperation.

Ideological Proclivities: Liberalism and Romanticism
While the politics, economics, and social developments of the period 1850-1939 influenced migration, so also did ideology. The rationalizations offered to support or discourage migration describe a broad area of ideological transformation. Some of these ideas were largely theoretical and cultural, others more mundane and concrete. Several different major ideological themes coloured the migration debates of the period as apologists and opponents justified their positions by references to contemporary beliefs. Liberal, romantic, nationalist, imperialist, and conservative theories all found spokesmen. Just how and when these themes appeared reflected once again the changes in the secular spheres just discussed.

During the period 1850-1939, the liberal theme revealed itself in several guises. First, the civilized-progressive version of Canada that appeared so often in immigration propaganda described an essentially liberal society. Canada's enlightened educational system with its comprehensive public schools, its representative government with easy citizenship access, its tradition of law and order protecting both property and civil rights, its freedom of speech, press, and assembly guaranteeing expression and movement, and its laissez faire economy all harmonized with the best European liberal programs. Second, in the two generations before the Great War the ideal of free trade made rapid advances, especially in western Europe. Free trade in turn was accompanied by the spread of liberal doctrines eliminating controls on both personal property and individual mobility. As noted above, passports and other restrictions on free movement largely went out of style in most countries during this period. Late-nineteenth-century labour therefore moved more freely than ever before. The age's railway and steamship innovations contributed directly to this movement. Indeed, a combination of the transportation revolution and the easing of restrictions on travel enabled the great European migrations characteristic of the time. The period's "birds of passage" phenomenon, that is, the movement of labourers from Europe to distant overseas lands and back again each year for seasonal work, dramatized this open, liberal system. The age's openness also facilitated migration by German job seekers to Germany's cities and to new transatlantic homes. Although Macdonald's restrictive tariffs remained in place in Canada until the Great War, they did not interfere with the limited numbers of German agrarians actively seeking Canadian farm land for settlement.

Third, the dominant role played by nonstate agencies in migration management, funding, and facilitating reflected the liberal credo of the age as well. Religious agencies staffed by clerics and lay people, and private philanthropic organizations with memberships of businesspersons, lobbyists, and individual do-gooders, played leading roles in the migration of Germans to Canada from the very earliest days. Their numbers, however, were particularly large in the era directly preceding 1914. Finally, the prolonged reluctance of Canada's federal government to step in and aggressively manage immigration matters reflected a traditional liberal hands-off policy. Even in Laurier's time, when Ottawa actively promoted immigration, the heavy reliance on the semiprivate Canadian Pacific Railway to implement Canada's immigration policies reflected liberal prejudices in favour of private enterprise and against overly intrusive government.

The First World War put an end to many of these liberal developments. World conflict made the "night watchman state" ideal of the previous generations anachronistic. To avoid national suicide, wartime governments now assumed greatly expanded roles in many areas of life. Marshalling for war meant conscripting troops, imposing censorship for "right" thinking, and also controlling economic production. An early victim of the new controls was the global economy based on free trade and labour movement. The new restrictions that stifled the free flow of goods and services included tariffs, confiscation of enemy or foreign property, and rationing of vital materials. Governments also introduced work permits, visas, and passports to monitor and control their wartime populations. Both Germany and Canada employed these measures, and thus experienced state officialdom interfering in migration as never before. This wartime interference continued beyond 1918. In the 1920s the state's role in the daily life of its subjects and citizens extended far beyond classical liberal boundaries. New, restrictive immigration laws that controlled not only the entry of acceptable immigrants but also the expulsion of the undesirable symbolized just how far the prewar liberal, open system had receded into the past.

The romantic theme, which matured and spread so widely in the Western world during the first half of the nineteenth century, also appeared in Canadian migration. As the discussion of image in Chapter 1 indicated, those who sought to induce Germans to abandon Europe and settle in North America presented the move as an escape to a more natural and hence superior civilization. The two halves of the Canadian image, the wild, natural, romantic land on the one hand and the democratic, ordered, liberal society on the other, were not always mutually inclusive. In fact, they offered a dual version of the dominion that corresponded to the traditional/modern dichotomy described above. The romantic image of virgin land, endless forests, exotic animals, and natural living in a salubrious environment was backward looking and reactionary. Nevertheless, for those tired of corrupt, chaotic, aged Europe who yearned for the unspoiled, unaffected, and natural, Canada seemed to be the answer. Canada's deliberate promotion of its romantic image reinforced the traditional direction of its larger immigration policy vis-à-vis Germany, of seeking only farmers for settlement in the dominion. Presumably, tillers of the soil fit more naturally and harmoniously into the landscape than those pursuing other vocations. The expansionists' agrarian myth for western Canada pushed so forcefully from the Macdonald period on reinforced this agricultural-only immigration policy in Germany. But recruiting under the agrarian sign was less effective than Canadian apologists hoped. Very few Germans living amid rapid industrialization, as it turned out, were attracted by this vision. Even in Canada itself, demographic, economic, and social developments were undermining the traditional romantic, agrarian version of the country. The majority of the country's population resided in urban centres and were increasingly impervious to the traditional images pandered by Canada's romantic apologists at home and abroad.

For purposes of attracting German immigrants to Canada, neither the romantic nor liberal-civilized renditions of the country enjoyed much success over the generations described in this book. With the exception of the first two decades after 1850, the romantic-reactionary version won few followers. Certainly it accorded with the ideals and wishes of those displaced peasants and artisans who migrated from Germany's south and west to Canada as families in the 1850s and 1860s. By the end of the century, however, there were no longer peasants in Germany for the romantic ideal to charm. The other part of the Canadian image, the liberal one, likewise did not win many followers in the second half of the nineteenth century, being too far advanced for popular acceptance during Bismarck's unification, and later incompatible with Germany's turn-of-the-century migration needs. In 1910 or 1925 displaced agricultural day labourers, factory workers, and the unemployed in general did not seek civil liberties so much as economic security. Since farming was virtually the only vocation open in Canada to immigrating Reich Germans, the economic motive necessary for prompting significantly large migration never materialized. Then, in the 1930s Germany's capture by the National Socialists also decreed the irrelevance of the civilized, liberal version of Canada's image. Democratic institutions, free speech, and liberal education were officially passé in the land of Hitler.

Ideological Proclivities: Nationalism
Throughout the emigration debate, the liberal theme of free movement was normally discussed in terms of not only the individual's rights and needs but also national development. Another important ideological influence on the migration of German people to Canada from 1850 to 1939 was therefore modern nationalism. Since the spread of national consciousness among

Germans entailed shifting loyalties from the local to the national, it necessarily inserted a new set of considerations into political, economic, and
social issues. This national criterion applied to migration as well. In Germany, evaluation of emigration in terms of the nation's present status and
future well-being appeared as early as 1848. The periodic debates which
arose thereafter, especially in times of heavy out-migration, always struggled
with the threshold question of the whether the out-migration helped or
hindered the nation's development.

Although migration as a question of national policy was discussed in
Germany's revolutionary assemblies during the 1848 revolution, only after
national political disunity ended in 1870 could the issue be dealt with real-
istically. The first substantial debate over migration's significance occurred
in Germany in the 1880s. At that time, a new interpretation and argument
supporting qualified emigration was added to the traditional safety valve
justification. Opposing out-migration in general, the new nationalist interpretation held that when it was inevitable, emigrants should not be abandoned. Instead, state officials or private individuals should try to steer those
leaving Germany to countries where the exiles could be useful to the fatherland. Proponents of such guided emigration defined usefulness in both economic and political terms. Economically German émigrés could serve as a
market for German goods abroad; politically they would form a sympathetic pressure group which could be valuable in case of international threats
arising against Germany.

This kind of national concern gave rise in the 1880s and 1890s to a spate
of societies with self-proclaimed missions to influence migration in a positive national way. Many of these remained active up to the outbreak of war
in 1914, and the belief that emigrants should be cultivated as valuable national assets and assisted in retaining their German ties continued after
1918. Indeed, Otto Preusse-Sperber's argument for sending migrants to South
America, where they could best remain German and so continue to be useful to Germany, essentially restated in the 1920s the position taken by
Friedrich Fabri and other colonial apologists in the 1880s. In the 1930s, the
Nazis went even further in calling for the unity of the Volk wherever they
might reside. Ideally, those who had emigrated from Germany before Hitler's
coming were to be brought back home and reincorporated into the German
nation. If that were physically impossible, then at least the scattered Volk
should be culturally and emotionally reattached to the fatherland. A number of agencies received the charge to bring back these distant brothers and
sisters: the Deutsche Ausland-Institut and the Volksbund für das Deutschtum
im Ausland were enlarged and their budgets expanded. The volkish and
racial theories that had influenced German nationalism so profoundly by
the 1920s were enunciated more loudly, more often, and more broadly in
the 1930s. The volkish emphasis upon the sanctity of German blood and

soil and the necessity for the Volk's attachment to both ended the debate on emigration. To the masses of Germans who bought into volkish ideology, National Socialist opposition to out-migration appeared both consistent and justified.

Thus, over the years 1850-1939 the influence of nationalism on Germany's emigration policy had become stronger. If in the early period, the contest between the rights of the individual (free movement in particular) and the material needs of the nation-state (economic, military, and political power) had manifested a certain balance, after 1900 the scales tipped in favour of the nation-state. In the decade before the Great War and in the years immediately following, German patriots argued passionately against permitting the nation's strength to be drained away by emigration, and government officials operating with limited means did their best to obstruct or dissuade Germans from abandoning their country. Frequent complaints by Canadian officials about German officialdom prohibiting agent recruitment or interfering with the transit of intended emigrants in Europe reflected this intransigence. By 1935, German nationalism's most extreme form, embodied in National Socialist totalitarianism, had conquered the field of emigration policy completely. To the Nazis, the demands of the nation took precedence over any individual rights or needs whatsoever, including the historic right to move freely.

Matters in Canada over the period 1850-1939 developed somewhat differently. During the 1850s and 1860s evidence of nationalism playing a role in determining immigration policy was scarce. The closest the English-speaking parts of eastern Canada came to group consciousness was a sense of being members of the Anglo-Saxon race and British by tradition. At mid-century, fear of annexation by the United States was the strongest sentiment binding British North Americans together. After Confederation, an emerging sense of Canadian national awareness began to affect immigration policy. In his effort to build an empire for Canada through an advancing western frontier, Macdonald used his National Policy to rally English Canadian support.[3] Macdonald tried to guarantee the future of the dominion against American intrusion not only by promoting a national railway and building a wall of tariff protection but also by actively recruiting more and more immigrants. Macdonald's use of nationalism to justify an expanded immigration recruitment program had parallels elsewhere in the Western Hemisphere. For example, Chile's nationalists argued just as strongly in the 1890s for more immigrants to thwart the expansionist threat posed by the more heavily populated Argentina.[4] Although Macdonald's policy made sense as a defensive move, the problem lay in his initial reliance on recruiting European immigrants solely in Great Britain: the preferred Britishers did not come in sufficient numbers. Because time was of the essence for frustrating the American threat, Macdonald launched Canada's first serious solicitation of non-Anglo-Celtic immigrants, including some Germans. The prime minister's effort at recruiting significant numbers of such new settlers largely failed, however. Success had to wait for better objective conditions and a more determined government.

Both conditions were fulfilled in the ensuing decade, as the economy improved and Wilfrid Laurier followed the precedent set by Macdonald with even more rigorous recruitment of non-English, non-French immigrants. Laurier had basically the same reasons Macdonald had; that is, to prevent the United States from trumping Canada in the land-grabbing business. Although the Laurier government's aggressive immigration policy was supported by Eastern financial, commercial, and industrial interests, Ottawa's justification always sounded less crass. Immigration would serve the country's larger interests by enabling the Canadian nation to acquire new territories in which its free government and British institutions could expand to the benefit of all. Ironically, the hundreds of thousands of non-English, non-French, "foreign others" who entered Canada before the First World War fundamentally altered the ethnic makeup of the dominion. These "others" not only brought with them different languages and cultures but often distinct political and social traditions as well. Thus, the Anglo-Celtic nativist tradition of describing the essential Canadian nation, that is, the English-speaking portion of Canada's population, as a branch of the civilized British people became more problematic than ever.

When war broke out in August 1914, Canada promptly fell into line behind the mother country. Immigration was immediately affected as Ottawa closed the country's doors, especially to persons hailing from the Central Powers. Germans in particular incurred the wrath of Canada's nativist, pro-British community, and as enemy aliens they were prohibited from entering the dominion. This prohibition continued after the war, because in 1919 Ottawa amended the country's immigration laws to expand the prohibited classes to include former enemy aliens. Throughout, the Canadian government justified these restrictions with nationalist rhetoric. Not until 1923 did the country's doors swing open again. Just as in the Laurier and Macdonald eras, nationalist exclusionist policy was replaced by a nationalist inclusionist one. Patriots argued in 1923, as they had in 1870 and 1900, that Canada needed more persons not only to tap its national wealth but to maintain its independence from the United States. In the tapping process, Germans figured only as humble farmers.

The inclusion hiatus was brief, however, for the Depression forced Ottawa to accede to nationalist demands for renewed restrictions on immigration. In 1931 all classes and occupations with only five exceptions were denied entry into Canada. The exceptions were British and US subjects with sufficient means to sustain themselves, family members of Canadian citizens, farmers with independent means, and those betrothed to Canadian citizens who also could pass the means test. Such exclusion, its nativist proponents argued, was necessary to prevent Canada from being flooded with impoverished foreigners who would overwhelm relief efforts and exacerbate an already disastrous labour market by creating even more unemployment. The 1931 law all but guaranteed the exclusion of Reich Germans from Canada, for a German farmer who possessed enough assets to satisfy Canada's immigration officials would never have been allowed by the Hitler government to take his wealth out of the country. The only exceptions able to avoid Canada's prohibitions and Germany's interference were political refugees, such as the Sudeten German social democrats who came to Canada without means but with the blessing and financial support of the British government.

Ideological Proclivities: Imperialism and Racism

The admission of the Sudeten Germans to Canada only after pressure from the mother country illustrates another theme affecting German-Canadian migration, namely, imperialism. This imperialist theme, in turn, had a Canadian, a British, and a German expression, all exhibiting exuberant and often conflicting claims. In Canada, imperialism was initially a strictly British matter. From the British conquest of New France in the eighteenth century until after the establishment of the Dominion of Canada in 1867, British North Americans considered themselves inhabiting a distant colony and outpost of the British Empire. With the uniting of the Maritime provinces with Upper and Lower Canada and the addition shortly thereafter of extensive western lands, the Macdonald government moved to create a separate Canadian empire in North America. In displacing the resident Native peoples while describing the land as uninhabited, only awaiting white settlement, the Canadian expansion into the west resembled America's experience more than some Canadian critics of "Yankee" imperialism would care to admit.[5] And the element of competition with the United States was always present in building Canada's North American empire. With the exception of the First World War and the Depression, Canada's immigration policy consistently reflected both competition with and imitation of America's successful westward expansion. Indeed, the Dominion Lands Act of 1872 that provided free homestead lands in western Canada was based upon the US Homestead Act.[6]

What distinguished Canada's expansion from the American one was not so much its nature or historical progression but rather its utilization of British models and claims for justification. This should come as no surprise, for Great Britain's imperialist adventure reached its apogee at the same time that Laurier and Clifford Sifton were moving masses of new migrants into Canada's west. Canada developed its own version of the "white man's burden" so popular in Victorian England. This Canadian version extended not only to the Métis and displaced First Nations but also to the recent arrivals from eastern and southern Europe. Defenders of Canada's empire building as different as Sifton the politician, and J.S. Woodsworth the social worker exhibited the same kind of social Darwinist racist attitudes toward the new immigrants and employed the same institutional and cultural justifications that Joseph Chamberlain and Cecil Rhodes were applying to Britain's imperialist aggressions in Africa and Asia. In order to do this, Canada's Anglo-Celtic spokesmen developed what Richard Day has called the "Great Chain of Race Theory," which placed Canada's ethnic groups in a kind of vertical chain descending from best to worst.[7] Since the English were clearly the "superior" group, a kind of *noblesse oblige* required them to do their duty, pick up the burden, and try to enlighten the inferior "others" by passing on to them British culture and traditions.

In his 1909 book *Strangers within Our Gates*, J.S. Woodsworth, perhaps the best-known exponent of the Great Chain of Race theory, trenchantly described the issue confronting British Canada in the age of mass immigration. Comparing the new immigration to a great and dangerous flood, Woodsworth categorized the immigrants in order of their presumed usefulness or value to Canada. Value he imputed quite simply to their ability to learn British Canadian conventions and assimilate into British Canadian society. He rendered his judgments on adaptability and worth by considering such factors as the immigrant's language skills, dress, diet, morality, work ethic, religion, and political inclinations. Quite logically, Woodsworth ranked British immigrants at the top because, in his words, they brought to Canada "more of our own blood" and thus could "assist us to maintain in Canada our British traditions and to mould the incoming armies of foreigners into loyal British subjects."[8]

The missionary zeal with which he preached his warning to his fellow British Canadians came to him naturally, for he was a minister by vocation and a disciple of the social gospel theories so widespread at the time. Woodsworth had spent several years in Winnipeg, the jumping-off place for the thousands of new immigrants who came to settle the West, working at the All People's Mission. In his time at the mission, he had, as he described it, "acted like a focusing glass to direct rays of assimilation energy into the homes of immigrant families."[9] As a result of his Winnipeg exposure, Woodsworth believed he had become familiar enough with the new immigrants to render judgment on them as potential future Canadian citizens. He concluded forthwith that not all the "others" could be saved. Some were clearly incapable of integrating into British Canada, of accepting British ways, even of learning English properly. The Aboriginal, Asian, and African peoples, for example, were simply too "other" to be assimilated. The answer to those who could not be transformed lay in exclusion: Canada's immigration laws should be changed to prohibit the entry of Asians, blacks,

Jews, and other "lessers" into the country. Too racially inferior to receive the ministrations of the enlightened and enlightening British Canadians, they posed a mortal threat to the livelihood of Canada's society and her blessed British traditions.

The widespread acceptance of such racist theories in Canada before the First World War made intolerance natural and rendered the plight of Canada's German immigrants that much worse when war broke out in 1914. Before then, the Germans had ranked quite high on the Great Chain of Race. Immigration officers of earlier periods had consistently considered Germans very desirable immigrants, albeit not the equal of the top-ranking British. Germans had certainly appeared more meritorious than the Slavs or Italians. After the war broke out, a hatred for Germans, German culture, and things German developed quickly in the dominion, and had not entirely dissipated when Ottawa lifted the ban on German immigration in 1923. Indeed, remnants of anti-German xenophobia carried over into the Depression years as well. When the Sudeten German socialist refugees arrived in Canada in the spring of 1939, they encountered surprising anti-German resentment directed at them. It did not matter that they had resisted Hitler, nor that the Nazis had forced them to settle in Canada.

The cultural and racial theories that inspired British and Canadian imperialism at the end of the nineteenth century influenced German imperialists as well. Indeed, belated German unification decreed that Germany, like Canada, consciously followed Great Britain's lead. While Canada began its most dramatic imperial efforts in the 1870s, shortly after the dominion's creation, Germany moved more slowly into imperialist expansion and its imperial manoeuvres peaked in the 1890s. The success and support of Germany's imperial adventure were linked to the economic advancements of that period and the Reich's new place in the world's economy. Theorists calling for colonies and empire had, however, been raising their cry in Germany since the economic troubles of the 1870s. From the beginning, the German imperialist theme exhibited social and economic planning elements as well as the social Darwinist ideas and missionary zeal so characteristic of Canada's effort. As we have seen, Friedrich Fabri epitomized this stage of Germany's imperialism with his plea for closed agricultural colonies in South America and commercial colonies in Africa and the East. His claim that such colonies fulfilled both a German right to build the nation and a responsibility to civilize the natives reflected contemporary British pretensions and assertions as well.

Some of the demands Fabri raised in the late 1870s became reality shortly thereafter, when Germany acquired overseas colonies. Like a sundog, however, the Reich's empire beyond Europe lasted only briefly, lost upon its defeat in the Great War. Nevertheless, the dream of empire did not die. Fabri's ideas about German settlements in South America received renewed attention in the 1920s. Moreover, the volkish movement, which Ernst Ritter rightly characterized as a kind of Pan-German ideological imperialism, spread widely among the *Volksdeutsche* living outside the Reich during the interwar years.[10] After 1933 Germany's imperial appetite waxed noticeably, and conquest and imperial expansion emerged as integral to the new German nationalism. The racist social Darwinist theme also reappeared, only this time the "inferiors" were not Africans or Asians but Slavs and Jews. After 1939 Hitler sought to solidify his "new order" in the east by first cleansing it of "inferior peoples" and then moving Germans into the former Slav lands as settlers and exploiters. As a result, the call went out to all members of the Volk to return to the Reich. Volkish spokesmen in the Third Reich appealed to all Germans living abroad, both recent emigrants and the descendants of earlier ones, to return to their true fatherland. Although volkish apologists in Hitler's Reich had scant success in luring Germans out of Canada or the United States during the war, the Third Reich's planners believed that after a German victory their appeal would be answered. Thus the National Socialist program ultimately envisioned a reversal of the out-migration that had drained so many of the Volk from Germany during the previous century and a half.

Technological Influences
In 1939 bringing Germans back to the Reich (or deporting them from Canada, for that matter) required far less time and effort than it once had. This change was due less to the increasing efficiency of governments or the organizing skills of philanthropic organizations than to the technological advances and innovations developed since 1850. Technology had always affected both the transportation of migrants and the availability of knowledge about migration itself. Since the physical ability to move and the desire to do so represented two of the necessary preconditions for migration, technology's impact was crucial. In the sphere of technology, innovation was even more apparent than in the realms of immigration policies and ideological commitments.

From 1850 to 1939 the capacity of the Canadian government and its agents to publicize their positions on immigration, and the capacity of their German audiences to receive their messages, increased substantially. The latter condition, which was not entirely technologically driven, relates to the ability of prospective immigrants to read. Throughout Europe during the nineteenth century literacy increased as mass education spread. The Germans set the pace in advancing education, for by 1830 almost all Germans could read and write. By the end of the century, the rate of illiteracy in Germany was estimated at only 0.05 percent.[11] Hence, throughout the period covered by this book, the printed word was nearly universally accessible there. Publication capacity, on the other hand, depended on the promoter's ability to exploit the available printing technology, which developed rapidly during the nineteenth century in conjunction with the spreading Industrial Revolution. By midcentury steam power had been introduced to drive revolving cylindrical presses that could produce more than 800 copies per hour. Mechanization of the paper-feeding process by using a continuous roll of paper followed, and the first roll-fed rotary press appeared in 1865. Cutting and folding devices were added shortly thereafter. In the 1880s the German-born Ottmar Mergenthaler invented the Linotype, a typesetting compositor that could set up to 7,000 pieces of type per hour. Comparable breakthroughs occurred in the technology for reproducing images in print as photographic techniques were adapted for the publishing process. The steady development of innovations facilitating mass production, increasing speed, and reducing costs continued into the twentieth century. Since the majority of the new technology appeared first in either Great Britain or the United States, Canada was ideally situated to take advantage of these innovations in its expanding propaganda campaign to win immigrants for the dominion. A comparison of brochures advertising Canada published in the 1860s with those from the end of the nineteenth century makes clear the increased sophistication available in printing and publishing.

Although these changes in reproducing and publishing technology were dramatic, they seem dwarfed by the contemporary innovations in transportation, which directly modernized migration. The most important changes involved the application of steam power to travel on land and water. The railroad had already evolved so far by 1850 that its revolutionary impact could be seen by even the least discerning. After 1850 the railroad became the chief means of facilitating mass migration within both the sending and receiving lands. In Germany, where economic development at midcentury lagged well behind the British pacesetters, railroad construction had nevertheless already made great strides. Pushed particularly in Prussia, Germany's rail system, unlike Britain's, preceded much of the country's industrial development. When industrialization did come, with its attendant social and economic displacement, the railroad made the movement of millions out of Germany not only feasible but possible. Without a modernizing rail system, it is difficult to imagine how the migrating millions would have made it to Hamburg, Bremen, or the other embarkation sites. Similarly, in Canada the railway predated both political unification and industrialization. Although steamboats plying the St. Lawrence River and the Great Lakes initially handled more of Canada's immigrant traffic, this changed rapidly after Macdonald's time. In the era of Laurier, the national railways carried Canada's massive numbers of new settlers to the opening West. Not without reason, Canadian historians have traditionally attributed the key role in ensuring the nation's survival in the face of the American threat to the national railway as much as to the huge influx of new settlers.

On water, the modest advancements made by shallow-draft steamboats in the first half of the nineteenth century were dramatically eclipsed by the transoceanic steamers that proliferated after midcentury. From 1850 to 1914 the technology of ocean travel changed dramatically and rapidly as shipping firms sought to keep up with the rising demand for more carriers. The first casualties of the new developments, sailing vessels, had all but ceased to play a meaningful role in the Atlantic crossing trade by 1870. In the last third of the nineteenth century, competition on the North Atlantic passenger run was fierce. Steamship companies built ever larger ships, and iron hulls replaced wooden ones. The single-screw propeller, which had replaced the paddle wheel in the 1860s, disappeared in favour of multiple propellers. At the turn of the century great ocean liners ferrying passengers between Europe and North America conducted business under several flags. British, Canadian, American, and German firms competed for the lucrative transatlantic carrying trade. Innovations in ocean transportation revolutionized migration travel: increased speed and size equated to greater safety and more comfort aboard ship, and the whole process became easier and less expensive.

Conclusion

As we have seen, all aspects of German-Canadian migration were profoundly transformed by forceful modernization between 1850 and 1939. Politics, economics, social structure, ideology, and technology, all spheres of human activity or organization that influenced the migration phenomenon, felt the impact of this progressive modernization. In 1850 German-Canadian migration lacked not only direction but definition, and transoceanic migration from Germany to British North America was an extremely difficult and dangerous undertaking. Over the four ensuing generations the migration of German peoples to Canada was transformed almost unrecognizably, becoming well organized, whether through private or state means, closely defined in legal and policy terms, and far less difficult to undertake. Modern economic developments spurred by the spread of industrialization created not only new products and new markets but also new labour categories and demands. While some labourers became redundant, others found new opportunities in new fields. The social alterations occurring in conjunction with such economic growth in turn created greater social mobility, whether desired or not. From the socially and economically displaced a pool of potential migrants appeared. Political change, most obviously expressed in the development of the modern German and Canadian states, made the control of migration both possible and necessary. Modern technology then provided the means to inform potential German migrants on the opportunities in Canada while at the same time transforming the journey out of Germany to Canada from dangerous and lengthy to safe and short. Finally, all of the above developments were justified and opposed by reference to what were believed to be appropriate ideological systems. Between 1850 and 1939 migration rhetoric incorporated such wide-ranging abstractions as civilization, nation, freedom, culture, Volk, and race.

In the history of German-Canadian migration these developments did not occur without conflict or resistance. Throughout, both German and Canadian policy makers struggled to interpret the meaning of migration to their respective states. From 1850 to 1939 Germany's emigration policy moved from opposition to indifference to ambivalence to firm opposition. Canada's policy, on the other hand, evolved from nonexistence to luke-warm support to enthusiastic endorsement to near-total prohibition. In both countries, the negative and positive meanings of migration derived from perceived needs that varied from time to time, being in turn influenced by such things as population level, economic performance, and political desires or fears. Since apparent needs varied so much, both Canadian and German perceptions of migration's meaning frequently differed as well, often resulting in disagreements or obstructionist policies. Because over the generations the views and approaches in both countries changed periodically, no consistent policy could develop in either country. Consistent from 1850 to 1939 for both Canada and Germany, however, was the tension created by the favour/disfavour, support/opposition, loss/gain, benefit/burden dichotomies that arose in the course of the migration debates.

This dynamic was not unique to Canada and Germany, being shared by the other participants in the period's great Atlantic migration. In Australia, the United States, and Brazil, for example, interested public and private parties also struggled with justifying, accommodating, inducing, or prohibiting migration. In these several receiving lands, as in Canada, nativist fears and social conventions clashed with perceived economic needs. In Ireland, Italy, Austria, and the Scandinavian lands, meanwhile, those who participated in the migration debate agonized over the departure of their sons and daughters, with some supporting, some opposing, some seeing migration as a positive national gain, others a clear loss. At various times, the several sending lands all tried to encourage or prevent the out-migration of their nationals just as Germany did. Whether receiving or sending, the numerous lands involved in this massive transoceanic movement from Europe to North and South America and beyond were nearly always responding to pressures and changes induced by social, economic, political, and ideological factors, often only vaguely perceived but nearly always spawned by that watershed development, modern industrialization.

Notes

Note: Documents for which no author or publisher is cited can be assumed to lack the information in the original publication.

Introduction

1 Manfred von Bresler to his parents, 27 September 1927, in *Troubles in Paradise: Letters to and from German Immigrants in Canada, 1925-1939,* ed. Jonathan F. Wagner (St. Katharinen: Scripta Mercaturae Verlag, 1998), 93.
2 See Dirk Hoerder, *Cultures in Conflict: World Migrations in the Second Millennium* (Durham, NC: Duke University Press, 2002).
3 Frank Thistlethwaite, "Migration from Europe Overseas in the Nineteenth and Twentieth Centuries," in *A Century of European Migrations, 1830-1930,* ed. Rudolph J. Vecoli and Suzanne M. Sinke (Urbana: University of Illinois Press, 1991), 28.
4 Dirk Hoerder, "Migration in the Atlantic Economies: Regional European Origins and World-wide Expansion," in *European Migrants: Global and Local Perspectives,* ed. Dirk Hoerder and Leslie Page Moch (Boston: Northeastern University Press, 1996), 37.
5 See, for example, Walter Nugent, *Crossings: The Great Transatlantic Migrations, 1870-1914* (Bloomington: University of Indiana Press, 1992).
6 James H. Jackson Jr. and Leslie Page Moch, "Migrations and the Social History of Modern Europe," *Historical Methods* 22 (1989): 27-36.
7 For a recent summary and critique of modernization theory with specific reference to German migration, see Steve Hochstadt, *Mobility and Modernity: Migration in Germany, 1820-1989* (Ann Arbor: University of Michigan Press, 1999), 7-54. In this work, Hochstadt discusses both the theory's history and its leading practitioners.
8 For an overview of Canada in 1850, see John Warkentin and R.C. Harris, *Canada before Confederation* (New York: Oxford University Press, 1974).
9 See, for example, R. Tilly, "The Take Off in Germany," in *Oceans Apart? Comparing Germany and the United States,* ed. E. Angermann and M.L. Frings (Stuttgart: Klett-Cotta, 1981), 47-59.
10 William L. Marr and Donald G. Paterson, *Canada: An Economic History* (Toronto: Macmillan of Canada, 1980), 195.
11 David Blackbourn, *The Long Nineteenth Century: A History of Germany, 1780-1918* (New York: Oxford University Press, 1998), 116. See also James Sheehan, *German History 1770-1866* (Oxford: Oxford University Press, 1989), 763-80.
12 See Heinz Lehmann, *Das Deutschtum in Ostkanada* (Stuttgart: Deutsche Ausland-Institut, 1931), 1-5; and Werner Bausenhart, *German Immigration and Assimilation in Ontario 1783-1918* (New York: Legus, 1989), 38-49.
13 Gerhard P. Bassler, *The German Canadian Mosaic Today and Yesterday: Identities, Roots and Heritage* (Ottawa: German Canadian Congress Press, 1991), 124.
14 K.M. McLaughlin, *The Germans in Canada* (Ottawa: Canadian Historical Association, 1985), 8; and Bausenhart, *German Immigration,* 50-74.

15 Udo Sauttner, "Deutsche in Kanada," in *Deutsche im Ausland, Fremde in Deutschland*, ed. Klaus J. Bade (Munich: C.H. Beck, 1992), 189.

16 The term *chain migration* describes movement induced by connections between individuals who had emigrated at an earlier time and those still remaining in the old country. Traditionally information passed from those abroad, usually in the form of personal letters to relatives or acquaintances in the former homeland, inspired later emigrants to join the earlier ones. Having connections in the receiving country seemed to assure those contemplating migration both a definite place to settle and assistance and security once the newcomers arrived in the new homeland. Considerable literature exists on chain migration. For a definition and general discussion, see John S. Macdonald and Leatrice E. Macdonald, "Chain Migration, Ethnic Neighborhood Formation and Social Networks," *Milbank Memorial Fund Quarterly* 42 (1964): 82-97; and Walter Kamphoefner, *The Westphalians: From Germany to Missouri* (Princeton: Princeton University Press, 1987), 70-105. On German chain migration to America, see the Kamphoefner work just noted, as well as Wolfgang Helbich, "The Letters They Sent Home: The Subjective Perspective of German Immigrants in the Nineteenth Century," *Yearbook of German-American Studies* 22 (1987): 22-42; and Robert W. Frizzell, "Migration Chains to Illinois: The Evidence from German-American Church Records," *Journal of American Ethnic History* 7 (1987): 59-73. For representative literature on chain migration among non-German immigrants to America, see the Macdonald essay cited above for Italians, and for Norwegians, Jon Gjerde, "Chain Migration from the West Coast of Norway," in Vecoli and Sinke, *Century of European Migrations*, 158-81.

17 Robert J. Kleiner, Tom Sorensen, Odd Stefan Dalgard, Torbjorn Moum, and Dale Drews, "International Migration and Internal Migration: A Comprehensive Theoretical Approach," in *Migrations across Time and Nations: Population Mobility in Historical Contexts*, ed. Ira A. Glazier and Luigi De Rosa (New York: Holmes and Meier, 1986), 307.

18 Marcus L. Hansen, *The Immigrant in American History* (Cambridge: Harvard University Press, 1940), 192.

19 Carl Strickwerda, "Tides of Migration, Currents of History: The State, Economy, and the Transatlantic Movement of Labor in the Nineteenth and Twentieth Centuries," *International Review of Social History* 44 (1999): 371.

20 For a sampling of recent research and publications dealing with European remigration, see Ewa Morawska, "Return Migration: Theoretical and Research Agenda," in Vecoli and Sinke, *Century of European Migrations*, 277-92. More specifically, for German American remigration note the works of Alfred Vagts, *Deutsch-Amerikanische Rückwanderung* (Heidelberg: C. Winter, 1960); Günter Moltmann, "American-German Return Migration in the Nineteenth and Early Twentieth Centuries," *Central European History* 13 (1980): 378-92; Walter D. Kamphoefner, "The Volume and Composition of German-American Return Migration," in Vecoli and Sinke, *Century of European Migrations*, 296-9; J.D. Gould, "European Inter-Continental Emigration – The Road Home: Return Migration from the U.S.A.," *Journal of European Economic History* 9 (1980): 41-112; and Mark Wyman, *Round-Trip to America: The Immigrants Return to Europe 1880-1930* (Ithaca, NY: Cornell University Press, 1993).

21 Wyman, *Round-Trip*, 189.

22 Nugent, *Crossings*, 71-2.

Chapter 1: Migration in the 1850s and 1860s

1 For an account of the revolution and the ensuing conservative reaction, see the relevant chapters in James J. Sheehan, *German History 1770-1866* (Oxford: Oxford University Press, 1989).

2 On Bismarck and the unification movement, see Otto Pflanze, *Bismarck and the Development of Germany*, 3 vols. (Princeton: Princeton University Press, 1990); T.S. Hamerow, *The Social Foundations of German Unification, 1858-1871*, 2 vols. (Princeton: Princeton University Press, 1969-72); and H. Böhme, *The Foundations of the German Empire* (Oxford: Oxford University Press, 1971).

3   For a discussion of opposition to Bismarckian unity, see N.M. Hope, *The Alternative to German Unification: The Anti-Prussian Party: Frankfurt, Nassau and the Two Hessen 1859-1867* (Wiesbaden: F. Steiner, 1973).

4   Wilhelm Monckmeier, *Die deutsche überseeische Auswanderung* (Jena: Gustav Fischer Verlag, 1912), 54-5.

5   For background on Canada in the 1860s, see, for example, Donald Creighton, "The 1860s," in *The Canadians*, ed. J.M.S. Careless and R.C. Brown (Toronto: Macmillan, 1967), 3-36; W.L. Morton, *The Critical Years* (Toronto: Macmillan of Canada, 1964); and F.H. Underhill, *The Image of Confederation* (Toronto: Canadian Broadcasting Corporation, 1964).

6   On Canadian-American relations at the time of Confederation, see C.P. Stacey, *Canada and the Age of Conflict: A History of Canadian External Relations*, vol. 1, *1867-1921* (Toronto: Macmillan of Canada, 1977); and John Bartlet Brebner, *North Atlantic Triangle: The Interplay of Canada, the United States and Great Britain* (New Haven: Yale University Press, 1966). For a more detailed discussion of American annexationist pressure and the Canadian response to it, see Donald F. Warner, *The Idea of Continental Union: Agitation for the Annexation of Canada to the United States, 1849-1893* (Lexington: University of Kentucky Press, 1960).

7   Brebner, *North Atlantic Triangle*, 177.

8   David P. Gagen, "Land, Population, and Social Change: The 'Critical Years' in Rural Canada West," *Canadian Historical Review* 59 (1978): 293-317.

9   Creighton, "1860s," 17.

10 For the classic account of the realization of Confederation, see Donald Creighton, *The Road to Confederation* (Toronto: Houghton Mifflin, 1965).

11 On Macdonald, see Donald Creighton, *John A. Macdonald: The Old Chieftain* (Toronto: Macmillan, 1955); Donald Swainson, *Sir John A. Macdonald: The Man and the Politician* (Kingston: Quarry Press, 1989); and Peter B. Waite, "The Political Ideas of John A. Macdonald," in *The Political Ideas of the Prime Ministers of Canada*, ed. Marcel Hamelin (Ottawa: Éditions de l'Université d'Ottawa, 1969), 51-67.

12 For a discussion of the National Policy, see Robert Craig Brown, *Canada's National Policy, 1883-1900: A Study in Canadian-American Relations* (Princeton: Princeton University Press, 1964).

13 On the take-off, see W. Hoffmann, "The Take-Off in Germany," in *The Economics of Take-Off into Sustained Growth*, ed. W.W. Rostow (New York: St. Martin's Press, 1963), 95-118.

14 See R. Fremdling, "Railroads and German Economic Growth," *Journal of Economic History* 37 (1977): 583-604.

15 David Blackbourn, *The Long Nineteenth Century: A History of Germany, 1780-1918* (New York: Oxford University Press, 1998), 177-91.

16 See Walter D. Kamphoefner, "At the Crossroads of Economic Development: Background Factors Affecting Emigration from Nineteenth-Century Germany," in *Migration across Time and Nations: Population Mobility in Historical Contexts*, ed. Ira A. Glazier and Luigi De Rosa (New York: Holmes and Meier, 1986), 175-201.

17 Ibid., 177-91.

18 J.A. Perkins, "The Agricultural Revolution in Germany 1850-1914," *Journal of European Economic History* 10 (1981), 72.

19 Ibid., 116.

20 Klaus J. Bade, "Die deutsche überseeische Massenauswanderung im 19. und frühen 20. Jahrhundert: Bestimmungsfaktoren und Entwicklungsbedingungen," in *Auswanderer, Wanderarbeiter, Gastarbeiter: Bevölkerung, Arbeitsmarkt und Wanderung in Deutschland seit der Mitte des 19. Jahrhunderts*, vol. 1, ed. Klaus J. Bade (Ostfildern: Scripta Mercaturae Verlag, 1984), 259-91.

21 On Canadian economic history, consult the following: Kenneth Norrie and Douglas Owram, *A History of the Canadian Economy* (Toronto: Harcourt Brace Jovanovich, 1990); William Marr and Donald G. Paterson, *Canada: An Economic History* (Toronto: Macmillan of Canada, 1980); and W.T. Easterbrook and Hugh J. Aitken, *Canadian Economic History* (Toronto: Macmillan Company of Canada, 1958).

22 Randy William Widdis, *With Scarcely a Ripple: Anglo-Canadian Migration into the United States and Western Canada 1880-1920* (Montreal and Kingston: McGill-Queen's University Press, 1998), 50.
23 Creighton, "1860s," 6.
24 See George P. de T. Glazebrook, *A History of Transportation in Canada* (Toronto: McClelland and Stewart, 1964), vol. 2, 14-15; and Norrie and Owram, *History of the Canadian Economy*, 224-32.
25 Norrie and Owram, *History of the Canadian Economy*, 232-43. On land usage and availability and migration from Upper Canada, see Widdis, *With Scarcely a Ripple*.
26 Reg Whitaker, *Canadian Immigration Policy since Confederation* (Ottawa: Canadian Historical Association, 1991), 3.
27 See the exchanges between proponents Conger and McGee and opponent Macdougal in Province of Canada, *Parliamentary Debates 1862-1865* (21 August 1863), pp. 23-4.
28 Canada, *Senate Debates* (7 May 1868), p. 219 (Senator Macpherson).
29 Dr. Becker to Viscount Monck, Governor General, 1 October 1868, Library and Archives Canada (hereafter cited as LAC), RG 6-C1, vol. 312, file 586.
30 William Raich to Minister of Agriculture, 15 March 1869, LAC, RG 17, vol. 27, no. 2396.
31 For a more complete discussion of documentary restriction on movement in Germany in the nineteenth century, see John Torpey, *The Invention of the Passport: Surveillance, Citizenship and the State* (Cambridge: Cambridge University Press, 2000), 57-92.
32 Peter Marschalck, *Deutsche Überseewanderung im 19. Jahrhundert* (Stuttgart: Ernst Klett Verlag, 1973), 55.
33 Walter D. Kamphoefner, *Westfalen in der Neuen Welt: Eine Sozialgeschichte der Auswanderung im 19. Jahrhundert* (Munster: F. Coppenrath Verlag, 1982), 22-56.
34 Bade, "Die deutsche überseeische Massenauswanderung," 267.
35 Marschalck, *Deutsche Überseeauswanderung*, 27.
36 Ibid., 50.
37 For a discussion of such movement south, see Marcus Lee Hansen, *The Mingling of the Canadian and American Peoples* (New Haven: Yale University Press, 1940).
38 Richard J.F. Day, *Multiculturalism and the History of Canadian Diversity* (Toronto: University of Toronto Press, 1987), 122.
39 See Helge W. Nordvik, "Norwegian Emigrants and Canadian Timber: Norwegian Shipping to Quebec 1850-1875," in *Maritime Aspects of Migration,* ed. Klaus Friedland (Cologne: Böhlau, 1989), 279-291.
40 Gustav Beling, Bericht des preussischen Consul zu Quebec vom Jahre 1863, Staatsarchiv Bremen (hereafter cited as StAB), 2-C.4.b.6.d.2.
41 "Einwanderung in Quebec im Jahre 1868," *Deutsche Auswanderer-Zeitung* (Bremen) (hereafter cited as *DAZ*), 29 March 1869; and "Liste der Schiffs-Passagierbeförderung über Bremen im Jahre 1969," *DAZ*, 10 January 1870.
42 Mabel F. Timlin, "Canada's Immigration Policy, 1896-1910," *Canadian Journal of Economics and Political Science* 26 (1960): 521.
43 Dr. Schreiner, "Bericht von Dr. Schreiner: Manitoba," in *Canada: Die Berichte der vier Delegierten über ihre Reise nach Canada im Herbst 1881,* ed. Otto Hahn (Reutlingen: Eduard Schauwecker, 1883), 49; Monckmeier, *Deutsche überseeische Auswanderung,* 207.
44 "Kanada," *Allgemeine Auswanderungszeitung* (Rudolstadt; hereafter cited as *AA*), 25 August 1865.
45 Rheinhard R. Doerries, "German Transatlantic Migration from the Early Nineteenth Century to the Outbreak of World War II," in *Population, Labour and Migration in 19th and 20th Century Germany*, ed. Klaus J. Bade (New York: St. Martin's Press, 1987), 115.
46 Philip Taylor, *The Distant Magnet* (New York: Harper and Row, 1971), 71.
47 Ibid., 73-6.
48 See Walter Kamphoefner, *News from the Land of Freedom* (Ithaca: Cornell University Press, 1991).
49 Merle Curti and K. Birr, "The Immigrant and the American Image in Europe," *Mississippi Valley Historical Review* 37 (1950): 207.
50 Quoted ibid., 221.

51 Preston A. Barba, "Cooper in Germany," *Indiana University Studies* 21 (1914): 52.
52 Ibid., 53.
53 Preston A. Barba, "Emigration to America Reflected in German Fiction," *German American Annals* (1914): 197.
54 Schmidt quoted in Barba, "Cooper in Germany," 55.
55 Ibid., 64-5.
56 A.J. Prahl, "America in the Works of Gerstäcker," *Modern Language Quarterly* 4 (1943): 224.
57 Barba, "Cooper in Germany," 70.
58 Barba, "Emigration to America," 215.
59 See Ray Allen Billington, *Land of Savagery, Land of Promise: The European Image of the American Frontier* (New York: W.W. Norton), 1981.
60 "Canada," *DAZ*, 17 January 1852.
61 "Canada," *AA*, 27 May 1871.
62 "Canada," *DAZ*, 7 January 1854.
63 *Canada: Zur Unterrichtung für Auswanderer und Ansiedler,* pamphlet (Berlin, 1858), 5, Staatsarchiv Hamburg.
64 "Canada," *AA,* 31 August 1865.
65 *Canada* (Berlin, 1858), Handelskammer Archiv Bremen (hereafter cited as HKAB) II.A., III 1K, no. 72b.
66 "Canada," *AA,* 17 January 1862.
67 "Zum Census von Canada," *DAZ,* 27 January 1854.
68 "Canada," *AA,* 9 March 1865.
69 "Canada," *AA,* 21 September 1865.
70 Ingrid Schöberl, "Auswanderung durch Information: Amerikanische Broschuren in Deutschland im späten 19. und frühen 20. Jahrhundert," *Amerikastudien* 27 (1982): 327.
71 "Canada," *AA,* 14 September 1865.
72 "Canada," *AA,* 10 August 1865.
73 "Canada," *AA,* 22 August 1862.
74 "Canada," *AA,* 21 June 1859.
75 "Canada," *AA,* 25 April 1867.
76 "Canada," *AA,* 7 June 1861.
77 "Aus Canada," *AA,* 28 November 1867.
78 "Canada," *DAZ,* 17 May 1853.
79 "Briefe aus Canada," *DAZ,* 27 June 1853.
80 William Wagner, "Briefe eines deutschen Ansiedlers in Kanada," *DAZ,* 10 May 1853.
81 William Wagner, *Canada: Ein kurzer Abriss von dessen geographischer Lage, sowie Production, Klima und Bodenbeschaffenheit, Erziehungs und Municipal Wesen, Fischereien, Eisenbahnen u.s.w.,* pamphlet (Berlin: L. Burckhardt, 1860), 15, Staatsarchiv Hamburg.
82 "Canada," *AA,* 26 June 1857.
83 "Canada," *AA,* 26 June 1857.
84 Wagner, *Canada: Ein kurzer Abriss,* 19.
85 Wagner, "Briefe eines deutschen Ansiedlers."
86 "Skitzen aus Neu-Schottland und Neu-Brunswick," *DAZ,* 30 July 1853.
87 "Literatur," *DAZ,* 24 June 1861.
88 "Canada," *AA,* 31 May 1861.
89 "Canada," *AA,* 7 February 1862.
90 Monckmeier, *Deutsche überseeische Auswanderung,* 192.
91 Ibid., 29.
92 Kristian Hvidt, "Emigration Agents: The Development of a Business and Its Methods," *Scandinavian Journal of History* 3 (1978): 180.
93 Norman Macdonald, *Canada: Immigration and Colonization, 1841-1903* (Toronto: University of Toronto Press, 1968), 40-1.
94 "Landschenkungen in Canada," *DAZ,* 15 September 1856.
95 "Zur Nachricht für Deutsche Auswanderer," 1853, HKAB, II-A, III.1.F., nr. 183.
96 "Briefe eines deutschen Ansiedlers," *DAZ,* 15 August 1853.

97   William Wagner, *Auszug aus den consolidirten Statuten von Canada, Britisches Nord-Amerika,* pamphlet (Berlin: Selbstverlage des Verfassers, 1860), 12, Staatsarchiv Hamburg.

98   Gerhard P. Bassler, "German Overseas Migration to North America in the Nineteenth and Twentieth Centuries," *German Canadian Yearbook* 7 (1983): 8-21.

99   A. Schumacher, "Bericht an den Direction des Nachrichtenbureaus für Auswanderer Bremen," 30 October 1854, HKAB, II-A.I, no. 141.

100   Macdonald, *Canada: Immigration and Colonization,* 42.

101   "Quebec," *AA,* 18 July 1856 and 28 July 1856.

102   "Die Anklagen gegen Herrn W. Sinn in Quebec und seine Rechtfertigung," *DAZ,* 12 February 1857.

103   *Canada 1862: Zur Nachricht für Einwanderer,* pamphlet (Preston, ON: Wilhelm Schluter, 1862), 19, Geheimes Staatsarchiv Preussischer Kulturbesitz (hereafter cited as GSPK).

104   Sinn to S. Stafford, Emigration Agent at Quebec, 14 April 1868, LAC, RG 17, vol. 20, no. 1728.

105   Paul W. Gates, "Official Encouragement to Immigration by the Province of Canada," *Canadian Historical Review* 15 (1931): 30.

106   Macdonald, *Canada: Immigration and Colonization,* 82-3.

107   Cited in Peter Hessel, "German Immigration to the Ottawa Valley in the 19th Century," *German Canadian Yearbook* 8 (1984): 77.

108   Macdonald, *Canada: Immigration and Colonization,* 82; Karin R. Gurttler, *Geschichte der deutschen Gesellschaft zu Montreal 1835-1985* (Montreal: Deutsche Gesellschaft Montreal, 1985), 27.

109   Ibid., Macdonald, 77-8.

110   Gates, "Official Encouragement," 31.

111   Montreal German Society to T.D. McGee, Minister of Agriculture, 10 October 1866, LAC, RG 17, vol. 12, no. 931.

112   "Canada," *AA,* 11 November 1869.

113   "Verkauf von Billeten der Grand Trunk Railway Company of Canada," Staatsarchiv Hamburg, cl. VII, lit. Kanada nr. 9z, vol. 13e.

114   Brenda Lee-Whiting, "Why So Many German Immigrants Embarked at Liverpool," *German Canadian Yearbook* 9 (1986): 76.

115   Walter Nugent, *Crossings: The Great Transatlantic Migrations, 1870-1914,* (Bloomington: University of Indiana Press, 1992), 43.

116   Otto Preusse-Sperber, *Deutschlands Auswanderungsfrage* (Leipzig: Dietrich, 1924), 25.

117   Peter Marschalck, *Deutsche Überseewanderung im 19. Jahrhundert* (Stuttgart: Ernst Klett Verlag, 1973), 47.

118   Hartmut Bickelmann, "Auswanderungsvereine, Auswandererverkehr und Auswandererfürsorge in Deutschland 1815-1930," in *Von Deutschland nach Amerika: Zur Sozialgeschichte der Auswanderung im 19. und 20. Jahrhundert,* ed. Günter Moltmann (Stuttgart: Institute for Foreign Cultural Relations, 1991), 13.

119   Ibid., 89-90.

120   Ibid., 157-67.

121   Gurttler, *Geschichte der deutschen Gesellschaft,* 15.

122   Gates, "Official Encouragement," 25.

123   Schöberl, "Auswanderung durch Information," 300-3.

124   Ibid., 304.

125   Wagner, *Canada: Ein kurzer Abriss,* 24.

126   Schöberl, "Auswanderung durch Information," 307.

127   Wagner, *Canada: Ein kurzer Abriss,* 9.

128   *Canada 1862,* 3.

129   *Canada: Zur Unterrichtung,* 8.

130   Wagner, *Canada: Ein kurzer Abriss,* 22.

131   *Canada 1862,* 9.

132   Wagner, *Canada: Ein kurzer Abriss,* 36-7.

133   *Canada: Zur Unterrichtung,* 14.

134   *Canada 1862,* 1.

135   Wagner, *Canada: Ein kurzer Abriss,* 32.

136 *Canada 1862,* 19.

137 Marschalck, *Deutsche Überseewanderung,* 19.

138 Hans Martin Schwarzmaier, "Auswandererbriefe aus Nordamerika: Quellen im Grenzbereich von geschichtlicher Landeskunde, Wanderungsforschung und Literatursoziologie," *Zeitschrift für die Geschichte des Oberrheins* 126 (1978): 313.

139 C.B., "Briefe eines deutschen Ansiedlers in Canada," *DAZ,* 11 January 1853.

140 For examples and discussions of letters from the United States, see Kamphoefner, *News from the Land of Freedom;* and Wolfgang Helbich, "The Letters They Sent Home: The Subjective Perspective of German Immigrants in the Nineteenth Century," *Yearbook of German American Studies* 22 (1987): 22-42. Helbich estimates that 100 million letters were sent from the United States back to Germany in the course of the nineteenth century.

141 Eugen von Philippovich, *Auswanderung und Auswanderungspolitik in Deutschland: Berichte über die Entwicklung und den gegenwärtigen Zustand des Auswanderungswesens in den Einzelstaaten und im Reich* (Leipzig: Dunker und Humbolt, 1882), ix.

142 Christine Hansen, "Die deutsche Auswanderung im 19. Jahrhundert: Ein Mittel zur Lösung sozialer und sozialpolitischer Probleme?" in *Deutsche Amerikaauswanderung im 19. Jahrhundert,* ed. Günter Moltmann (Stuttgart: Metzlersche Verlag, 1976), 121.

143 Monckmeier, *Deutsche überseeische Auswanderung,* 240-2.

144 Bade, "Die deutsche überseeische Massenauswanderung," 291.

145 Hansen, *Deutsche Auswanderung im 19. Jahrhundert,* 39.

146 Günter Moltmann, "Nordamerikanische Frontier und deutsche Auswanderung – soziale Sicherheitsventil im 19. Jahrhundert?" in *Industrielle Gesellschaft und politisches System, Beiträge zur politischen Sozialgeschichte,* ed. Dirk Stegmann, Bernd-Jurgen Wendt, and Peter-Christian Witt (Bonn: Verlag Neue Gesellschaft, 1978), 288.

147 Hansen, "Deutsche Auswanderung im 19. Jahrhundert," 38-41.

148 Ibid., 41-5.

149 Moltmann, "Nordamerikanische Frontier," 289.

150 Hansen, *Deutsche Auswanderung im 19. Jahrhundert,* 49.

151 Monckmeier, *Deutsche überseeische Auswanderung,* 242.

152 Hessel, "German Immigration to the Ottawa Valley," 77.

153 Mack Walker, *Germany and the Emigration 1816-1885* (Cambridge: Harvard University Press, 1964), 175.

154 William Sinn, "Einwanderung in Canada im Jahre 1854," *DAZ,* 5 April 1855.

155 British government Protest to Presidium of the Diet of German Confederation, February 1855, Hauptstaatsarchiv Württemberg, e. 46-8, bu. 893, nos. 10-12.

156 Alexander Malet to Governments of Bremen, Frankfurt and Württemberg, December 1855, Hauptstaatsarchiv Württemberg, e. 46-8, bu. 893, nos. 14-15.

157 See Hugh J.M. Johnston, *British Emigration Policy 1815-1830: Shoveling Out Paupers* (Oxford: Clarendon Press, 1972).

158 Gerhard P. Bassler, "The Inundation of British North America with the Refuse of Foreign Pauperism," *German Canadian Yearbook* 4 (1978): 104-5.

159 Hartmut Bickelmann, "The Venture of Travel," in *Germans to America: 300 Hundred Years of Immigration 1683-1983,* ed. Günter Moltmann (Stuttgart: Institute for Foreign Cultural Relations, 1982), 130.

160 Birgit Gelberg, *Auswanderung nach Übersee: Soziale Probleme der Auswandererbeförderung in Hamburg und Bremen von der Mitte des 19. Jahrhunderts bis zum Ersten Weltkrieg* (Hamburg: Hans Christians Verlag, 1973), 6-10.

161 Ibid., 15-21.

162 Ibid., 28-31.

163 Edwin C. Guillet, *The Great Migration: The Atlantic Crossing by Sailing Ship since 1770* (Toronto: University of Toronto Press, 1963), 48.

164 Gelberg, *Auswanderung nach Übersee,* 48.

165 Ibid., 48-9.

166 Günter Moltmann, "Steamship Transport of Emigrants from Europe to the United States, 1850-1914: Social, Commercial and Legislative Aspects," in *Maritime Aspects of Migration* ed. Klaus Friedland (Cologne: Böhlau, 1989), 311.

167 Hessel, "German Immigration to the Ottawa Valley," 84.

168 Gustav Beling, Bericht des Bremischen Consulats zu Quebec vom Jahre 1863, StAB, 2-C.4.b.6.d.2.
169 Rolf Engelsing, *Bremen als Auswandererhafen 1683-1880,* Veröffentlichen aus dem Staatsarchiv der Freien Hansestadt Bremen, booklet 29 (Bremen: Carl Schunemann, 1961), 110; and "Canada," *DAZ,* 10 January 1870.
170 "Canada," *DAZ,* 2 April 1868.
171 Thomas W. Page, "The Transportation of Immigrants and Reception Arrangements in the Nineteenth Century," *Journal of Political Economy* 19 (1911): 737.
172 Gelberg, *Auswanderung nach Übersee,* 49-50.
173 Marcus L. Hansen, *The Immigrant in American History* (Cambridge: Harvard University Press, 1940), 48.
174 "Faust Recht" means the law of the fist, or the most powerful. Ibid., 36.
175 "Canada," *AA,* 5 April 1866.
176 Gelberg, *Auswanderung nach Übersee,* 40-2.
177 Mittelberger cited in Bickelmann, "Venture of Travel," 47.
178 Cited in Guillet, *Great Migration,* 96-7.
179 Gelberg, *Auswanderung nach Übersee,* 43-4.
180 "Die Einwanderung in Canada im Jahre 1854," *DAZ,* 4 May 1855.
181 Marjorie P. Kohli, "Immigrants to Canada: Ships Arriving at Quebec 1866," www.dcs.uwaterloo.ca/~marj/genealogy/ships/ships1866.html, 15 August 2002.
182 Monckmeier, *Deutsche überseeische Auswanderung,* 235-6.
183 Zu Wohlgeborendem Königliche Preussischen Consul zu Quebec, 3 July 1860, GSPK, I H.A., rep. 77, tit. 226, no. 11, bd. 15.
184 George Pemberton to Reinhard Hebeler, Prussian Consul in London, 16 August 1861, GSPK, I H.A., rep. 77, tit. 226, no. 11, bd. 15.
185 Report of the Consulat des Norddeutschen Bundes, 2 June 1869, StAB, 2-P.8.C.1.b.
186 Report of the Consulat des Norddeutschen Bundes, 4 June 1869, StAB, 2-P.8.B.C.1.b.
187 Gurttler, *Geschichte der deutschen Gesellschaft,* 26.
188 On Grosse Isle, see Marianna O'Gallagher, *Grosse Île: Gateway to Canada 1832-1937* (St. Foy: Carraig Books, 1984) and Padraic O'Laighin, "Grosse Ile: The Holocaust Revisited," in *The Untold Story: The Irish in Canada,* ed. Robert O'Driscoll and Lorna Reynolds (Toronto: Celtic Arts of Canada, 1988), vol. 1, 75-101.
189 Ninette Kelley and Michael Trebilcock, *The Making of the Mosaic: A History of Canadian Immigration Policy* (Toronto: University of Toronto Press, 1998), 83-4.
190 Brown cited in Guillet, *Great Migration,* 177.
191 "1854 New Route Now Open, the Great Western Railway from Hamilton to Detroit," flyer, Government Education Department, Quebec, 1854, StAB, 2-B.13.b.1.a.2.II.
192 A.C. Buchanan to Superintendent, Grand Trunk Railway Station Point Levi, 8 June 1867, and circular no. 484, Grand Trunk Railway, 14 June 1867, LAC, RG 17, vol. 16, nos. 1327-35.

Chapter 2: Migration in the Age of Bismarck and Macdonald, 1870-90

 1 For general background information on the new Germany and its constitutional arrangements, see, for example, Gordon A. Craig, *Germany 1866-1945* (Oxford: Oxford University Press, 1978); and Wolfgang J. Mommsen, *Imperial Germany 1867-1918: Politics, Culture, and Society in an Authoritarian State* (New York: St. Martin's Press, 1995).
 2 On the *Kulturkampf,* see the relevant chapters in Craig, *Germany 1866-1945;* Margaret L. Anderson, *Windthorst: A Political Biography* (Oxford: Oxford University Press, 1981); and David Blackbourn, *Marpingen: Apparitions of the Virgin Mary in a Nineteenth-Century German Village* (New York: Knopf, 1993).
 3 For Bismarck's campaign against the Social Democrats and his social insurance program, see Vernon L. Lidtke, *The Outlawed Party: Social Democracy in Germany, 1878-1890* (Princeton: Princeton University Press, 1966); and Theodore S. Hamerow, "Bismarck and the Emergence of the Social Question in Imperial Germany," in *Imperial Germany,* ed. Volker Dürr, Kathy Harms, and Peter Hayes (Madison: University of Wisconsin Press, 1985), 17-31.

4 For brief, general accounts of the Bismarckian and Wilhelmian Empire, see Hans-Ulrich Wehler, *The German Empire 1871-1918* (Leamington Spa: Berg, 1989); and Volker R. Berghahn, *Imperial Germany, 1871-1914: Economy, Society, Culture and Politics* (Providence: Berghahn Books, 1994).

5 For a brief account of Macdonald and his political career, see Donald Swainson, *Sir John A. Macdonald: The Man and the Politician* (Kingston, ON: Quarry Press, 1989); and Peter B. Waite, "The Political Ideas of John A. Macdonald," in *The Political Ideas of the Prime Ministers of Canada,* ed. Marcel Hamelin (Ottawa: Éditions de l'Université d'Ottawa, 1969), 51-68.

6 Donald F. Warner, *The Idea of Continental Union: Agitation for the Annexation of Canada to the United States, 1849-1893* (Lexington: University of Kentucky Press, 1960), 60-141.

7 Carl E. Solberg, *Immigration and Nationalism: Argentina and Chile, 1890-1914* (Austin: University of Texas Press, 1970), 7.

8 On the Dominion Lands Act and dominion land policy, see Chester Martin, *Dominion Lands Policy* (Toronto: McClelland and Stewart, 1973).

9 See Carl E. Solberg, "Land Tenure and Land Settlement: Policy and Patterns in the Canadian Prairies and the Argentine Pampas, 1880-1930," in *Argentina, Australia and Canada: Studies in Comparative Development 1870-1965,* ed. D.C.M. Platt and Guido di Tella (New York: St. Martin's Press, 1985), 53-75.

10 See John Dales, *The Protective Tariff in Canada's Development* (Toronto: University of Toronto Press, 1966).

11 On the National Policy, see Robert Craig Brown, *Canada's National Policy, 1883-1900: A Study in Canadian-American Relations* (Princeton: Princeton University Press, 1964).

12 For the story of the railway's building, see Pierre Berton, *The National Dream: The Great Railway, 1871-1881* (Toronto: McClelland and Stewart, 1970); and his *The Last Spike: The Great Railway, 1881-1885* (Toronto: McClelland and Stewart, 1971).

13 Gerald Friesen, *The Canadian Prairies: A History* (Toronto: University of Toronto Press, 1984), 245.

14 On the North-West Rebellion, see Bob Beal and Rob Macleod, *Prairie Fire: The 1885 North West Rebellion* (Edmonton: Hurtig, 1984).

15 For background on the provincial rights movements in the time of Macdonald, see Ramsay Cook, *Provincial Autonomy, Minority Rights and the Compact Theory, 1867-1921* (Ottawa: Queen's Printer, 1969); and Peter B. Waite, *Canada 1874-1896: Arduous Destiny* (Toronto: McClelland and Stewart, 1971).

16 For standard histories treating German industrialization in this period, see W.O. Henderson, *The Rise of German Industrial Power, 1834-1914* (Berkeley: University of California Press, 1975); and A. Sommariva and G. Tullio, *German Macroeconomic History, 1880-1979* (London: St. Martin's Press, 1987).

17 For a brief discussion of the German industrial take-off and ensuing "Great Depression," see Berghahn, *Imperial Germany,* 11-17.

18 Ibid., 1.

19 See ibid., 1-31; Mommsen, *Imperial Germany,* 101-18; and David Blackbourn, *The Long Nineteenth Century: A History of Germany, 1780-1918* (New York: Oxford University Press, 1998), 313-50.

20 "Über die Ursachen der deutschen Auswanderung," *Deutsche Auswanderer-Zeitung* (Bremen; hereafter cited as *DAZ*), 24 June 1872.

21 For a discussion of this issue, see M.C. Urquhart, "New Estimates of Gross National Product, Canada, 1870-1916: Some Interpretations for Canadian Economic Development," in *Long-Term Factors in American Economic Growth,* NBER Studies in Income and Growth 51, ed. Stanley L. Engerman and Robert E. Gallman (Chicago: University of Chicago Press, 1986), 9-88.

22 For a discussion of migration from Ontario to New York, see Randy W. Widdis, "Scale and Context: Approaches to the Study of Canadian Migration Patterns in the Nineteenth Century," *Social Science History* 12 (1988): 269-89. On migration from Quebec to New England, note, for example, Bruno Ramirez, "The Crossroad Province: Quebec's Place in

International Migrations, 1870-1915," in *A Century of European Migrations, 1830-1930,* ed. Rudolph J. Vecoli and Suzanne M. Sinke (Urbana: University of Illinois Press, 1991), 243-60.

23 See Kenneth Norrie and Douglas Owram, *A History of the Canadian Economy* (Toronto: Harcourt Brace Jovanovich, 1990), 317-33.

24 Ibid., 335-87.

25 For an account of the CPR's role in western development, consult John A. Eagle, *The Canadian Pacific Railway and the Development of Western Canada 1896-1914* (Montreal and Kingston: McGill-Queen's University Press, 1989).

26 Kenneth McNaught, *The History of Canada* (New York: Praeger, 1970), 170.

27 Warwick Armstrong, "The Social Origins of Industrial Growth: Canada, Argentina and Australia, 1870-1930," in *Argentina, Australia and Canada,* ed. Platt and di Tella, 76-94.

28 Reg Whitaker, *Canadian Immigration Policy since Confederation* (Ottawa: Canadian Historical Association, 1991), 4.

29 Canada, "Report of the Select Standing Committee on Immigration and Colonization," *Sessional Papers,* 1877, 10.

30 Ibid., 39.

31 Ibid., 45.

32 John Lowe, Secretary of Agriculture, to Dr. Hahn, 30 May 1879, Library and Archives Canada (hereafter cited as LAC), RG 25, accession A-1, vol. 3, 11.

33 See Sir John A. Macdonald's commentary upon a memo from the minister of agriculture dated 15 October 1872, LAC, RG 2, Orders in Council, vol. 302, no. 981.

34 Edwin Corbett in Berne to the Earl of Derby, 16 March 1877, LAC, RG 7, vol. 311, file G-21, no. 1085.

35 Elise de Koerber to Governor General of Canada, 24 February 1879, LAC, RG 7, vol. 311, file G-21, no. 1085.

36 Elise de Koerber to W. Armand, Colonial Office, 20 December 1877, LAC, RG 7, vol. 311, file G-21, no. 1085.

37 Ambassador Odo Russell to the Marquis of Salisbury, 4 December 1878, LAC, RG 7, vol. 311, file G-21, no. 1085.

38 Elise de Koerber to Governor General of Canada, 24 February 1879, LAC, RG 7, vol. 311, file G-21, no. 1085.

39 Elise de Koerber to Governor General of Canada, 12 February 1879, LAC, RG 7, vol. 311, file G-21, no. 1085.

40 Elise de Koerber to Governor General of Canada, 27 February 1879, LAC, RG 7, vol. 311, file G-21, no. 1085.

41 Minutes of Committee for the Control and Protection of Female Immigration, Ottawa, 14 February 1879, LAC, RG 7, vol. 311, file G-21, no. 1085.

42 Elise de Koerber letter to Major de Winton, 22 May 1879, LAC, RG 7, vol. 311, file G-21, no. 1085.

43 Peter Marschalck, *Deutsche Überseewanderung im 19. Jahrhundert* (Stuttgart: Ernst Klett Verlag, 1973), 49.

44 "Canada," *DAZ,* 18 September 1871, 5 February 1872, and 27 January 1873.

45 Peterson on Auswärtige Angelegenheiten, 17 April 1885, Geheimes Staatsarchiv Preussischer Kulturbesitz (hereafter cited as GSPK), I H.A., rep. 77, tit. 226, no. 11, bd. 6.

46 Wilhelm Monckmeier, *Die deutsche überseeische Auswanderung* (Jena: Gustav Fischer Verlag, 1912), 192.

47 Duncan McDougall, "Immigration into Canada, 1851-1920," *Canadian Journal of Economics and Political Science* 27 (1961): 168.

48 Wilhelm C. Munderlow to Auswärtiges Amt, 15 May 1882, GSPK, I H.A., rep. 77, tit. 226, no. 11, bd. 6.

49 Marschalck, *Deutsche Überseewanderung,* 45.

50 Ibid., 80.

51 Ibid., 72-84.

52 Heinz Lehmann, *Das Deutschtum in Westkanada* (Berlin: Junker und Dunnhaupt Verlag, 1939), 56-93.

53 Ibid., 99-101.

54 Ibid.
55 Ibid., 60-8.
56 Ibid., 87.
57 Otto Hahn, ed., *Canada: Die Berichte der vier deutschen Delegierten* (Reutlingen: Eduard Schau-wecker, 1883), 3.
58 Douglas Owram, *Promise of Eden: the Canadian Expansionist Movement and the Idea of the West 1856-1900* (Toronto: University of Toronto Press, 1980), 59-78.
59 Ibid., 107.
60 Ibid., 65.
61 *Manitoba: Die letzte Berichte über Manitoba und den Nord-Westen von Canada,* pamphlet (Amsterdam, 1885), 4-5, GSPK.
62 *Manitoba und der Grosse Nordwesten Amerika's 200 Million Acres zu Ansiedlungszwecken* (Liverpool: Turner and Dunnett, 1883), 1, GSPK.
63 Ibid., 8.
64 Ibid., 9.
65 *Manitoba und die Nordwestlichen Territorien für Ansiedler,* pamphlet (1884), 10, GSPK.
66 Owram, *Promise of Eden,* 165.
67 *Manitoba: Die letzte Berichte,* 11.
68 *Manitoba und der Grosse Nordwesten,* 9.
69 Ibid., 5.
70 Ibid., 17.
71 *Manitoba und die Nordwestlichen Territorien,* 8.
72 John Lowe, Secretary of Agriculture, to Sir Charles Tupper, High Commissioner, 11 May 1886, LAC, RG 25, vol. 13, series 1, accession A-1, 6.
73 Heinrich Lemcke, *Canada, das Land und seine Leute: Ein Führer und geographisches Handbuch* (Leipzig: Eduard Heinrich Meier Verlag, 1887), 179-202.
74 Ibid., 164.
75 Ibid., 150.
76 Ibid., 107.
77 Ibid., 109.
78 Ibid., 108.
79 Ibid., 110.
80 Ibid., 112.
81 Specifically, on 30 May 1879, Hahn was appointed "Resident Agent of the [Agricultural] Department in Germany at a salary of $500, together with an allowance of $300 for print-ing and advertising." J. Lowe to Sir A.T. Galt, High Commissioner, 23 April 1881, LAC, RG 25, vol. 3, accession A-1, pp. 12-13.
82 J. Lowe, Secretary of Agriculture, to Sir A.T. Galt, High Commissioner, 10 December 1881, LAC, RG 25, accession A-1, vol. 4, p. 22.
83 Hahn, *Canada: Die Berichte der vier Delegierten,* 3.
84 Ludwig Glock, "Bericht von Ludwig Glock," in Hahn, *Canada: Die Berichte der vier Delegier-ten,* 65.
85 Ibid., 66.
86 Ibid., 67.
87 Ibid., 69.
88 Ibid., 70.
89 Otto Hahn, "Bericht von Otto Hahn," in Hahn, *Canada: Berichte der vier Delegierten,* 79-80.
90 Ibid., 80.
91 Ibid., 83.
92 Ibid., 85.
93 Ernst A. Stadler, "Karl May: The Wild West under the German Umlaut," *Bulletin of the Missouri Historical Society* 21 (1965): 297-8.
94 See also R.H. Cracoft, "The American West of Karl May," *American Quarterly* 19 (1967): 249-58.
95 John Lowe, Deputy Minister of Agriculture, to Sir Charles Tupper, High Commissioner for Canada, 26 July 1888, LAC, RG 25, vol. 15, file "External Affairs High Commissioner's Office."

96 *Manitoba: Die letzte Berichte*, 15.
97 Reichardt to Puttkamer and Bismarck, 17 October 1887, GSPK, I H.A., rep. 120, CXIII 20, no. 18, bd. 1.
98 Ober-Präsident der Provinz Hanover to Bismarck, 1 July 1886, GSPK, I H.A., rep. 77, tit. 226, no. 11, bd. 7.
99 Agnes Bretting and Hartmut Bickelmann, *Auswanderungsagenturen und Auswanderungsvereine um 19. und 20. Jahrhundert* (Stuttgart: Franz Steiner Verlag, 1991), 71-3.
100 Reichardt to Puttkamer and Bismarck, 17 October 1887, GSPK, I H.A., rep. 120, CXIII 20, no. 18, bd. 1.
101 Philip Taylor, *The Distant Magnet* (New York: Harper and Row, 1971), 78-80.
102 Cited in James B. Hedges, "The Colonization Work of the Northern Pacific Railroad," *Mississippi Valley Historical Review* 13 (1926): 315.
103 Ibid., 330-1.
104 Beschwerde über den deutschen Konsul Richard Kind in Antwerpen Seitens des Kaufmannes Richard Berns derselbst, Antwerpen, 22 March 1873, GSPK, III. H.A., 2.4.1 III, no. 14368; and Ober-Präsident von Elsass-Lotharingen to Reichskanzler Bismarck, 3 May 1873, GSPK, III. H.A., 2.4.1 III, no. 14368.
105 Reichskonsul Timmers to Bismarck, 27 June 1872, GSPK, III. H.A., 2.4.1 III, no. 14368.
106 Gottlieb Leibbrandt, *Little Paradise: Aus Geschichte und Leben der Deutschkanadier in der County Waterloo, Ontario, 1800-1975* (Kitchener: Allprint Company Ltd., 1977), 261.
107 John Dyke to Lord Odo Russell, 28 February 1873, LAC, C-4769, vol. 106, file 17988.
108 For the details on this matter and its resolution, see the correspondence contained in LAC, C-4769, vol. 106, file 17988.
109 John Lowe, Secretary, Department of Agriculture, to John Dyke, Dominion Immigration Agent, Liverpool, 13 October 1882, LAC, RG 25, vol. 6, file "External Affairs High Commissioner's Office, London."
110 Agriculture Secretary Pope to A.T. Galt, 15 March 1882, LAC, RG 25, vol. 5, series 1, file "External Affairs High Commission Office London."
111 John Lowe, Secretary, Department of Agriculture, to Henry Eilber, 17 March 1885, LAC, RG 25, vol. 11, series 1, file "External Affairs London High Commissioner's Office."
112 Jastrow to Minister of External Affairs in Berlin, 2 March 1886, GSPK, I H.A., rep. 77, tit. 226, no. 11, bd. 14.
113 Ingrid Schöberl, "Auswanderung durch Information: Amerikanische Broschuren in Deutschland im späten 19. und frühen 20. Jahrhundert," *Amerikastudien* 27 (1982): 327.
114 Almut Mehner, "Hamburgs Auswanderungs-Missionen bis zum Ersten Weltkrieg," *Zeitschrift des Vereins für Hamburgische Geschichte* 63 (1977): 127-44.
115 *100 Jahre Innere Mission in Bremen, 1849-1949,* pamphlet (Bremen: H.M. Hauschild, 1949), 20-1, Staatsarchiv Bremen; and Birgit Gelberg, *Auswanderung nach Übersee: Soziale Probleme der Auswandererbeförderung in Hamburg und Bremen von der Mitte des 19. Jahrhunderts bis zum Ersten Weltkrieg* (Hamburg: Hans Christians Verlag, 1973), 34-6.
116 Mehner, "Hamburgs Auswanderungs-Missionen," 144; and Reinhard R. Doerries, "Zwischen Staat und Kirche: Peter Paul Cahensly und die katholischen deutschen Einwanderer in den Vereinigten Staaten von Amerika," in *Russland, Deutschland, Amerika: Festschrift für Fritz T. Epstein zum 80. Geburtstag,* ed. A. Fischer, G. Moltmann, and K. Schwabe (Wiesbaden: Steiner Verlag, 1978), 88-104.
117 Mehner, "Hamburgs Auswanderungs-Missionen," 150.
118 Victor Mohr, "Die Geschichte des Raphaels-Werkes: Ein Beispiel für die Sorge um den Menschen unterwegs," *Zeitschrift für Kulturaustausch* 39 (1989): 354-62.
119 Gelberg, *Auswanderung nach Übersee,* 33-6.
120 Mehner, "Hamburgs Auswanderungs-Missionen," 146.
121 Ibid., 151.
122 Klaus J. Bade, "Die deutsche überseeische Massenauswanderung im 19. und fruhen 20. Jahrhundert: Bestimmungsfaktoren und Entwicklungsbedingungen," in *Auswanderer, Wanderarbeiter, Gastarbeiter: Bevölkerung, Arbeitsmarkt und Wanderung in Deutschland seit der Mitte des 19. Jahrhunderts,* vol. 1, ed. Klaus J. Bade (Ostfildern: Scripta Mercaturae Verlag, 1984), 293.

123 Klaus J. Bade, *Friedrich Fabri und der Imperialismus in der Bismarckzeit* (Freiburg im Breisgau: Atlantis Verlag, 1975), 80-135.
124 Bretting and Bickelmann, *Auswanderungsagenturen und Auswanderungsvereine*, 203.
125 Ibid., 39.
126 Bade, "Die deutsche überseeische Massenauswanderung im 19. und fruhen 20. Jahrhundert: Bestimmungsfaktoren und Entwicklungsbedingungen," 296-7.
127 Deutsche Gesellschaft Montreal to the Oberpräsident der Provinz Westpreussen, 6 July 1888, GSPK, I H.A., rep. 120, C X III 20, no. 18, bd. 1.
128 Reinhardt to Bismarck, 18 September 1888, GSPK, I H.A., rep. 77, tit. 226, no. 11, bd. 6.
129 Hoger letter to Konigliche Landrathsamt in Glogau, 3 June 1887, GSPK, I H.A., rep. 77, tit. 226, no. 11, bd. 8.
130 Bretting and Bickelmann, *Auswanderungsagenturen und Auswanderungsvereine*, 59.
131 Resultat der Ermittlungen über die Thätigkeit der sich angeblich mit der Beförderung der Auswanderung nach Canada befassenden Personen, Königliche Regierung, Abteilung des Innern, Düsseldorf, 25 January 1888, GSPK, I H.A., rep. 77, tit. 226, no. 11, bd. 6.
132 Der Oberpräsident der Provinz Hanover to Bismarck, 27 September 1886, and Interior Minister Jastrow to the Oberpräsident zu Schleswig, Hanover, and Kassel, 5 October 1885, GSPK, I H.A., rep. 77, tit. 226, no. 11, bd. 7.
133 Engeleck to Landrathsamt, 6 August 1886, GSPK, I H.A., rep. 77, tit. 226, no. 11, bd. 7.
134 Staatsanwalt Gunther to Minister Friedberg in Berlin, 7 July 1887, GSPK, I H.A., rep. 120, C X III 20, no. 18, bd. 1.
135 Reichskanzler, Reichsamt des Innern to K.B. Stadtsministerium, 18 October 1884, GSPK, I H.A., rep. 77, tit. 226, no. 11, bd. 6.
136 Trade Ministry to Bismarck, 12 August 1886, GSPK, I H.A., rep. 120, C X III 20, no. 18, bd. 1.
137 Interior Ministry to Graf Ledlitz-Trutzschler in Posen, 11 November 1886, GSPK, I H.A., rep. 77, tit. 226, no. 11, bd. 9.
138 Staatsanwalt Laue to Landrath of Neufeldersleben, 2 August 1886, GSPK, I H.A., rep. 77, tit. 226, no. 11, bd. 7.
139 Peterson letter to Foreign Office, 17 April 1885, GSPK, I H.A., rep. 77, tit. 226, no. 11, bd. 6.
140 *Allgemeine Instruction für die Agenten der Gesellschaft, HAPAG*, Abteilung, 1 January 1888, GSPK, I H.A., rep. 120, C X III 20, no. 18, bd. 1.
141 Edwin C. Guillet, *The Great Migration: The Atlantic Crossing by Sailing Ship since 1770* (Toronto: University of Toronto Press, 1963), 245.
142 Cited in David Budlong Tyler, *Steam Conquers the Atlantic* (New York: D. Appleton-Century, 1939), 371.
143 Günter Moltmann, "Steamship Transport of Emigrants from Europe to the United States, 1850-1914: Social, Commercial and Legislative Aspects," in *Maritime Aspects of Migration*, ed. Klaus Friedland (Cologne: Böhlau, 1989), 312.
144 United States Public Health and Marine Hospital Service, *Report of the Immigration Service, by John M. Woodworth, M.D. Supervising Surgeon U.S. Marine-Hospital Service* (Washington, DC: US Government, 1873), 10.
145 H.J. Maas to W.J. Wells, Government Immigrant Agent, Ottawa, 4 March 1882, LAC, RG 25, vol. 5, file "External Affairs High Commission Office London."
146 See Lars Ljungmark, *For Sale – Minnesota: Organized Promotion of Scandinavian Immigration, 1866-1873* (Goteborg: Laromedelsforl, 1971), 264-5.
147 Walter Nugent, *Crossings: The Great Transatlantic Migrations, 1870-1914* (Bloomington: University of Indiana Press, 1992), 96-8.

Chapter 3: Migration in the Generation before the Great War, 1890-1914

1 See the following discussions of the politicizing and factionalizing trends in the Wilhelmian Empire: Geoff Eley, *Reshaping the German Right: Radical Nationalism and Political Change after Bismarck* (New Haven: Yale University Press, 1980); George Mosse, *The Nationalization of the Masses: Political Symbolism and Mass Movements in Germany from the Napoleonic Wars through the Third Reich* (New York: H. Fertig, 1975); Woodruff D. Smith, *The German Colonial Empire* (Chapel Hill: University of North Carolina Press, 1978); E. Kehr, *Battleship*

Building and Party Politics in Germany (Chicago: University of Chicago Press, 1975); Roger Chickering, *We Men Who Feel Most German: A Cultural Study of the Pan-German League, 1886-1914* (London: Allen and Unwin, 1984); and Richard J. Evans, *Society and Politics in Wilhelmian Germany* (London: Croom Helm, 1978).

2 For a discussion of the centripetal and centrifugal forces in the imperial political system, see Volker R. Berghahn, *Imperial Germany, 1871-1914: Economy, Society, Culture and Politics* (Providence: Berghahn Books, 1994), 191-261.

3 On Wilhelmian foreign policy, see Imanuel Geiss, *German Foreign Policy, 1871-1914* (Boston: Routledge and Kegan Paul, 1976); and Volker R. Berghahn, *Germany and the Approach of War in 1914* (London: Macmillan, 1984).

4 David Blackbourn, *The Long Nineteenth Century: A History of Germany, 1780-1918* (New York: Oxford University Press, 1998), 313.

5 See W.O. Henderson, *The Rise of German Industrial Power 1834-1914* (Berkeley: University of California Press, 1975).

6 Blackbourn, *Long Nineteenth Century,* 318; and Berghahn, *Imperial Germany,* 21-2.

7 See Wolfgang J. Mommsen, *Imperial Germany 1867-1918: Politics, Culture, and Society in an Authoritarian State* (New York: St. Martin's Press, 1995), 163-88; and Hans-Ulrich Wehler, *The German Empire 1871-1918* (Leamington Spa: Berg, 1989), 170-81.

8 Bismarck cited in Otto Stolberg-Wernigerode, *Deutschland und die Vereinigten Staaten vom Amerika im Zeitalter Bismarcks* (Berlin: W. De Grugter and Company, 1933), 199.

9 Gerhard Brunn, *Deutschland und Brasilien 1889-1914* (Cologne: Böhlau Verlag, 1971), 127-33.

10 For an overview of the Laurier age, see Robert Craig Brown and Ramsay Cook, *Canada, 1896-1921: A Nation Transformed* (Toronto: McClelland and Stewart, 1974); Richard Clippingdale, *Laurier: His Life and World* (Toronto: McGraw-Hill Ryerson, 1979); and Paul Stevens, "Wilfrid Laurier: Politician," in *The Political Ideas of the Prime Ministers of Canada,* ed. Marcel Hamelin (Ottawa: Éditions de l'Université d'Ottawa, 1969), 69-85.

11 On immigration and western settlement, see the appropriate sections in Brown and Cook, *Canada, 1896-1921;* and Gerald Friesen, *The Canadian Prairies: A History* (Toronto: University of Toronto Press, 1984).

12 Kenneth H. Norrie, "The Rate of Settlement of the Canadian Prairies, 1870-1911," in *Perspectives on Canadian Economic History,* ed. Douglas McCalla (Toronto: Copp Clark Pitman, 1987), 172-8.

13 H. Blair Neatby, "The New Century," in *The Canadians 1867-1967,* ed. J.M.S. Careless and R.C. Brown (Toronto: Macmillan, 1967), 142.

14 On Sifton, see D.J. Hall, "Clifford Sifton: Immigration and Settlement Policy, 1896-1905," in *The Settlement of the West,* ed. Howard Palmer (Calgary: Comprint Publishing, 1977), 60-85; and Hall's two-volume biography, *Clifford Sifton* (Vancouver: University of British Columbia Press, 1981-5).

15 On the founding of the Prairie provinces, see Friesen, *Canadian Prairies;* John Archer, *Saskatchewan: A History* (Saskatoon: Western Producer Prairie Books, 1980); and Howard Palmer and Tamara Palmer, *Alberta: A New History* (Edmonton: Hurtig, 1990).

16 Kenneth H. Norrie and Douglas Owram, *A History of the Canadian Economy* (Toronto: Harcourt Brace Jovanovich, 1990), 321.

17 Ibid., 322.

18 Harold Troper, *Only Farmers Need Apply* (Toronto: University of Toronto Press, 1972), 18.

19 Ninette Kelley and Michael Trebilcock, *The Making of the Mosaic: A History of Canadian Immigration Policy* (Toronto: University of Toronto Press, 1998), 118-20.

20 Richard J.F. Day, *Multiculturalism and the History of Canadian Diversity* (Toronto: University of Toronto Press, 1987), 122-7.

21 Valerie Knowles, *Strangers at Our Gates: Canadian Immigration and Immigration Policy 1540-1990* (Toronto: Dundurn Press, 1992), 82.

22 Freda Hawkins, *Critical Years in Immigration: Canada and Australia Compared* (Montreal and Kingston: McGill-Queen's University Press, 1989), 8-24.

23 Knowles, *Strangers at Our Gates,* 51-3.

24 Kelley and Trebilcock, *Making of the Mosaic,* 158.
25 Ibid., 160.
26 Hawkins, *Critical Years in Immigration,* 22-3.
27 Canada, House of Commons, "Report of Select Standing Committee on Agriculture and Colonization" (29 April 1908), *Journals* 43 (1907-8): 363.
28 Knowles, *Strangers at Our Gates,* 60.
29 Barbara Roberts, *Whence They Came: Deportation from Canada 1900-1935* (Ottawa: University of Ottawa Press, 1988), 5.
30 Canada, House of Commons, "Report of Frank Pedley, Superintendent of Immigration" (April 1903), *Journals* (1901-3), Session 9, 1-3.
31 Canada, House of Commons, "Report of Standing Committee on Agriculture and Colonization," (29 April 1908), *Journals* 43 (1907-8): 328.
32 Ibid.
33 Secretary John Lowe to Mr. Trow, 6 July 1891, Library and Archives Canada (hereafter cited as LAC), C-4689, vol. 30, 682.
34 T. Mayne Daly to Sir Charles Tupper, 28 June 1893, LAC, C-4689, vol. 30, 682.
35 Sir Charles Tupper to T. Mayne Daly, 18 April 1895, LAC, C-4689, vol. 30, 682.
36 Troper, *Only Farmers Need Apply,* 148.
37 Tupper cited ibid., 156.
38 Heinz Lehmann, *Das Deutschtum in Westkanada* (Berlin: Junker und Dunnhaupt Verlag, 1939), 88.
39 Franksen to Reichskanzler von Bülow, 28 November 1905, Geheimes Staatsarchiv Preussischer Kulturbesitz (hereafter cited as GSPK), I H.A., rep. 77, tit. 226, no. 11, bd. 14.
40 Lehmann, *Deutschtum in Westkanada,* 59-108.
41 Peter Marschalck, *Deutsche Überseewanderung im 19. Jahrhundert* (Stuttgart: Ernst Klett Verlag, 1973), 76.
42 Ibid., 76-82.
43 Frank Thistlethwaite, "Migration from Europe Overseas in the Nineteenth and Twentieth Centuries," in *A Century of European Migrations, 1830-1930,* ed. Rudolf J. Vecoli and Suzanne M. Sinke (Urbana: University of Illinois Press, 1991), 25-6.
44 See, for example, Charlotte J. Erickson, "Who Were the English and Scots Immigrants to the United States in the Late Nineteenth Century?" in *Population and Social Change,* ed. D.V. Glass and Roger Revelle (London: E. Arnold, 1972), 22-49; and the following studies, which show an awareness among migration scholars in the early twentieth century of such "swallow-like" activity among Greek, Italian, and Polish migrants: Robert F. Foerster, *Italian Emigration of Our Times* (Cambridge: Harvard University Press, 1919), 21-37; Henry P. Fairchild, *Greek Immigration to the United States* (New Haven: Yale University Press, 1911), 75-8; and William I. Thomas and Florian W. Zaniecke, *The Polish Peasant in Europe and America* (New York: Dover Publications, 1958), 192.
45 Sellin cited in Wilhelm Monckmeier, *Die deutsche überseeische Auswanderung* (Jena: Gustav Fischer Verlag, 1912), 171.
46 W.D. Kamphoefner, "'Entwurzelt' oder 'verpflantz'? Zu Bedeutung der Kettenwanderung für die Einwandererakkulturation," in *Auswanderer, Wandarbeiter, Gastarbeiter: Bevölkerung, Arbeitsmarkt und Wanderung in Deutschland seit der Mitte des 19. Jahrhunderts,* ed. Klaus J. Bade (Ostfildern: Scripta Mercaturae Verlag, 1984), 339.
47 Marschalck, *Deutsche Überseewanderung,* 48-9.
48 Franksen to Chancellor Hohenlohe-Schillingsfürst, 8 August 1900, Staatsarchiv Hamburg (hereafter cited as StAH), Senatskommission, 2379.
49 Monckmeier, *Deutsche überseeische Auswanderung,* 193.
50 Brunn, *Deutschland und Brasilien,* 153.
51 *Canada: Das Land der Zukunft,* pamphlet (1901), 1, StAH.
52 *Kanada, Eine kurze Beschreibung über Landes und Ansiedlungs-Verhältnisse,* pamphlet (1907), 5, StAH.
53 *Die Ernte in Canada,* pamphlet (1903), 1, StAH.
54 *Canada: Das Land der Zukunft,* 1.

55 Ibid., 3.
56 Karl May's most celebrated novel of the American West, *Winnetou,* was written in 1892. By 1895, 100,000 copies had been sold. At the turn of the century over a million copies of May's works were circulating. For more on May, see Ernst A. Stadler, "Karl May: The Wild West under the German Umlaut," *Bulletin of the Missouri Historical Society* 21 (1965): 297-8; and R.H. Cracoft, "The American West of Karl May," *American Quarterly* 19 (1967): 249-58.
57 J.F. Hansen, *Der deutsche Farmer in Kanada* (Toronto: Union Trust Company of Canada, 1905), 22.
58 *Canada: Das Land der Zukunft,* 1.
59 *Die Ernte in Canada,* 1-2.
60 Ibid., 3-4.
61 Anonymous report on German prospects in Canada, GSPK, I H.A., rep. 77, 67.226, no. 11, bd. I.
62 Freiherr von Freilitzsch to Interior Ministry, 27 February 1894, Staatsarchiv Bremen (hereafter cited as StAB), 2-B.13.b.1.a.2. a.
63 Franksen to von Bülow, 12 December 1905, GSPK, I H.A., rep. 77, tit. 226, no. 11, bd. 14.
64 General Consul Lang to Reichskanzler Bethmann-Holweg, 9 December 1912, GSPK. I H.A., rep. 77, tit. 226, no. 11, bd. 17.
65 Bopp to Reichskanzler, 11 November 1902, StAH, Bestand, Politische Polizei, 351.
66 Otto Zwarg to Hans Schmidt, Friedenau b/Berlin, 2 March 1905, GSPK, I H.A., rep. 77, tit. 226, no. 11, bd. 13.
67 Lehmann, Zentral-Auskunftsstelle für Auswanderer, Berlin, 2 March 1905, GSPK, I H.A., rep. 120, C X III 20, no. 18, bd. 3.
68 Knowles, *Strangers at Our Gates,* 65.
69 Franksen to Reichskanzler von Bülow, 25 June 1906, GSPK, I H.A., rep. 77, tit. 226, no. 11, bd. 7.
70 Ibid.
71 Strom to Behörde für das Auswandererwesen in Hamburg, 11 December 1906, GSPK, I H.A., rep. 77, tit. 226, no. 17, bd. 15.
72 Karlsberg's sworn testimony, Hamburg, 24 December 1906, GSPK, I H.A., rep. 77, tit. 226, no. 11, bd. 15.
73 Franksen to Reichskanzler's Office, Berlin, 17 July 1905, GSPK, I H.A., rep. 77, tit. 226, no. 11, bd. 6.
74 Farmer's Auxiliary Association to Oskar Schmidt, 16 November 1904, GSPK, I H.A., rep. 120 C X III 20, no. 18, bd. 3.
75 John A. Eagle, *The Canadian Pacific Railway and the Development of Western Canada* (Montreal and Kingston: McGill-Queen's University Press, 1989), 186.
76 Lehmann of Auswärtiges Amt to Hamburg Senate, 22 April 1909, StAH, Senatskommission, 2379.
77 J.V. Wolff, Head of Central Information Office for Emigrants, to Auswärtiges Amt, 8 March 1909, StAH, Senatskommission, 2379.
78 Lang to von Bülow, 25 May 1909, StAB, A. 4, no. 235.
79 J.V. Wolff, Head of Central Information Office for Emigrants, to Auswärtiges Amt, 8 March 1909, StAH, Senatskommission, 2379.
80 Ibid.
81 Wolff to Auswärtiges Amt, 20 March 1909, StAH, Senatskommission, 2379.
82 Von Brettreich for Staatsministerium des Innern to Prasidien der K. Regierungen, Munich, 9 May 1909, StAB, vol. 2, no. 453.
83 J.V. Wolff to Auswärtiges Amt, 20 March 1909, StAH, Senatskommission, 2379.
84 *100 Jahre Innere Mission in Bremen, 1849-1949,* pamphlet (Bremen: H.M. Hauschild, 1949), 92, StAB.
85 *Der deutsche Auswanderer,* pamphlet (Witzenhausen, 1914), StAB, A.4, no. 490.
86 *St. Raphaels-Blatt, Organ des deutschen St. Raphaels-Vereins zum Schutze kathol. Auswanderer,* E. V. no. 1, February 1913.
87 "Kanada als Kolonizationsland," *St. Raphaels-Blatt,* January 1911, 8-12.
88 "Der Vertrauensmann in Hamburg," *St. Raphaels-Blatt,* January 1908, 24-5.

89 Ibid.
90 "Canada," *St. Raphaels-Blatt,* July 1904, 337.
91 "Canada," *St. Raphaels-Blatt,* June 1913, 23.
92 "Canada," *St. Raphaels-Blatt,* February 1913, 955.
93 "Canada," *St. Raphaels-Blatt,* June 1913, 28.
94 "Canada," *St. Raphaels-Blatt,* February 1913, 955.
95 "Canada," *St. Raphaels-Blatt,* September 1913, 998-9.
96 Statistik vom 1. April bis 30. September, 1902, and Statistik vom 1 Oktober 1902 bis 30 September 1903, Zentral-Auskunftsstelle für Auswanderer, Handelskammer Archiv Bremen (hereafter cited as HKAB), II – AII6.
97 Walter Nugent, *Crossings: The Great Transatlantic Migrations, 1870-1914* (Bloomington: University of Indiana Press, 1992), 48.
98 E.A. Fabarius to Robert von Zedlitz, 27 February 1903, GSPK, I H.A., rep. 120, C X III 20, no. 18, bd. 3.
99 Kaiserlich Deutsches Konsulat für Kanada to Reichskanzler, 23 January 1913, GSPK, I H.A., rep. 77, tit. 226, no. 11, bd. 6.
100 Ibid.
101 *Denkschrift über die Auskunftserteilung an Auswanderungslustige, insbesondere über die Zentral-Auskunftsstelle für Auswanderer,* pamphlet (Berlin 1905), HKAB, II.AII.6.
102 Monckmeier, *Deutsche überseeische Auswanderung,* 260.
103 Deutsch Kolonialgesellschaft Zentral-Auskunftsstelle für Auswanderer, *Kanada,* pamphlet (Berlin: Rudolf Mosse, 1902), 7-8, GSPK.
104 Ibid., 9.
105 Monckmeier, *Deutsche überseeische Auswanderung,* 254.
106 Ibid., 255.
107 Ibid., 256.
108 Ibid., 256.
109 John Torpey, *The Invention of the Passport: Surveillance, Citizenship and the State* (Cambridge: Cambridge University Press, 2000), 103.
110 Monckmeier, *Deutsche überseeische Auswanderung,* 257.
111 Secretary John Lowe to James Trow, 6 July 1891, LAC, C-4689, vol. 30, 682.
112 Sir Charles Tupper to T. Mayne Daly, 27 September 1895, LAC, C-4689, vol. 30, file 682.
113 John Dyke to J.G. Colmer, 15 February 1894, LAC, C-4689, vol. 30, file 682.
114 Unsigned letter to John Ennis from Spiro and Company, 19 January 1895, LAC, C-4689, vol. 30, file 682.
115 John Lowe to James Trow, 6 July 1895, LAC, C-4689, vol. 30, file 682.
116 William Wagner to the Deputy Minister of the Interior, November 1894, LAC, C-4689, vol. 30, file 682.
117 T. Mayne Daly to Sir Charles Tupper, 3 April 1895, LAC, C-4689, vol. 30, file 682.
118 John Dyke to J.G. Colmer, 26 January 1894, LAC, C-4689, vol. 30, file 682.
119 John Dyke to J.G. Colmer, 15 February 1894, LAC, C-4689, vol. 30, file 682.
120 J.G. Colmer to Sir Charles Tupper, 9 March 1895, LAC, C-4689, vol. 30, file 682.
121 Sir Charles Tupper to T. Mayne Daly, 27 September 1895, LAC, C-4689, vol. 30, file 682.
122 See Memorandum regarding Mr. Bosworth's Complaint as to the Operation of German Control Stations, 2 December 1913, and other documents describing this issue in LAC, RG 25, vol. 1136, file 1300.
123 United States Senate, *Steerage Conditions: Partial Report on Behalf of the Immigration Commission on Steerage Conditions* (Washington, 1909), 10.
124 Hansen, *Der deutsche Farmer,* 32-7.
125 Terry Coleman, *The Liners: A History of the North Atlantic Crossing* (New York: Putnam, 1979), 40-6.
126 United States Senate, *Steerage Conditions,* 4-11.
127 An die Senatskommission bei der Behörde für das Auswanderungswesen in Bremen, 27 June 1910, StAB, A. 4, no. 347.
128 John Henderson, "Steerage to Canada," *Reynolds's Newspaper* (London), 18 September 1910.
129 Kelley and Trebilcock, *Making of the Mosaic,* 138.

Chapter 4: Interwar Migration, 1919-39

1 Carl Strickwerda, "Tides of Migration, Currents of History: The State, Economy, and the Transatlantic Movement of Labor in the Nineteenth and Twentieth Centuries," *International Review of Social History* 44 (1999): 385.

2 For general accounts of Canada during the Great War, see Desmond Morton and J.L. Granatstein, *Marching to Armageddon: Canadians and the Great War, 1914-1919* (Toronto: Lester and Orpen Dennys, 1989); and Daniel Dancocks, *Spearhead to Victory: Canada and the Great War* (Edmonton: Hurtig, 1987).

3 On the prohibition of the German press, see Werner A. Bausenhart, "The Ontario German Language Press and Its Suppression by Order of Council in 1918," *Canadian Ethnic Studies* 4 (1972): 35-48.

4 Robert Craig Brown and Ramsay Cook, *Canada 1896-1921: A Nation Transformed* (Toronto: McClelland and Stewart, 1974), 227.

5 For general background information on the 1920s, see John Herd Thompson and Allen Seager, *Canada, 1922-1939: Decades of Discord* (Toronto: McClelland and Stewart, 1985).

6 For a general account of the war's origins and a discussion of its course, see Gordon A. Craig, *Germany 1866-1945* (Oxford: Oxford University Press, 1978), 302-95.

7 For accounts dealing with the after-effects of the war in Germany, see Richard Bessel, *Germany after the First World War* (Oxford: Clarendon Press, 1993); Craig, *Germany*, 396-468; A.J. Ryder, *The German Revolution of 1918* (Cambridge: Cambridge University Press, 1968); and Gerald Feldman, *The Great Disorder: Politics, Economics and Society in the German Inflation, 1914-1924* (New York: Oxford University Press, 1993).

8 On the Canadian economy during the 1920s, see the relevant chapters in Michael Bliss, *Northern Enterprise: Five Centuries of Canadian Business* (Toronto: McClelland and Stewart, 1987); W.L. Marr and Donald G. Paterson, *Canada: An Economic History* (Toronto: Macmillan of Canada, 1980); and Kenneth H. Norrie and Douglas Owram, *A History of the Canadian Economy* (Toronto: Harcourt Brace Jovanovich, 1990).

9 Peter Pulzer, *Germany 1870-1945: Politics, State Formation, and War* (Oxford: Oxford University Press, 1997), 111. See also Feldman, *Great Disorder;* and Gustav Stolper, *The German Economy from 1870 to the Present Day* (New York: Harcourt Brace and World, 1967).

10 See Carl Johannes Fuchs, *Deutsche Agarpolitik vor und nach dem Krieg* (Stuttgart: W. Kohlhammer, 1927); and Willi Klatt, *Geschichtliche Entwicklung der Landarbeiterverhältnisse in Ostpreussen* (Strassfurt: N.p., 1929).

11 On the fall of Weimar and the rise of Hitler, see Edgar J. Feuchtwanger, *From Weimar to Hitler, 1918-1933* (London: Macmillan, 1994); and Anthony J. Nichols, *Weimar and the Rise of Hitler* (New York: St. Martin's Press, 1979).

12 On Canadian Depression politics in general, see H. Blair Neatby, *The Politics of Chaos: Canada in the Thirties* (Toronto: Macmillan of Canada, 1972). For Mackenzie King, refer to H. Blair Neatby, *William Lyon Mackenzie King, 1932-1939: The Prism of Unity* (Toronto: University of Toronto Press, 1976); and for R.B. Bennett's time in office, see Richard Wilber, *The Bennett Administration* (Ottawa: Canadian Historical Association, 1969).

13 For Canada's Depression economy, see A.E. Safarian, *The Canadian Economy and the Great Depression* (Toronto: University of Toronto Press, 1970).

14 For material on the Depression's impact and Canadian responses to it, see R.D. Francis and H. Ganzevoort, *The Dirty Thirties in Prairie Canada* (Vancouver: Tantalus Research, 1980); and Michiel Horn, *The Dirty Thirties: Canadians in the Great Depression* (Toronto: Copp Clark, 1972).

15 See H. James, *The German Slump: Politics and Economics, 1924-1936* (Oxford: Clarendon Press, 1984); and Jürgen von Kruedener, *Economic Crisis and Political Collapse: The Weimar Republic 1924-1933* (Providence: St. Martin's Press, 1989).

16 On the structure and functioning of Nazi Germany, see Karl Bracher, *The German Dictatorship: The Origins, Structure, and Consequences of National Socialism* (Harmondsworth: Penguin, 1977); and Michael Burleigh, *The Third Reich, a New History* (London: Macmillan, 2000).

17 See R.J. Overy, *War and Economy in the Third Reich* (Oxford: Clarendon Press, 1995).

18 John Torpey, *The Invention of the Passport: Surveillance, Citizenship and the State* (Cambridge: Cambridge University Press, 2000), 122-31.

19 Ibid., 131-43.

20 Hartmut Bickelmann, *Deutsche Überseeauswanderung in der Weimarer Zeit* (Wiesbaden: Franz Steiner Verlag, 1980), 10-12.

21 See W.A. Carrothers, *Emigration from the British Isles: With Special Reference to the Development of the Overseas Dominions* (London: P.S. King and Son, 1965).

22 See Stephen Constantine, "Empire Migration and Social Reform 1880-1930," in *Migrants, Emigrants, and Immigrants: A Social History of Migration,* ed. Colin G. Pooley and Ian D. Whyte (London: Routledge, 1991), 62-86.

23 Ninette Kelley and Michael Trebilcock, *The Making of the Mosaic: A History of Canadian Immigration Policy* (Toronto: University of Toronto Press, 1998), 164-215.

24 R. Alberti to F.C. Blair, 28 August 1919, Library and Archives Canada (hereafter cited as LAC), C-4689.

25 F.C. Blair to August Schreiner, 19 December 1922, LAC, C-4689.

26 W.J. Egan, Deputy Minister, to Sir Joseph Pope, Under Secretary of State for External Affairs, Ottawa, 8 February 1924, LAC, C-4689.

27 Deputy Minister of Department of Immigration to L. Kempff, German General Consul, 8 January 1927, Bundesarchiv Berlin (hereafter cited as BAB), R1501/1794.

28 The following articles represent such sentiment: W.A. Carrothers, "The Immigration Problem in Canada," *Queen's Quarterly* 36 (1929): 517-31; and F.W. Baumgartner, "Central European Immigration," *Queen's Quarterly* 37 (1930): 183-92.

29 Kelley and Trebilcock, *Making of the Mosaic,* 216-18.

30 Ibid., 216-49.

31 Henry Drystek, "'The Simplest and Cheapest Mode of Dealing with Them': Deportation from Canada before World War II," *Histoire Sociale/Social History* 15 (1982): 436-7.

32 Jonathan F. Wagner, ed., *Troubles in Paradise: Letters to and from German Immigrants in Canada 1925-1939* (St. Katharinen: Scripta Mercaturae Verlag, 1998), 194-8.

33 Ibid., 245-53.

34 Heinz Lehmann, *Das Deutschtum in Westkanada* (Berlin: Junker und Dunnhaupt Verlag, 1939), 109-15.

35 Bickelmann, *Deutsche Überseeauswanderung,* 150.

36 Cited in Lehmann, *Deutschtum in Westkanada,* 121.

37 Bickelmann, *Deutsche Überseeauswanderung,* 156.

38 Ibid., 157.

39 Ibid., 155.

40 Lehmann, *Deutschtum in Westkanada,* 109-31.

41 Bickelmann, *Deutsche Überseeauswanderung,* 34.

42 See Gerhard P. Bassler, *The German Canadian Mosaic Today and Yesterday: Identities, Roots, and Heritage* (Ottawa: German Canadian Congress Press, 1991), 49.

43 Interdepartmental Correspondence, Agents for the Canadian Pacific Railway Germany, Hamburg, 15 February 1929, Kirchenkreis Alt-Hamburg Archiv (hereafter cited as KAHA), Auswanderermission no. 18.

44 Hermann Wagner, Statistik der Auswanderer, die durch Vermittlung der reichsdeutschen Vertretung unter dem Schutz der Lutheran Immigration Board vom 1.1.-10.11.27 nach Kanada reisten, KAHA, Auswanderermission no. 18.

45 Wagner, *Troubles in Paradise,* 34.

46 Jonathan F. Wagner, "Heim ins Reich: The Story of Loon River's Nazis," *Saskatchewan History* 29 (1976): 41.

47 Jonathan F. Wagner, "British Columbia's Anti-Nazi Germans, the Tupper Creek Refugees," *B.C. Studies,* no. 39 (1978): 3-19; and Jonathan F. Wagner, "Saskatchewan's Sudetendeutsche: The Anti-Nazi Germans of St. Walburg," *Saskatchewan History* 33 (1980): 90-101.

48 Otto Preusse-Sperber, *Deutschlands Auswanderungsfrage* (Leipzig: Dietrich, 1924), 7-8.

49 Luigi di Comite and Ira A. Glazier, "Socio-demographic Characteristics of Italian Emigration to the United States from Ship Passenger Lists: 1990-1914," *Ethnic Forum* 4 (1984): 89.

50 Bickelmann, *Deutsche Überseeauswanderung*, 22.
51 Karl Thalheim, *Das deutsche Auswanderungsproblem der Nachkriegzeit* (Crimmitschau: Rohland and Berthold Verlag, 1926), 85.
52 D. Gleiss to Ludwig Kempff, 1 October 1924, KAHA, Auswanderermission no. 18.
53 Edith von Schilling, "Ein Besuch bei den Deutschen in Loon River," *Der Auslandsdeutsche* 19 (July 1936): 449.
54 Kerby A. Miller, "Emigration as Exile: Cultural Hegemony in Post-Famine Ireland," in *A Century of European Migrations, 1830-1930*, ed. Rudolf J. Vecoli and Suzanne M. Sinke (Urbana: University of Illinois Press, 1991), 339.
55 Manfred von Bresler to his parents, 3 May 1927, in Wagner, *Troubles in Paradise*, 100.
56 Julius Soriba to his family, 26 December 1927, in Wagner, *Troubles in Paradise*, 137.
57 Hermann Merkens to Pastor Pasewaldt, 25 January 1935, in Wagner, *Troubles in Paradise*, 255.
58 Preusse-Sperber, *Deutschlands Auswanderungsfrage*, 30.
59 *Verband für Evangelische Auswandererfürsorge, Jahresbericht 1929*, pamphlet (Bremen, 1929), 1, Landeskirchliches Archiv der Bremischen Evangelischen Kirche (hereafter cited as LABEK).
60 Ludwig Kempff, *Kanada und seine Probleme* (Berlin and Leipzig: Deutsche Verlagsanstalt Stuttgart, 1926), 7.
61 Roth is quoting Johann Gottfried Seume, the former Hessian soldier and early literary contributor to the evolution of a Canadian image in Germany. See Hermann Boeschenstein, "Is There a Canadian Image in German Literature?" *Seminar* 3 (1967): 6.
62 Dr. F. Roth, "Das Deutschtum in Westcanada," manuscript, BAB R57/37.
63 C.R. Hennings, "Vom Deutschen in Kanada," *Der Auslandsdeutsche* 17 (1934): 142.
64 "Deutsche in Urwald und Prairie," *Der Volksdeutsche* 2 (1934): 36.
65 D. Erich Koch, "Kanadische Eindrücke," *Vossische Zeitung*, 23 January 1927.
66 W.A. Boepler, "Die lutherische Einwanderungsbehörde Canadas," *Die Abendschule* (1927): 586.
67 D. Erich Koch, "Deutsche Auswanderungspolitik," *Vossische Volkszeitung*, 19 February 1927.
68 "Deutsche Auswanderung nach Canada," editorial, *Nordische Volkszeitung* (Berlin), 8 September 1927.
69 Heinz Jordan to his parents, 4 April 1926, in Wagner, *Troubles in Paradise*, 80.
70 Henry Fricke to his mother and sister, 11 December 1928, in Wagner, *Troubles in Paradise*, 161.
71 Ibid., 161.
72 Gerhard Einstmann to his family, 18 April 1929, in Wagner, *Troubles in Paradise*, 193.
73 Martin Broszat, "Die völkische Ideologie und der National-Sozialismus," *Deutsche Rundschau* 89 (1958): 62.
74 George Mosse, *The Crisis of German Ideology* (New York: Grosset and Dunlap, 1964).
75 F.C. Blair's report on his trip to Europe, 14 April 1928, LAC, RG 30, vol. 5636, file 5510-1.
76 Karl Götz, *Brüder über dem Meer* (Stuttgart: J. Engelhorns, 1938), 150-1.
77 Colin Ross, *Zwischen USA und dem Pol* (Leipzig: F.A. Brockhaus, 1934), 192.
78 Ibid., 196.
79 Ibid., 190-2.
80 Ibid., 310.
81 Gisela Sigrist, "Kanada-Wunschraum, Kanada-Wunschtraum, zur Wahrnehmung Kanadas in deutschen Reisebeschribungen," *Zeitschrift für Kulturaustausch* 45 (1995): 214-15.
82 "Kanada," in *Handwörterbuch des Grenz und Auslandsdeutschums* (Breslau, 1938), s.v.
83 Götz, *Brüder*, 141.
84 Hermann Merkens to Herr Pasewaldt in Hamburg, 25 January 1935, in Wagner, *Troubles in Paradise*, 255-6.
85 Heinrich Brakelmann to Gotthold Roth, 9 May 1939, in Wagner, *Troubles in Paradise*, 317-18.
86 Reichsstelle für das Auswanderungswesen, reports from Schmidt, 20 October 1927, and Hintrager, 28 November 1927, Staatsarchiv Hamburg (hereafter cited as StAH), Auswanderugsamt I, IIAV9.

87 Reg Whitaker, *Canadian Immigration Policy since Confederation* (Ottawa: Canadian Historical Association, 1991), 14.
88 Ludwig Kempff to Auswärtiges Amt, 3 November 1925, StAB, 3-A. 4, no. 552.
89 W.J. Egan, Deputy Minister, Office of the Deputy Minister of Immigration and Colonization, Ottawa, Canada, to Lugwig Kempff, 3 November 1925, StAB, 3-A. 4, no. 552.
90 Reichsminister des Innern to Norddeutschen Lloyd, Canadian Pacific Railway, et al., 19 September 1924, StAB, 4.49.-II.E.7.a.
91 Reichsminister des Innernto Dr. Schroder of the Canadian Pacific Railway, 13 December 1927, StAB 4, 19-30.
92 Zehnte Übersicht der vorhandenen Auswanderungsagenten, January 1929, StAB, 3-A, no. 494.
93 Canadian Pacific Railway, Einreisebestimmungen für Canada, 15 February 1929, KAHA, Auswanderermission no. 18.
94 Hintrager to Reichsministerium des Innern, 3 February 1927, and Reichsministerium des Innern to Auswärtiges Amt, Department VI, 16 February 1927, BAB, R1501/1794.
95 Memorandum from F.C. Blair, Department of Immigration and Colonization, 24 November 1928, LAC, C-10256, file 377272, vol. 350.
96 Manager's Annual Report, Canadian Lutheran Immigration Aid Society, 1930, BAB, R57 neu/1163-42.
97 Jung cited in Thalheim, *Das Deutsche Auswanderungsproblem*, 124.
98 Ibid., 130.
99 Ibid., 135.
100 Ibid., 137-8.
101 Jochen Oltmer, "Migration and Public Policy in Germany, 1918-1939," in *Crossing Borders: The Exclusion and Inclusion of Minorities in Germany and the United States*, ed. Larry E. Jones (New York: Berghahn Books, 2001), 53.
102 See Klaus J. Bade, "Das Amt der verlorenen Worte: Das Reichswanderungsamt 1918 bis 1924," *Zeitschrift für Kulturaustausch* 39 (1989): 312-5.
103 Bickelmann, *Deutsche Überseeauswanderung*, 81-9.
104 John S. Macdonald and L.E. Macdonald, "Chain Migration, Ethnic Neighborhood Formation and Social Networks," *Milbank Memorial Fund Quarterly* 42 (1964): 83.
105 Kempff to Auswärtiges Amt, 19 April 1921, Politisches Archiv des Auswärtigen Amtes (hereafter cited as PAAA), R77314, abt. III, Politik Canada, no. 2.
106 "Nordamerika," *Nachrichtenblatt des Reichswanderungsamtes*, 1920, 195.
107 Memorandum to the Executive Covering the Managers' Trip to Winnipeg, February 1927, LAC, C-7389, vol. 240, file 147188.
108 Oskar Hintrager to Reichswirtschaftsministerium, 6 January 1927, BAB, R1501/1794.
109 Oskar Hintrager to Reichswirtschaftsministerium, 3 February 1927, BAB, R1501/1794.
110 "Nordamerika," *Nachrichtenblatt des Reichswanderungsamtes*, 12 January 1926.
111 "Nordamerika, Welche Aussichten bestehen für einen Deutschen Landwirt in Kanada," *Nachrichtenblatt des Reichsstelle für des Auswanderungswesen*, 1930, 222.
112 Ibid.
113 "Nordamerika," *Nachrichtenblatt des Reichswanderungsamtes*, 12 January 1926.
114 "Kanada," *Nachrichtenblatt des Reichswanderungsamtes*, 1930, 222.
115 Ibid.
116 "Kanada," *Nachrichtenblatt des Reichswanderungsamtes*, 2 January 1925.
117 "Nordamerika," *Nachrichtenblatt des Reichswanderungsamtes*, 18 August 1925.
118 "Nordamerika, Kanada," *Nachrichtenblatt des Reichswanderungsamtes*, 20 August 1928.
119 "Nordamerika, Kanada," *Nachrichtenblatt des Reichswanderungsamtes*, 1930, 68.
120 "Welche Aussichten Bestehen für einen Deutschen Landwirt in Kanada?" *Nachrichtenblatt des Reichswanderungsamtes*, 1930, 223.
121 Reichsministerium des Innern to Auswärtiges Amt, Department VI, 19 February 1927, BAB, R1501/1480.
122 Bickelmann, *Deutsche Überseeauswanderung*, 53.
123 Ibid., 207-8.

124 Ibid., 62-3.
125 Ibid., 214-15.
126 See Victor Mohr, "Die Geschichte des Raphaels-Werkes: Ein Beispiel für die Sorge um den Menschen unterwegs," *Zeitschrift für Kulturaustausch* 39 (1989): 357; and Peter Hahn S.A.C., "Achtzig Jahre S. Raphaels-Verein: 1871-1951," *Mitteilung Raphaels-Werk* (1951): 13.
127 Grant Grams, *German Emigration to Canada and the Support of its Deutschtum during the Weimar Republic* (Frankfurt am Main: Peter Lang, 2001), 135.
128 Minutes of Executive Meeting of the Canada Colonisation Association, Office of Superintendent of Colonisation, CPR, Winnipeg, 10 February 1927, Glenbow Museum and Archive, Calgary, Alberta, M2269, file 648.
129 Grams, *German Emigration to Canada,* 160-5.
130 Ibid., 172-8.
131 Ibid., 178.
132 Helmut Talazko, "Aus der Geschichte der evangelischen Arbeit für Auswanderer und Ausgewanderete," *Zeitschrift für Kulturaustausch* 3 (1989): 345.
133 Cited ibid., 349.
134 D. Hosemann, An die obersten Kirchenbehörden der im Deutschen Evangelischen Kirchenbund zusammengeschlossen Landeskirchen, 12 November 1930, LABEK.
135 *Verband für Evangelische Auswandererfürsorge, Jahresbericht 1926,* pamphlet (Bremen, 1926), 14, LABEK.
136 *Verband für Evangelische Auswandererfürsorge, Jahresbericht 1927,* pamphlet (Bremen, 1927), 6, LABEK.
137 *Verband für Evangelische Auswandererfürsorge, Jahresbericht 1930-31,* pamphlet (Bremen, 1931), 3, LABEK.
138 *Verband für Evangelische Auswandererfürsorge, Jahresbericht 1931-32,* pamphlet (Bremen, 1932), 22, LABEK.
139 Bericht über die Arbeit der Evangelischen Auswanderermission für die Zeit vom 1 Januar bis 30. November 1930, KAHA, Auswanderermission no. 18.
140 Verband für Evangelische Auswandererfürsorge, Jahresbericht 1929, 2, LABEK.
141 Unterredung mit Pastor Schmok, 14 January 1927, KAHA, Auswanderermission no. 40.
142 Denkschrift über die Vertretung der Lutheran Immigration Board, StAH, 373 Auswanderungsamt I, IIF 18, bd. 1, p. 3.
143 Unterredung mit Pastor Schmok, 14 January 1927, KAHA, Auswanderermission no. 40.
144 Undated letter from Dr. Wagner, recipient unknown, Ev-lutherische Auswanderermission Hamburg, StAH, 373-7I, Auswanderungsamt I, II F18, bd. I.
145 Ibid.
146 H.W. Harms, Memorandum, 1 September 1926, KAHA, Auswanderungsamt no. 40.
147 Denkschrift über die Vertretung der LIB, 18 September 1926, StAH, 373-71, Auswanderungsamt, I, IIF, bd. I.
148 H.W. Harms to Dr. Schroeder in Hamburg, StAH, 373-71, Auswanderungsamt I, IIF 18, bd. I.
149 Hintrager Circular, Reichsstelle für das Auswanderungswesen, 3 September 1925, StAH, 373-71, Auswanderungsamt I, IIF 18, bd. I.
150 Karl Witte, "Zum 70. Geburtstag Dr. H. Wagner," *Die Kirche in Hamburg Wochenzeitung* 18 (1961): 6.
151 H. Wagner to the Behörde für das Auswandererswesen, 31 December 1925, StAH, 373-71, Auswanderungsamt I, II F 18, bd. I.
152 H. Wagner to O. Hintrager, 29 September 1925, StAH, 373-71, Auswanderungsamt I, II F 18, bd. I.
153 H. Wagner to O. Hintrager, 17 February 1926, KAHA, Auswanderermission no. 40.
154 Hermann Wagner, *Von Küste zu Küste: Bei deutschen Auswanderern in Kanada* (Hamburg: Verlag der Ev. Luth. Auswanderermission, 1929).
155 Hermann Wagner, "Eine Reise durch Kanada," KAHA, Auswanderersmission no. 44, 2.
156 Ibid., 2.
157 Ibid.
158 Ibid., 9.
159 O. Hintrager to H. Wagner, 21 January 1929, KAHA, Auswanderermission no. 15.

160 H. Brakelmann to M. Bodenstein, 11 March 1935, in Wagner, *Troubles in Paradise*, 292-3.
161 W. Muller to H. Wagner, 8 January 1931, in Wagner, *Troubles in Paradise*, 262.
162 H. Wagner to W. Muller, 13 February 1931, in Wagner, *Troubles in Paradise*, 263-4.
163 Das Deutsche Ausland-Institut Stuttgart, *Was ist das D.A.I.?* pamphlet (Stuttgart, 1923), StAH.
164 *Das Deutsche Ausland-Institut im Jahre 1928*, pamphlet (Stuttgart, 1928), 2, StAH.
165 CNR western manager W.J. Black to J.S. McGowan, 26 April 1929, CNR Inter-Departmental Correspondence, LAC, RG 30, vol. 5629, files 5133-1 to 5133-2.
166 W.J. Black, memo, 1 August 1929, LAC, RG 30, vol. 5629, files 5133-1 to 5133-2.
167 W.J. Black to J.S. McGowan, 26 April 1929, CNR Inter-Departmental Correspondence, LAC, RG 30, vol. 5629, files 5133-1 to 5133-2.
168 Grisebach letter of introduction for C.C. Kelly, District Agriculturist, Prince George, BC, 1 August 1929, LAC, RG 30, vol. 5689, files 5133-1 to 5133-2.
169 T.G. Wanner, DAI, to W.J. Black, 30 September 1929, LAC, RG 30, vol. 5629, files 5133-1 to 5133-2.
170 Ernst Ritter, *Das Deutsche Ausland-Institut in Stuttgart 1917-1945: Ein Beispiel Deutscher Volkstumarbeit zwischen den Weltkriegen* (Wiesbaden: Steiner Verlag, 1976), 95.
171 Ibid., 148-9.
172 Strölin report on resettling Germans from North America back in the Reich, December 1940, BA, RT57/105.
173 Fragebogen zur Erfassung auslandsdeutscher Familien, example Heinrich Hubert of Riverside, Ontario, BA, R57 (neu) 363.
174 M. Grisebach to Karl Gerhardt, 29 January 1936, BA, R57/181/9.
175 See Götz's autobiographical sketch in *Die Heimstätter: Ein deutsches Schicksal in Kanada* (Leipzig: Philipp Reclam, 1940), 72-7.
176 Paul Abele to K. Götz, 16 September 1936, BAB, R57/1102.
177 Ritter, *Deutsche Ausland-Institut*, 163.
178 "Karl Götz als beliebter Erzahler in Winnipeg," *Deutsche Zeitung für Kanada*, 9 September 1936.
179 Ritter, *Deutsche Ausland-Institut*, 164.
180 Karl Götz, "Deutsche Arbeit in Kanada," in *Deutsche Leistung in Amerika* (Berlin: Zentralverlag der NSDAP, 1940), 65-72; and Götz, *Die Heimstätter*, 53-4, 73.
181 For an elaboration on this theme see Götz's novel, *Die Heimstätter* (The Homesteader), which describes the plight of a Saskatchewan immigrant in the 1930s, including his homesickness, his poverty, his being exploited, and his final decision to return to his real home, Germany.
182 See Grisebach to Hamm, 17 December 1936; Grisebach to Schlecker, 10 February 1937; Grisebach to Abele, 1 September 1937, BAB, R57/1102.
183 K. Götz to K. Strölin, 9 September 1936, BAB, R57/1102.
184 M. Grisebach to H.H. Reimer, 17 December 1936, BAB, R57/1102.
185 See Grams, *German Emigration to Canada*, 98-115.
186 For background on the VDA, see Ritter, *Deutsche Ausland-Institut;* and Hans-Adolf Jacobsen, ed., *Hans Steinacher, Bundesleiter des VDA 1933-1937: Erinnerungen und Dokumente* (Boppard am Rhein: Boldt, 1970).
187 Hans Steinacher, "Denkschrift Steinachers vom 10.4.1933 zur Reorganization der Volkstumpolitik," in Jacobsen, *Hans Steinacher,* 84.
188 Hans Steinacher, "Grundlagen und Ziele der Volkstumarbeit," in Jacobsen, *Hans Steinacher,* 74.
189 Ibid., 69.
190 Ibid., 72.
191 Ibid., 69.
192 Hans Steinacher, "Rundschreiben des Hauptreferenten für Übersee des VDA, Ostern, 1934," in *Die diplomatische Beziehungen des Dritten Reiches zu Argentinien,* ed. Arnold Ebel (Landau/ Pflaz: A. Kraemer, 1970), 216.
193 Hans Steinacher, "Jahresbericht des Volksbund für das Deutschtum im Ausland," in Jacobsen, *Hans Steinacher,* 120-1.
194 Ibid., 129.

195 "Deutsch-Canadischer Verband von Saskatchewan: Bericht des ersten vorsitzenden Herrn J.N. Destein," 2 July 1934, BAB, R57 (neu), 1163/3-41.
196 Sitzungsbericht der Sitzung vom 14. Juli 1934 zwischen dem Komitee des Deutschen Vereins Harmonie und dem Vorsitzenden der DAGO Herrn Straubinger, BAB, R57 (neu), 1163/3-41.
197 Schoenfeldt to Rolf Hoffmann, 15 June 1939, BAB, NS42/vorl. 19.
198 Quoted in Elizabeth Barbara Gerwin, "A Survey of the German-Speaking Population of Alberta" (master's thesis, University of Alberta, 1938), 153-4.
199 See "Der Deutsche Tag der Provinz Ontario in Canada," *Der Volksdeutsche,* November 1936; and Agnes Schroeder, "Deutsche Schriftleitung in Kanada," *Der Volksdeutsche,* May 1936.
200 "Das Deutschtum in Kanada," *Der Volksdeutsche,* January 1934.
201 Heinrich Seelheim to Auswärtiges Amt, 7 November 1935, PAAA, VIA, Volksbund für das Deutschtum im Ausland, Deutschtum 2, VDA, bd. 14.
202 B. Bott, Denkschrift zur Lage, PAAA, VIA, Förderung des Deutschtums, Deutschtum 1, bd. 2.
203 DAI to Auslands-Organization, 25 February 1935, BAB, R/181/40.
204 "Informationsdienst für die Gestapo in Kanada," *Deutsche Arbeiter Zeitung,* 23 October 1935.
205 For an account of Bott's pro-Nazi activities in Canada, see Jonathan F. Wagner, *Brothers beyond the Sea* (Waterloo, ON: Wilfrid Laurier University Press, 1981), 64-118.
206 Oltmer, "Migration and Public Policy," 61.
207 Ibid., 11-15.
208 *Überfahrtsbedingungen und Einreisebestimmungen nach Kanada, Hamburg-Amerika Linie,* October 1927, 25, StAB, 3-A.4, no. 552.
209 Ibid., 3.

Conclusion

1 John Torpey, *The Invention of the Passport: Surveillance, Citizenship and the State* (Cambridge: Cambridge University Press, 2000), 6.
2 C.R. Hennings, "Vom Deutschtum in Kanada," *Der Auslandsdeutsche* 17 (1934): 142.
3 Walter Nugent, "Frontiers and Empires in the Late Nineteenth Century," *Western Historical Quarterly* 20 (1987): 393-408.
4 Carl E. Solberg, *Immigration and Nationalism: Argentina and Chile, 1890-1914* (Austin: University of Texas Press, 1970), 22.
5 Richard J.F. Day, *Multiculturalism and the History of Canadian Diversity* (Toronto: University of Toronto Press, 1987), 117.
6 See Chester Martin, *Dominion Lands Policy* (Toronto: McClelland and Stewart, 1973), 116-28.
7 See Richard J.F. Day, *Multiculturalism and the History of Canadian Diversity* (Toronto: University of Toronto Press, 1987).
8 Woodsworth cited in Day, *Multiculturalism,* 136.
9 Ibid.
10 See Ernst Ritter, *Das Deutsche Ausland-Institut in Stuttgart 1917-1945: Ein Beispiel deutscher Volkstumsarbeit zwischen den Weltkriegen* (Wiesbaden: Franz Steiner Verlag, 1976).
11 Gordon A. Craig, *Germany 1866-1945* (Oxford: Oxford University Press, 1978), 187.

Bibliography

Archival Sources
The main archives consulted for this book are the Library and Archives Canada (LAC), Ottawa; the Bundesarchiv Berlin (BAB); Archiv des Auswärtigen Amtes, Bonn; Staatsarchiv Hamburg (StAH); Staatsarchiv Bremen (StAB); Geheimes Staatsarchiv Preussischer Kulturbesitz (GSPK), Berlin; Bayerisches Haupt Staatsarchiv, Munich; Archiv des Kirchenkreis Alt-Hamburg (KAHA) in der Nordelbischen Evangelisch-lutherischen Kirche, Hamburg; and Landeskirchliches Archiv der Bremischen Evangelischen Kirchenbund zusammengeschlossen Landeskirchen (LABEK), Bremen. All specific archival references from the above, as well as other less frequently used archives, are detailed in notes to the text.

Pamphlets
Allgemeine Instruction für die Agenten der Gesellschaft, HAPAG. Abteilung, 1 January 1888. GSPK.
Canada: Das Land der Zukunft. 1901. StAH.
Canada 1862: Zur Nachricht für Einwanderer. Preston, ON: Wilhelm Schluter, 1862. GSPK.
Canada: Zur Unterrichtung für Auswanderer und Ansiedler. Berlin, 1858. StAH.
Denkschrift über die Auskunftserteilung an Auswanderungslustige, insbesondere über die Zentral-Auskunftsstelle für Auswanderer. Berlin, 1905. Handelskammer Archive Bremen.
Deutsch Kolonialgesellschaft Zentral-Auskunftsstelle für Auswanderer, *Kanada.* Berlin: Rudolf Mosse, 1902. GSPK.
Das Deutsche Ausland-Institut im Jahre 1928. Stuttgart, 1928. StAH.
Das Deutsche Ausland-Institut Stuttgart. *Was ist das D.A.I.?* Stuttgart, 1923. StAH.
Der deutsche Auswanderer. Witzenhausen, 1914. StAB.
Die Ernte in Canada. 1903. StAH.
Kanada: Eine kurze Beschreibung über Landes und Ansiedlungs-Verhältnisse. 1907. StAH.
Manitoba: Die Letzte Berichte über Manitoba und den Nord-Westen von Canada. Amsterdam, 1885. GSPK.
Manitoba und der grosse Nordwesten Amerika's 200 Millionen Acres zu Ansiedlungzwecken. Liverpool: Turner and Dunnett, 1883. GSPK.
Manitoba und die Nordwestlichen Territorien für Ansiedler. 1884. GSPK.
100 Jahre Innere Mission in Bremen, 1849-1949. Bremen: H.M. Hauschild, 1949. StAB.
Verband für Evangelische Auswandererfürsorge, Jahresbericht 1926. Bremen, 1926. LABEK.
Verband für Evangelische Auswandererfürsorge, Jahresbericht 1927. Bremen, 1927. LABEK.
Verband für Evangelische Auswandererfürsorge, Jahresbericht 1929. Bremen, 1929. LABEK.
Verband für Evangelische Auswandererfürsorge, Jahresbericht 1930-31. Bremen, 1931. LABEK.
Verband für Evangelische Auswandererfürsorge, Jahresbericht 1931-32. Bremen, 1932. LABEK.
Wagner, William. *Auszug aus den consolidirten Statuten von Canada, Britisches Nord-Amerika.* Berlin: Selbstverlage des Verfassers, 1860. StAH.

–. *Canada: Ein kurzer Abriss von dessen geographischer Lage, sowie Production, Klima und Bodenbeschaffenheit, Erziehungs und Municipal Wesen, Fischereien, Eisenbahnen u.s.w.* Berlin: L. Burckhardt, 1860. StAH.

Other Sources

Abella, Irving, and Harold Troper. *None Is Too Many: Canada and the Jews of Europe, 1933-1948.* Toronto: University of Toronto Press, 1982.

Adams, Willi Paul. *Die deutschspachige Auswanderung in die Vereinigten Staaten: Berichte über Forschungsstand und Quellenbestände.* Berlin: John F. Kennedy Institut für Nordamerika-studien Freie Universität, 1980.

Akermann, Sune. "Towards an Understanding of Emigrational Processes." In *Human Migration: Patterns and Policies,* ed. William McNeill and Ruth Adams, 287-306. Bloomington: University of Indiana Press, 1978.

Anderson, Margaret L. *Windthorst: A Political Biography.* Oxford: Oxford University Press, 1981.

Appel, L. "Official Encouragement of Immigration to Minnesota during the Territorial Period." *Minnesota History Bulletin* 5 (1923): 167-203.

Archer, John. *Saskatchewan: A History.* Saskatoon: Western Producer Prairie Books, 1980.

Armstrong, Elisabeth. *The Crisis in Quebec, 1914-19.* Toronto: McClelland and Stewart, 1974.

Armstrong, Warwick. "The Social Origins of Industrial Growth: Canada, Argentina, and Australia, 1870-1965." In *Argentina, Australia and Canada: Studies in Comparative Development, 1870-1965,* ed. D.C.M. Platt and Guido di Tella, 76-94. New York: St. Martin's Press, 1985.

Ashliman, D.L. "The Novel of Western Adventure in Nineteenth Century Germany." *Western American Literature* 3 (1968): 133-45.

Avery, Donald H. *Reluctant Host: Canada's Response to Immigrant Workers, 1896-1994.* Toronto: McClelland and Stewart, 1995.

Bade, Klaus J. "Das Amt der verlorenen Worte: Das Reichswanderungsamt 1918-1924." *Zeitschrift für Kulturaustausch* 39 (1989): 312-25.

–. *Deutsche im Ausland, Fremde in Deutschland.* Munich: C.H. Beck, 1992.

–. "Die deutsche überseeische Massenauswanderung im 19. und frühen 20. Jahrhundert: Bestimmungsfaktoren und Entwicklungsbedingungen." In *Auswanderer, Wanderarbeiter, Gastarbeiter: Bevölkerung, Arbeitsmarkt und Wanderung in Deutschland seit der Mitte des 19. Jahrhunderts,* vol. 1, 259-99. Ostfildern: Scripta Mercaturae Verlag, 1984.

–. *Europa in Bewegung: Migration vom späten 18. Jahrhundert bis zur Gegenwart.* Munich: C.H. Beck, 2000.

–. *Friedrich Fabri und der Imperialismus in der Bismarckzeit.* Freiburg im Breisgau: Alantis Verlag, 1975.

–. "From Emigration to Immigration: The German Experience in the Nineteenth and Twentieth Centuries." *Central European History* 28 (1995): 507-35.

–. "German Emigration to the United States and Continental Immigration to Germany in the Late Nineteenth and Early Twentieth Centuries." *Central European History* 13 (1980): 348-77.

–. "Historische Migrationsforschung." *IMIS-Beiträge* 20 (2002): 21-44.

–. "Immigration, Naturalization and Ethno-national Traditions in Germany: From the Citizenship Law of 1913 to the Law of 1999." In *Crossing Borders: The Exclusion and Inclusion of Minorities in Germany and the United States,* ed. Larry E. Jones, 29-49. New York: Berghahn Books, 2001.

–. "Labour, Migration and the State: Germany from the Late 19th Century to the Onset of the Great Depression." In *Population, Labour and Migration in 19th and 20th Century Germany,* 59-85. New York: St Martin's Press, 1987.

Barba, Preston A. "Cooper in Germany." *Indiana University Studies* 21 (1914): 52-104.

–. "Emigration to America Reflected in German Fiction." *German American Annals* (1914): 193-227.

Bartl, Cornelia. "The Loss of the German-Canadian Image." *German Canadian Yearbook* 13 (1989): 307-23.

Bassler, Gerhard P. "Die Anfänge deutschen Massenwanderung nach British Nordamerika um 19. Jahrhundert." *Annalen-Annals-Annales German Canadian Studies* 2 (1978): 4-18.

–. "Auswanderungsfreiheit und Auswandererfürsorge in Württemberg 1815-1855." *Zeitschrift für Württembergische Landesgeschichte* 33 (1974): 117-160.

–. *The German Canadian Mosaic Today and Yesterday: Identities, Roots and Heritage.* Ottawa: German Canadian Congress Press, 1991.

–. "German Overseas Migration to North America in the Nineteenth and Twentieth Centuries." *German Canadian Yearbook* 7 (1983): 8-21.

–. "The Inundation of British North America with the Refuse of Foreign Pauperism." *German Canadian Yearbook* 4 (1978): 93-113.

Baumgartner, F.W. "Central European Immigration." *Queen's Quarterly* 37 (1930): 183-92.

Bausenhart, Werner. *German Immigration and Assimilation in Ontario 1783-1918.* New York: Legus, 1989.

–. "The Ontario German Language Press and Its Suppression by Order of Council in 1918." *Canadian Ethnic Studies* 4 (1972): 35-48.

Beal, Bob, and Rob Macleod. *Prairie Fire: The 1885 North West Rebellion.* Edmonton: Hurtig, 1984.

Bek, William G. "Gottfried Dudens Report, 1824-1827." *Missouri Historical Review* 12 (1917): 1-9.

–. "Gottfried Dudens Report, 1824-1827." *Missouri Historical Review* 13 (1919): 251-81.

Berghahn, Volker R. *Germany and the Approach of War in 1914.* London: Macmillan, 1984.

–. *Imperial Germany, 1871-1914: Economy, Society, Politics and Culture.* Providence: Berghahn Books, 1994.

Berton, Pierre. *The Last Spike: The Great Railway, 1881-1885.* Toronto: McClelland and Stewart, 1971.

–. *The National Dream: The Great Railway, 1871-1881.* Toronto: McClelland and Stewart, 1970.

Bessel, Richard. *Germany after the First World War.* Oxford: Clarendon Press, 1993.

Bessell, Georg. *100 Jahren Innere Mission in Bremen: Ein Stück verborgener Geschichte 1849-1949.* Bremen: H.M. Hauschild, 1949.

Bickelmann, Hartmut. "Auswanderungsvereine, Auswandererverkehr und Auswandererfürsorge in Deutschland 1815-1930." In *Von Deutschland nach Amerika: Zur Sozialgeschichte der Auswanderung im 19. und 20. Jahrhundert,* no. 4, ed. Günter Moltmann. Stuttgart: Institute for Foreign Cultural Relations, 1991.

–. *Deutsche Überseeauswanderung in der Weimarer Zeit.* Wiesbaden: Franz Steiner Verlag, 1980.

–. "The Emigration Business." In *Germans to America: 300 Years of Immigration 1683-1983,* ed. Günter Moltmann, 134-43. Stuttgart: Institute for Foreign Cultural Relations, 1982.

–. "The Venture of Travel." In *Germans to America: 300 Years of Immigration 1683-1983,* ed. Günter Moltmann, 46-133. Stuttgart: Institute for Foreign Cultural Relations, 1982.

Billington, Ray Allen. *Land of Savagery, Land of Promise: The European Image of the American Frontier.* New York: W.W. Norton, 1981.

Blackbourn, David. *The Long Nineteenth Century: A History of Germany, 1780-1918.* New York: Oxford University Press, 1998.

–. *Marpingen: Apparitions of the Virgin Mary in a Nineteenth-Century German Village.* New York: Knopf, 1993.

Bliss, Michael. *Northern Enterprise: Five Centuries of Canadian Business.* Toronto: McClelland and Stewart, 1987.

Boeschenstein, Hermann. "Is There a Canadian Image in German Literature?" *Seminar* 3 (1967): 1-20.

Böhme, H. *The Foundations of the German Empire.* Oxford: Oxford University Press, 1971.

Bonsor, N.R.P. *North Atlantic Seaway.* Prescot, Lancashire: T. Stephenson, 1955.

Bothwell, Robert, Ian Drummond, and John English. *Canada 1900-1945.* Toronto: University of Toronto Press, 1987.

Bracher, Karl. *The German Dictatorship: The Origins, Structure, and Consequences of National Socialism.* Harmondsworth: Penguin, 1977.

Brebner, John Bartlet. *North Atlantic Triangle: The Interplay of Canada, the United States and Great Britain.* New Haven: Yale University Press, 1966.

Bretting, Agnes. "The Old Home and the New: The Problem of Americanization." In *Germans to America: 300 Years of Immigration 1683-1983,* ed. Günter Moltmann, 152-9. Stuttgart: Institute for Foreign Cultural Relations, 1982.

Bretting, Agnes, and Hartmut Bickelmann. *Auswanderungsagenturen und Auswanderungsvereine um 19. und 20. Jahrhundert.* Stuttgart: Franz Steiner Verlag, 1991.

Broszat, Martin. "Die völkische Ideologie und der National-Sozialismus." *Deutsche Rundschau* 89 (1958): 53-68.

Brown, Robert Craig. *Canada's National Policy, 1883-1900: A Study in Canadian-American Relations.* Princeton: Princeton University Press, 1964.

Brown, Robert Craig, and Ramsay Cook. *Canada 1896-1921: A Nation Transformed.* Toronto: McClelland and Stewart, 1974.

Brunn, Gerhard. *Deutschland und Brasilien 1889-1914.* Cologne: Böhlau Verlag, 1971.

Burleigh, Michael. *The Third Reich, a New History.* London: Macmillan, 2000.

Burnet, Jean R., and Howard Palmer. *"Coming Canadians": An Introduction to a History of Canada's Peoples.* Toronto: McClelland and Stewart, 1988.

Butler, William F. *The Great Lone Land.* London: S. Low, Marston and Seark, 1872.

Canada. House of Commons. "Report of Frank Pedley, Superintendent of Immigration" (April 1903), *Journals* (1901-3), Session 9.

–. "Report of the Select Standing Committee on Immigration and Colonization." *Sessional Papers.* 1877.

–. Select Standing Committee on Agriculture and Colonization (29 April 1908). *Journals* 43 (1907-8).

Carrothers, W.A. *Emigration from the British Isles: With Special Reference to the Development of the Overseas Dominions.* London: P.S. King and Son, 1929.

–. "The Immigration Problem in Canada." *Queen's Quarterly* 36 (1929): 517-31.

Chickering, Roger. *We Men Who Feel Most German: A Cultural Study of the Pan-German League, 1886-1914.* London: Allen and Unwin, 1984.

Clippingdale, Richard. *Laurier: His Life and World.* Toronto: McGraw-Hill Ryerson, 1979.

Coleman, Terry. *The Liners: A History of the North Atlantic Crossing.* New York: Putnam, 1977.

Constantine, Stephen. "Empire Migration and Social Reform 1880-1930." In *Migrants, Emigrants and Immigrants: A Social History of Migration,* ed. Colin G. Pooley and Ian D. Whyte, 62-86. London: Routledge, 1991.

Cook, Ramsay. *Provincial Autonomy, Minority Rights and the Compact Theory, 1867-1921.* Ottawa: Queen's Printer, 1969.

Cowen, Helen L. *British Emigration to British North America.* Toronto: University of Toronto Press, 1961.

Cracoft, R.H. "The American West of Karl May." *American Quarterly* 19 (1967): 249-58.

Craig, Gordon A. *Germany 1866-1945.* Oxford: Oxford University Press, 1978.

Creighton, Donald. "The 1860s." In *The Canadians,* ed. J.M.S. Careless and R.C. Brown, 3-36. Toronto: Macmillan, 1967.

–. *John A. Macdonald: The Old Chieftain.* Toronto: Macmillan, 1955.

–. *The Road to Confederation.* Toronto: Houghton Mifflin, 1965.

Cross, Michael S., and Gregory S. Kealey. *The Consolidation of Capitalism, 1896-1929.* Toronto: McClelland and Stewart, 1983.

Curti, Merle, and K. Birr. "The Immigrant and the American Image in Europe." *Mississippi Valley Historical Review* 37 (1950): 203-30.

Dales, John. *The Protective Tariff in Canada's Development.* Toronto: University of Toronto Press, 1966.

Dancocks, Daniel. *Spearhead to Victory: Canada and the Great War.* Edmonton: Hurtig, 1987.

Day, Richard J.F. *Multiculturalism and the History of Canadian Diversity.* Toronto: University of Toronto Press, 1987.

Di Comite, Luigi. "Aspects of Italian Emigration, 1881-1915." In *Migration across Time and Nations,* ed. Ira A. Glazier and Luigi De Rosa, 148-59. New York: Holmes and Meier, 1986.

Di Comite, Luigi, and Ira A. Glazier. "Socio-demographic Characteristics of Italian Emigration to the United States from Ship Passenger Lists: 1880-1914." *Ethnic Forum* 4 (1984): 78-90.

Doerries, Rheinhard R. "German Transatlantic Migration from the Early Nineteenth Century to the Outbreak of World War II." In *Population, Labour and Migration in 19th and 20th Century Germany*, ed. Klaus J. Bade, 115-34. New York: St. Martin's Press, 1987.

–. "Zwischen Staat und Kirche: Peter Paul Cahensly und die Katholischen Deutschen Einwanderer in der Vereinigten Staaten von Amerika." In *Russland, Deutschland, Amerika: Festschrift für Fritz T. Epstein zum 80. Geburtstag*, ed. A. Fischer, G. Moltmann, and K. Schwabe, 88-104. Wiesbaden: Steiner Verlag, 1978.

Drystek, Henry. "'The Simplest and Cheapest Mode of Dealing with Them': Deportation from Canada before World War II." *Histoire Sociale/Social History* 15 (1982): 407-41.

Eagle, John A. *The Canadian Pacific Railway and the Development of Western Canada 1896-1914*. Montreal and Kingston: McGill-Queen's University Press, 1989.

Easterbrook, W.T., and Hugh J. Aitken. *Canadian Economic History*. Toronto: Macmillan Company of Canada, 1958.

Easterlin, Richard A. "Influences in European Overseas Emigration before World War I." *Economic Development and Cultural Change* 9 (1961): 331-51.

Eberhard, Julius. "Bericht von Julius Eberhard." In *Canada: Die Berichte der vier deutschen Delegierten über ihre Reise nach Canada im Herbst 1881*, ed. Otto Hahn, 53-64. Reutlingen: Eduard Schauwecker, 1883.

Eley, Geoff. *Reshaping the German Right: Radical Nationalism and Political Change after Bismarck*. New Haven: Yale University Press, 1980.

Ellis, L.E. *Reciprocity, 1911: A Study in Canadian-American Relations*. New Haven: Yale University Press, 1939.

Engelsing, Rolf. *Bremen als Auswandererhafen 1683-1880*. Veröffentlichen aus dem Staatsarchiv der Freien Hansestadt Bremen, booklet 29. Bremen: Carl Schunemann, 1961.

Erickson, Charlotte J. "Who Were the English and Scots Immigrants to the United States in the Late Nineteenth Century?" In *Population and Social Change in the Late Nineteenth Century*, ed. D.V. Glass and Roger Revelle, 22-49. London: E. Arnold, 1972.

Evans, Richard J. *Society and Politics in Wilhelmian Germany*. London: Croom Helm, 1978.

Fairchild, Henry P. *Greek Immigration to the United States*. New Haven: Yale University Press, 1911.

Feldman, Gerald. *The Great Disorder: Politics, Economics and Society in the German Inflation, 1914-1924*. New York: Oxford University Press, 1993.

Feuchtwanger, Edgar J. *From Weimar to Hitler, 1918-1933*. London: Macmillan, 1994.

Firestone, O.J. *Canada's Economic Development 1867-1953*. London: Bowes and Bowes, 1958.

Foerster, Robert F. *Italian Emigration of Our Times*. Cambridge: Harvard University Press, 1919.

Francis, R.D., and H. Ganzevoort. *The Dirty Thirties in Prairie Canada*. Vancouver: Tantalus Research, 1980.

Fremdling, R. "Railroads and German Economic Growth." *Journal of Economic History* 37 (1977): 583-604.

Friesen, Gerald. *The Canadian Prairies: A History*. Toronto: University of Toronto Press, 1984.

Frizzell, Robert W. "Migration Chains to Illinois: The Evidence from German-American Church Records." *Journal of American Ethnic History* 7 (1987): 59-73.

Fuchs, Carl Johannes. *Deutsche Agarpolitik vor und nach dem Krieg*. Stuttgart: W. Kohlhammer, 1927.

Gagen, David P. "Land, Population, and Social Change: The 'Critical Years' in Rural Canada West." *Canadian Historical Review* 59 (1978): 293-317.

Gates, Paul W. "Official Encouragement to Immigration by the Province of Canada." *Canadian Historical Review* 15 (1931): 24-38.

Geiss, Imanuel. *German Foreign Policy, 1871-1914*. Boston: Routledge and Kegan Paul, 1976.

Gelberg, Birgit. *Auswanderung nach Übersee: Soziale Probleme der Auswandererbeförderung in Hamburg und Bremen von der Mitte des 19. Jahrhunderts bis zum Ersten Weltkrieg*. Hamburg: Hans Christians Verlag, 1973.

Gerwin, Elizabeth Barbara. "A Survey of the German-Speaking Population of Alberta." Master's thesis, University of Alberta, 1938.

Gjerde, Jon. "Chain Migration from the West Coast of Norway." In *A Century of European Migrations 1830-1930*, ed. Rudolf J. Vecoli and Suzanne M. Sinke, 158-81. Urbana: University of Illinois Press, 1991.

Glazebrook, George P. de T. *A History of Transportation in Canada*. Toronto: McClelland and Stewart, 1964.

Glock, Ludwig. "Bericht von Ludwig Glock." In *Canada: Die Berichte der vier deutschen Delegierten über ihre Reise nach Canada im Herbst 1881*, ed. Otto Hahn, 65-72. Reutlingen: Eduard Schauwecker, 1883.

Goetsch, Paul. "The Image of Canada in Nineteenth-Century German Travel Literature." *German Canadian Yearbook* 7 (1983): 121-35.

Götz, Karl. *Brüder über dem Meer*. Stuttgart: J. Engelhorns, 1938.

–. *Deutsche Leistung in Amerika*. Berlin: Zentralverlag der NSDAP, 1940.

–. *Die Heimstätter: Ein deutsches Schicksal in Kanada*. Leipzig: Philipp Reclam, 1944.

Gould, J.D. "European Inter-Continental Emigration 1815-1914: Patterns and Causes." *Journal of European Economic History* 8 (1979): 593-679.

–. "European Inter-Continental Emigration, the Road Home: Return Migration from the U.S.A." *Journal of European Economic History* 9 (1980): 41-112.

Grams, Grant. *German Emigration to Canada and the Support of its Deutschtum during the Weimar Republic*. Frankfurt am Main: Peter Lang, 2001.

–. "Der Verein für das Deutschtum im Ausland and Its Observations of Canada Prior to World War One." *Canadian Ethnic Studies* 33 (2001): 117-25.

Granatstein, J.L. *Mackenzie King: His Life and World*. Toronto: McGraw-Hill Ryerson, 1977.

Guillet, Edwin C. *The Great Migration: The Atlantic Crossing by Sailing Ship since 1770*. Toronto: University of Toronto Press, 1963.

Gurttler, Karin R. *Geschichte der deutschen Gesellschaft zu Montreal 1835-1985*. Montreal: Deutsche Gesellschaft Montreal, 1985.

Guttsman, W.L. *The German Social Democratic Party, 1875-1933*. London: Allen and Unwin, 1981.

Hahn, Otto. "Bericht von Otto Hahn." In *Canada: Die Berichte der vier deutschen Delegierten über ihre Reise nach Canada im Herbst 1881*, ed. Otto Hahn, 73-87. Reutlingen: Eduard Schauwecker, 1883.

Hall, D.J. *Clifford Sifton*. 2 vols. Vancouver: University of British Columbia Press, 1981-5.

–. "Clifford Sifton: Immigration and Settlement Policy, 1896-1905." In *The Settlement of the West*, ed. Howard Palmer, 60-85. Calgary: Comprint Publishing, 1977.

Hamelin, Marcel. *The Political Ideas of the Prime Ministers*. Ottawa: Éditions de l'Université d'Ottawa, 1969.

Hamerow, Theodore S. "Bismarck and the Emergence of the Social Question in Imperial Germany." In *Imperial Germany*, ed. Volker Dürr, Kathy Harms, and Peter Haye, 17-31. Madison: University of Wisconsin Press, 1985.

–. *The Social Foundations of German Unification, 1858-1871*. 2 vols. Princeton: Princeton University Press, 1969-72.

Hansen, Christine. "Die deutsche Auswanderung im 19. Jahrhundert: Ein Mittel zur Lösung sozialer und sozialpolitischer Probleme?" In *Deutsche Amerikaauswanderung im 19. Jahrhundert*, ed. Günter Moltmann, 9-61. Stuttgart: Metzlersche Verlag, 1976.

Hansen, J.F. *Der Deutsche Farmer in Kanada*. Toronto: Union Trust Company of Canada, 1905.

Hansen, Marcus L. *The Atlantic Migration 1607-1860*. New York: Harper, 1961.

–. *The Immigrant in American History*. Cambridge: Harvard University Press, 1940.

–. *The Mingling of the Canadian and American Peoples*. New Haven: Yale University Press, 1940.

Hawkins, Freda. *Critical Years in Immigration: Canada and Australia Compared*. Montreal and Kingston: McGill-Queen's University Press, 1989.

Hedges, James B. *Building the Canadian West: The Land and Colonization Policies of the Canadian Pacific Railway*. New York: Russell and Russell, 1971.

–. "The Colonization Work of the Northern Pacific Railroad." *Mississippi Valley Historical Review* 13 (1926): 311-42.

–. "Promotion of Immigration to the Pacific Northwest by the Railroads." *Mississippi Valley Historical Review* 15 (1928): 183-203.

Helbich, Wolfgang. "The Letters They Sent Home: The Subjective Perspective of German Immigrants in the Nineteenth Century." *Yearbook of German-American Studies* 22 (1987): 22-42.

Henderson, W.O. *The Rise of German Industrial Power, 1834-1914.* Berkeley: University of California Press, 1975.

Hennig, Morton. *Auswanderung und Auswanderer Fürsorge: Festschrift zum 90. Jährigen Bestehen der Ev.-Luth. Auswanderermission in Hamburg.* Hamburg, 1961.

Hessel, Peter. "German Immigration to the Ottawa Valley in the 19th Century." *German Canadian Yearbook* 8 (1984): 67-94.

Hippel, Wolfgang von. *Auswanderung aus Südwestdeutschland: Studien zur württembergischen Auswanderung und Auswanderungspolitik im 18. und 19. Jahrhundert.* Stuttgart: Klett-Cotta, 1984.

Hochstadt, Steve. "Migration and Industrialization in Germany, 1815-1977." *Social Science History* 5 (1981): 445-68.

–. *Mobility and Modernity: Migration in Germany, 1820-1989.* Ann Arbor: University of Michigan Press, 1999.

–. "The Socioeconomic Determinants of Increasing Mobility." In *European Migrants: Global and Local Perspectives,* ed. Dirk Hoerder and Leslie Page Moch, 141-69. Boston: Northeastern University Press, 1996.

Hoerder, Dirk. "Changing Paradigms in Migration History: From 'to America' to Worldwide Systems." *Canadian Review of American Studies* 24 (1994): 105-26.

–. *Creating Societies: Immigrant Lives in Canada.* London, Montreal, and Kingston: McGill-Queen's University Press, 1999.

–. *Cultures in Contact: World Migrations in the Second Millennium.* Durham, NC: Duke University Press, 2002.

–. "Immigration and the Working Class: The Remigration Factor." *International Labor and Working Class History* 21 (1982): 28-41.

–. "Migration in the Atlantic Economies: Regional European Origins and Worldwide Expansion." In *European Migrants: Global and Local Perspectives,* ed. Dirk Hoerder and Leslie Page Moch, 21-51. Boston: Northeastern University Press, 1996.

Hoerder, Dirk, and Jorg Nagler. *People in Transit: German Migrations in Comparative Perspective, 1820-1930.* New York: Cambridge University Press, 1995.

Hoerder, Dirk, and Horst Rossler. *Distant Magnets: Expectations and Realities in the Immigrant Experience.* New York: Holmes and Meier, 1993.

Hoffmann, W. "The Take-Off in Germany." In *The Economics of Take-Off into Sustained Growth,* ed. W.W. Rostow, 95-118. New York: St. Martin's Press, 1963.

Hope, N.M. *The Alternative to German Unification: The Anti-Prussian Party: Frankfurt, Nassau and the Two Hessen 1859-1867.* Wiesbaden: F. Steiner, 1973.

Horn, Michiel. *The Dirty Thirties: Canadians in the Great Depression.* Toronto: Copp Clark, 1972.

Hvidt, Kristian. "Emigration Agents: The Development of a Business and Its Methods." *Scandinavian Journal of History* 3 (1978): 179-203.

Innis, Harold A. *A History of the Canadian Pacific Railway.* Toronto: University of Toronto Press, 1971.

Jackson, James H., Jr. "Alltagsgeschichte, Social Science, History and the Study of Migration in 19th Century Germany." *Central European History* 23 (1990): 242-63.

Jackson, James H., Jr., and Leslie Page Moch. "Migrations and the Social History of Modern Europe." *Historical Methods* 22 (1989): 27-36.

Jacobsen, Hans-Adolf, ed. *Hans Steinacher, Bundesleiter des VDA 1933-1937, Erinnerungen und Dokumente.* Boppard am Rhein: Boldt, 1970.

James, H. *The German Slump: Politics and Economics, 1924-1936.* Oxford: Clarendon Press, 1984.

Johnson, Stanley C. *A History of Emigration from the United Kingdom to North America 1763-1912*. London: G. Routledge and Sons, 1913.

Johnston, Hugh J.M. *British Emigration Policy 1815-1830: Shovelling Out Paupers*. Oxford: Clarendon Press, 1972.

Jones, Maldwyn A. "Aspects of North Atlantic Migration: Steerage Conditions and American Law." In *Maritime Aspects of Migration*, ed. Klaus Friedland, 321-31. Cologne: Böhlau, 1989.

Kamphoefner, Walter D. "At the Crossroads of Economic Development: Background Factors Affecting Emigration from Nineteenth-Century Germany." In *Migration across Time and Nations: Population Mobility in Historical Contexts*, ed. Ira A. Glazier and Luigi De Rosa, 175-201. New York: Holmes and Meier, 1986.

–. "'Entwurzelt' oder 'verpflantz'? Zur Beduetaung der Kettenwanderung für die Einwandererkulturation in Amerika." In *Auswanderer, Wandarbeiter, Gastarbeiter: Bevölkerung, Arbeitsmarkt und Wanderung in Deutschland seit der Mitte des 19. Jahrhunderts*, ed. Klaus J. Bade. Ostfildern: Scripta Mercaturae Verlag, 1984.

–. *News from the Land of Freedom*. Ithaca: Cornell University Press, 1991.

–. "Südamerika als Alternative? Bestimmungsfaktoren der deutschen Überseewanderung im 19. Jahrhundert." *Jahrbuch für Wirtschaftsgeschichte* 1 (2000): 199-215.

–. "The Volume and Composition of German-American Return Migration." In *A Century of European Migration, 1830-1930*, ed. Rudolf J. Vecoli and Suzanne M. Sinke, 296-9. Urbana: University of Illinois Press, 1991.

–. *Westfalen in der Neuen Welt: Eine Sozialgeschichte der Auswanderung im 19. Jahrhundert*. Münster: F. Coppenrath Verlag, 1982.

–. *The Westphalians: From Germany to Missouri*. Princeton: Princeton University Press, 1987.

Kehr, E. *Battleship Building and Party Politics in Germany*. Chicago: University of Chicago Press, 1975.

Kelley, Ninette, and Michael Trebilcock. *The Making of the Mosaic: A History of Canadian Immigration Policy*. Toronto: University of Toronto Press, 1998.

Kempff, Ludwig. *Kanada und seine Probleme*. Berlin and Leipzig: Deutsche Verlagsanstalt Stuttgart, 1926.

Kennedy, Paul M. *The Rise of the Anglo-German Antagonism*. London: Allen and Unwin, 1980.

Klatt, Willi. *Geschichtliche Entwicklung der Landarbeiterverhältnisse in Ostpreussen*. Strassfurt, 1929.

Kleiner, Robert J., Tom Sorensen, Odd Stefan Dalgard, Torbjorn Moum, and Dale Drews. "International Migration and Internal Migration: A Comprehensive Theoretical Approach." In *Migration across Time and Nations: Population Mobility in Historical Contexts*, ed. Ira A. Glazier and Luigi De Rosa. New York: Holmes and Meier, 1986.

Knowles, Valerie. *Strangers at Our Gates: Canadian Immigration and Immigration Policy 1540-1990*. Toronto: Dundurn Press, 1992.

Koch-Kraft, Andrea. *Deutsche in Kanada: Einwanderung und Adaption*. Bochum: Universitäts Verlag, 1990.

Kohli, Marjorie P. "Immigrants to Canada: Ships Arriving at Quebec 1866." www.dcs.uwaterloo.ca/~marj/genealogy/ships/ships1866.html. 15 August 2002.

Kollmann, Wolfgang, and Peter Marschalck. "German Emigration to the United States." In *Perspectives in American History VII*, ed. Donald Fleming and Bernard Bailyn, 499-547. Cambridge: Harvard University Press, 1973.

Kraut, Alan M. *The Huddled Masses: The Immigrant in American Society, 1880-1921*. Arlington Heights, IL: Harlan Davidson, 1982.

Kruck, Alfred. *Geschichte des Alldeutschen Verbandes 1890-1939*. Wiesbaden: Fritz Steiner Verlag, 1954.

Kruedener, Jürgen von. *Economic Crisis and Political Collapse: The Weimar Republic 1924-1933*. Providence: St. Martin's Press, 1989.

Larson, Karl. *Die in die Fremde zogen Auswanderer: Schicksale in Amerika 1873-1912*. Berlin: Erich Reiss Verlag, 1913.

Lee-Whiting, Brenda. "Why So Many German Immigrants Embarked at Liverpool." *German Canadian Yearbook* 9 (1986): 71-9.

Lehmann, Heinz. *Das Deutschtum in Ostkanada.* Stuttgart: Deutsche Ausland-Institut, 1931.
–. *Das Deutschtum in Westkanada.* Berlin: Junker und Dunnhaupt Verlag, 1939.
–. *Zur Karte des Deutschtums in den Kanadischen Prärieprovinzen.* Leipzig: Hirzel Verlag, 1938.
Leibbrandt, George. "The Emigration of the German Mennonites from Russia to the United States and Canada in 1873 to 1880." *Mennonite Quarterly Review* 6 (1932): 205-26, and 7 (1933): 5-41.
Leibbrandt, Gottlieb. *Little Paradise: Aus Geschichte und Leben der Deutschkanadier in der County Waterloo, Ontario, 1800-1975.* Kitchener: Allprint Company Ltd., 1977.
Lemcke, Heinrich. *Canada, das Land und seine Leute: Ein Führer und geographisches Handbuch.* Leipzig: Eduard Heinrich Meier Verlag, 1887.
Lidtke, Vernon L. *The Outlawed Party: Social Democracy in Germany, 1878-1890.* Princeton: Princeton University Press, 1966.
Ljungmark, Lars. *For Sale – Minnesota: Organized Promotion of Scandinavian Immigration, 1866-1873.* Göteborg: Laromedelsforl, 1971.
Lucassen, Jan, and Leo Lucassen. *Migration, Migration History, History: Old Paradigms and New Perspectives.* New York: Peter Lang, 1997.
Luebke, David. "German Exodus: Historical Perspectives on the Nineteenth Century Emigration." *Yearbook of German-American Studies* 20 (1985): 1-17.
Macdonald, John S., and Leatrice E. Macdonald. "Chain Migration, Ethnic Neighborhood Formation and Social Networks." *Milbank Memorial Fund Quarterly* 42 (1964): 82-97.
Macdonald, Norman. *Canada: Immigration and Colonization, 1841-1903.* Toronto: University of Toronto Press, 1968.
McDougall, Duncan M. "Immigration into Canada 1851-1920." *Canadian Journal of Economics and Political Science* 27 (1961): 162-75.
McKegney, Patricia P. "A Study in War-Time Propaganda in Berlin, Ontario 1914-18." *German Canadian Yearbook* 13 (1990): 288-306.
McLaughlin, K.M. *The Germans in Canada.* Ottawa: Canadian Historical Association, 1985.
McNaught, Kenneth. *The History of Canada.* New York: Praeger, 1970.
McNaught, Kenneth, and David Bercuson. *The Winnipeg Strike: 1919.* Don Mills, ON: Longman Canada, 1974.
Marr, William, and Donald G. Paterson. *Canada: An Economic History.* Toronto: Macmillan of Canada, 1980.
Marschalck, Peter. "The Age of Demographic Transition: Mortality and Fertility." In *Population, Labour and Migration in 19th and 20th Century Germany*, ed. Klaus J. Bade, 15-33. Leamington Spa: Berg, 1987.
–. *Deutsche Überseewanderung im 19. Jahrhundert.* Stuttgart: Ernst Klett Verlag, 1973.
Martin, Chester. *Dominion Lands Policy.* Toronto: McClelland and Stewart, 1973.
Mehner, Almut. "Hamburgs Auswanderungs-Missionen bis zum Ersten Weltkrieg." *Zeitschrift des Vereins für Hamburgische Geschicht* 63 (1977): 127-65.
Miller, Kerby A. *Emigrants and Exiles: Ireland and the Irish Exodus to North America.* New York: Oxford University Press, 1985.
–. "Emigration as Exile: Cultural Hegemony in Post-Famine Ireland." In *A Century of European Migrations, 1830-1930*, ed. Rudolf J. Vecoli and Suzanne M. Sinke, 339-63. Urbana: University of Illinois Press, 1991.
Mohr, Victor. "Die Geschichte des Raphaels-Werkes: Ein Beispiel für die Sorge um den Menschen unterwegs." *Zeitschrift für Kulturaustausch* 39 (1989): 354-62.
Moltmann, Günter. "American-German Return Migration in the Nineteenth and Early Twentieth Centuries." *Central European History* 13 (1980): 378-92.
–. *Deutsche Amerikaauswanderung im 19. Jahrhundert: Sozialgeschichte Beiträge.* Stuttgart: Metzler, 1976.
–. "Migrations from Germany to North America: New Perspectives." *Reviews in American History* 14 (1986): 580-96.
–. "Nordamerikanische Frontier und deutsche Auswanderung: soziale Sicherheitsventile im 19. Jahrhundert?" In *Industrielle Gesellschaft und politisches System, Beiträge zur politischer Sozialgeschichte*, ed. Dirk Stegmann, Brend-Jurgen Wendt, and Peter-Christian Witt, 279-96. Bonn: Verlag Neue Gesellschaft, 1978.

–. "Stand und zukünftige Aufgaben der deutschen Überseewanderungsforschung mit besonderer Berücksichtigung Hamburgs." In *Die Deutsche und Skandinavische Amerikaauswanderung im 19. und 20. Jahrhundert*, ed. Kai Detlev Sievers, 15-34. Studien zur Wirtschafts- und Sozialgeschichte Schleswig-Holsteins, vol. 3. Bonn: Neue Gesellschaft, 1978.

–. "Steamship Transport of Emigrants from Europe to the United States, 1850-1914: Social, Commercial and Legislative Aspects." In *Maritime Aspects of Migration*, ed. Klaus Friedland, 309-20. Cologne: Böhlau, 1989.

–. "300 Years of German Emigration to North America." In *Germans to America: 300 Years of Immigration 1683-1983*, ed. Günter Moltmann, 8-15. Stuttgart: Institute for Foreign Cultural Relations, 1982.

Mommsen, H. *The Rise and Fall of Weimar Democracy*. Chapel Hill: University of North Carolina Press, 1996.

Mommsen, Wolfgang J. *Imperial Germany 1867-1918: Politics, Culture and Society in an Authoritarian State*. New York: St. Martin's Press, 1995.

Monckmeier, Wilhelm. *Die deutsche überseeische Auswanderung*. Jena: Gustav Fischer Verlag, 1912.

Morawska, Ewa. "Return Migrations: Theoretical and Research Agenda." In *A Century of European Migrations, 1830-1930*, ed. Rudolf J. Vecoli and Suzanne M. Sinke, 277-92. Urbana: University of Illinois Press, 1991.

Morton, Desmond. *A Short History of Canada*. Edmonton: Hurtig, 1966.

Morton, Desmond, and J.L. Granatstein. *Marching to Armageddon: Canadians and the Great War, 1914-1919*. Toronto: Lester and Orpen Dennys, 1989.

Morton, Desmond, and G. Wright. *Winning the Second Battle: Canadian Veterans and the Return to Civilian Life, 1915-1920*. Toronto: University of Toronto Press, 1987.

Morton, W.L. *The Critical Years*. Toronto: Macmillan of Canada, 1964.

–. *The Kingdom of Canada*. Toronto: McClelland and Stewart, 1963.

Mosse, George. *The Crisis of German Ideology*. New York: Grosset and Dunlap, 1964.

–. *The Nationalization of the Masses: Political Symbolism and Mass Movements in Germany from the Napoleonic Wars through the Third Reich*. New York: H. Fertig, 1975.

Neatby, H. Blair. "The New Century." In *The Canadians*, ed. J.M.S. Careless and R.C. Brown, 137-71. Toronto: Macmillan, 1967.

–. *The Politics of Chaos: Canada in the Thirties*. Toronto: Macmillan of Canada, 1972.

–. *William Lyon Mackenzie King, 1932-1939: The Prism of Unity*. Toronto: University of Toronto Press, 1976.

Nichols, Anthony J. *Weimar and the Rise of Hitler*. New York: St. Martin's Press, 1979.

Nordvik, Helge W. "Norwegian Emigrants and Canadian Timber: Norwegian Shipping to Quebec 1850-1875." In *Maritime Aspects of Migration*, ed. Klaus Friedland, 279-91. Cologne: Böhlau, 1989.

Norrie, Kenneth H. "The Rate of Settlement of the Canadian Prairies, 1870-1911." In *Perspectives on Canadian Economic History*, ed. Douglas McCalla, 168-81. Toronto: Copp Clark Pittman, 1987.

Norrie, Kenneth H., and Douglas Owram. *A History of the Canadian Economy*. Toronto: Harcourt Brace Jovanovich, 1990.

Nugent, Walter. *Crossings: The Great Transatlantic Migrations, 1870-1914*. Bloomington: University of Indiana Press, 1992.

–. "Frontiers and Empires in the Late Nineteenth Century." *Western Historical Quarterly* 20 (1987): 393-408.

O'Gallagher, Marianna. *Grosse Île: Gateway to Canada 1832-1937*. St. Foy, QC: Carraig Books, 1984.

O'Grada, Cormac. "Across the Briny Ocean: Some Thoughts on Irish Emigration to America, 1800-1850." In *Migration across Time and Nations: Population Mobility in Historical Contexts*, ed. Ira A. Glazier and Luigi De Rosa, 79-94. New York: Holmes and Meier, 1986.

O'Laighin, Padraic. "Grosse Île: The Holocaust Revisited." In *The Untold Story: The Irish in Canada*, vol. 1, ed. Robert O'Driscoll and Lorna Reynolds, 75-101. Toronto: Celtic Arts of Canada, 1988.

Oltmer, Jochen. "Deutsche Migrationsverhältnisse neuere Forschungsergebnisse zur Wanderungsgeschichte im Kaiserreich und in der Weimarer Republik." *Historische Jahrbuch* 122 (2002): 483-520.

–. "Migration and Public Policy in Germany, 1918-1939." In *Crossing Borders: The Exclusion and Inclusion of Minorities in Germany and the United States,* ed. Larry E. Jones, 50-69. New York: Berghahn Books, 2001.

Opdenhövel, Patrick. *Die kanadisch-deutschen Beziehungen in der Zwischenkriegzeit, Handel und Aussenpolitik 1919-1939.* Frankfurt am Main: Lang, 1993.

Oppel, Alwin. "Das Deutschtum in Kanada." *Deutsche Erde* 5 (1906): 47-54.

Ostergren, Robert C. "Swedish Migration to North America in Transatlantic Perspective." In *Migration across Time and Nations: Population Mobility in Historical Contexts,* ed. Ira A. Glazier and Luigi De Rosa, 125-47. New York: Holmes and Meier, 1986.

Overy, R.J. *War and Economy in the Third Reich.* Oxford: Clarendon Press, 1995.

Owram, Douglas. *Promise of Eden: The Canadian Expansionist Movement and the Idea of the West 1856-1900.* Toronto: University of Toronto Press, 1980.

Page, Thomas W. "Transportation of Immigrants and Reception Arrangements in the Nineteenth Century." *Journal of Political Economy* 19 (1911): 732-49.

Palmer, Howard, and Tamara Palmer. *Alberta: A New History.* Edmonton: Hurtig, 1990.

Perkins, J.A. "The Agricultural Revolution in Germany 1850-1914." *Journal of European Economic History* 10 (1981): 71-118.

Pflanze, Otto. *Bismarck and the Development of Germany.* 3 vols. Princeton: Princeton University Press, 1990.

Philippovich, Eugen von. *Auswanderung und Auswanderungspolitik in Deutschland: Berichte über die Entwicklung und den gegenwärtigen Zustand des Auswanderungswesens in den Einzelstaaten und im Reich.* Leipzig: Dunker und Humbolt, 1882.

Pierenkemper, Toni. "Labour Market, Labour Force and Standard of Living: From Agriculture and Industry." In *Population, Labour and Migration in 19th and 20th Century Germany,* ed. Klaus J. Bade, 35-57. New York: St. Martin's Press, 1987.

Prahl, A.J. "America in the Works of Gerstäcker." *Modern Language Quarterly* 4 (1943): 213-24.

Prentice, Alison, Paula Bourne, Gail Cuthbert Brandt, Beth Light, Wendy Metchinson, and Naomi Black. *Canadian Women: A History.* Toronto: Harcourt Brace Jovanovich, 1988.

Preston, Richard. "The Evolution of Urban Canada: The Post-1867 Period." In *Readings in Canadian Geography,* ed. R.M. Irving, 19-46. Toronto: Holt Rinehart and Winston of Canada, 1978.

Preusse-Sperber, Otto. *Deutschlands Auswanderungsfrage.* Leipzig: Dietrich, 1924.

Pulzer, Peter. *Germany 1870-1945: Politics, State Formation, and War.* Oxford: Oxford University Press, 1997.

Ramella, Franco. "Emigration from an Area of Intense Industrial Development: The Case of Northwestern Italy." In *A Century of European Migrations, 1830-1930,* ed. Rudolf J. Vecoli and Suzanne M. Sinke, 261-74. Urbana: University of Illinois Press, 1991.

Ramirez, Bruno. "The Crossroad Province: Quebec's Place in International Migrations, 1870-1915." In *A Century of European Migrations, 1830-1930,* ed. Rudolf J. Vecoli and Suzanne M. Sinke, 243-60. Urbana: University of Illinois Press, 1991.

Ritter, Ernst. *Das Deutsche Ausland-Institut in Stuttgart 1917-1945: Ein Beispiel Deutscher Volkstumarbeit zwischen den Weltkriegen.* Wiesbaden: Steiner Verlag, 1976.

Roberts, Barbara. *Whence They Came: Deportation from Canada 1900-1935.* Ottawa: University of Ottawa Press, 1988.

Röder, Werner. "Die Emigration aus dem nationalsozialistischen Deutschland." In *Deutsche im Ausland, Fremde in Deutschland,* ed. Klaus J. Bade, 345-67. Munich: C.H. Beck, 1992.

Ross, Colin. *Zwischen USA und dem Pol.* Leipzig: F.A. Brockhaus, 1934.

Ryder, A.J. *The German Revolution of 1918.* Cambridge: Cambridge University Press, 1968.

Safarian, A.E. *The Canadian Economy in the Great Depression.* Toronto: University of Toronto Press, 1970.

Sauer, Angelika E. "A Matter of Domestic Policy? Canadian Immigration Policy and the Admission of Germans, 1945-1950." *Canadian Historical Review* 74 (1993): 226-63.

Sauttner, Udo. "Deutsche in Kanada." In *Deutsche im Ausland, Fremde in Deutschland,* ed. Klaus J. Bade, 185-97. Munich: C.H. Beck, 1992.

Schöberl, Ingrid. "Auswandererwerbung durch Information: Amerikanische Broschüren in Deutschland im späten 19. und frühen 20. Jahrhundert." *Amerikastudien* 27 (1982): 299-339.

–. "Auswanderungspolitik in Deutschland und Einwanderungspolitik in den Vereinigten Staaten." *Zeitschrift für Kulturaustausch* 32 (1982): 324-9.

Schorske, C.E. *German Social Democracy, 1905-1917.* Cambridge: Harvard University Press, 1972.

Schreiner. "Bericht von Dr. Schreiner: Manitoba." In *Canada: Die Berichte der vier deutschen Delegierten über ihre Reise nach Canada im Herbst 1881,* ed. Otto Hahn, 48-52. Reutlingen: Eduard Schauwecker, 1883.

Schwarzmaier, Hans Martin. "Auswandererbriefe aus Nordamerika. Quellen im Grenzbereich von Geschichtlicher Landskunde, Wanderungsforschung und Literatursoziologie." *Zeitschrift für die Geschichte des Oberrheins* 126 (1978): 302-69.

Schwebel, Karl H. *Veröffentlichungen aus dem Staatsarchiv der Freien Hansastadt Bremen.* Bremen: Selbstverlag des Staatsarchiv Bremen, 1961.

Sheehan, James J. *German History 1770-1866.* Oxford: Oxford University Press, 1989.

Sigrist, Gisela. "Kanada – Wunschraum, Kanada – Wunschtraum, Zur Wahrnehmung Kanadas in deutschen Reisebeschreibungen." *Zeitschrift für Kulturaustausch* 45 (1995): 208-18.

Smith, Woodruff D. *The German Colonial Empire.* Chapel Hill: University of North Carolina Press, 1978.

Solberg, Carl E. *Immigration and Nationalism: Argentina and Chile, 1890-1914.* Austin: University of Texas Press, 1970.

–. "Land Tenure and Land Settlement: Policy and Patterns in the Canadian Prairies and the Argentine Pampas, 1880-1930." In *Argentina, Australia and Canada: Studies in Comparative Development 1870-1965,* ed. D.C.M. Pratt and Guido di Tella, 53-75. New York: St. Martin's Press, 1985.

–. *The Prairies and the Pampas: Agrarian Policy in Canada and Argentina, 1880-1930.* Stanford: Stanford University Press, 1987.

Sommariva, A., and G. Tullio. *German Macroeconomic History, 1880-1979.* London: St. Martin's Press, 1987.

Stacey, C.P. *Canada and the Age of Conflict: A History of Canadian External Relations.* 2 vols. Toronto: Macmillan of Canada, 1977.

Stadler, Ernst A. "Karl May: The Wild West under the German Umlaut." *Bulletin of the Missouri Historical Society* 21 (1965): 295-307.

Steinacher, Hans. "Rundschreiben des Hauptreferenten für Übersee des VDA, Ostern, 1934." In *Die diplomatische Beziehungen des Dritten Reiches zu Argentinien,* ed. Arnold Ebel. Landau and Pfalz: A. Kraemer, 1970.

Stelter, Gilbert, and Allan F.J. Artibise. *The Canadian City.* Toronto: Carleton University Press, 1977.

Stevens, Paul. "Wilfrid Laurier: Politician." In *The Political Ideas of the Prime Ministers of Canada,* ed. Marcel Hamelin, 69-85. Ottawa: Éditions de l'Université d'Ottawa, 1969.

Stolberg-Wernigerode, Otto. *Deutschland und die Vereinigten Staaten vom Amerika im Zeitalter Bismarcks.* Berlin: W. De Grugter and Company, 1933.

Stolper, Gustav. *The German Economy from 1870 to the Present Day.* New York: Harcourt Brace and World, 1967.

Strickwerda, Carl. "Tides of Migration, Currents of History: The State, Economy, and the Transatlantic Movement of Labor in the Nineteenth and Twentieth Centuries." *International Review of Social History* 44 (1999): 367-94.

Swainson, Donald. *Sir John A. Macdonald: The Man and the Politician.* Kingston: Quarry Press, 1989.

Talazko, Helmut. "Aus der Geschichte der evangelischen Arbeit für Auswanderer und Ausgewanderete." *Zeitschrift für Kulturaustausch* 3 (1989).

Taylor, Phillip. *The Distant Magnet.* New York: Harper and Row, 1971.

Thalheim, Karl C. *Das deutsche Auswanderungsproblem der Nachkriegzeit.* Crimmitschau: Rohland and Berthold Verlag, 1926.

Thistlethwaite, Frank. "Migration from Europe Overseas in the Nineteenth and Twentieth Centuries." In *A Century of European Migrations, 1830-1930,* ed. Rudolph J. Vecoli and Suzanne M. Sinke, 17-49. Urbana: University of Illinois Press, 1991.

Thomas, William I., and Florian W. Zaniecke. *The Polish Peasant in Europe and America.* New York: Dover Publications, 1958.

Thompson, John Herd. *The Harvest of War: The Prairie West, 1914-1919.* Toronto: McClelland and Stewart, 1988.

Thompson, John Herd, and Allen Seager. *Canada, 1922-1939: Decades of Discord.* Toronto: McClelland and Stewart, 1985.

Tilly, Charles. "Migration in Modern European History." In *Human Migration: Patterns and Policies,* ed. William McNeill and Ruth Adams, 48-72. Bloomington: University of Indiana Press, 1978.

Tilly, R. "The Take Off in Germany." In *Oceans Apart? Comparing Germany and the United States,* ed. E. Angermann and M.L. Frings, 47-59. Stuttgart: Klett-Cotta, 1981.

Timlin, Mabel F. "Canada's Immigration Policy 1896-1910." *Canadian Journal of Economics and Political Science* 26 (1960): 517-34.

Torpey, John. *The Invention of the Passport: Surveillance, Citizenship and the State.* Cambridge: Cambridge University Press, 2000.

Treplin, Ulrike. "Die deutsche Kanada-Auswanderung in der Weimarer Zeit und die evangelisch-lutherische Auswanderermission in Hamburg." *Zeitschrift der Gesellschaft für Kanada-Studien* (1987): 167-92.

Troper, Harold. *Only Farmers Need Apply.* Toronto: University of Toronto Press, 1972.

Turney, Roberta Stevenson. "The Encouragement of Immigration in West Virginia." *West Virginia History* 12 (1950): 46-60.

Tyler, David Budlong. *Steam Conquers the Atlantic.* New York: D. Appleton-Century, 1939.

Underhill, F.H. *The Image of Confederation.* Toronto: Canadian Broadcasting Corporation, 1964.

United States Public Health and Marine Hospital Service. *Report of the Immigration Service, by John M. Woodworth, M.D. Supervising Surgeon U.S. Marine-Hospital Service.* Washington, DC: US Government, 1873.

Urquhart, M.C. "New Estimates of Gross National Product, Canada, 1870-1916: Some Interpretations for Canadian Economic Development." In *Long-Term Factors in American Economic Growth,* NBER Studies in Income and Growth 51, ed. Stanley L. Engerman and Robert E. Gallman, 9-88. Chicago: University of Chicago Press, 1986.

Vagts, Alfred. *Deutsch-Amerikanische Rückwanderung.* Heidelberg: C. Winter, 1960.

Wade, Mason. *The French Canadians: 1750-1945.* Toronto and New York: St. Martin's Press, 1955.

Wagner, Hermann. *Evangelische Kirche und Auswanderung.* Munich: Kaiser Verlag, 1932.

–. *Von Küste zu Küste: Bei Deutschen Auswanderern in Kanada.* Hamburg: Verlag der Ev. Luth. Auswanderermission, 1929.

Wagner, Jonathan F. "British Columbia's Anti-Nazi Germans, the Tupper Creek Refugees." *B.C. Studies,* no. 39 (1978): 3-19.

–. *Brothers beyond the Sea: National Socialism in Canada.* Waterloo, ON: Wilfrid Laurier University Press, 1981.

–. "Heim ins Reich: The Story of Loon River's Nazis." *Saskatchewan History* 29 (1976): 41.

–. Saskatchewan's Sudetendeutsche: The Anti-Nazi Germans of St. Walburg." *Saskatchewan History* 33 (1980): 90-101.

–, ed. *Troubles in Paradise: Letters to and from German Immigrants in Canada 1925-1939.* St. Katharinen: Scripta Mercaturae Verlag, 1998.

Waite, Peter B. *Canada, 1874-1896: Arduous Destiny.* Toronto: McClelland and Stewart, 1971.

–. "The Political Ideas of John A. Macdonald." In *The Political Ideas of the Prime Ministers of Canada,* ed. Marcel Hamelin, 51-68. Ottawa: Éditions de l'Université d'Ottawa, 1969.

Walker, Mack. *Germany and the Emigration 1816-1885*. Cambridge: Harvard University Press, 1964.

Warkentin, John, and R.C. Harris. *Canada before Confederation*. New York: Oxford University Press, 1974.

Warner, Donald F. *The Idea of Continental Union: Agitation for the Annexation of Canada to the United States, 1849-1893*. Lexington: University of Kentucky Press, 1960.

Wehler, Hans-Ulrich. *The German Empire 1871-1918*. Leamington Spa: Berg, 1989.

Whitaker, Reg. *Canadian Immigration Policy since Confederation*. Ottawa: Canadian Historical Association, 1991.

Widdis, Randy William. "Scale and Context: Approaches to the Study of Canadian Migration Patterns in the Nineteenth Century." *Social Science History* 12 (1988): 269-89.

–. *With Scarcely a Ripple: Anglo-Canadian Migration into the United States and Western Canada 1880-1920*. Montreal and Kingston: McGill-Queen's University Press, 1998.

Wiedersheim. "Bericht von Dr. Wiedersheim: Canada Land und Leute." In *Canada: Die Berichte der vier deutschen Delegierten über ihre Reise nach Canada im Herbst 1881*, ed. Otto Hahn, 11-47. Reutlingen: Eduard Schauwecker, 1883.

Wilber, Richard. *The Bennett Administration*. Ottawa: Canadian Historical Association, 1969.

Witte, Karl. "Zum 70. Geburtstag Dr. H. Wagner." *Die Kirche in Hamburg Wochenzeitung* 18 (1961): 6.

Wyman, Mark. *Round-Trip to America, the Immigrants Return to Europe, 1880-1930*. Ithaca, NY: Cornell University Press, 1993.

Zolberg, A.R. "Global Movements, Global Walls: Responses to Migration, 1885-1925." In *Global History and Migrations*, ed. W. Gungwu, 279-307. Boulder, CO: Westview Press, 1997.

Index